LIBRARY
Our Lady of Holy Cross College
New Orleans, Louisiana

For Reference

Not to be taken from this room

REFERENCE BOOKS
for Elementary and Junior High School Libraries

Second Edition

by

Carolyn Sue Peterson

The Scarecrow Press, Inc.

Metuchen, N.J.   1975

Library of Congress Cataloging in Publication Data

Peterson, Carolyn Sue, 1938-
    Reference books for elementary and junior high school libraries.

    1. Children's reference books--Bibliography.
I. Title.
Z1037.1.P4   1975   028.52   75-8537
ISBN 0-8108-0816-1

Copyright © 1975 by Carolyn Sue Peterson

Printed in the United States of America

PREFACE

The second edition of Reference Books for Elementary and Junior High School Libraries is truly a new work, having undergone a thorough and complete revision. Since the first edition, published in 1970, much has happened concerning reference books and reference services for children in grades k-9. As more and more school systems are converting to plans for individualized instruction, more attention has been focused upon the delivery of information to students via the school library (media center, instructional materials center, resource center, etc.). Correspondingly, considerably more reference books in a variety of subject fields have been published specifically for children.

The purpose of this book is to provide a buying guide of many suggested sources for elementary and junior high school libraries. Nearly 900 titles are included, providing a wide enough range of materials for each individual librarian (media specialist) to make selections based precisely upon the needs of the students and faculty of her school. It is hoped that Reference Books for Elementary and Junior High School Libraries will also serve as a valuable guide to available titles for students in education and library science classes dealing with materials selection and reference media. Still another use of this book relates to reference services. When searching for a difficult-to-find answer, perhaps the librarian can simplify the task by scanning annotations of possible sources to determine which title is most likely to contain appropriate information.

The scope of materials included is deliberately broad, attempting to cover the wide span of interests, curriculum needs, and levels of difficulty of youngsters from preschool through ninth grade. All major areas of the curriculum are covered as well as special interests and hobbies. For each there are titles ranging from very simple (primary level, when such materials are available) to scholarly adult titles suitable for scholastically talented fourteen-year-olds. Although the number of titles included in this work could easily be expanded, the size of the book has been deliberately restrained for two reasons. First, elementary school libraries, in general, do not need vast quantities of titles in their reference collections; instead, they need a reasonable number reflecting a variety of viewpoints. Secondly, the titles selected for inclusion represent qualitative suggestions, either recommended by accepted reviewing sources or tested and tried in actual reference situations. While an attempt was made to provide titles published within the last five years, many older ones are included. It must be remembered that some titles do not easily lose their timeliness, while others are out-of-date before their publication.

Materials included in this book are arranged both by type of reference book and by subject areas. Works of a general nature are included in the former category: encyclopedias, dictionaries, yearbooks, indexes, atlases, and bibliographies. In the second grouping are chapters on biographical reference books, foreign language dictionaries, music and art, philosophy and religion, geography, history, social sciences, ethnic groups, natural science and mathematics, applied science, and recreation and hobbies. In most chapters, a number of subject headings further divide titles into specific areas. When level of difficulty is important, the titles within one grouping are arranged in this manner, always beginning with the simplest. When the level of difficulty is neither easily discernible nor important, titles appear in alphabetical order under a topic. In each instance, ease of use rather than consistency has been of prime concern.

It cannot be emphasized too strongly that this book is merely a guide, a compilation of sound, usable titles for young students. Which ones should or should not be available in a school library remains as always the decision of the individual librarian based upon the demands of her peculiar situation. It is hoped that Reference Books for Elementary and Junior High School Libraries will serve as a useful tool to lighten the load of the librarian in building a serviceable reference collection.

Prices quoted throughout this volume, which will not remain accurate for long, were those in effect as of Fall 1974. They are included here only as a helpful guideline and to facilitate comparisons by selectors.

I would like to acknowledge with gratitude the assistance of a number of persons and companies who contributed to the completion of the manuscript. The companies who sent books for review aided considerably by making materials readily available; their cooperation is greatly appreciated. Thanks are due to the author's mother, Clara Peterson, for proofreading and to Barbara Marquess and Belinda Jones for typing the manuscript. To Ann D. Fenton the author especially acknowledges gratitude and appreciation for conducting bibliographic searches, for indexing, and for offering encouragement.

CSP
November 1974

CONTENTS

Preface	iii
Introduction	1
Sample Basic Reference Collection for Primary Grades	5
Sample Basic Reference Collection for Intermediate Grades	6
Sample Basic Reference Collection for Junior High Schools	10
General Encyclopedias	15
English Language Dictionaries	30
Picture Dictionaries	31
School Dictionaries	34
Adult and College Dictionaries	39
Unabridged Dictionaries	43
Factbooks and Yearbooks	47
Factbooks	47
Yearbooks	51
Indexes	55
Atlases	60
Map Skills	60
Introductory Atlases	62
Mature Atlases	64
Special Purpose Atlases	72
Historical Atlases	74
World History Atlases	74
American History Atlases	75
Biographical Reference Books	77
Biographical Indexes	78
General Biographical Dictionaries	79
American Biographical Dictionaries	81
British Biographical Dictionaries	82
Authors and Illustrators	83
Political Figures	87
Scientists	88
Composers and Musicians	89
Foreign Language Dictionaries	91
French	91

German	93
Italian	93
Latin	94
Russian	94
Spanish	95
English and Language Arts	**97**
General Works	97
Drama	101
Fiction	103
Folklore and Mythology	105
Poetry	108
Quotations	110
Spelling and Grammar	111
Word Books	112
Music and Art	**118**
Music	118
Art	123
Philosophy and Religion	**129**
Philosophy	129
Religion	130
Geography	**137**
History	**148**
World History--Bibliographies	148
World History--General Works	150
Ancient and Medieval History	151
Modern World History	154
American History--Bibliographies	156
American History--General Works	157
American History--Specific Topics	160
American History--Documents	162
American History--Names, Symbols, and Stories	164
Flags	165
The Social Sciences	**167**
General Works	167
Citizenship	168
Costume	169
Economics	170
Etiquette	171
Festivals and Holidays	172
International Relations	174
Parliamentary Procedure	174
Political Science	175
Transportation	178
Vocations and Careers	180
Ethnic Groups in America	**184**
General Works	184

Series	186
American Indians	189
Asian Americans	190
Black Americans	190
Jewish Americans	193
Spanish-Speaking Americans	194
Natural Sciences and Mathematics	196
Bibliographies	196
General Works	197
Biological Sciences	200
Zoology	203
Botany	211
Mathematics	214
Physical Sciences	215
Astronomy	215
Chemistry and Physics	216
Geology	217
Oceanography	218
Applied Science	220
General Works	220
Child Care	221
Cooking	222
Ecology	223
Gardening	224
Health and Medicine	225
Home Repairs and Tools	227
Mechanics	228
Pets	230
Sewing	231
Space	232
Recreation and Hobbies	234
Hobbies--General Works	234
Hobbies--Collecting	235
Miscellaneous Hobbies	237
Bicycling and Motorcycling	239
Crafts	240
Games	242
Model Building	244
Photography	245
Outdoor Recreation	246
Sports	246
Bibliographies	254
Review Sources	270
Directory of Publishers	275
Author and Title Index	283
Subject Index	305

INTRODUCTION

Attempting to make the process of acquiring a formal education as relevant as possible for each student, educators in elementary and junior high schools have increasingly explored methods of individualized instruction. In recent years such concepts as modular scheduling, work contracting, packet programing, dial access, programed learning, and the like have become familiar terms in the constant striving to discover techniques which successfully meet each student's unique learning needs. More and more schools are departing from the standardized classroom in which both teaching and textbooks are geared to a fabled "average" student, with both slow and gifted learners struggling to be a part of that group. Correspondingly, as traditional teaching fades slowly from the current education scene, passive learning is also disappearing. Emphasis is increasingly being placed upon the process of learning as opposed to teaching; students learn, they are not taught. Learning is student-centered rather than teacher-centered.

Quite naturally, as education has progressed into an active, individualized activity, schools have been placing greater and greater demands upon the library, by whatever term it may be called. New schools built specifically to house individualized instructional programs are designed so that all rooms, pods, spaces, etc., are adjacent to the library. As a vital part of the educational program, the library must contain a wide selection of materials of high quality representing a broad range of reading levels. Basic to the collection is a useful selection of reference materials, and basic to the program is a viable pattern of reference service.

Over the years the school librarian's role in reference service has evolved through a number of stages, each appropriate to the type of educational program conducted in the school. When basal texts dominated the classroom, the librarian's responsibility was generally to assist the teaching staff by providing instruction in simple "library skills." Either presented to individual children as the need arose, as a unit to an entire class, or at a large group instruction session, these skills normally consisted of how to use the card catalog, understand the Dewey classification system, and perhaps how to use the dictionary and encyclopedia. Following the advent of the space age with its accompanying upgrading of academic curricula, educational programs began incorporating research projects into every subject field, gradually moving down from senior high into junior high and later even into elementary schools. Again, the librarian's role as a member of the instructional team was revamped to cope with the more sophisticated curricula. Not only did she seriously have to embellish the reference collection for young students; she had to convert her library skills course into a program designed to teach basic research techniques including the use of the more specialized reference tools.

With the growing prevalence of independent learning in the elementary and junior high school, the librarian once again is being called upon to reassess her contributions to the educational program. For, regardless of the types of individualized or independent learning situations which exist in the schools, their success will be somewhat dependent upon the quality of reference service in the school library. Perhaps the time has come for school librarians to view their roles not as teachers but as full-fledged reference librarians. Unfortunately, reference service has generally been construed as necessary only for older students, adults, and specialists. Perhaps this service should be extended to the younger student whose educational program will lead him to seek information because he genuinely wants to know, not merely to fulfill a class assignment. Although both school and public librarians have stressed showing the child how to find information rather than doing his homework for him, perhaps they should now concentrate on locating the materials for him. Even in public libraries there are experiments in answering telephone reference questions via cable television.

In considering the library's role in today's independent learning situations for students from grades k through 9, perhaps the children should be regarded as specialists whose time is exceedingly valuable, for into it must be crammed unbelievable quantities of skills and thought processes. Imagine a scientist approaching the librarian in a special library and asking for available material on the research he is conducting. Imagine the librarian suggesting to him that she will be glad to show him how to use the card catalog! But picture the eleven-year-old asking the school librarian for available material for the research he is conducting. Picture the librarian saying that she will have a collection of information for him within the hour and that she will ask the district media center to deliver additional materials the following day! Considering the short amount of time that the youngster will have to learn all that he must learn, his time will certainly be more valuably spent analyzing, comparing, and synthesizing information than copying notations from the card catalog and periodical indexes and compiling his own stack of materials. In other words, the child's time should logically be spent not in locating information, but in assimilating it.

If the librarian is going to provide reference service to research-oriented students, she needs to review reference interview procedures in general. She should allow adequate time for the interview in order to listen to what the child is requesting. She should clarify the question to determine that she and the child are discussing the same problem. She should restate the question to the inquirer, perhaps interpolating to further crystallize the topic.

Introduction

She should determine whether the student needs only a definition or a number of sources interpreting the subject. She should find out the student's reading and comprehension levels and match reference materials accordingly. Her method of delivery of reference service should resemble closely that given to adults in public, academic, and special libraries. Young students' questions and research are as serious and valid, if not more so, than those of adults.

No student is too young to benefit from research. Even six-year-olds who must utilize audiovisual reference materials or must have print materials read to them can gain from the experience. At that age they can learn to check and compare several sources, learn to assimilate information from various sources rather than just copy a paragraph from an encyclopedia, encounter challenging subject matter beyond their limited reading skills, practice decision-making by selecting interesting pertinent facts to use in oral reports, and so on. A child who has conquered these milestones at age six reaches junior high school capable of producing documented studies.

To provide a delivery technique for reference services capable of supporting independent learning programs in the schools, the librarian should assess her reference collection carefully. Obviously, the quantity, range of reading levels, and range of subjects must exceed any holdings adequate for traditional self-contained classroom, textbook teaching approaches. She should systematically prepare long-range plans for developing the reference collection in accordance with her projected budget. Knowledge of the strengths and weaknesses of her collection and anticipation of the current and future needs of her students are essential for preparing a well-planned purchasing schedule.

What constitutes a reference collection? Conceivably, every single item in the library could reasonably be considered reference material, for nearly all books, films, filmstrips, slides, transparencies, recordings, pamphlets, periodicals provide information of some sort. Depending upon the kind of information sought and the amount of time available for searching, every piece of media, even books of fiction, can render background facts to the researcher. Some types of books, however, are designed to provide quantities of factual information with little expenditure of effort on the part of the searcher. It is generally accepted that a reference book <u>per se</u> is one designed by arrangement and treatment to be consulted for definite items of information rather than to be read from cover to cover. Fitting this definition are encyclopedias, dictionaries, indexes, yearbooks, factbooks, bibliographies, atlases, etc. Although some boys and girls may read an encyclopedia from A to Z or the <u>Guinness Book of World Records</u> in its entirety, most children will consult them for specific facts.

In building a reference collection for children, one notes quickly that serious gaps persist in juvenile reference materials. The situation is much improved, however, and will continue improving as children, teachers, and librarians demand the production of elementary level reference books. Meanwhile, children can utilize available juvenile sources and less scholarly adult ones.

To select materials for the reference collection, one should review the basic criteria for evaluating such titles.

A. Authority
 1. What is the editor's or author's background?
 2. What work has he/she already done?
 3. How much time has he/she devoted to it?
 4. What is the reputation of the publisher?
 5. Is the book new or revised? If revised, what type of revision has been employed?

B. Scope
 1. Has the author succeeded in the purposes as stated in the preface?
 2. What is the range of the subject matter?
 3. What are the book's limitations?
 4. How does it compare with similar books?
 5. How recent is the material included in the bibliographies?
 6. In spot-checking familiar topics, does the material appear to be up-to-date?

C. Treatment of Material
 1. How complete and accurate are the facts?
 2. Is the content objective?
 3. Is equal space allotted to subjects of equal importance?
 4. Is the type clear and readable?

D. Arrangement
 1. Is the sequence of materials alphabetical, classified, geographical, chronological, tabular, or statistical?
 2. Are the indexes full and accurate?
 3. Are there appendixes?
 4. Are cross-references used?

E. Format
 1. Does the format aid or hamper use of the book?
 2. How many volumes and/or pages does it contain?
 3. Is the binding durable and attractive?
 4. What is the quality of the paper?
 5. How clear and readable is the type?
 6. Are the illustrations attractive, accurate, and well-placed within the text?

F. Special Features
 1. Are there special devices to facilitate use?
 2. Does the book feature outstanding names as consultants?
 3. In what way is the book unique?

The remaining chapters in this book will list and evaluate

Introduction 5

various types of reference books, from general encyclopedias to hobby dictionaries. While few schools will need or want all the material described, most will find a growing need to include much of it in their reference collections. For those who are just beginning to build reference collections, sample basic collections for primary, intermediate, and junior high schools follow. These lists are merely suggested samples of first purchase material and should not be regarded as standardized selections for all situations. It cannot be emphasized too firmly that only the librarian can know what should be available to satisfy the needs of her unique clientele.

SAMPLE BASIC REFERENCE COLLECTION FOR PRIMARY GRADES

Britannica Junior Encyclopaedia
Childcraft
Compton's Precyclopedia
New Book of Knowledge
My Pictionary
My First Picture Dictionary
My Second Picture Dictionary
My Fun-with-Words Dictionary
New Golden Dictionary
Charlie Brown Dictionary
Rainbow Dictionary
The Weekly Reader Beginning Dictionary
World Book Dictionary
My World
New Book of Knowledge Annual
Subject Index to Children's Magazines
Subject Index to Books for Primary Grades
How to Use Maps and Globes
How to Read a City Map
How to Read a Highway Map
My First World Atlas
Rand McNally Classroom Atlas Indexed
Goode's World Atlas
Hammond Citation World Atlas
Something About an Author
Presidents
Cat in the Hat Beginner Dictionary in French
Mi Diccionario Illustrado
Fairy Elves
Marguerite DeAngeli's Book of Nursery and Mother Goose Rhymes
Time for Poetry
Index to Children's Poetry
Index to Poetry for Children and Young People
In Other Words
Music Dictionary
Stories of Favorite Operas
More Stories of Favorite Operas

Royal Book of Ballet
Golden Song Book
Famous Paintings
The Costume Book
Etiquette
Giant Nursery Book of Things That Go
Richard Scarry's Hop Aboard
Richard Scarry's What Do People Do All Day
Now You Know About People at Work
Building Bridges of Understanding
Multicultural Bibliography for Preschool through Second Grade
Black Experience in Children's Books
Black Experience in Children's Audio Visual Materials
Libros en Espanol
Now You Know About Animals
Beginning Knowledge Book of Turtles
Beginning Knowledge Book of Snakes
Doubleday First Guide to Insects
Now You Know About Plants
Doubleday First Guide to Trees
Doubleday First Guide to Wild Flowers
Beginning Knowledge Book of Backyard Flowers
Beginning Knowledge Book of Stars
Doubleday First Guide to Rocks
Mammals
Birds
What Is a Simple Machine
Joe Kaufman's What Makes It Go
Recipes for Art and Craft Materials
Let's Do Fingerplays
Games for Younger Children
Children's Books in Print
Subject Guide to Children's Books in Print
Children's Catalog
Elementary School Library Collection
I Read, You Read, We Read ...
Multi Media Approach to Children's Literature
Reading Ladders for Human Relations
Resources for Learning

SAMPLE BASIC REFERENCE COLLECTION FOR INTERMEDIATE GRADES

Britannica Junior Encyclopaedia
Collier's Encyclopedia
Compton's Encyclopedia
Encyclopedia International
Merit Students Encyclopedia
New Book of Knowledge
World Book Encyclopedia
Charlie Brown Dictionary

Introduction

Rainbow Dictionary
Webster's Elementary Dictionary
Thorndike-Barnhart Beginning Dictionary
Thorndike-Barnhart Intermediate Dictionary
Barnhart Dictionary of New English Since 1963
American Heritage Dictionary
Webster's New Collegiate Dictionary
Webster's New World Dictionary
Webster's Third New International Dictionary
World Book Dictionary
First Book of Facts and How to Find Them
Famous First Facts
Guinness Book of World Records
Webster's Dictionary of Proper Names
New Book of Knowledge Annual
World Book Year Book
Compton Yearbook
Information Please Almanac
Reader's Digest Almanac
World Almanac and Book of Facts
Abridged Readers' Guide to Periodical Literature
Subject Index to Children's Magazines
Subject Index to Books for Intermediate Grades
How We Use Maps and Globes
How to Read a City Map
How to Read a Highway Map
Hammond Illustrated Atlas for Young America
Rand McNally Classroom Atlas Indexed
Intermediate World Atlas
Goode's World Atlas
Hammond Medallion World Atlas
Rand McNally New Cosmopolitan World Atlas
Merit Atlas
World Book Atlas
Atlas Moderno Universal
Hammond Comparative World Atlas
Hammond Atlas of World History
Hammond Atlas of United States History
American Heritage Pictorial Atlas of United States History
History Atlas of America
Index to Young Readers' Collective Biographies
Index to Short Biographies
Current Biography Yearbook
Webster's Biographical Dictionary
Concise Dictionary of American Biography
Something About an Author
Junior Book of Authors
More Junior Authors
Third Book of Junior Authors
Facts About the Presidents
Asimov's Biographical Encyclopedia of Science and Technology
Great Composers 1300-1900
Composers Since 1900

Larousse Illustrated French-English/English-French Dictionary
Mi Diccionario Illustrado
Mi Primer Diccionario
Reader's Encyclopedia
Lincoln Library of Language Arts
Index to Children's Plays in Collections
Subject and Title Index to Short Stories for Children
Dragons, Unicorns, and Other Magical Beasts
Fairy Elves
Index to Fairy Tales
Folklore
Dictionary of Mythology, Mainly Classical
Time for Poetry
One Thousand Poems for Children
Index to Children's Poetry
Index to Poetry for Children and Young People
Golden Book of Quotations
Familiar Quotations
Instant English Handbook
Perfect Speller
In Other Words
Junior Thesaurus
Young People's Thesaurus Dictionary
New Roget's Thesaurus of the English Language in Dictionary Form
How Man Made Music
Music Dictionary
Golden Encyclopedia of Music
Stories of Favorite Operas
More Stories of Favorite Operas
Royal Book of Ballet
American Heritage Songbook
Famous Paintings
History of Art for Young People
Encyclopedia of Art
Book of Art
Britannica Encyclopedia of American Art
World's Great Religions
Handbook of World's Religions
Golden Bible Atlas
Common Bible
Holy Scriptures
Bible Encyclopedia for Children
Webster's New Geographical Dictionary
Encyclopedia of World Geography
Lands and Peoples
Other Lands, Other Peoples
Worldmark Encyclopedia of Nations
Europa Yearbook
American Heritage New Pictorial Encyclopedic Guide to the United
    States
Encyclopedia of World History
Dictionary of Chivalry
Atlas of Discovery

Introduction 9

Record of America
Encyclopedia of American History
Concise Dictionary of American History
Freedom Encyclopedia
How Documents Preserve Freedom
Voices from America's Past
What So Proudly We Hail
Stories of the States
Flags of the World
Flag Book of the United States
America Is My Country
The Costume Book
Dictionary of Costume
Etiquette
Emily Post Book of Etiquette for Young People
Customs and Holidays Around the World
Red Letter Days
American Book of Days
First Book of How to Run a Meeting
Complete Junior Encyclopedia of Transportation
Now You Know About People at Work
Concise Handbook of Occupations
Building Bridges of Understanding
In America Series
Great Indian Tribes
Black Experience in Children's Books
Black Experience in Children's Audio Visual Materials
Junior History of the American Negro
Negro Almanac
Junior Jewish Encyclopedia
Libros en Espanol
Manana Is Now
Book of Popular Science
Discovering Natural Science
Animal Atlas of the World
Botany
Mathematics Illustrated Dictionary
Metric System Simplified
Earth and Space
ABC's of Astronomy
ABC's of Chemistry
Rocks and Minerals
Concise Color Encyclopedia of Nature
Mammals
Birds
Reptiles and Amphibians
Fishes
Insects
Fossils
Standard First Aid and Personal Safety
Joe Kaufman's What Makes It Go
The Way Things Work
New Illustrated Space Encyclopedia

Hobby Collections A-Z
Recipes for Art and Craft Materials
Games
Concise Encyclopedia of Sports
Junior Illustrated Encyclopedia of Sports
Children's Books in Print
Subject Guide to Children's Books in Print
Children's Catalog
Elementary School Library Collection
I Read, You Read, We Read ...
Multi Media Approach to Children's Literature
Periodicals for School Libraries
Reading Ladders for Human Relations
Resources for Learning

SAMPLE BASIC REFERENCE COLLECTION
FOR JUNIOR HIGH SCHOOLS

Collier's Encyclopedia
Compton's Encyclopedia
Encyclopedia Americana
Encyclopedia International
Lincoln Library of Essential Information
Merit Students Encyclopedia
New Book of Knowledge
New Encyclopaedia Britannica
World Book Encyclopedia
American Heritage School Dictionary
Thorndike-Barnhart Intermediate Dictionary
Webster's Intermediate Dictionary
Thorndike-Barnhart Advanced Dictionary
Barnhart Dictionary of New English Since 1963
American Heritage Dictionary
Funk & Wagnalls Standard College Dictionary
Webster's New Collegiate Dictionary
Webster's New World Dictionary
Funk & Wagnalls Standard Dictionary (International Edition)
Webster's Third New International Dictionary
World Book Dictionary
Famous First Facts
Guinness Book of World Records
Abbreviations Dictionary
Webster's Dictionary of Proper Names
Handbook of Pseudonyms and Personal Nicknames
New Century Cyclopedia of Names
New Book of Knowledge Annual
World Book Year Book
Compton Yearbook
Collier's Yearbook
Facts on File
Information Please Almanac
Reader's Digest Almanac

Introduction

World Almanac and Book of Facts
Abridged Readers' Guide to Periodical Literature
Ayer Directory
Book Review Digest
Vertical File Index
Hammond Illustrated Atlas for Young America
Hammond Headline World Atlas
Goode's World Atlas
National Geographic Atlas of the World
Hammond Medallion World Atlas
Rand McNally New Cosmopolitan World Atlas
Merit Atlas
World Book Atlas
New York Times Atlas of the World
Britannica Atlas
Atlas Moderno Universal
Hammond Comparative World Atlas
Muir's Historical Atlas
Shepherd's Historical Atlas
Hammond Atlas of World History
Hammond Atlas of United States History
American Heritage Pictorial Atlas of United States History
Index to Young Readers' Collective Biographies
Index to Short Biographies
Current Biography Yearbook
Webster's Biographical Dictionary
Who's Who in the World
McGraw-Hill Encyclopedia of World Biography
Concise Dictionary of American Biography
Encyclopedia of American Biography
Something About an Author
Junior Book of Authors
More Junior Authors
Third Book of Junior Authors
Twentieth Century Authors
Twentieth Century Authors: First Supplement
American Authors
British Authors Before 1800
British Authors of the Nineteenth Century
European Authors 1000-1900
Who's Who in American Politics
Facts About the Presidents
Asimov's Biographical Encyclopedia of Science and Technology
McGraw-Hill Modern Men of Science
Great Composers 1300-1900
Composers Since 1900
Cassell's New French Dictionary
Cassell's New German Dictionary
Cassell's Italian Dictionary
Cassell's New Latin Dictionary
Dictionary of Spoken Russian
Appleton's New Cuyas Dictionary: English-Spanish/Spanish-English

Reader's Encyclopedia
Brewer's Dictionary of Phrase and Fable
Concise Oxford Companion to English Literature
Dictionary of Fictional Characters
Oxford Classical Dictionary
Oxford Companion to Classical Literature
Oxford Companion to American Literature
Lincoln Library of Language Arts
Dictionary of Literary Terms
Play Index
McGraw-Hill Encyclopedia of World Drama
Short Story Index
Index to Fairy Tales
Folklore
Dictionary of Mythology, Mainly Classical
Funk & Wagnalls Dictionary of Folklore, Mythology, and Legend
Index to Children's Poetry
Index to Poetry for Children and Young People
Granger's Index to Poetry
Poetry Handbook
Familiar Quotations
Home Book of Quotations
Instant English Handbook
Perfect Speller
Misspeller's Dictionary
Young People's Thesaurus Dictionary
Webster's New Dictionary of Synonyms
New Roget's Thesaurus of the English Language in Dictionary Form
Complete Rhyming Dictionary
Dictionary of American Slang
Golden Encyclopedia of Music
Concise Dictionary of Music
New Encyclopedia of the Opera
Dictionary of Modern Ballet
Folk Songs of the World
Rock Encyclopedia
History of Art for Young People
Encyclopedia of Art
Britannica Encyclopedia of American Art
McGraw-Hill Dictionary of Art
Eastern Religions
Handbook of World's Religions
Dictionary on Non-Christian Religions
Atlas of the Bible Lands
Common Bible
Holy Scriptures
Harper's Bible Dictionary
Home Book of Bible Quotations
Who's Who in the Old Testament
Who's Who in the New Testament
Webster's New Geographical Dictionary
Columbia-Lippincott Gazetteer
Encyclopedia of World Geography

Introduction 13

Lands and Peoples
Other Lands, Other Peoples
Worldmark Encyclopedia of Nations
Fact Book of the Countries of the World
Europa Yearbook
American Heritage New Pictorial Encyclopedic Guide to the United States
Pictorial Travel Atlas of Scenic America
Encyclopedia of World History
Who's Who in the Ancient World
Who's Who in the Middle Ages
New Century Classical Handbook
Dictionary of Chivalry
Atlas of Discovery
Chronology of the Expanding World
Chronology of the Modern World
Harper Encyclopedia of the Modern World
Record of America
Webster's Guide to American History
Oxford Companion to American History
Encyclopedia of American History
Encyclopedia of American Facts and Dates
Album of American History
Concise Dictionary of American History
Freedom Encyclopedia
Voices from America's Past
Documents of American History
What So Proudly We Hail
Stories of the States
Flags of the World
Flag Book of the United States
Lincoln Library of Social Sciences
American Citizens Handbook
Dictionary of Costume
What People Wore
Economics Reference Book
New Seventeen Book of Etiquette
Customs and Holidays Around the World
National Holidays Around the World
American Book of Days
Chronology and Fact Book of the United Nations
Roberts Rules of Order
Dictionary of American Politics
Book of States
U.S. Government Organization Manual
Almanac of American Politics
Official Congressional Directory
Complete Junior Encyclopedia of Transportation
Encyclopedia of Careers and Vocational Guidance
Occupational Outlook Handbook
Lovejoy's Career and Vocational Guide
Lovejoy's College Guide
Building Bridges of Understanding

Makers of America
Great Indian Tribes
American Negro Reference Book
Ebony Success Library
Ebony Pictorial History of Black America
Multi Media Materials for Afro-American Studies
Negro Almanac
Junior Jewish Encyclopedia
Manana Is Now
Book of Popular Science
Audubon Nature Encyclopedia
Animal Atlas of the World
Illustrated Encyclopedia of the Animal Kingdom
Botany
Mathematics Illustrated Dictionary
Mathematics Dictionary
Metric System Simplified
Pocket Encyclopedia of Physical Sciences
ABC's of Astronomy
ABC's of Chemistry
Handbook of Chemistry and Physics
Larousse Encyclopedia of the Earth
Mammals
Birds
Reptiles and Amphibians
Fishes
Insects
Fossil Book
Gerrish's Technical Dictionary
New Encyclopedia of Child Care
Complete Ecology Fact Book
Standard First Aid and Personal Safety
Stein and Day International Medical Encyclopedia
Drugs from A to Z
The Way Things Work
New Space Encyclopedia
Teenagers Guide to Collecting Practically Anything
Games
Concise Encyclopedia of Sports
Encyclopedia of Sports
Books in Print
Subject Guide to Books in Print
I Read, You Read, We Read ...
Junior High School Library Catalog
Periodicals for School Libraries
Reading Ladders for Human Relations
Spoken Records
Senior High School Library Catalog

GENERAL ENCYCLOPEDIAS

An encyclopedia, according to the American Library Association, is "a work containing informational articles on subjects in every field of knowledge, usually arranged in alphabetical order, or a similar work limited to a special field or subject." General encyclopedias by their very nature represent one of the more basic sources for reference material. Historically, encyclopedias date back to the time of Aristotle, as individuals attempted to summarize and classify knowledge. In fact, the word "encyclopedia" is frequently defined as a systematic summary of all information significant to mankind. With the vast knowledge explosion in recent years, this definition appears somewhat absurd. Until mechanical devices for information storage and retrieval are widely available and more economicaly, it is obvious that existing encyclopedias cannot contain "all information significant to mankind."

Realizing the impossibility of summarizing "all information significant to mankind" in 15 to 30 volumes, encyclopedia editors usually aim for broad subject coverage but with emphasis on certain specific areas. Necessarily, an elementary or junior high library must contain a variety of sets representing different subject emphases rather than rely on one encyclopedia to carry the burden of summarized information. Students very quickly learn which set is most likely to answer specific questions. More and more, encyclopedia editors are attempting to gear their sets to specific grade levels and to maintain a writing style appropriate for the intended user. The New Book of Knowledge, for example, is designed for use by children as young as seven years old, and its readability for second graders is carefully checked. Since the average sixth grade will include children with reading skills ranging from second grade through high school, it is essential that elementary and junior high libraries acquire encyclopedias on varying levels of difficulty. Within one junior high class, students will likely need both Encyclopaedia Britannica and Britannica Junior.

Besides choosing encyclopedias with differing subject emphases and with varying readability levels, the librarian selecting sets for young people should evaluate them carefully. The following questions may assist in determining the quality of the work being examined.

1. Who is the publisher and what else has he published?

2. Who are the editors and contributors and what are their qualifications?
3. Are articles signed by the contributors?
4. Is the work sponsored by a significant organization or association?
5. Does the work have a stated purpose?
6. How long and thorough are the articles?
7. Is the subject coverage well balanced?
8. How does the set compare with similar works?
9. What is the date of the latest copyright?
10. Is there a policy of continuous revision?
11. Is there a yearbook or supplement to assist in maintaining currency?
12. Are statistical data, illustrative material, and bibliographies up to date?
13. How is the material arranged, i.e., alphabetical, topical, etc.?
14. Do cross references aid in locating related material?
15. How extensive and how useful is the index?
16. How are controversial subjects treated?
17. Is the style scholarly or popular?
18. For what intellectual level is the material intended?
19. Is the binding attractive and durable?
20. What quality of paper is used?
21. Is the page make-up pleasing?
22. What quality of illustrative material, maps, etc., are included?
23. Is the type face and size pleasing?
24. Are bibliographies listed?
25. Does it feature any type of study aid?

Numerous works aiming at encyclopedic coverage are available; some are excellent and some are quite the contrary. In addition to the older, standard sets, several new titles have been produced in relatively recent years. Some of the most recent entirely new sets include Encyclopedia International (1963-1964), New Book of Knowledge (1966), the Merit Students Encyclopedia (1967), and the Young Students Encyclopedia (1972). Since all the encyclopedias discussed in the following pages are recommended, no attempt is made to suggest order of purchase. Each set is superior in some part to all other sets. The final decision as to which sets should be acquired is dependent entirely upon the individual situation. In other words, each librarian must determine the needs of the students in his school and further determine which encyclopedias fulfill these needs. It is highly recommended that many titles be available rather than multiple copies of one or two titles.

Britannica Junior Encyclopaedia for Boys and Girls. By the editors of Encyclopaedia Britannica. Chicago: Encyclopaedia Britannica, Inc. (William Benton, Publisher), 1973. 15 vols. $109.50.

General Encyclopedias

Britannica Junior, first published under this title in 1934, was based upon and expanded from Weedon's Encyclopedia, published between 1931-1932. Edited by the staff of Encyclopaedia Britannica, it is not a junior version of the massive set but is designed as a preparatory reference work for children in grades four through eight. The Britannica staff receives editorial advice from the faculties of the University of Chicago and the University Laboratory School. Broad in scope but with some emphasis on science and social studies, it is geared to the elementary school curriculum and the needs and interests of children. Utilizing letter-by-letter alphabetical arrangement, its broad topic entries are long and well developed. In a graded approach, the articles begin with basic information and proceed to detailed and background knowledge. The many subheadings, clear explanations, and simple vocabulary make the set easily usable by young children and by older children with reading disabilities.

Supplementing the broad-entry text is the 644-page Ready Reference Index in Volume 1, which includes pronunciation, brief fact notations, and "see also" references for 24,600 entries. Abundant cross references within the text aid in locating related material. Reliable and accurate, the set undergoes a complete revision every five to six years, supplemented by annual revision and updating. It does not provide a yearbook, but the Britannica Book of the Year can be used to update it as well as the Encyclopaedia Britannica. A list of nearly 780 distinguished authorities (editors, artists, and special consultants), with their qualifications and contributions, is included in volume one. Profusely illustrated with over 12,000 photographs, drawings and maps, the set contains excellent pictures both in full color and black and white. In addition to nearly 800 maps distributed throughout the text, Britannica Junior features a complete atlas in Volume 15 with its own useful index. The 143 maps included are produced by Encyclopaedia Britannica Cartography, Hammond, Inc., Rand McNally, and Greco. Although bibliographies do not accompany specific subjects, a lengthy list appears under the article "Children's Literature." The format in general is more attractive than in earlier editions. Particularly appealing is the large, clear 10-point type printed on fine non-glare paper. Britannica Junior provides a good introduction to more mature encyclopedias and should be included in elementary school libraries and in junior high libraries where students have reading problems.

Childcraft--The How and Why Library. Chicago: Field Enterprises Educational Corp., 1974. 15 vols. $77.50.

Although Childcraft--The How and Why Library is not an encyclopedia as such, it contains such an array of information that it can be considered in this category. Designed for use by and with pre-school and primary level children, its contents are carefully selected on the basis of young children's interests and curiosities as indicated by existing research. The material included substantiates the editor's claim in this respect, and also reflects the judgments of the outstanding educational and library consultants who are associated with the set. Arranged by subjects, the 15 volumes, each of which is devoted to a separate general topic, bear the following titles: vol. 1, Poems and Rhymes; vol. 2, Stories and Fables; vol. 3, Children Everywhere; vol. 4, World and Space; vol. 5, About Animals; vol. 6, The Green Kingdom; vol. 7, How Things Work; vol. 8, How We Get Things; vol. 9, Holidays and Customs; vol. 10, Places to Know; vol. 11, Make and Do; vol. 12, Look and Learn; vol. 13, Look Again; vol. 14, About Me; and vol. 15, Guide and Index.

Volumes one, two and three are anthologies of high quality literature, both traditional and contemporary, representing outstanding authors and poets. Science and nature are of primary concern in volumes four, five, and six, covering such topics as weather, astronomy, animals, plants, and earth formations. In volume seven are explanations of the workings of more than 500 simple machines and other devices, such as how a steam iron works and how a faucet works. The work that people do and the products they produce for daily living are the subjects of volume eight. Much-needed information on holidays is incorporated in volume nine. Introducing children to the cultural heritage of man, volume ten describes more than 275 famous places around the world. More than 400 creative activities for preschool and elementary school children are detailed in volume 11. A variety of visual communication is discussed in volume 12; more than 150 examples are presented, ranging from color to letters to numerals to trademarks. Volume 13 introduces children to famous works of art through 217 reproductions created by more than 190 artists. Using 400 photographs to illustrate the text, volume 14 depicts the child as a complete being, emotional, physical, rational, and social. Volume 15, the Guide and Index, is the key to Childcraft. Directed to parents and teachers, it contains sections on how Childcraft aids in child development and guidance, and how it relates to the various areas of the school curriculum. The general index is full, accurate, and easy to use.

Distributed throughout the set are hundreds of illustrations, many in full color and many being excellent photographs. Generous use of illustrations by outstanding children's artists, including many Caldecott Medal winners, enhances the quality of illustrative material. The format of the set has commendable features: sturdy, rainbow-colored binding; durable, high quality paper; and clear, legible print. All in all, while Childcraft is not an encyclopedia, it contains such a wealth of material valuable to teachers and children that it should definitely be considered as a basic reference source. Its information and appeal easily justify the expense.

Collier's Encyclopedia, With Bibliography and Index. William Halsey, editorial director. Louis Shores, editor-in-chief. New York: Macmillan Educational Corp., 1974. 24 vols. $299.00.

This excellent adult encyclopedia was first published in 1949-1951 in 20 volumes and was expanded to 24 volumes in 1962. Principally designed to be used by junior and senior high school, college and university students, it appeals to and can readily be used by upper elementary grade children. The broad entry articles are arranged alphabetically letter-by-letter, with more important topics receiving longer coverage. Writing throughout is clear but scholarly. In many areas the text is correlated to school curricula. While subject coverage is comprehensive and expertly balanced, political science, biography, fine arts, religion, science, technology, classics, and philosophy are all especially well treated. Striving for an objective viewpoint at all times, the editors submit controversial subjects to authorities representing all sides. If two or more standpoints are presented and no decision can be made, all are printed in the article. Outstanding accuracy and reliability are maintained by nearly 5,000 editors and international authorities who contribute to the set. All major articles are signed, with the total list of contributors and their qualifications identified in Volume 1. A large permanent staff carries on a vigorous program of continuous revision. Up to date in all vital areas, the set is reprinted to include current information. It is supplemented by the highly recommended Collier's Encyclopedia Year Book ($4.95 to set owners).

For a large adult encyclopedia, Collier's is extremely well illustrated, with 17,000 illustrations, including some 1,400 in color, distributed throughout the set. Besides the black and white and full color illustrative material, some three-dimensional acetate color transparencies are included. Appropriately located in the text, the many Rand McNally maps are current, legible, and accurate, with gazetteer information for states, provinces, and major countries printed on map versos. A unique and outstanding feature of Collier's is the bibliography, designed for self-education. A 200-page section in Volume 24 lists over 11,500 important titles arranged alphabetically by subject, briefly annotated, and graded by level of difficulty; various audio-visual materials, including 16mm films, are included. The excellent analytical index of more than 400,000 entries and numerous "see" and "see also" references within the text assist in linking related material. Superior in physical makeup, the set is printed in clear, easy-to-read type on fine quality, non-glare, white paper. As a whole, Collier's rates as one of the three foremost adult encyclopedias. Scholarly, reliable, attractive, and readable, it should most certainly be available in elementary and junior high school libraries. It is probably the easiest adult set for children to use and therefore provides a smooth transition from encyclopedias coordinated with school curricula to those designed for mature users.

Compton's Encyclopedia and Fact Index. Donald E. Lawson, ed.
    Helen Hemingway Benton, publisher. Chicago: F. E.
    Compton Co., a division of Encyclopaedia Britannica, 1974.
    26 vols. $144.00.

Compton's Encyclopedia, first published in 1922, is suitable for children from elementary levels through high school. Geared to the requirements of school curricula, the subject coverage is well balanced and well selected. It is especially fine on science and on subjects of particular interest to children, such as magic, fairies and fairy stories, pets, etc. Arrangement is alphabetical letter-by-letter, using the broad form of entry. The well written articles are designed to stimulate children to further reading. Insuring a high degree of readability, the articles are graded to cover a wide age range. Study guides accompany many major articles. In addition to the long articles in the main text, the set features a Fact-Index which incorporates in its thousands of entries brief biographies, tables and charts, and dictionary-type definitions. The Fact-Index is distributed throughout the set with each volume containing the corresponding section of the index. Supplementing the Fact-Index are "see also" cross references indicating related articles in the text, and "see" references guiding users from the text to the Fact-Index. Accurate, reliable, and up to date, it undergoes continuous revision with at least two printings a year and is supplemented by the Compton Yearbook ($7.95 to set owners). A list of the specialists, consultants, and editors who contribute to the set is included. Articles are not signed, but areas of responsibility of each authority are clearly indicated. Compton's contains 25,000 illustrations, including full color pictorial material and acetate transparencies, which aid in clarifying the text. Current, accurate maps, prepared by Hammond, Inc. and staff cartographers, are appropriately placed in the text. Gazetteer entries are indexed on the versos. Graded bibliographies of books and films follow major articles. Attractive in format, the set is printed in excellent type on fine, heavy paper. Long considered a favorite encyclopedia, Compton's maintains a steady quality and definitely belongs on the reference shelf.

Compton's Precyclopedia. (William Benton, Publisher). Chicago: F. E. Compton Co., 1973. 16 vols. and Teaching Guide and Index. $74.95.

Based on the Young Children's Encyclopedia, which is published by Encyclopaedia Britannica and directed to the home market, Compton's Precyclopedia is a school and library edition designed to introduce the pre-school and early-school child to a variety of learning experiences. Created as a "trainer or browsing encyclopedia," it is aimed at children of approximately four to ten years of age. Although the articles in the set appear to be arbitrarily selected, they are generally on topics of high interest appeal to young children. Included is material on the social sciences, literature, language arts, the humanities, and new mathematics, with heavy emphasis on science articles. Entries are unsigned and vary in length from two to several pages. A list of contributors appears in volume 1, and a page indicating areas of responsibility is printed in the back of each volume.

Making no apparent attempt at comprehensiveness, the set is designed to attract the attention and interest of children. Consistent with this goal is the inclusion of material written in a variety of styles: fictional, conversational, and poetic. In addition to factual articles, the set contains stories, poems, riddles, jokes, and more than 24,000 illustrations. Throughout the set the size of type varies, with large print used for articles primarily of interest

General Encyclopedias   21

to the very young, and smaller type for topics presented in considerably more detail. Most articles end with "see also" references to related information in other volumes.

Preceding the main alphabetical sequence of the text in each volume is a 24-page introductory section called "Things to Do." Included in it are the numbers, the letters of the alphabet, and stories, poems, and games designed to help children get ready to read. Chosen for this section is high interest, participation material.

The paperback "Teaching Guide and Index to Compton's Precyclopedia" is a helpful tool for adults who may be assisting children in the use of the set. Following a brief introduction to the "Things to Do" material, the cross-referenced index locates topics throughout the set. Printed on blue paper in the back of the tool is the "Teaching Guide," which subdivides information into possible units for study based on topics usually taught in the primary grades. Topics covered include: about make-believe; being me; pioneers; home, school, and family; health and safety; the community is people; communication; transportation; exploring; our earth; animals; plants; and getting ready for mathematics. Under each topic is a list of related articles with their location in the set.

Although the Compton's Precyclopedia is open to a number of valid criticisms, e.g., the arbitrary inclusion and exclusion of topics, the sparse guide words, the inconsistent style, the lack of balance in coverage, etc., basically the set succeeds in its purpose of providing an introduction to encyclopedias for the very young. In general the material is truly of interest to children and the format is attractive. Keeping in mind its limitations, i.e., that it is in no way a comprehensive encyclopedia, it should be included in all primary school libraries.

The Encyclopedia Americana. Bernard S. Cayne, ed. in chief.
    New York: Americana Corp., 1974. 30 vols. $400.00.

The oldest American encyclopedia still in print, The Encyclopedia Americana was begun in 1829 under the direction of Francis Lieber, a German political exile. Completed in 1833 in thirteen volumes, it was based on the German encyclopedia, Brockhaus' Konversations-Lexikon and was designed to provide readable material in a popular style. From 1900 to 1911, the Americana was owned by the Scientific American and under this influence developed a fine reputation for information in science and technology, a reputation it still holds today.

The Americana was expanded to its present thirty volumes between 1917 and 1919 and is now revised annually. The 1974 edition contains comprehensive subject coverage, and in addition to its able handling of the sciences and technology is especially strong in topics of American interest as well as in literature, history, geography, and biography. While remaining American in emphasis, the Americana is international in content.

Some of the Americana's special features include book-length articles on several major countries, comprehensive articles on the U.S. states and the Canadian provinces, long entries on each of the centuries A.D., digests of literary classics and operas, literary and mythological allusions, the texts of historical documents, and glossaries of technical or otherwise difficult terms.

Designed for junior high and up, the Americana is also suitable for upper elementary grade children. The articles are written in excellent scholarly style yet are easy to understand. In fact, according to the publishers, the overwhelming majority of the words used in the set are contained in the recent revision of Webster's Seventh New Collegiate Dictionary.

The Americana's articles, which are alphabeted word-by-word, are well developed on limited topics but are much longer for the more important ones. There is a carefully planned balance between short and long articles. The many brief articles provide separate capsules of information on each of thousands of persons, places, ideas, and things of all description. The longer articles furnish extensive and detailed surveys of many "big" subjects. Thus the Americana provides readers with quick, short answers to specific questions, as well as the wealth of information that may be needed on major subjects. The Americana's articles are known for their accuracy and reliability.

The Americana contains thousands of high-quality illustrations, many in full color. Hammond Incorporated specially prepared the major maps for the set, while staff or free-lance cartographers are responsible for the remainder. Maps of the states, provinces, and countries list detailed gazateer information on the versos. Accurate, legible, and up to date, they are consistently of superior quality.

Extensive bibliographies follow all major articles, and briefer "Further Readings" accompany shorter articles. The comprehensive and accurate index volume is supplemented by numerous "see also" references within articles, lists of related articles, and tables of contents for major articles. Excellent glare-free, white paper and clear, easy-to-read print add to the appeal of the set.

All in all, Encyclopedia Americana is an extremely valuable reference work for elementary and junior high schools and beyond. Its scholarly content in readable style makes it a usable tool for those students who need more information than is contained in juvenile encyclopedias. The encyclopedia is supplemented by The Americana Annual (8.95 to set owners), a highly recommended, authoritative yearbook.

Encyclopedia International. Edward Humphrey, ed. New York: Grolier Incorporated, 1974. 20 vols. $199.50.

New in concept and first published in 1964, Encyclopedia International required $4,000,000 and four years to produce. In its new and completely revised edition in 1974, it has matured into an outstanding reference work. It is created for use by young people from fifth grade up, especially in high school and early college. Its balanced subject coverage is based on nationwide surveys of secondary school reference needs. Social studies receive outstanding treatment, as do vocational material, sports and recreation. It includes numerous biographical entries, a high proportion of

General Encyclopedias 23

which are of contemporary persons. Alphabetically arranged, letter by letter, it contains 36,000 specific entries. The length of entry is determined by the importance of the subject, and the extensive index is supplemented by "see" and "see also" references and by lists of related articles. Written in clear, short-sentence style, and thoroughly tested for readability, its explanations of complicated topics are lucid and easy to understand. Up to date, reliable, and accurate, it is subject to continuous revision by its permanent editorial staff. Its currency is further maintained by its highly recommended Yearbook (7.95 to set owners) which reviews the previous year's events in addition to updating published sections of the main set. Listing as contributors more than 2,000 qualified specialists, the Encyclopedia International includes the full names and qualifications of contributors for all but the briefest articles. The set contains 19,000 well-chosen and well located illustrations, many in full or duo-color. Particularly outstanding are the 32 pages of full color reproductions of famous works of art. Fine political, topographic, resource and other special purpose maps produced by Hammond, Inc., Jeppesen Co. and staff cartographers appear in the set. Gazetteer information appears on the back of maps for the states, provinces, and major countries. Excellent bibliographies accompany the more important articles. The format is superior, featuring clear, legible type and bold headings and subheadings. All in all, Encyclopedia International is carefully researched and edited and it is a valuable reference set which should be included in elementary and junior high school libraries.

The Lincoln Library of Essential Information. Anson B. Barber, ed. Columbus, Ohio: Frontier Press Co., 1974. 2 vols. $63.95.

Designed for ready reference and as a self-instruction device for general cultural information, the Lincoln Library of Essential Information is suitable for students in elementary, junior and senior high schools, and colleges. Closely correlated to school curricula, it contains a comprehensive subject coverage and is especially strong on literature, fine arts, music, education, and biography. Arrangement is classified, with twelve broad subject areas: English language, literature, history, geography and travel, science, mathematics, economics and useful arts, government and politics, fine arts, education, biography, and miscellany. Ease of use is facilitated by the fine analytical index of more than 25,000 entries and by many cross references. Tables and charts succinctly show large quantities of information, and special dictionaries of subjects and terms provide further factual material. Many subject specialists contributed to the work. While articles are unsigned, each authority's area of responsibility is clearly stated. Written in a concise and detailed style, articles are consistently accurate and reliable. Continuous revision, with a new edition published annually, insures the currency of the material. It is supplemented by the Lincoln Library of the Social Studies, the Lincoln Library of the Language Arts, and the Lincoln Library of the Fine Arts. About 1,000 quality illustrations in color and halftone are well located throughout. An atlas section contains a number of pages of multicolor maps. Extensive bibliographies of well selected titles follow each of the major subject divisions. A special feature is the inclusion of thousands of test questions and answers for self-education. Sturdily bound, Lincoln Library has clear, legible type on thin but strong paper. Easy to use and bountiful in current information, it is a valuable two-volume encyclopedia that definitely belongs in elementary and junior high school libraries.

Merit Students Encyclopedia. William D. Halsey, editorial director. Louis Shores, senior library advisor. New York: Macmillan Educational Corp., 1974. 20 vols. $165.00.

First published in 1967, the Merit Students Encyclopedia required seven years and $7,000,000 for compilation and publication. It is created for children from fifth grade through high school and is geared to curriculum materials from all states. Its subject coverage, while outstanding in all areas, is especially strong on states and countries, particularly Canada, science, technology, fine arts, literature, and vocational guidance. The articles are clearly written and are prepared primarily for the grade levels at which the subject is taught. Exceedingly accurate, each article is reviewed or written and signed by one of the many contributing specialists. The encyclopedia is continuously revised and is reprinted at least once each year to include important happenings. It contains more than 19,000 illustrations, with more than 5,000 in full color, and with many having transparent acetate overlays. More than 1,350 maps of all types are included--physical, political, economic, historical, and thematic. The main series of maps is based on the Rand McNally Cosmo series; others are by staff cartographers. The political maps have gazetteer indexes on the versos. Distributed throughout the text, the maps are up to date, legible, and accurate. Articles, arranged alphabetically letter by letter under specific entry, each begin with a dictionary definition, including pronunciation. Using extensive cross references to link related material, the set includes a 400-page index with 125,000 entries. "Fact Boxes" and "Student Guides" further assist in quick location of essential data. Bibliographies of graded titles appear with major articles. The outstanding format features clear printing with bold headings on fine quality paper. Updated by the supplement, Merit Students Year Book (identical to Collier's Year Book), an authoritative survey of national and international developments, the Merit Students Encyclopedia is comprehensive, well organized, and up to date. Sophisticated and scholarly without being too difficult, it is a valuable addition to the reference books for young people.

New Book of Knowledge. Martha Glauber Shapp, ed. New York: Grolier, Inc., 1974. 20 vols. $199.50.

Replacing the Book of Knowledge (1910-1965), the New Book of Knowledge, first published in 1966, is, indeed, entirely new.

At a reputed cost of $32 million and 15 years of work, the fifteenth edition of Encyclopaedia Britannica emerged as a structurally new encyclopedia. Dubbed the Britannica 3, the work is the only major encyclopedia to be presented in three parts: the Propaedia: Outline of Knowledge; the Macropaedia: Knowledge in Depth; and the Micropaedia: Ready Reference and Index. The "Propaedia" in one volume attempts to classify knowledge into ten major areas: Matter and energy; the Earth; Human life; Human society; Art; Technology; Religion; The history of mankind; and The branches of knowledge. Each topic is outlined in minute detail with index references to the Macropaedia in order to provide the user with an effective tool for self-education. Also included in this volume are the lists of advisors, contributors, and consultants for the set.

The "Micropaedia: Ready Reference and Index" consists of more than 102,000 short articles in ten volumes. Articles in this section are limited in length from one sentence to 750 words. Nearly 16,000 illustrations, about one-fourth in color, enhance this text. Arranged with three columns per page, the "Micropaedia" contains concise, easy to locate information in a clear, attractive format. In addition to providing accessible ready reference material, this portion of the set doubles as an index to the entire set by providing "see" references to topics within the "Micropaedia" and "see also" references to topics in the "Micropaedia" and in the "Macropaedia."

The final 19 volumes of the Britannica 3 consist of the "Macropaedia: Knowledge in Depth," a collection of 4,207 broad coverage articles. Resembling former editions of Britannica, the "Macropaedia" articles range from about 1,000 words to complete book-length entries. Written in the traditional scholarly style, this section provides in-depth information according to broad general topics, e.g., African Peoples, Arts of; Electricity; Women, Status of. About 8,000 illustrations appear in this section, including some fine maps by Rand McNally. Excellent bibliographies follow each article.

The Britannica 3 attempts to provide a universal approach to a vast amount of accumulated knowledge, and contains contributions from 4,277 persons from all continents. Since it is virtually a new encyclopedia, it has the advantage of being well-balanced in its coverage, especially in the areas of contemporary knowledge and discoveries. The three-part arrangement, a serious departure from traditional encyclopedia structure, will lend itself to more efficient use by junior high school students. Youngsters who previously might have steered away from the broad entry format can now use the ready reference volumes to locate specific facts quickly as well as aid in approaching the long scholarly articles in the "Macropaedia." The New Britannica is definitely recommended for junior high school libraries, especially those requiring serious, mature material.

Our Wonderful World. Arthur Louis Joquel II, exec. ed. New York: Grolier Incorporated, 1972. 18 vols. O.P.

First published by Spencer Press (then affiliated with Sears,

Roebuck and Co.) in 1955 to 1957 and acquired by Grolier Incorporated in 1961, Our Wonderful World evolved under the founding editorship of Herbert S. Zim, a well-known juvenile writer. This fine thematic set was last published in 1972; since, unfortunately, it is going out of print, librarians should keep their copies as long as they are serviceable.

Totally original in concept, the set bears the subtitle: "An Encyclopedic Anthology for the Entire Family." In conceiving Our Wonderful World, the editors, instead of asking subject specialists to contribute, decided to utilize excellent material already written. They collected 13,000 books, 200 files of magazines, and 40,000 pamphlets. These were checked against readability formulas such as those by Flesch and Dale-Chall. Having accumulated the material, the editorial staff developed a thematic arrangement, with each volume covering a particular theme or themes. The subject units were incorporated in thirty major themes of general knowledge. Stories and poems on the theme were included with the factual material. In 1967 a new unit entitled "Negro History" was added, and in 1968 another addition, "Family," was incorporated. Most of the contents are excerpts from previously published materials taken from about 4,000 books, pamphlets, and magazines; however, some articles were specially commissioned. Approximately 2,500 authors and contributors are listed.

Written in an appealing narrative style, and designed as supplementary material with a high reading motivation for upper elementary grades through high school, the set is closely related to school curricula and is particularly useful for material on vocations and hobbies. The work contains thousands of illustrations, many in full color. Maps, produced by the Jeppesen Co., are of fine quality and are distributed throughout the text. Various bibliographies within the set list titles for further reading. Because of the thematic arrangement, the outstanding analytical index is essential. Besides the 246-page index in Volume 18, cross references in the text and lists of related subject articles aid in locating material. Clear print on good paper and overall superior production combine to make an attractive format. Although Our Wonderful World is less efficient for ready reference than alphabetically arranged encyclopedias, it nonetheless contains much information not included in the quick-reference sets. Its demise is truly unfortunate for both elementary and junior high libraries.

The World Book Encyclopedia. William H. Nault, ed. Chicago: Field Enterprises Educational Corp., 1974. 22 vols. $239.50.

Sustaining its popularity for many years, World Book Encyclopedia was first published in 1917 and has been published in special Braille and extra large print editions for use by the blind or partially sighted. The purpose of the set as stated in the encyclopedia is to present "information from man's vast reservoir of knowledge in the most accessible and usable form." Geared for children in elementary grades through high school, World Book is attractive, easy to read, and versatile. The coverage is superb and well balanced, with entries chosen to correspond to school curricula and the interests and needs of young people. It is especially strong in vocational guidance, science, literature, and art, and contains numerous fine biographical entries. This set is arranged alphabetically word by word under specific entry. The style is clear, concise, and factual, with articles written to meet different age requirements and checked against a readability chart. The length of the articles is determined by the importance of the topic, some being treated in depth and others briefly and concisely. The entries are accurate, up to date, and reliable, and are constantly and thoroughly checked for exactness. More than 3,000 contributors, including internationally known subject specialists, are listed with their qualifications and areas of contribution. In addition, a large permanent editorial staff is maintained. All major articles are signed by both contributor and critical reviewer.

World Book Encyclopedia is continuously revised and is supplemented by the World Book Year Book ($5.95 to schools and libraries). The 29,000 expertly prepared illustrations add greatly to the set. Maps, mostly in color and distributed throughout the text, include political, physical, terrain, and thematic sequences and are produced by Rand McNally and cartographers of the World Book staff. Gazetteers accompany the maps of all the states, provinces, and major countries of the world.

An important feature added to World Book Encyclopedia in 1972 is the final volume, Research Guide/Index. It begins with an introduction to research, giving step by step advice on how to proceed. The bulk of the volume, however, is occupied by the index. Listing more than 150,000 entries, the index provides a detailed approach to the information contained in the set. Incorporated in the alphabetical sequence of the index are 200 reading and study guides, each of which gives suggested topics for study, short graded bibliographies, a list of other resources, and a list of other sources of information. The elaborate system of cross-referencing throughout the set supplements the separate index. Outstanding in format, World Book features clear, legible type with bold headings and subheadings printed on fine quality art paper. Clearly written, easy to use, and carefully edited, it definitely belongs in elementary and junior high school libraries.

Young Students Encyclopedia. Specially prepared with the staff of My Weekly Reader. Editorial Director, George H. Wolfson. Middletown, Conn.: American Education Publications, a Xerox Co., 1972. 15 vols. 2600p. $55.30.

Prepared by the editors of My Weekly Reader and Funk & Wagnalls, Young Students Encyclopedia is a reliable, but limited, entry into the encyclopedia arena. Concerned primarily with coverage of those ideas most often included in school curricula, variation in reading abilities, and encouragement of active reader participation, the set attempts "to provide a basic introduction to man's ideas, language and world." More than 2,400 articles are arranged alphabetically letter by letter. The articles are quite well balanced, with science and technology receiving slightly heavy coverage.

General Encyclopedias

Although articles are unsigned, contributors and their specific areas of responsibility are listed in volume one. Throughout the set the editors have attempted to present familiar topics at a reading level comprehensible by young children, and complicated ones at a more difficult reading level.

The format of the set is in general attractive. The large, clear print is easy to read and the two-column arrangement usable. Included in the excessively wide margins are numerous illustrations. A large number of full color pictures as well as charts, tables, and maps are utilized. Maps are few and rather inadequate; those included for states and countries are very simple political-physical maps drawn with little detail and painted in drab colors. Other illustrative material, while small in size, is relatively attractive. An important feature of this encyclopedia is the "Learning by Doing" segments, printed in blue type, and designed to encourage students to participate in the activities being discussed. Scattered throughout the text, they include such items as how to make an abacus, how plants grow, and how Newton's Laws of Motion work. Consistent with this aim is the inclusion of numerous children's games. In the margins adjacent to a number of articles are concise bits of related material, such as glossaries of terms, collections of specific data (e.g., facts about states and countries), and tables of information (e.g., the Morse code).

In the back of volume 15 is the 80-page Index. Besides providing a finding list for specific subjects, it gives the pronunciation of hard words, the birth and death dates of people, and the scientific names of plants and animals. To supplement the Index, "also read" references follow each article and point out related material in the set. "See" references are also incorporated in the main alphabetical sequence.

While the Young Students Encyclopedia cannot be thought of as a standard comprehensive juvenile encyclopedia, it certainly should be considered as a supplement to other more complete works. Although the editors' intent is limited, they have succeeded in their purpose. The well written and attractive set provides reliable information at a relatively low cost. It will serve well in elementary schools.

ENGLISH LANGUAGE DICTIONARIES

A dictionary is a book of the words of a language, arranged alphabetically or in some definite order, with definitions and often other appropriate information, e.g., etymologies, pronunciation. Ranging in scope from multi-volume histories of a language to simple picture editions, dictionaries exist for almost every age and intellectual level. In an elementary or junior high school library, the collection should include selections from the entire range--from unabridged to picture dictionaries. Price range extends from $300.00 historical dictionaries to less-than-a-dollar paperbacks. Price and quality, however, are not synonymous. To choose wisely requires determining which dictionaries within a specific price range are of the finest quality.

To evaluate dictionaries for purchase and use, several criteria are applicable. Authority is fundamental and can be determined by the reputation of the publisher, the qualifications of the editors and contributors, and the recency and extent of revisions (a recent publication date does not insure that the work is current). The scope of the dictionary, which can usually be gleaned from the title page, is a determining factor. Does it include colloquial and slang words, foreign words and phrases, and abbreviations? Does it contain encyclopedic material? Observing the word treatment, the evaluator should note spelling, pronunciation, syllabication, etymology, definition, quotations, synonyms and antonyms, and syntax. Equally important, the format, or physical make-up of the work, should be examined. Is the binding sturdy? Is the type clear and large? Are illustrations numerous, accurate, and recent? Is the paper thick enough so that the type does not show through? Is the arrangement suitable for maximum efficiency of use?

Those choosing appropriate editions for elementary and junior high schools must select from a surprising number of titles. Even at the picture dictionary level, there are many variations in quality, coverage, and price. It is essential, therefore, to determine needs carefully before examining titles for purchase.

In this chapter the dictionary titles are arranged under the following subheadings: picture dictionaries, school dictionaries, adult and college dictionaries, and unabridged dictionaries. In the first two divisions the titles are arranged according to level of

English Language Dictionaries   31

difficulty, beginning with the simplest. Titles in the last two categories are arranged alphabetically since their levels of difficulty are similar. At least one title from each of the four groups should be included in both elementary and junior high school libraries.

PICTURE DICTIONARIES

Greet, W. Cabell, Marion Monroe and Andrew Schiller. My Pictionary. New York: Lothrop, 1970. 95p. $4.75.
Greet, W. Cabell, William A. Jenkins and Andrew Schiller. My First Picture Dictionary. New York: Lothrop, 1970. 192p. $5.50.
Greet, W. Cabell, William A. Jenkins and Andrew Schiller. My Second Picture Dictionary. New York: Lothrop, 1971. 384p. $5.95.

These colorful beginning picture dictionaries are designed to be used with primary reading programs, specifically the Scott, Foresman Reading Systems. My Pictionary and My First Picture Dictionary are arranged by nine subjects and are color-coded accordingly, e.g., green--people, yellow--animals, pink--storybook characters, etc. They contain 524 and 800 words respectively and both contain an alphabetical index. The second volume begins to make the transition to a standard dictionary format; its entries are alphabetically arranged within each color-coded category. Each entry is in the singular with the plural appearing in blue type. Illustrative sentences use both the singular and plural form of the word. My Second Picture Dictionary is alphabetically arranged and contains material adapted from the 1968 Thorndike-Barnhart Beginning Dictionary. Each entry is in bold face type, then is divided by syllables. Each contains a definition, and some have illustrative sentences which appear in italics. In addition to the Lexicon, this dictionary contains a gazetteer consisting of the states of the United States arranged alphabetically, and giving the flag, flower, a map with the capitol, tree, bird, and fish for each. In general, these three sequential dictionaries are outstanding for primary use.

O'Donnell, Mabel and Willmina Townes. Words I Like to Read and Write. New York: Harper, 1973. 128p. $2.16.
O'Donnell, Mabel and Willmina Townes. Words to Read, Write, and Spell. New York: Harper, 1973. 224p. $3.54.

Prepared for average and superior first graders, Words I Like to Read and Write contains nearly 800 listings alphabetically arranged. Each entry gives the plural, an illustrative sentence, and a color picture. It is printed in a type strongly resembling manuscript to facilitate correlation of the child's own handwriting to the printed page. Appended is "The Alphabet," which shows the letter in both upper and lower case and gives illustrations in color, and a section which shows the numerals from one to twenty with the printed word and illustrative pictures. Designed as a sequel for grades two, three, and four, Words to Read, Write, and Spell consists of 937 main entries with definitions, illustrative sentences, and in many cases, pictures in full color. Updated and expanded from the 1963 editions, these two dictionaries are attractive choices for primary levels.

Scarry, Richard. Richard Scarry's Best Word Book Ever. New York: Golden Press, 1963. 91p. $3.95.

Designed by the inimitable Richard Scarry, this picture dictionary consists of 91 pages packed with humorous drawings of objects of interest to children, such as toys, food, flowers, airplanes, and animals, with each illustration labeled. It is fun to read as well as being an introductory word book.

Geisel, T. S. and Philip D. Eastman. The Cat in the Hat Beginner Book Dictionary. New York: Random, 1964. 133p. $3.95.

According to the title page of The Cat in the Hat Beginner Book Dictionary, it is written "by the Cat himself and P. D. Eastman." This alphabetically arranged dictionary, illustrated with rollicking funny drawings by the popular author-illustrators, explains word meanings with sentences and pictures.

Scarry, Richard. Richard Scarry's Storybook Dictionary. New York: Golden Press, 1966. 125p. $3.95.

More than 700 entries and over 1,600 variant forms and labels appear in the Storybook Dictionary. Each entry tells a separate and complete story with setting, characters, and plot, and is colorfully illustrated with Richard Scarry's popular drawings. Entry words appear in bold type with variants following when appropriate in light face type. The entry word is in bold type whenever it appears in the little story illustrating it.

Ertel, James. The My-Fun-With-Words Dictionary. Nashville: Southwestern, 1974. 2 vols. $19.95.

This unique picture dictionary attempts really to define words rather than merely to imply meanings through illustrations. Each page is divided into three equal parts, each painted a soft pastel and each providing the background for an entry word. The entry word itself appears in large dark print and is accompanied by a cartoon drawing in bold colors, definitions, and sentence illustrations. The text throughout is written in a casual, humorous style somewhat akin to a child's speech patterns. Although this dictionary is expensive, it is definitely recommended for primary level students.

Parker, Bertha Morris. The New Golden Dictionary. New York: Golden Press, 1972. 118p. $4.95.

English Language Dictionaries 33

Based on Ellen Wales Walpole's The Golden Dictionary, the New Golden Dictionary has 1,712 words, including 1,262 defined words, 450 words used as labels of pictured items, and 880 variants. It contains over 2,000 full color illustrations, at least one for each entry. Both text and illustrations reflect a variety of environments, e.g., urban, suburban, rural, home, school and community. Two or more sentences illustrate each entry word. In a section addressed to adults are a series of dictionary games designed to make dictionary work enjoyable. According to the publisher, the book "invites three to seven year olds to explore their own world of words."

Schultz, Charles M. The Charlie Brown Dictionary. New York: World, 1973. 399p. $6.95.

Illustrated with cartoons of Charlie Brown, Snoopy, Lucy, et al., this picture dictionary will be chosen by primary students for the popular drawings alone. They will, however, be getting a bargain, for this dictionary is a new one based on the Rainbow Dictionary. Both the illustrations and definitions are new, but in general the vocabulary is that of the earlier book. Additions and deletions were made to reflect changes in the language that children speak, read, and hear, especially on television. Altogether, this book contains 2,400 entries, consisting of both main entries and related forms, and has over 580 pictures in full color.

Wright, Wendell W. The Rainbow Dictionary for Young Readers. Cleveland: World, 1972. 463p. $3.95.

Intended as an introduction to words for children in grades one through four, this picture dictionary contains 2,300 carefully chosen words appearing most frequently in eight word lists. Concerned only with spelling and simple definitions, it defines words clearly and illustrates them by use in sentences. It omits etymologies, synonyms, encyclopedic material, biographical and geographical terms, abbreviations, slang, and foreign words and phrases. An oversized book with large, well spaced type and colorful illustrations, it is attractive and easy to use.

Watters, Garnette and Stuart A. Courtis. The Picture Dictionary for Children. Completely rev. New York: Grosset, 1968. 383p. $3.95.

First published in 1938, the Picture Dictionary for Children contains 5,079 entries, 2,177 of which are basic words and 2,902 variants. Illustrated throughout with black and white drawings, it is intended for elementary grades one through six. It serves as a very simple introduction to the use of words, meanings, and spellings. Each entry is amplified by one or more illustrative sentences. One unique feature of this picture dictionary is having the entry word appear both in manuscript and in cursive writing. The compilers of this dictionary are also responsible for the Curtis-Watters Illustrated Golden Dictionary for Young Readers, a considerably more sophisticated work for the same grade levels.

Daniels, Leo Francis. International Visual Dictionary. Los Angeles: Clute International Institute, 1973. 710p. $9.95. Dist. by Carroll Book Service, North Tarrytown, N.Y.

The International Visual Dictionary is designed for children in the early elementary grades and for adults learning English. Geared as a tool for learning the English language, the book aims to aid in improving one's vocabulary, expressing oneself more easily and confidently in English, and developing certain dictionary skills. Listing over 2,800 entries, the dictionary explains entry words by (1) using the word in a sentence, and (2) explaining the word in a sentence or as many sentences as necessary to depict the various uses of the word. The Word-Usage Finder, in essence an index, locates words used throughout the dictionary in addition to the main entry to provide added insight into word meanings. The approach to word definitions in this book is useful and interesting, the print is large and readable, and the entry words are clearly printed in bold type. The book as a whole, however, is marred by nondescript illustrations and thin paper which allows both print and pictures to show through. Despite these drawbacks, it will be useful to students in the elementary grades.

SCHOOL DICTIONARIES

Morris, William. The Weekly Reader Beginning Dictionary. New York: Grosset, 1973. 352p. $6.95.

Published also under the title, Ginn Beginning Dictionary, The Weekly Reader Dictionary is designed to span the gap between picture dictionaries and standard juvenile dictionaries of 18,000 plus entries. It contains over 5,000 entries illustrated with 600 color pictures. The strong feature of this dictionary is the very attractive format. Entry words appear in the left-hand column in large bold type. In the middle column is an actual definition in simple language followed by an illustrative sentence. In the right-hand column are one or more color illustrations of entry words. Large clear type and wide margins add to the appeal of this book which will probably best be utilized by third and fourth grade students.

Perry, Day A. Dictionary of Basic Words. Chicago: Children's Press, 1969. 614p. $19.95.

Prepared as a bridge between the picture dictionary and the regular intermediate dictionary, the Dictionary of Basic Words contains 21,000 entries. The main entry appears in bold type and is followed by the pronunciation, part-of-speech label, numbered definitions, sentence explanations, and variant forms of the word. More than 2,000 full color illustrations fill the book. The useful section, "How to Use the Dictionary," is easy to read and to understand. This dictionary is very attractive and should fill the gap between beginning and intermediate dictionaries; however, the rather

English Language Dictionaries

exorbitant price should cause librarians to assess their needs to determine whether this expensive title can be justified.

Thorndike, E. L. and Clarence L. Barnhart. Thorndike-Barnhart Beginning Dictionary. 7th ed. Glenview, Ill.: Scott, Foresman, 1972. 735p. $6.95.

The first of three progressive Thorndike Barnhart school dictionaries, the Thorndike-Barnhart Beginning Dictionary contains 20,500 entries and 33,500 meanings. Most of the vocabulary was selected from words used in text and trade books for grades three and four. Definitions, which list the most common meaning first, are illustrated liberally with sentences and phrases. People and places are included in the main alphabet. Foreign words and phrases and slang expressions are omitted. An outstanding section entitled "How to Use This Dictionary" consists of 58 lessons on locating words, finding meanings, using pronunciations, and using the dictionary for spelling and writing. The illustrations, large clear print, good paper, and sturdy binding make this an attractive book.

Webster's Elementary Dictionary; a Merriam-Webster. Springfield, Mass.: Merriam, 1971. 595p. $3.95.

An easy to use dictionary prepared for fourth, fifth, and sixth grade students, Webster's Elementary Dictionary contains over 18,000 entries and is abridged from larger Merriam-Webster publications. Words chosen for inclusion were selected after editors had read ninety per cent of the text books used in intermediate grades throughout the United States as well as hundreds of issues of children's periodicals. Appearing in the front of the dictionary is a section entitled "Getting Acquainted with Your Dictionary." Following the main alphabet are appendices listing Presidents of the United States, states of the United States, nations of the world, largest cities of the world, and weights and measures. Clear, simple definitions, illustrative sentences and phrases, and more than 1,600 line drawings adequately explain entries. Large easy-to-read print on good paper adds to the appeal of this dictionary.

Courtis, Stuart A. and Garnette Watters. The Courtis Watters Illustrated Golden Dictionary for Young Readers. Rev. ed. New York: Golden Press, 1965. 666p. $3.95.

First published in 1951 and revised and expanded in 1965, this book is excellent for young children of approximately grades two to five. Indicating usage with over 20,000 illustrative sentences, it defines clearly and simply over 10,000 basic words. Pronunciation symbols are so simple that it is not usually necessary to refer to the keys given in the front and back of the book. It contains over 3,000 black and white drawings throughout the text and a section of color illustrations. Little encyclopedic material is included and no synonyms, antonyms, derivations, biographical and geographical terms, abbreviations, slang and foreign words and phrases. Uncluttered, with fine large type, this book is well suited for the intended grade levels.

Kenward, James, comp. The Faber Junior Dictionary. London:
  Faber, 1964. 619p. $6.75.

The Faber Junior Dictionary, prepared for youngsters aged
8 to 14, suggests a three-fold purpose: (1) to find out what words
mean; (2) to make sure of spelling; and (3) to add new words to
one's vocabulary. Utilizing a simple format with one column per
page, it resembles a thesaurus more than a standard dictionary.
Each entry word is in bold type with pronunciation given when necessary, followed by a part of speech label and a very brief definition with an illustrative phrase. Entries are quite brief, with
most confined to one line of text. Although the dictionary is British, it is useful for American students also. It should, however,
because of its format be used in conjunction with a standard classroom dictionary.

Webster's New Elementary School Dictionary; a Merriam-Webster.
  Philip Babcock Gove, ed. New York: American Book,
  1970. 611p. $5.84.

Derived from Webster's Third New International Dictionary,
Webster's New Elementary School Dictionary is available only in a
school text edition and is geared specifically for upper elementary
school children. Its 31,000 entries give simple definitions, brief
etymologies, synonyms, and examples of usage. In addition to the
main body of text, the book has a fine introduction on the use of
the dictionary, rules for spelling and grammar, etc. Additional
material in the appendix includes, for example, abbreviations; lists
of the Presidents, Vice Presidents, and states of the United States;
and signs and symbols. This fine dictionary features a good binding, clear type, and in general, an attractive format.

The American Heritage School Dictionary. New York: American
  Heritage and Houghton Mifflin, 1972. 992p. $7.95.

Intended for use by students in grades 3 to 9, this dictionary
lists 35,000 main entries and 50,000 variant forms of words.
Clear definitions, simple pronunciation, and sample sentences make
this dictionary easy to understand. Entries include pronunciation,
part of speech, numbered definitions, illustrative phrases and sentences, and other forms of the word. Using three columns per
page, the book's bold yellow center column contains illustrations,
word histories, grammar and usage notes, and anecdotal matter to
promote understanding and enjoyment of language. The introductory
sections, "The Making of This Dictionary" and "How to Use Your
Dictionary," provide interesting information for the reader. Extremely attractive, this dictionary will appeal to the intended age
group of users.

Holt Basic Dictionary of American English. New York: Holt, 1966.
  848p. $4.36.

Also published and sold by Scholastic Book Services as the

English Language Dictionaries 37

Scholastic Dictionary of American English, the Holt Basic Dictionary of American English contains 40,000 entries and is designed for children aged ten and eleven. For each entry, the dictionary gives the pronunciation, definitions, illustrative sentences and phrases, and variant forms of the word. Preceding the main body of text is a 42-page section called "You and Your Dictionary" which teaches such dictionary skills as how to find words, word meanings, pronunciation, spelling, how to use words, and word histories. Appended tables include such topics as the metric system simplified, sixty Indian tribes of North America, domestic weights and measures, Presidents of the United States, etc. Illustrated throughout with drawings, the book has a clear, easy-to-use format.

Guralnik, David B. Webster's New World Dictionary for Young Readers. New ed. of the Elem ed. New York: World, 1971. 808p. $4.95.

A very fine and popular dictionary prepared specifically for students in grades four through eight, Webster's New World Dictionary for Young Readers is based on the outstanding college work, Webster's New World Dictionary--Second College Edition. The new edition of the elementary edition contains 44,000 words in one alphabet, including proper names, abbreviations, suffixes, prefixes, and compounds. The main entry gives pronunciation, a part-of-speech label, numbered definitions, and outstanding phrase and sentence illustrations of the various meanings in context. The section "Guide to Using the Dictionary" acquaints the reader with the vast information provided in the text.

The Harcourt Brace School Dictionary. Harrison Gray Platt, ed. New York: Harcourt, 1968. 864p. $4.80.

Prepared for students in grades four through eight, The Harcourt Brace School Dictionary contains 46,000 entries correlated with modern textbooks. Entries, arranged in a single alphabet, contain easy to understand definitions and illustrative sentences. A second color is used to designate cross references, synonym notes, usage notes, etymologies, and specific areas of maps and diagrams. Guide words also appear in color. Preceding the main text are sections entitled "How to Use Your Dictionary" (text material for grades four and five) and "How to Get the Most from Your Dictionary" (text work for grades six through eight).

The Winston Dictionary for Schools; 1700 Pictorial Illustrations, 10 Color Plates, 16 Maps in Color. New York: Holt, 1967. 966p. $4.84.

The Winston Dictionary for Schools is designed for intermediate grade children and contains 46,000 entries. Entries contain the entry word in large bold type, pronunciation, part of speech, numbered definitions, synonyms, and additional forms of the word. The useful appendices include a sixteen-page, full-color atlas of the world; tables of weights and measures; foreign monetary units; signs and symbols; Presidents, states, and chief cities of the United States; and area and population of foreign countries. The book has large, clear print and, in general, an attractive format.

Flexner, Stuart Berg. The Random House Dictionary of the English Language. School ed. New York: Random, 1973. 908p. $5.32.

Based on the unabridged and college editions of the Random House Dictionary of the English Language, the School Edition also uses word frequency lists to determine its entries. It contains a single alphabetical sequence of more than 47,500 entries, including biographical and geographical entries, abbreviations, and contractions. Entries include the pronunciation, part of speech, definitions, and examples used in sentences and phrases. Meanings of words appear in order of frequency with the most common meaning first. A lengthy section called the "Student's Guide to the Dictionary" and the "Explanatory Notes for a Specimen Page" will be beneficial to the user. The 15 pages of maps by Rand McNally and the tables of weights and measures further extend the usefulness of this dictionary. Designed for fourth to eighth grade students, it should definitely have a space on the school reference shelf.

Thorndike, E. L. and Clarence L. Barnhart. Thorndike-Barnhart Intermediate Dictionary. Garden City, N.Y.: Doubleday, 1971. 990p. $6.95.

Designed for grades five to eight, the Thorndike-Barnhart Intermediate Dictionary is a completely new work listing more than 56,700 entries and 67,700 meanings in a single alphabet. More than 33,000 illustrative sentences and phrases and 1,300 maps, drawings, and diagrams explain definitions. Etymologies for some 1,800 entries are included in this volume. Entries contain any or all of the following: homograph number, pronunciation, restrictive label, definition, illustrative sentence, part of speech label, inflected forms, etymology, run-on entry, idioms. The section entitled "How to Use This Dictionary" covers such topics as initial consonant sounds, spellings of vowel sounds, additional spelling hints, suggestions for dividing words, and parts of a dictionary entry. This three-column dictionary is a first purchase item for both upper elementary and junior high school libraries.

Webster's Intermediate Dictionary; a New School Dictionary. Springfield, Mass.: Merriam, 1972. 910p. $6.50.

Planned to follow Webster's New Elementary Dictionary and to precede Webster's New Students Dictionary, the Intermediate Dictionary is prepared specifically for the junior high school student. It contains more than 57,000 entries, over 1,000 etymologies, and 800 pictorial illustrations. A fifty-page section, "Using Your Dictionary," includes instruction with short check-up tests for each section. The vocabulary supposedly represents current language including new words from environment and ecology, the drug scene, space exploration, genetics, black culture, sex education, biology and other technical and scientific fields. Tables throughout the text provide such information as the chemical elements; weights and measures; the metric system; the Braille alphabet; the signs of the zodiac; and the Books of the Bible. Appended tables list the Presidents, Vice-Presidents, and states of the United States; the provinces of Canada; the nations of the world; and arbitrary signs and symbols. Throughout the book the guide words, the alphabet, and the pronunciation key appear in blue print, giving them fine visibility. Although on first impact its appearance is a bit juvenile, Webster's Intermediate Dictionary deserves a thorough examination for it will most assuredly be useful and popular with the junior high school crowd.

Webster's New Students Dictionary; a Merriam Webster. New York: Merriam, 1974. 1060p. $6.95.

Succeeding Webster's Students Dictionary, Webster's New Students Dictionary is virtually a new work rewritten in 1964 and based on Webster's Third New International Dictionary and Webster's Seventh New Collegiate Dictionary. Listing 57,000 entries of words most often encountered by junior and senior high school students, it gives in one alphabet synonyms, foreign words and phrases, and slang expressions. Abbreviations, signs and symbols, and biographical and geographical material are included as supplementary. Intended as a bridge between elementary and collegiate dictionaries, Webster's New Students Dictionary is outstanding and should be included in the reference collection of elementary and junior high school libraries.

Thorndike, E. L. and Clarence L. Barnhart. Thorndike-Barnhart Advanced Dictionary. Garden City, N.Y.: Doubleday, 1973. 1186p. $9.50.

The most mature of the Thorndike-Barnhart school dictionaries, the Thorndike-Barnhart Advanced Dictionary represents a thorough revision, updating, and amplification of the Thorndike-Barnhart High School Dictionary. Prepared for grades 7 to 12, it contains in a single alphabet 55,000 main entries and 95,000 total entries illustrated with 1,300 maps, charts, and tables. New entries included in the revision are new math and science terms, new common vocabulary entries, more place names and political unions, broadened biographical coverage, etc. In the section called "Using This Dictionary" the editors have listed and illustrated thirteen parts of a dictionary entry. Upholding the tradition of excellence, this dictionary should be in all junior high school libraries and should be considered for upper elementary school libraries as well.

ADULT AND COLLEGE DICTIONARIES

Barnhart, Clarence L. and others. The Barnhart Dictionary of New English Since 1963. New York: Harper, 1973. 512p. $12.95.

Included in this unique source are more than 5,000 recent terms required or created by scientific researches and achievements, technical and cultural activities, and social environments. The very long entries include pronunciation, etymologies, and usage notes, plus one or more quotations to clarify meanings. This dictionary should be available to supplement standard dictionaries in both elementary and junior high school libraries.

The American College Dictionary. Clarence L. Barnhart, ed. New York: Random, 1969. 1444p. $6.95.

Prepared under the editorship of the well-known lexicographer, Clarence L. Barnhart, The American College Dictionary is an outstanding abridged dictionary containing 132,000 entries. All information is listed in one alphabet including biographical information, geographical data, abbreviations, foreign words and phrases, and slang expressions. Definitions appear with the most common meaning listed first. In addition to the material given in the main body of text, American College Dictionary includes a section on how to use the dictionary, proof marks, punctuation, colleges and universities in the United States, signs and symbols, and given names. Having a good format with clear type, it is easy to use and should be considered for the elementary and junior high reference collection. According to its general introduction, it is designed "to meet the essential needs of the reader, speaker, and writer who want to know the meaning of a word, how to pronounce it, how to spell it, its history, or some important fact of usage."

The American Heritage Dictionary of the English Language. William Morris, ed. Boston: American Heritage and Houghton Mifflin, 1969. 1550p. $8.95.

A recent publication, The American Heritage Dictionary of the English Language contains 155,000 entries, including biographical and geographical names, representing basic current vocabulary. An independent compilation not based on an unabridged dictionary, this desk dictionary utilizes 20,000 sample sentences and phrases, 6,000 quotations, and 4,000 marginal drawings to illustrate and further explain definitions. According to the editors, "The first definition is the central meaning about which the other senses may be most logically organized." Entries include syllabication, pronunciation, part of speech, field and usage labels, definitions, illustrative material, etymology, synonyms, and usage notes. An up-to-date reference book produced by the use of computers, this dictionary should be considered for both elementary and junior high school libraries.

Concise Oxford Dictionary of Current English. H. W. Fowler and F. G. Fowler, eds. 5th ed., rev. by E. Freidrichsen. New York: Oxford University Press, 1964. 1558p. $8.75.

Based on the vast historical Oxford English Dictionary, the Concise Oxford Dictionary is an authoritative reference to the history and meaning of words. Containing 70,000 entries, it lists definitions in historical order with the common meaning last. Etymologies, synonyms, and excellent, detailed illustrations of usage follow definitions. The main body of text incorporates foreign words and phrases and slang terms. Biographical and geographical material is omitted entirely, but abbreviations are included in an appendix. A guide to the use of the dictionary is contained in the preface. An excellent format with small but legible type adds to the usefulness of this work. Although the Concise Oxford Dictionary is British and is indeed concerned with British usage, it should be available to complement American dictionaries. It is an ideal and inexpensive supplement to the good American works that omit British terms. Upper elementary and junior high school students can easily use this dictionary, and it is recommended for purchase at these levels.

Funk and Wagnalls Standard College Dictionary. New York: Funk and Wagnalls, 1973. 1606p. $6.95.

Edited and compiled by four famous linguists, Albert H. Marckwardt, Fredric G. Cassidy, S. I. Hayakawa, and James B. McMillan, Funk and Wagnalls Standard College Dictionary is a completely new dictionary first published in 1963 and based on the Funk and Wagnalls Standard Dictionary--International Edition. Numbering 150,000 entries, the main alphabet includes geographical names, biographical names, mythological terms, abbreviations, foreign words and phrases, and slang expressions. Definitions are arranged with the most common meaning first. Included in appendices are weights and measures, colleges and universities, signs and symbols, given names, proof marks, punctuation, and capitalization. Continuously revised and easy to use, this fine abridged dictionary earns consideration for purchase for elementary and junior high school libraries.

Oxford Illustrated Dictionary. J. Coulson, C. T. Carr, M. L. Hutchinson, and D. S. Eagle, eds. New York: Oxford University Press, 1962. 974p. $15.00.

Based on the Concise Oxford Dictionary, the Oxford Illustrated Dictionary is virtually a combination dictionary and small encyclopedia. Following Oxford dictionary tradition, it lists definitions in historical order, with the most common meaning given last. The 39,000 entries contain brief etymologies and illustrative quotations, foreign words and phrases, slang expressions, abbreviations, and geographical biographical names are incorporated in the main alphabet; 1,700 terms are further defined with pictures and diagrams. Encyclopedic information, e.g., lists of Roman Emperors, weights and measures, etc., is contained in the ten supplementary appendices. An unusual reference work, the Oxford Illustrated Dictionary could be quite useful for junior high libraries.

The Random House Dictionary of the English Language: College Edition. Laurence Urdang and Stuart Berg Flexner, eds. New York: Random, 1968. 1568p. $6.95.

Based on the unabridged Random House Dictionary of the English Language, The Random House Dictionary: College Edition takes its place with the finest of college dictionaries. Since it is new, it is outstanding on new and recently recognized material, containing words, phrases, and geographical names which have come into current use. It contains 155,000 entries in its main alphabet, including biographical and geographical names, abbreviations, idiomatic expressions, and current scientific terms. Entries list the most common meaning first. Following the definitions are illustrative sentences and phrases, etymologies, usage and field labels, and synonyms and antonyms. Prefatory material includes the "Guide to the Dictionary" and "Historical Sketch of the English Language." Various appendices provide such information as signs and symbols, lists of colleges and universities in the United States and Canada, English given names, weights and measures, and foreign alphabets. A thorough style manual, including proofreading symbols, is also appended. Up to date and reliable, the Random House Dictionary: College Edition lists over 350 qualified consultants. Readable, easy to use, and current, it merits consideration for elementary and junior high school libraries.

Webster's New Collegiate Dictionary. 8th ed. Springfield, Mass.: Merriam, 1973. 1536p. $7.95.

Claimed by the publisher to be the most comprehensive desk dictionary ever published by Merriam, the Webster's New Collegiate Dictionary contains an increase of 22,000 vocabulary entries over the Seventh New Collegiate published in 1963. It lists 152,000 entries which include definitions in historical order with the earliest meaning given first, etymologies, examples of usage, synonyms, foreign words and phrases, slang expressions, and abbreviations. 760 synonym groups and 1,115 antonyms appear in the eighth edition. Several appendices list supplementary material. Included are biographical and geographical names, colleges and universities of the United States and Canada, and a "Handbook of Style." Using larger type and attractive page layouts has improved the format and appeal of this college dictionary. Providing clear, concise definitions, it should be considered for both elementary and junior high schools.

Webster's New Ideal Dictionary; a Merriam-Webster. Springfield, Mass.: Merriam, 1968. $3.49.

A small dictionary designed for upper high school and college use, Webster's New Ideal Dictionary contains 41,000 entries in the main alphabet. In addition it lists abbreviations, foreign words and phrases, and a population table for American towns. No geographical names, biographical names, mythological names, or etymologies are included. Although the scope of this dictionary is extremely limited, it is valuable as a small work because its definitions are easy to understand and reliable. Elementary and junior high students will probably find it more useful than will the older students for whom it is intended.

Webster's New World Dictionary. 2nd College ed. David B. Guralnik, ed. New York: World, 1972. 1692p. $7.95.

The second college edition of Webster's New World Dictionary was published in 1970 and updated in 1972. It contains 157,000 entries, approximately five thousand more than in the previous edition. Emphasizing American usage, it includes some 14,000 Americanisms. Its single alphabet contains a vocabulary of American English, biographical names, geographical names, foreign words and phrases, slang, abbreviations, legendary, Biblical and classical names. Each entry word is followed by the pronunciation, part of speech label, inflected forms if irregular, etymology, and definitions. Definitions are simple, precise, and clear and are followed by etymologies. Illustrative phrases and drawings help to clarify meanings. Additional material in the dictionary includes an expanded list of colleges, universities, and junior colleges in the United States and Canada; a "Guide to Punctuation, Mechanics, and Manuscript Form"; proofreaders' marks; tables of weights and measures; and special signs and symbols. This authoritative and up-to-date title should be considered for first purchase among college edition dictionaries for both elementary and junior high school libraries.

UNABRIDGED DICTIONARIES

Funk and Wagnalls New Standard Dictionary of the English Language. New York: Funk and Wagnalls, 1963. 2816p. $62.50.

Originally compiled by Isaac K. Funk with the assistance of 380 scholars and consultants, and issued under the title Standard Dictionary in 1893, Funk and Wagnalls New Standard Dictionary received its current title in 1913 when it was thoroughly revised. A comprehensive collection of words, it contains 458,000 entries including much encyclopedic information. Entries provide definitions with the most current meaning given first, spelling, pronunciation, etymologies, synonyms and antonyms, and illustrative quotations chosen from both popular and classical writing. More than 7,000 drawings illustrate the entries. Listed in the main alphabet are 65,000 Biblical, mythological, and proper names; 30,000 biographical and geographical terms; and slang expressions. Supplementary material includes foreign words and phrases, rules for simplified spelling, population statistics, and a supplement of new words. Although the New Standard Dictionary is well edited, reliable, and comprehensive, it is in need of revision. Since the last completely revised edition in 1913, it has been subject to a policy of continuous revision which has proved inadequate. For all of its fine qualities, it is simply not as up to date as other unabridged dictionaries. Because of its scope and reliability, however, it can still be recommended for purchase for elementary and junior high libraries to complement other dictionaries with differing emphases.

Funk and Wagnalls Standard Dictionary of the English Language:
International Edition. New York: Funk and Wagnalls. 2
vols. $29.95.

 A comprehensive intermediate dictionary, Funk and Wagnalls
Standard Dictionary: International Edition lists 175,000 entries.
First published in 1958 under the editorship of Charles Earle Funk
assisted by 150 authorities, it is revised annually and includes new
words with each revised printing. Included in the main alphabet
are biographical, geographical, and proper names, foreign words
and phrases; and slang terms. Especially strong on new words in
science and technology, it also attempts to keep abreast of new
words in the arts, trades, and professions. Entries list definitions
with the most common meaning first, etymologies, examples of usage, and synonyms. Additional material includes a guide to the
use of the dictionary, a list of abbreviations, Nobel Prize winners,
and world populations. Current and easy to use, Funk and Wagnalls
Standard Dictionary: International Edition deserves consideration for
purchase by elementary and junior high school libraries.

The Random House Dictionary of the English Language. Unabridged
ed. Jess Stein, ed. New York: Random, 1966. 2059p.
$30.00.

 Entirely new and modern in concept, the Random House Dictionary was first published in 1966 after its editorial staff spent
seven years compiling its contents. It represents contributions by
over 200 subject specialists including such well known authorities
as Henry Steele Commager, Gilbert Highet, and Charles Goren.
According to the preface, the purpose of the dictionary is to provide the contemporary user with a means for keeping pace with the
rapid growth of his language. Accordingly, the Random House Dictionary contains only 260,000 entries based on current usage, as
compared with other unabridged dictionaries which contain about
450,000 entries. Highly technical words, obsolete and archaic
words are omitted. Emphasizing current terms, the dictionary contains a high proportion of popular vocabulary which will require
frequent revisions. Included in the main alphabet are literary,
Biblical, biographical, mythological, and geographical names; also
included are abbreviations, proverbs and mottoes, and foreign words
and phrases. Definitions are presented with the most common
meanings first. Illustrative sentences and phrases and levels of
usage follow the definitions. In addition to the main alphabet, supplementary material includes a 64-page atlas by Hammond; French,
German, Spanish, and Italian bilingual dictionaries; a gazetteer; a
list of independent countries of the world; a list of the states of
the United States; geographical information; a directory of the colleges and universities of America; a style manual; a list of major
dates in world history; and the Presidents and Vice-Presidents of
the United States. Although the Random House Dictionary contains
hardly enough entries to be considered unabridged, it is most certainly a valuable reference source and could be utilized in elementary and junior high schools.

English Language Dictionaries

Webster's New Twentieth Century Dictionary of the English Language. Based on the broad foundations laid down by Noah Webster. Jean L. McKechnie, ed. 2nd ed. Cleveland: World, 1958. 2318p. $49.95.

The smallest of the very large unabridged dictionaries, Webster's New Twentieth Century Dictionary contains 320,000 entries. First published in 1941, it was extensively revised in the second edition issued in 1955, so much so that it was virtually a new work. With each printing new words are incorporated into the text. Entries in this dictionary include definitions, pronunciation, parts of speech, etymologies, synonyms, and some illustrative quotations. Including much encyclopedic information in the main body of text, Webster's New Twentieth Century Dictionary lists in separate sections biographical data; geographical material; noted names in fiction, mythology, and legend; foreign words and phrases; abbreviations; signs and symbols; forms of address; and weights and measures. Generously illustrated with 3,000 drawings, it contains many full color plates and 16 full-page color maps. Having an exceptionally fine physical make-up, it has large, easy to read type printed on good paper and is well bound. While it is not as comprehensive as other unabridged dictionaries currently available, it is authoritative and usable and could be valuable in elementary and junior high school libraries.

Webster's Third New International Dictionary of the English Language. Springfield, Mass.: Merriam, 1971. 3194p. $54.50.

Edited by Philip Babcock Gove with the assistance of over 300 specialists and consultants, Webster's Third New International Dictionary is an unabridged compendium of present day terms and meanings. Although it is descended from earlier Merriam-Webster dictionaries, it is completely revised. Appreciably smaller than its predecessors, Webster's Third contains 450,000 entries and excludes words obsolete before 1755, thus omitting the vocabulary of Chaucerian and Elizabethan literature. Entries provide the phonetic spelling, part of speech, etymologies, synonyms and antonyms, usage, and illustrative quotations, many of which are taken from contemporary sources. Definitions follow Webster tradition and appear in chronological order. Much encyclopedic information is included; for example, the Braille alphabet, the Morse code, the perpetual calendar, and the chemical elements. Incorporated in the main alphabet are foreign words and phrases, abbreviations, and slang terms. Excluded from this edition is geographical and biographical information. Criticized because of its limitations and philosophy, Webster's Third New International Dictionary is nonetheless up to date, concentrating on contemporary words and usage, and authoritative. It is an essential complement to school dictionaries for elementary school libraries and a first purchase unabridged dictionary for secondary schools.

World Book Dictionary. Clarence L. Barnhart, ed. Chicago: Field Enterprises, 1974. 2 vols. $50.20.

The World Book Dictionary, a Thorndike-Barnhart dictionary, is produced as a joint project of Field Enterprises, Thorndike-Barnhart, and Doubleday and Company; it was completely new in 1963 and is revised annually. New words, appearing first in the World Book Year Book, are included in the next year's revision of the dictionary. Designed as a companion reference work to the World Book Encyclopedia, the World Book Dictionary is suitable for students from grade four through college. The 200,000 entries give definitions (most common meaning first), usage notes, etymologies, and illustrative sentences and phrases, and slang expressions. All encyclopedic information, including biographical and geographical entries, is omitted. A supplement to the main body of text provides extremely useful information including "A Guide to the Dictionary" and "Handbook of Style." Accurate and up to date, the dictionary lists many advisors and special consultants, all highly qualified subject specialists, in addition to the editorial staff of Mr. Barnhart, Field Enterprises, and Doubleday and Company. Carefully edited and easy to use, World Book Encyclopedia Dictionary is a must for elementary and junior high school libraries.

FACTBOOKS AND YEARBOOKS

Factbooks and yearbooks are designed to locate quick reference or current information that might otherwise be difficult to find. Factbooks usually deal with specific areas and present minute details of unusual subjects. These are of particular interest to intermediate grade students who notoriously concern themselves with specifics. Most of these cover such fascinating material that the user can spend hours just browsing through them.

Yearbooks also contain vital facts and statistics but, most importantly, provide a record of the previous year's events. Since they are revised annually, they present up-to-date information. Available in many formats and arrangements, they run the gamut from encyclopedia supplements, such as Britannica Book of the Year and New Book of Knowledge Annual, to almanacs such as Information Please Almanac and World Almanac. These tools can vitalize almost every area of the curriculum with current, pertinent facts and statistics. While it is unnecessary to purchase yearbooks for each set of encyclopedias, the inclusion of two or three titles, depending upon the need for duplicate material, will aid in providing current information.

FACTBOOKS

Whitney, David C. The First Book of Facts and How to Find Them. New York: Franklin Watts, 1966. 66p. $3.95.

Small, inexpensive, illustrated in color, The First Book of Facts is a fine introduction to reference work. It illustrates various kinds of facts and shows what kinds of tools will locate them. It explains clearly the kinds of alphabetical arrangement, the differences in forms of names, and shows how facts can be used in critical thinking.

Unstead, R. J. My World: A First Picture Encyclopedia in Full Color. New York: Herder and Herder, 1970. 191p. $6.95.

This one-volume source of interesting information is hardly full enough to be considered an encyclopedia; however, it is useful as a compendium of facts for younger students. Divided into a number of topics, it includes: What men make; By land and sea;

Up in the air; Fruit, flowers, and food; Getting to know animals; Birds, fish, reptiles, insects; and Look and find out A-Z. The first six sections contain full color pictures for each subject upon which each item is numbered with the corresponding word name at the bottom of the page. The "Look and Find Out A-Z" is an alphabetical listing of items appearing throughout the pictorial text with each described in rather long one-half to two-column entries. This book will be enjoyed both for reference and browsing by primary and middle grade children.

Elting, Mary. The Answer Book. New York: Grosset and Dunlap, 1959. 153p. $4.95.

Elting, Mary. Answers and More Answers. New York: Grosset and Dunlap, 1961. 153p. $4.95.

These two factbooks are filled with questions and answers of interest to children. The Answer Book is arranged by broad topics with a table of contents listing each question in order of appearance. Arranged somewhat differently, Answers and More Answers has the questions grouped together by similarities rather than in broad subjects. Typical questions follow. What is the Milky Way? What happens inside a cat when it purrs? What makes gelatin jell? How did people learn to talk? Why does frost on windows look like ferns? Entries are one-half to one page in length with illustrations on most pages. In the index numerals in italics refer to pictures, and entries printed in capital letters refer to the question titles.

Leokum, Arkady. Tell Me Why. New York: Grosset and Dunlap, 1965. 480p. $6.49.

Leokum, Arkady. More Tell Me Why. New York: Grosset and Dunlap, 1967. 480p. $6.49.

Leokum, Arkady. Still More Tell Me Why. New York: Grosset and Dunlap, 1968. 480p. $6.49.

Leokum, Arkady. Lots More Tell Me Why. New York: Grosset and Dunlap, 1972. 480p. $6.49.

The "Tell Me Why Library" provides answers to nearly 1,700 hard to answer questions that intermediate level children ask. More than 400 questions are answered in each book with average answers running about a page in length. All four books are organized according to five broad categories: The World around us, How other creatures live, All about human beings, How things began, and What makes it work. Typical questions are: How does a broken bone heal? What makes a boomerang return? Do dogs dream? Why does thunder follow lightning? and How did the handshake originate? Printed in large type with two color drawings and diagrams, the books will attract browsers as well as provide facts.

Kane, Joseph Nathan. Famous First Facts; A Record of Happenings, Discoveries, and Inventions in the United States. 3rd ed. New York: Wilson, 1964. 1165p. $22.00.

Factbooks and Yearbooks 49

An adult work suitable for use by children, Famous First Facts, 3rd edition, is a greatly enlarged version of a standard reference book. It alphabetically identifies and explains first events, first discoveries, and first inventions in America. Some examples include the first deaf students' magazine, the first American flag flown in battle, the first national park containing an active volcano, and the first railroad accident. Easy to use and quite comprehensive, it is a valuable addition to all reference collections.

Fogel, Barbara R. What's the Biggest? New York: Random House, 1969. 115p. $3.50.

This juvenile book of comparisons is divided into three major categories: Living things, Man-made things, and the Earth and the universe. Included in the book are entries describing recordholders for size among animals, birds, fish, human beings, buildings, tunnels, dams, telescopes, mountains, caves, waterfalls, planets, stars, and many more. Entries are from one to several pages in length and incorporate many facts about the subject besides the specific statistical data. In a preliminary essay the author discusses big, bigger, and biggest and traces man's attempts to measure. A short bibliography and a brief index are useful. This book, like the Guinness Book of World Records, can provide valuable facts but is also intriguing browsing material for the elementary school child.

McWhirter, Norris and Ross McWhirter. Guinness Book of World Records. 1974 Rev. Am. ed. New York: Sterling, 1973. 672p. $6.95.

Alphabetically arranged, this extremely popular factbook deals only with superlatives, e.g., highest, lowest, biggest, smallest, fastest, slowest, oldest, newest, loudest, greatest, hottest, coldest, strongest. For example, under the entry "Birds," some of the information given includes largest, smallest, rarest, most abundant, longest-lived, fastest-flying, longest flights, highest flights, most acute night vision, largest and smallest eggs, longest feathers, largest turkey, and most talkative bird. The book not only settles arguments but stimulates further research. Children enjoy it and many own paperback copies.

DeSola, Ralph. Abbreviations Dictionary. 4th ed. New York: American Elsevier, 1974. 442p. $24.50.

This useful key to today's many abbreviations offers abbreviations, acronyms, contractions, initials, nicknames, signs and symbols defined, including civil and military time systems, Greek alphabet, international civil aircraft markings, numbered abbreviations, proofreaders' marks, punctuation. Over 54,000 entries and 77,000 definitions are listed.

Shankle, George Earlie. American Nicknames; Their Origin and Significance. 2nd ed. New York: Wilson, 1955. 524p. $10.00.

In dictionary form this interesting factbook lists more than 4,000 American nicknames of people, cities, and states, political organizations, and military regiments. Cross references assist the user in identifying the owner of a particular nickname. Origins and meanings of nicknames appear with the entry and sources are given in footnotes.

Payton, Geoffrey. Webster's Dictionary of Proper Names. Springfield, Mass.: Merriam, 1971. 752p. $9.95.

This comprehensive dictionary lists and describes proper names. Covering a wide variety of subjects, it includes names from literature, initials, people, places, historical periods, food, sports, musical works, titles, and even comic strip characters. Specific entries range from Montezuma Castle to Apollo 13 to Arkansas Traveller to Ziegfeld Follies to All-Star Game to Zen to Little Red Ridinghood. Each item has a date and a descriptive paragraph or is cross-referenced to another entry. While this tool may be profitably used by upper elementary school children, it will be extremely valuable to junior high school students.

Sharp, Harold S., comp. Handbook of Pseudonyms and Personal Nicknames. Metuchen, N.J.: Scarecrow Press, 1972. 2 vols. $27.50.

This helpful handbook provides pseudonyms, stage names, appellations, nicknames, pen names, and sobriquets of people living in all time periods, in all countries, and from all occupations. The 15,000 main entries consist of the real names in capital letters with birth and death dates, some brief description, and the pseudonyms. Some 25,000 nicknames and/or pseudonyms appear in the single alphabet with cross-references to the main entry. This valuable source book should be helpful to the students, teachers, and librarians alike. A supplement will be published in 1975.

The New Century Cyclopedia of Names. New ed. Clarence L. Barnhart and William D. Halsey, eds. New York: Appleton-Century-Crofts, 1954. 3 vols. $47.45 set. $15.80 ea.

This comprehensive dictionary lists over 100,000 proper names including persons, places (both real and legendary), historical events, organizations, treaties, works of art, literature, and music. Edited by the lexicographer Clarence L. Barnhart of Thorndike-Barnhart dictionaries fame, the book contains a list of over 350 consulting editors. The well-written, readable, and concise entries are arranged alphabetically with the length of entries ranging from a few lines to half a page. Appended are the following: Chronological table of world history (by century, then country); Lists of rulers, chiefs of state, and other notables, by country; States of the United States and of the Confederacy; Genealogical charts; Members of the United Nations; Table of popes; Geological table; List of prenames used in this work with pronunciations. The New Century Cyclopedia of Names covers such a wealth of

Factbooks and Yearbooks 51

information on so many subjects that it constitutes a major reference source for all libraries. The price should not be a deterrent.

YEARBOOKS

The New Book of Knowledge Annual, _____, Highlighting Events of _____; the Young People's Book of the Year. New York: Grolier. $7.95.

The only major encyclopedia year book designed especially for children, The New Book of Knowledge Annual is a must for elementary school libraries. Well illustrated in both black and white and color, the volume is written in a style easily read by youngsters. While the information included is both noteworthy and newsworthy, it is chosen to match the interests of girls and boys. The main body is divided into a number of sections: "Our Changing World," e.g., Southeast Asia, the United States political system and Watergate, and a new Vice-President; "World of Science," e.g., The Energy Crisis, Comet Kohoutek, and the Health Food Boom; "Animal World," e.g., Animals in the News, Drive-Through Zoos, Raising a Skunk; "Living History," e.g., A Child's Paris, Circus World Museum; a Monster in Loch Ness?; "Fun to Read," e.g., Exciting New Books, Poetry, Women of the West; "Youth in the News," e.g., Olga Korbut, a Russian Pixie; The Sound of Michael Jackson; Junior Achievement; "Fun to Make and Do," e.g., Making an Organic Garden, Wire Sculpture; "World of Sports," e.g., Little League Baseball, Ballooning, Rodeo Today; and "The Creative World," e.g., The Waltons, Children's Theater, the Music Scene. A chronology section features two or more pages for each month and small paragraphs describing important events. An international statistical supplement and the dictionary index complete this useful book.

Encyclopedia Year Book, _____. New York: Grolier, _____. $7.95.

This year book is designed as a supplement to The Encyclopedia International. Very simply arranged, it contains a rather detailed chronology of events, a section of feature articles of the year, the alphabetically arranged "Review of the Year" which contains some special reports, the contributors, and the index. Special features included are newsworthy events, e.g., "The Year That Shook America," "The Energy Squeeze," and "The American Indian." The remainder of information occurs in the "Review of the Year," including "Obituaries" and "Biography."

Compton Yearbook, _____. Chicago: F. E. Compton. $7.95 to set owners only.

This yearbook carries the subtitle: a summary and interpretation of the events of _____ to supplement Compton's Encyclopedia. It features a chronology of the preceding year, embellished with color photographs; the events of the previous year, in alphabetical sequence; a calendar for the coming year; and a selection of articles which will appear in the forthcoming edition of the encyclopedia. It also includes feature articles on topics of current interest and a section of new words from Merriam Webster.

World Book Year Book,   , A Review of the Events of   .
       Chicago: Field Enterprises. $12.95, $7.30 to set owners.

Although designed to supplement the World Book Encyclopedia, the World Book Year Book is a valuable reference source unto itself. It contains a chronology of the previous year's events in capsule; a collection of articles entitled "The Year in Focus"; special reports, e.g., "How Can We Solve the Energy Crisis" and "The Rise and Falter of the Free Press," an article describing "A Year in Perspective"; an alphabetical supplement to the encyclopedia called "The Year on File," new and revised articles in "World Book Supplement," a supplement to the World Book Dictionary, and an extensive cumulative index covering this volume and the two preceding yearbooks.

Americana Annual, An Encyclopedia of the Events of the Year.
       New York: Americana Corporation, 1923 --. $8.95 to set owners.

A supplement to Encyclopedia Americana, the Americana Annual includes a record of events in the preceding year. The survey articles in the main body are alphabetically arranged and are signed by the contributor. Preceding the main text is a section devoted to timely feature articles on such subjects as environment, space exploration, political events, and other topics of special current interest. The monthly chronologies contain a day-by-day listing of major world events. An obituaries section contains information on hundreds of prominent persons who died during the year. Special photographic features, some of them in color, are also incorporated. The volume is fully indexed.

Britannica Book of the Year, 1938-   . Chicago: Encyclopaedia
       Britannica, 1938-   . $8.95 to set owners only.

Written in a popular style, the Britannica Book of the Year is designed to serve as an annual survey and as a supplement for both the Encyclopaedia Britannica and the Britannica Junior. The date in the title is the date of publication with the information included pertaining to the previous year. Feature articles devoted to important topics of the year precede a chronology of the Year's major events. In the main body of the book are signed articles, usually a half-page long. Photographs, charts, and statistics accompany appropriate entries. Some biographies and a necrology list are included. Following the index is a section entitled "States Statistical Supplement" which lists statistical data on such topics as population, church membership, births and deaths, national government (including members of the House of Representatives, Senate, and the Supreme Court), state government, taxation, living

Factbooks and Yearbooks 53

conditions, welfare, law enforcement, education, production, foreign aid and commerce, finance, and transport and communications.

Collier's Year Book, Covering the Year of ___. New York: Macmillan Educational Corp., 1939-___. $7.95 to set owners.

First issued as a supplement to the National Encyclopedia under the title National Yearbook, Collier's Year Book now serves to supplement Collier's Encyclopedia and Merit Students Encyclopedia and to provide an annual survey. The signed articles cover broad topics with cross references from more specific ones. Collier's features the inclusion of controversial subjects which were debated during the previous year. It contains "Special Articles of the Year," e.g., "Vietnam: America Leaves the War," "Children Make Films," and "Health Care: A Survey." Other special sections include "Books in Review," a list of outstanding books published during the year; the chronology, and an index.

Facts on File: A Weekly Digest of World Events With Cumulative Index. New York: Facts on File, 1940-___.
Facts on File Yearbook. New York: Facts on File, 1943-___.
1948-68 $40 ea.; 1969 $45.00; 1970-72 $52.50.

News digests from 4,000 newspapers, magazines, radio and television broadcasts, and press releases comprise the weekly issues of Facts on File. News items are recorded day by day in chronological order under one of the major topics, such as World Affairs, National Affairs, Foreign Affairs, Latin America, Finance and Economics, Arts and Science, Education and Religion, Sports, Obituaries, and Miscellaneous. The index of this loose leaf news digest is cumulated bi-weekly, monthly, quarterly, and annually. Facts on File Yearbook consists of a bound volume of the 52 weekly issues with a cross reference index. News items are arranged alphabetically by category. Facts are presented in unopinionated language. Because of the comprehensiveness and unbiased approach, these two reference tools are essential to a reference shelf.

Information Please Almanac, Atlas and Yearbook, 1947-___. Dan Golenpaul, ed. New York: Simon and Schuster, 1947-___. $3.95. $2.25 paper.

A general almanac similar to World Almanac, Information Please Almanac contains fewer statistics and data but is more readable because of larger, clearer type and heavier paper. Especially important are the reviews of the year on Washington, sports, theater, fiction, movies, music, and the performing arts. It also lists statistical and historical descriptions of the countries of the world, sports records, plus many kinds of general information. A day by day news chronology and special features are included. Although there is no specific pattern to the subject arrangement of the articles, the index locates specific facts easily.

The Official Associated Press Almanac 1974. Maplewood, N.J.:
Hammond Almanac, 1974. 1040p. $5.95.

Edited by Laurence Urdang, The Official Associated Press Almanac replaces the old New York Times Encyclopedia Almanac. Besides giving the previous year in review, it contains the usual statistical type information found in almanacs: United States history and government, taxes/expenditures, finance/industry/labor, travel/transportation, census/social services, United States crime summary, diplomatic affairs, military-affairs, communications/language, zip codes and population of United States towns and cities, sports, etc. Its index locates information in the topically arranged text.

Reader's Digest Almanac. Pleasantville, N.Y.: Reader's Digest Association, 1966- . $3.95. $2.95 paper.

This almanac begins with "World in Review," a month-by-month chronology of the major events and developments of the year. Following the chronology is a large amount of information arranged under alphabetical subject headings, e.g., Accidents and disaster; Awards and prizes; Books; Calendars, time and holidays; Cities; Climate and weather, etc. Easy to use, the book contains a rather full index.

Statesman's Year Book; Statistical and Historical Annual of the States of the World. New York: St. Martin's Press, 1864- . $13.95.

Over one hundred years old, the Statesman's Year Book is a concise, reliable manual of information about the governments of the world. Although material is more detailed on Great Britain and the United States, it provides for each country facts about its government, constitution, area, population, religion, social welfare, education, judicial system, finance, defense, production and industry, agriculture, commerce, navigation, communications, banking and credit, money, etc. A selected bibliography is given for each country. A valuable reference book, it suffers from thin paper and small hard-to-read type.

World Almanac and Book of Facts. George E. Delury, ed. New York: Newspaper Enterprise Association. 1868- . $4.95. $1.95 paperback.

Published annually for more than a century, World Almanac is a compendium of facts on such topics as population, economics, sports events, politics, religion, education, the United States, and other countries. It locates important institutions and organizations and gives many scientific facts. The chronology of events provides summary histories of the previous year. It includes everything from the best selling book of the preceding year to the cost of a fishing license. The extensive index appears in the front of the volume.

INDEXES

Considerable information pertinent to the curriculum of elementary and junior high schools is contained in periodicals, newspapers, pamphlets and anthologies. Untapped, these valuable sources of material become useless shelf-sitters, utilized only superficially. Properly used, they provide essential enrichment for young people's studies. For example, current quantitative standards for periodicals recommend 40 to 50 titles for elementary schools and 100 to 125 for junior highs. Obviously, this many magazines, even though filled with applicable information, if not correctly used as reference sources on current vital topics, will become expensive browsing material occupying an undue amount of shelf space. The same is true for anthologies and collected works in book format.

The key to reaching this type of information is the fine array of available indexes, such as the Readers' Guide to Periodical Literature, Subject Index to Books for Intermediate Grades, or the Media Review Digest. Some of these indexes are rather expensive. It is, therefore, important to check the library's holdings against the titles indexed in order to decide which indexes to purchase. At the same time the librarian should consider what indexing is provided in bibliographic sources, e.g., the excellent analytic entries in the Children's Catalog. The indexes described in this chapter all cover general information. Indexes dealing with specific subjects are listed in the chapters devoted to particular topics.

Abridged Readers' Guide to Periodical Literature, 1935- . New York: Wilson, 1935- . $15.00 yearly.

The H. W. Wilson Company conceived of the Abridged Readers' Guide to cater specifically to the needs of small libraries. It indexes only 44 of the 160 adult general periodicals listed in the Readers' Guide. Issued monthly from September through May, the abridged edition provides information identical to that given in the original. In deciding whether to subscribe to the Readers' Guide or the Abridged Readers' Guide, one should check the library's holdings against both lists. If an adequate number of holdings are included in the Abridged Readers' Guide, then the less expensive title should be obtained. On the other hand, if many of the library's magazines are omitted from the abridged edition and are included in the original, the additional cost of Readers' Guide is justified.

Ayer Directory of Publications. Leonard Bray, ed. Philadelphia: Ayer Press, 1880-   . $45.00.

About 23,000 newspapers and magazines published in America are listed in this annual directory. Its subtitle reads: a guide to publications printed and published in the United States and its Territories, the Dominion of Canada, Bermuda, the Republics of Panama and the Philippines; descriptions of the states, provinces, cities and towns in which they are published; classified lists; 70 maps. Arranged geographically, it includes an alphabetical index for locating publications when place of publication is unknown. Each entry gives the name, frequency of issue, price, circulation, editors, political affiliation, etc. It also contains classified lists, e.g., daily newspapers, daily periodicals, college publications, etc. Equally valuable as a geographical handbook, it provides information for each town, such as population, railroads, airlines, number of banks, gas meters, telephones, institutions, manufacturing, mining, and farming. Since many of the tiny towns listed in Ayer's are omitted in other gazetteers, it can be of untold worth.

Book Review Digest. New York: Wilson Co., 1905-   . Sold on service basis.

Listing a consensus of skillfully condensed critical opinion, both pro and con, about important book titles, the Book Review Digest, while dealing primarily with adult books, does include some juvenile works. Arranged alphabetically by the author, the book annually capsules reviews of more than 6,000 books from over seventy general magazines. It gives full reference to the magazines so that the reader can easily locate the review itself. To be included in the Digest, a non-fiction book must receive at least two reviews and fiction at least four. Each volume contains a subject and title index. Published monthly except in February and July, it is cumulated in an annual bound volume. The subject and title index cumulates every five years.

Book Review Index, 1965-   . Detroit: Gale Research, 1965-   . Annual cumulations, 1965-1968, $30.00 each; 1969-   , $45.00 each.

More comprehensive in coverage than the Book Review Digest, Book Review Index cites reviews from over 200 periodicals. Entries are alphabetical by author with no subject entries and no digests of reviews. Only one review is necessary to qualify a title for inclusion. Actually, these book review tools complement each other and should be used accordingly.

Essay and General Literature Index. New York: Wilson Co., 1900-   . Semiannual with a bound annual cumulation/permanent five-year cumulation. $22.00 a year. 1900-1969, 7 vols, $55.00 each.

Typical of the Wilson indexes, the Essay and General

Literature Index is an author-subject index to collections of essays covering many areas but stressing the humanities and social sciences, and with special emphasis on literary criticism. Although only works published in the twentieth century are indexed, authors of every age and nationality are listed. From the inception of the Index in 1900 through 1969, 9,917 titles have been analyzed. Libraries wishing to acquire the Index should purchase only those permanent volumes indexing collections of essays owned by the library.

Illustration Index. Roger C. Greer, ed. 3rd ed. Metuchen, N.J.: Scarecrow Press, 1973. 164p. $5.00.

A continuation of two previous indexes, the Illustration Index in its third edition indexes illustrations including photographs, charts, drawings, etc., in twelve periodicals and two books. Covering the period of time from July 1, 1963 to December 31, 1971, the book analyzes American Heritage Magazine, Ebony, Grade Teacher, Hobbies, Holiday, Instructor, Life, Look, National Geographic, School Arts, Sports Illustrated, and Travel. The two books listed are National Geographic's America's Wonderlands and Von Braun's History of Rocketry and Space Travel. In indexing material the editor has placed emphasis on the history and cultures of various people and countries, sporting activities, costumes, hobbies, and scientific subjects. Since this index covers periodicals which would probably be in elementary and junior high libraries, it is recommended as a valuable reference source for locating illustrative material. The two previous editions are recommended only for those libraries owning periodicals for the years preceding 1963.

Media Review Digest, 1973-74. Edited by C. Edward Wall, B. Penny Northern, Cynthia Rigg, and Richard LeSueur. Ann Arbor, Mich.: Pierian Press, 1974. Annual. $65.00.

Formerly called Multi Media Review Index, the Media Review Digest consists of about 40,000 citations and cross references to reviews of various media in periodicals. Separate sections cover films and videotapes, filmstrips, records and tapes, and miscellaneous media. Entries include title, series title, producer/distributor, release date, technical data, annotation, LC subject headings, Dewey number, grade level indications, source of review and coded summary of review content, quotation from review, and name of reviewer. The annual volume is up-dated by three supplements and monthly columns appearing in Audiovisual Instruction. Included in the supplements will be Media in Print and New Media in Print which will provide "mediagraphic" data on new and available audiovisuals whether or not they have been reviewed.

New York Times Index. By Joseph C. Gephert. New York: New York Times. Semi-monthly subscriptions $87.50; annual cumulations $87.50; combination $150.00 yearly.

While this semi-monthly tool is in actuality a subject index to the New York Times, it can serve usefully in locating material in other newspapers since it gives clues as to the dates of specific events. It not only locates events in the Times but provides brief summaries of articles which often answer questions without referring to the paper itself. Cumulated annually, it covers a variety of subjects including politics, economics, science, agriculture, military affairs, religion, fine arts, book reviews, plays, crime, deaths, motion pictures, speeches, sports, music, church activities, and letters to the editor. About 3,500 subject headings with numerous cross references are used. Entries tell the author, title, date, column, page, and cross references to related articles.

Readers' Guide to Periodical Literature, 1900-   . New York: Wilson, 1905-   . $35.00 yearly.

One of the most commonly used periodical indexes is Wilson's Readers' Guide. Indexing 160 adult general magazines frequently found in small libraries, it is published twice monthly (once a month in July and August). The bi-monthly issues are combined at intervals into larger editions and are cumulated annually in a bound volume. Alphabetically arranged by author and subject, each entry gives the author, title, name of periodical, volume number, inclusive paging, date, and if appropriate, illustrators and bibliographies. Cross references and sub-headings aid in locating material. Magazines indexed range in subject from Americas to Sky and Telescope and National Geographic Magazine to Sports Illustrated. While the titles included in Readers' Guide are of adult periodicals, a large portion of these are of interest to children and should appear among the library's holdings.

Speech Index: An Index to 259 Collections of World Famous Speeches, Orations, and Speeches for Various Occasions. Roberta Briggs Sutton, ed. 4th ed. Metuchen, N.J.: Scarecrow Press, 1966. 947p. $20.00. Fourth Edition Supplement, 1966-1970. 1972. 277p. $7.50.

The Speech Index, fourth edition, indexes speeches listed in 259 collected works published between 1935 and 1965, while the supplement indexes another 58 titles published between January 1966 and December 1970. The main body of text is arranged alphabetically by authors and subjects. In the back is a selected list of titles, which includes speech titles difficult to locate if the user does not know the author and if the meaning in the title bears no resemblance to the topic discussed, or if there are no key words in the title to guide him to the proper subject entry. This reference tool is recommended for junior high libraries having need to own many of the titles indexed.

Subject Index to Books for Intermediate Grades. Mary K. Eakin, comp. 3rd ed. Chicago: American Library Association, 1963. 308p. $8.00.

Similar to Subject Index to Books for Primary Grades, this tool indexes alphabetically by subject about 1,800 books of fiction, non-fiction, and school texts selected as valuable teaching material in the upper elementary school. Although intended for teachers, it can be used with little difficulty by intermediate level children. It supplements rather than duplicates specialized indexes, e.g., short stories, poetry, etc.

Subject Index to Books for Primary Grades. Mary K. Eakin and Eleanor Merritt, comps. 3rd ed. Chicago: American Library Association, 1967. 167p. $4.00.

Alphabetically arranged by subject, this indispensable reference book indexes a wide variety of both trade and text books suitable for use in the primary grades. Books for independent reading and for reading aloud are differentiated by grade and level symbols.

Subject Index to Children's Magazines. Gladys Cavanagh, editor. Madison, Wisconsin. Monthly (Aug.-May). $10.50 yearly.

This monthly periodical index is essential for an elementary school library. Using the same form of entry as the Readers' Guide, it indexes the valuable children's publications which contain invaluable information. Its list includes the juvenile weekly newspapers, e.g., Newstime and My Weekly Reader; varied titles, such as Boys' Life, Jack and Jill, Cricket, Humpty-Dumpty, Highlights for Children, Arizona Highways, Man and His Music, Ranger Rick's Nature Magazine; and regional historical magazines, for example, Illinois History and Wisconsin Trails. Indexing stories, poems, and plays as well as factual material, Subject Index to Children's Magazines is an indispensable tool for both children and teachers. It is now available from Gladys Cavanagh, 2223 Chamberlain Avenue, Madison, Wisconsin, 53705.

Vertical File Index; A Subject and Title Index to Selected Pamphlet Material. New York: Wilson. $9.00 yearly.

Issued monthly except August, the Vertical File Index lists selected free and inexpensive pamphlet material ranging in level from elementary to adult. Designed to locate pamphlet material for acquisition, it provides for each entry the title, paging, publisher, publication date, descriptive note, and price or conditions under which it may be acquired. Alphabetically arranged by subject with a title index, each issue lists current, available pamphlets, booklets, leaflets, and mimeographed material.

ATLASES

The first formal study of maps usually begins in the primary grades when the child learns to locate on simple maps his home within his community. This rudimentary introduction to map symbols and map reading provides the basis for the depth study which occurs in the intermediate levels. Whether choosing the simplest materials for beginners or the most comprehensive for experts, the librarian must evaluate and select carefully. Although price and quality are not necessarily synonymous, it is generally safe to conclude that the better atlases will be more costly. It is therefore recommended that the evaluator select the finest atlases available within a particular price range.

To assist in determining the quality of an atlas, those evaluating should answer the following questions. What is the reputation of the publisher, editor and staff, and cartographers? What is the country of origin? Is there a bibliography? What region is covered, e.g., world, continent, country, state? What kinds of maps are included? Does it contain a gazetteer or statistical information? What are the imprint, copyright, and revision dates? What are the dates on the individual maps? What dates are given for boundaries, census figures, and place names? What method of topographical representation is employed? Is the lettering legible? Is the color varied and pleasant? Are names in the vernacular or translated? In what order are the maps arranged? Is there a general index? In the case of historical atlases, what period of time is covered?

Listed below are a number of titles especially suitable for elementary and junior high school libraries. They are arranged under the following headings: Map Skills, Introductory Atlases, Mature Atlases, Special Purpose Atlases, and Historical Atlases.

MAP SKILLS

Stanek, Muriel. How We Use Maps and Globes. Chicago: Benefic Press, 1968. 48p. $2.40.

This useful little book, written on a second grade reading level, covers such topics as: how globes help us, how maps help us, what are directions, land and water on maps and globes, using the globe to learn about night and day, and the seasons, and how maps show distance. Complementing the simple text are the illustrations which bear the primary responsibility for explanations. Although map symbols are not shown as clearly as in the two books by Rhodes, the overall coverage of this work is much more extensive.

Rhodes, Dorothy. How to Read a City Map. Chicago: Elk Grove Press, 1967. 46p. $5.19.

How to Read a City Map contains but few simple words and relies heavily upon the symbols and drawings to convey explanations. More than two dozen common map symbols are used and explained. A glossary of fourteen terms appears at the back of the book. The overall usefulness of the book is marred by the lack of either an index or a table of contents; however, this problem is not insurmountable for the text is brief enough to permit the user to locate information with a minimum of browsing. Although designed as an introduction to map work for primary level students, the book could be used profitably by older students who have never accomplished the art of reading a city map.

Rhodes, Dorothy. How to Read a Highway Map. Chicago: Children's Press, 1970. 53p. $5.19.

Compared with the author's How to Read a City Map, this book contains much of the same material plus considerably more. A logical sequel, it has a longer text with a more difficult vocabulary and more detailed explanations. Relying heavily on illustrations, it has for each symbol one or more photographs, the symbol itself, and the symbol on a section of a map. A glossary of 48 terms appears at the back. As with the previous book, this one has no index nor table of contents, but is nonetheless useful to middle elementary and junior high students who are first encountering map reading.

Asimov, Isaac. Words on the Map. New York: Houghton Mifflin, 1962. 274p. $5.95.

Alphabetically arranged, Words on the Map consists of 250 one-page essays in which over 1,500 names are discussed. Covered in the text are all of the states and major cities of the United States, the major cities and countries of the world, mountains, rivers, lakes, and seas. While the author makes no attempt to be comprehensive, he provides an interesting, readable book which can serve as an introduction or as a complement to atlases used for study.

Rand McNally Answer Atlas. New York: Rand McNally, 1968. 71p. $2.95.

A unique and interesting volume, the Rand McNally Answer Atlas is designed to inspire children to study maps rather than to serve as an atlas per se. Arranged by geographical locale, it includes sections on Europe, Soviet Union, Mediterranean Lands, Asia, Africa, Australia and New Zealand, South America, North America, Canada, United States, Northern Lands and Seas, Southern Lands and Seas, and the World. For each there is a physical map, a brief political map, and a list of questions, followed by a map showing numbered answers in the margins connected by lines to appropriate spots on the map. Sample questions are "What three continents border the Mediterranean Sea?"; "In what country was Africa's lowest temperature recorded?"; and "What is the longest river in the world?" A set of tables show a variety of world facts and comparisons. The index gives page, latitude, and longitude for each of its entries.

INTRODUCTORY ATLASES

My First World Atlas. Maplewood, N.J.: Hammond Inc., 1973. 48p. $.88 paper.

Abridged from the Hammond Illustrated Atlas for Young America, My First World Atlas serves as a fine introduction to maps. It contains the same illustrations and maps as the parent volume, but omits all narrative text explaining concepts. The section called "How to Read Maps" contains all the illustrative material appearing in the original under the subdivision, "Maps and How to Use Them." Other sections include physical and political reference maps, reference tables, world history, and American history. Since the narrative explanations are valuable to the beginning map student, the parent volume is recommended as first choice; the abridged edition, however, could be valuable in some instances. For example, it would be a fine inexpensive selection to use on a one per child basis in elementary school map study.

Hammond Illustrated Atlas for Young America. Maplewood, N.J.: Hammond Inc., 1967. 95p. $4.50.

The Hammond Illustrated Atlas for Young America bears the subtitle "full color maps and up-to-date facts with new concepts about our physical and political world." Excellent for elementary students, it has an outstanding section, "Maps and How to Use Them," which provides a narrative text and illustrations to explain the following concepts: facts about our earth; maps and how they started; what is a map; how to use a map; what scale means; projections; and contours. The section entitled "Our Physical and Political World" includes a simple, uncluttered map and a story for each geographical area. In "Man's Story in Maps" world history and American history are depicted with good maps and a narrative text. On the back lining paper are charts showing oceans and seas of the world, and principal mountains of the world. A very brief index aids in locating specific information.

Atlases 63

Rand McNally Classroom Atlas Indexed. 6th ed. Chicago: Rand McNally, 1973 (c1970). 84p. $1.25.

    Designed for the beginner, the Rand McNally Classroom Atlas Indexed is produced in an attractive inexpensive paperback format. It includes a series of relief, political, and special (land use, population soils, climate, vegetation, races, languages, religions) maps. For each geographical unit it provides a merged relief map, a political map, and a comparative map. Tables on the inside cover show world facts and comparisons, continental comparisons, and largest metropolitan areas and cities. The world political information table shows the region or political division, the area in square miles, population in square miles, the capital, the largest city, and the form of government or ruling power. The back cover lists United States geographical and historical facts, territorial acquisitions, and the westward movement of the center of population. Easy to handle, appealing color, and uncluttered maps make this a desirable introductory atlas.

The First Book Atlas. 3rd ed. By the editors and cartographers of Hammond Inc. New York: Watts, 1973. 96p. $3.95.

    The First Book Atlas contains political and special maps of countries and continents. Information includes political boundaries, capitals, major cities, important rivers, seas, and other major physical features. For each continent special maps show resources and products and land use, and tables of data indicate area, population, highest point, lowest point, longest river and largest lake. Approximately one-third of the atlas is devoted to the United States. The fifty states are shown on sectional maps with detailed plans of leading cities and national parks outlined in cutaways. Although the muted brown and blue maps are not as attractive in color as those in some atlases, The First Book Atlas is reasonably priced and has the advantage of being a small and easy to handle volume.

Intermediate World Atlas. New Rev. Ed. Maplewood, N.J.: Hammond Inc., 1972. 63p. $1.28 paper.

    The Intermediate World Atlas, designed to correlate with the Hammond map transparency series, serves as a bridge between introductory classroom atlases and adult atlases. Featuring clear, uncluttered simple political/physical maps, it provides reasonably well balanced geographical coverage. Its brief Gazetteer-Index of the World contains an alphabetical listing of continents, major countries, colonial possessions, states of the United States, and Canadian provinces. For each entry it gives the area, population, and page reference, and designates members of the United Nations. The front inside cover consists of a Glossary of Geographical Terms, while the back of the cover shows maps of the Near and Far sides of the Moon. A short five-page index of the world lists major cities and geographical features. Since the atlas is printed in large, clear type and contains a minimum of information, it should be an excellent source for children in the middle elementary school grades.

Hammond Headline World Atlas. Maplewood, N.J.: Hammond Inc.,
1974. 50p. $1.00 paper.

Considerably more complete than the Intermediate World Atlas, the Headline World Atlas, also published as the Grosset World Atlas, can serve more mature students in the same fashion as the Intermediate serves younger ones. For all continents, major subdivisions, and countries it provides political, topographical, and special maps featuring agriculture, industry and resources. It also shows flags, capsule data summaries, and outline locations on small maps and globes. The gazetteer-index lists alphabetically the grand divisions, countries, states, and colonial possessions and gives the area, population, capital or chief town, and index references and page numbers. Following the main body of the atlas are a moon map and lists of principal islands of the world, principal mountains of the world, and longest rivers of the world.

MATURE ATLASES

Goode, John P. Goode's World Atlas; ed. by Edward B. Espenshade, Jr., and Joel L. Morrison. 14th ed. 50th anniversary. Chicago: Rand McNally, 1974. 372p. $9.95. $5.95 paper.

A respected standard atlas since its introduction in 1922, Goode's World Atlas is now in its fourteenth edition. Versatile enough to be used by mature middle elementary school children and also by college students, it provides a variety of maps in soft, soothing colors. The first section of the atlas, called "World Thematic Maps," lists 54 pages of special comparison maps depicting such topics as transportation, natural resources, landforms, vegetation, population density, population distribution, languages, religion, etc. Part 2, "Metropolitan Area Maps," consists of a series of urban maps of major cities of the world, e.g., New York, Chicago, Los Angeles, London, Paris, Tokyo, etc. Part 3, "Regional Section," arranged by continent, contains the bulk of the atlas. Here are the physical/political reference maps and environment maps for the various regions and countries. In Part 4, "Ocean Floor Maps" are maps of the Atlantic, Pacific, Indian, and Arctic Ocean floors. The last section "Geographical Tables and Indexes" includes world comparisons, principal countries and regions of the world, principal cities of the world, metropolitan area map index, glossary of foreign geographical terms, abbreviations and pronunciations, and a pronouncing index or over 30,000 geographical names.

Hammond Citation World Atlas. Maplewood, N.J.: Hammond Inc.,
1973. 352p. $12.95.

The Citation World Atlas is a medium-sized atlas in the Hammond series, containing the first 320 pages of the Medallion Atlas. Its maps correspond with those in the International World Atlas plus additional maps covering the United States. While this book contains classified indexes for each continent or country, it also lists an abbreviated world index of 25,000 entries. It includes a gazetteer-index of the world, an introduction to maps and indexes, geographical terms, airline distance tables, world statistics, and map projections. While this particular atlas is less valuable as a research source than the more expensive atlases, it may well be considered for elementary school students who might find the much larger cross-reference indexes confusing rather than helpful.

Rand McNally World Atlas. Family Ed. Chicago: Rand McNally, 1973. 317p. $9.95.

The Family Edition World Atlas inexpensively provides a wide range of information. While it is not adequate for research purposes, it is useful for young students. Divided into a number of parts, the atlas contains much encyclopedic information. The first section, "Earth: the Life-Supporting Planet," uses text, photographs, charts, tables, graphs, and special maps to describe such topics as mountains, oceans, pollution, food resources, mineral resources, water resources, energy resources, archaeology, weather, geology, etc. Abridged from "The Good Earth" in Earth and Man, this section effectively defines man's responsibility for the abundant earth. "Global Views" is a brief collection of maps showing the continents from an aerial view. "The Political World in Maps" consists of an 89-page section of Cosmos Series maps of the various continents and countries, one half of which is devoted to the United States. The index, one hundred pages long, provides pronunciation, population, and location for all entries. Two sections of supplemental material are noteworthy because of their clarity and extensiveness. The "United States Information" section lists geographical and historical facts about the United States, state areas and populations, and a general information table. The "World Facts and Comparisons" group of tables shows movements, measurements, inhabitants, surface and extremes of temperature and rainfall of the earth; approximate population of the world 1650-1973; largest countries of the world in population and area; principal lakes, rivers, islands, mountains; world air and steamship distance tables; and many others. A final section consists of a collection of historical maps. In general, although this atlas contains an inadequate number of maps to serve as an all-purpose atlas, it is recommended for young students, because of its additional material, as a supplement to more sophisticated works.

Hammond Ambassador World Atlas. Maplewood, N.J.: Hammond Inc., 1974. 480p. $16.95.

This highly recommended atlas is the second largest of the Hammond atlases. Identical to Part II of the comprehensive Medallion World Atlas, the Ambassador contains exactly the same maps plus the entire 100,000 entry A-to-Z cross index. In addition it includes supplemental material such as the gazetteer-index, an introduction to the maps and indexes, postal zip code maps for major United States cities, map projections and geographical terms. A section of world statistics tables covers topics such as elements of the solar system, oceans and seas of the world, great ship canals, principal lakes and inland seas, principal islands of the world, principal mountains of the world, and longest rivers of the world. Because of its comprehensiveness, its clear usable format, and its reasonable price, this atlas is definitely a good purchase for elementary and junior high school libraries.

National Geographic Atlas of the World. Melville Bell Grosvenor, ed. 3rd ed. Washington, D.C.: National Geographic Society, 1970. 331p. $18.75.

 Considered to be one of the finer atlases produced in the United States, the National Geographic Atlas of the World is comprehensive, attractive, and accurate. For each geographical region it provides political maps with some physical features and a descriptive gazetteer with the flag, a brief history, and vital statistics. A special addition for the United States is a section showing national parks, monuments and historic sites, and battlefields of the Civil War. Additional information includes global statistics (geographic extremes and comparisons), populations of major cities, temperatures, abbreviations, and a glossary of geographical terms. Exceedingly comprehensive, the index lists 139,000 entries. Altogether, this atlas is a good one that belongs on every reference shelf.

Hammond Medallion World Atlas. Maplewood, N.J.: Hammond Inc., 1973. 655p. $24.95.

 The Medallion World Atlas is the largest and most complete atlas in the Hammond series and is literally composed of five separate atlases. They are "Environment and Life," "Modern Maps and Indexes," "Atlas of the Bible Lands," "Historical Atlas," and "United States History Atlas." The first part is a collection of articles with maps, diagrams, and photographs covering such topics as the ice ages, environmental controls, the moon, and the structure of the earth. Comprising the second part are the 320 pages of maps of countries, states, and continents which are found also in the Hammond Citation and Ambassador atlases. The basic maps are political, showing international and internal boundaries and other limited detail. Each continental map is accompanied by special maps showing population distribution, vegetation, rainfall, average January temperature, average July temperature, and topography. Each political map is accompanied by a small topographical map; a special map showing agriculture, industry, and resources; flags; and tables of statistical data. A very useful additional feature is the presence of an individual index for each map. All these individual indexes are included in the excellent 110,000-entry index which follows the map collection. All entries give geographical identification, zip code if in the United States, page numbers, and location symbols. The map section itself is heavily weighted in favor of the United States with more than one third of the pages being devoted to this country.

Part three of the Medallion World Atlas is the "Atlas of the Bible Lands," which is also published under separate cover. Basically, it contains thirty-two pages of maps and photographs tracing the history of the Bible lands from 2000 B.C. to the present time. The "Hammond Historical Atlas," part four, is also published separately. It traces chronologically through maps the most significant periods and events in the development of western civilization. The final section, "United States History Atlas," is likewise issued as an independent title. It too proceeds chronologically, moving from the American Indians and the voyages of discovery of America to modern American politics. All in all, the Medallion is easy to use and comprehensive enough to serve the purposes of most elementary and junior high school libraries. It is definitely recommended for purchase.

Rand McNally New Cosmopolitan World Atlas. Enl. "Planet Earth" ed. Chicago: Rand McNally, 1973. 407p. $19.95.

Attractive and accurate, the Rand McNally Cosmopolitan World Atlas is a good choice for schools seeking atlases in the medium price range. Preceding the map section in this atlas are 55 pages of encyclopedic information. Included in it are topics entitled "The Planet Earth," "The Moon," "The Ocean World," and "Maps and Map Projections." In a series of photographs, drawings, charts, maps, and diagrams plus a minimal text, various geographical subheadings are discussed, such as: the planet earth in space, the solar system, the earth's atmosphere, weather systems from space, geology of the earth, man on the moon, etc. Also included in this preliminary material are the various maps of the ocean floor. The maps themselves, part of the well-known "Cosmos Series," are arranged region by region, with headings as follows: The world and special regions, Europe, Asia, Africa, Australia and Oceania, South America, North America, and The physical world in maps. Heavily weighted toward North America, it contains more than 60 pages of maps in that section out of a total of 140 map pages. The political-physical maps are done in pastel colors that are pleasing and easy to read.

The final part of the Cosmopolitan is entitled "Geographical Facts, Figures, and Information about the World and the United States." In this section are tables of information such as world political information; world facts and comparisons; principal mountains; great oceans and seas; principal lakes, rivers, and islands; world air and steamship distances; largest metropolitan areas and cities; and altitudes of selected world cities. Interspersed here is a group of metropolitan area maps of major world cities. Finally, there appears "Selected United States Information," listing geographical facts, general information tables, population by state or colony, and largest metropolitan areas followed by a section of United States metropolitan area maps.

The last 100 pages of the atlas comprise a fine comprehensive index to the political-physical maps. More than 82,000 entries locate every place and feature on the maps. The atlas as a whole is recommended to elementary and junior high schools as a reliable and popular source of maps, especially for Canada and the United States.

Reference Books

<u>Merit Atlas: Man's Earth and Universe.</u> Chicago: Rand McNally, 1973. (Dist. by Lexington, Andrews). 408p. $31.00.

    Published by Rand McNally, but sold by Lexington, Andrews as an adjunct to the <u>Merit Students Encyclopedia</u>, the <u>Merit Atlas</u> is an attractive and useful new work. Basically divided into two parts, the first section, "The Good Earth," is identical to the first part of <u>The Earth and Man</u>. It consists of 143 pages of text, color photographs, drawings, charts, diagrams, and maps depicting the evolution of earth and man. Under the subheadings "The structure of the earth," "Life on earth," "The resources of the earth," and "Man on earth," are topics covering the physical structure of the earth, its resources, and man's relationship to the earth including its abuse and pollution. This section is immediately followed by an index to its contents.

    Part II is the "World Atlas." Included here are the collection of famous "Cosmos Series" maps, arranged under the following headings: The world and special regions, Europe, Asia, Africa, Australia and Oceania, South America, and North America. Coverage emphasizes North America. Also contained in this section are special features: Maps and map projections, World political information table, World history in maps, Geographical facts, Figures and information about the World and the United States, and United States Presidential elections since World War II. An index of more than 80,000 entries including physical features, points of interest, and political names locates each entry by location reference and page number. The atlas is timely and appealing and should be a valuable addition to libraries in both elementary and junior high school.

<u>The Earth and Man: a Rand McNally World Atlas.</u> Chicago: Rand McNally, 1972. 439p. $35.00.

    <u>Earth and Man</u> is an unusual and attractive encyclopedic atlas. Designed to emphasize man's relationship to the earth and its preservation, the atlas is divided into two major sections. The first part, "The Good Earth," consists of 143 pages of text, photographs, drawings, charts, diagrams, and maps. Sub-topics under consideration include "The earth in space," "The structure of the earth," "Life on earth," "The resources of the earth," and "Man on earth." Using a series of two-page spreads for each specific subject, the book covers such diverse items as theories on the origin of the solar system, human nutrition, the structure of weather systems, the population problem, the abuse of the earth, and controlling pollution. Over 1,200 illustrations accompany the text.

    The second section of <u>Earth and Man</u> is "Maps," a collection of primarily Rand McNally "Cosmos Series" maps. Arranged by continent, the maps appear under the following major headings: Europe and the Soviet Union, Asia, Africa, Australia and New Zealand, Anglo America, and Latin America. Although the United States and Canada are presented in greater detail than other countries of the world, the maps are clear, accurate, and easy to use. Colored in soft gray shades with pastel political borders, these

Atlases 69

political-physical maps are pleasant to look at. Printed on blue paper following the maps is a section called "Geographical Facts, Figures and Information about the World and the United States." Listed here are tables of political information, population, and gazetteer facts. Also included in this section are the subject index to "The Good Earth" and the index of nearly 70,000 names appearing on the maps. In general, although this atlas has fewer maps than other atlases of the same price range, it is recommended for elementary and junior high school libraries because of its emphasis upon ecology, its attractiveness for the browser, and its accurate information for the researching student.

The World Book Atlas. Chicago: Field Enterprises, 1972. 392p. $31.20.

The World Book Atlas is prepared by the editorial staff of the World Book Encyclopedia, the cartographic staff of Rand McNally, and a special board of consultants. Although it is designed to supplement the World Book Encyclopedia, it can readily be used independently. To introduce the atlas, the editors have prepared a section called "how to get the most out of the World Book Atlas." In it are simple instructions and check-tests for learning how to find places on maps, find directions, find distances, understand symbols, understand populations, pronounce names of cities, and understand abbreviations and foreign geographic terms.

The map section, containing physical, political, physical-political, and historical maps, is divided by broad geographic regions. Included are the World; Europe; Asia; Africa; Australia, New Zealand and Pacific Islands; Polar Regions; Latin America; Canada; and the United States. A special section of maps, photographs, and facts about the moon follows. The final group of maps takes the form of a travel guide of the United States, including distance tables, highway maps, and brief descriptions of landmarks.

Supplementing the map collection is a block of information on population. Included here are populations of major world cities, a pronouncing gazetteer, the census of Canada, and the census of the United States. The index, printed on pale green paper, contains 82,000 entries giving identification, page numbers, and location references. The entire atlas is well-made and easy to use. Each of 14 major divisions is color-coded both in the index and on the pages to facilitate rapid use. Although the atlas is imbalanced in favor of the United States, it is reasonably comprehensive and accurate. It is definitely recommended for purchase for both elementary and junior high school libraries.

Oxford World Atlas. Saul B. Cohen, ed. Prepared by the Cartographic Dept. of Clarendon Press. New York: Oxford University Press, 1973. 190p. $19.95.

An entirely new work, the Oxford World Atlas required a reputed seven years for research and preparation. Attempting to show man's environment in relationship to man's activities, the atlas shows a variety of features on each map. The map section begins with three map pages showing the Ocean Islands, the Indian Ocean, the Atlantic Ocean, and the Pacific Ocean. The next section, "The Physical Environment," includes 10 pages showing the physical formations and altitudes of the continents. Part III is "The Human Environment," map pages showing population and cities, land use, highways, railroads, shipping, air traffic, mining, etc. The next 41 pages are "Topographic Maps" of regions throughout the world arranged by continent. Eighteen of these are of the United States and Canada as compared with three for Africa. A collection of urban maps depicts major cities around the world. The last map section, "Thematic Maps," consists primarily of world comparisons and includes such topics as soils, population, manufacturing, income, nutrition, selected crops, cereals, energy, iron ore/steel, foreign aid/trade, air communications, airports, etc.

    Prefatory material in this atlas consists of an introduction with full map keys, map projections, and material on the earth and the solar system. The tabular chart, "Countries of the World," shows capital city, population, density, area, and approximate land use in percentages. Another chart, "Selected World Geographical Name Changes from 1945," gives both old and new names of countries and cities. The gazetteer in the back of the atlas contains 30,000 entries and identifies each as well as giving map number, page, latitude, and longitude. This atlas is deceptively simple. It contains a vast amount of material on each map, but is not excessively difficult to use. It should definitely be considered for junior high school libraries and for elementary school libraries where such sophisticated information is needed.

<u>New York Times Atlas of the World</u>; in collaboration with the <u>Times of London</u>. New York: Quadrangle Books, 1972. 40, 144, 84p. $35.00.

    Published also as <u>The Times Concise Atlas of the World</u>, the <u>New York Times Atlas of the World</u> is designed to bring the best features of the <u>Times Atlas Comprehensive Edition</u> into a less expensive price range. Although much of the material in the <u>Concise Edition</u> is new, many of the maps are adapted directly from the <u>Comprehensive Edition</u>. The Concise Edition is divided into three main parts: Man, the World, and the Universe; the Maps; and the Index. Part I consists primarily of text and special maps covering a variety of topics. Some examples include the origin of the earth, geology, continental drift, volcanoes, earthquakes, land and sea forms, minerals, food and nutrition, population, fuel and energy, world tourism, patterns of world trade, the universe, the moon and stars.

    The map section consists of 144 pages of six-color physical-political maps. Prepared with considerable detail, the maps show both natural and cultural features, e.g., deserts, lakes, swamps, highways, railroads, canals, and airports. Thirty-three metropolitan area maps are included in this section; ten of these are located in the United States.

    A strong feature of this atlas is the index which includes

95,000 entries. According to the editors, it includes not every name on the maps, but all towns and physical features except the smallest. Each entry lists the entry word, the country, the page, and the location symbol. A valuable statistical table called "Countries of the World" gives for each country the capital, the square miles, and the population. An important collection of geographic comparison tables covers such items as lakes, rivers, oceans and seas, areas, mountains, populations 1970-71, and populations of metropolitan areas. Altogether, this atlas is accurate, reliable, and although it is rather difficult, should be considered for serious students in both elementary and junior high schools.

The International Atlas. Rev. 2nd ed. Chicago: Rand McNally, 1974. 534p. $35.00.
Britannica Atlas. Chicago: Encyclopaedia Britannica, 1974. 534p. $35.00.

Published jointly in 1969 by Rand McNally and Encyclopaedia Britannica, The International Atlas and Britannica Atlas are, in the 1974 edition, identical except for the Foreword. Considered the best atlas ever produced in the United States, it was created as a truly international atlas by more than 100 specialists from other countries, although it is basically the work of Rand McNally. The text throughout carries out the international intent, for it appears in English, French, German, and Spanish. Further, measurement is indicated by the metric system followed by Anglo-American terms (feet, miles, etc.). The scale is clearly marked and color-coded for quick recognition.

Well balanced in coverage, the map section is divided into the following sections: world, ocean, and continent maps; regional maps; Europe; Union of Soviet Socialist Republics; Asia; Africa; Australia/Oceania; Anglo-America; Latin America; and metropolitan area maps. Maps in the main series are physical and are supplemented by political, thematic, and 60 large-scale metropolitan maps. Both tastefully and accurately drawn, the maps show considerable detail, including natural features as well as man-made cultural ones.

A special section entitled "World Scene," prepared by Encyclopaedia Britannica, provides a valuable collection of thematic maps. Included are the world, July 1973; the world, January 1, 1914; the world, January 1, 1937; population; religions; languages; agricultural regions; forests and fisheries; minerals; energy production and consumption; gross national product; international trade; intercontinental air connections; great circle distances; continental transport routes; time zones; climate; surface configuration; earth structure and tectonics; natural vegetation; soils; and drainage regions and ocean currents.

Following the map sections are the glossary, world information tables, population of cities and towns, and the index. The index lists 160,000 separate names that appear on the maps. Each name is identified and located by page number, latitude and longitude. The International Atlas and the Britannica Atlas are recommended as outstanding atlases containing quality, reliable material. Although they may be too difficult for elementary school students who have not had a thorough grounding in map study, one of them should be available in junior high school libraries and also in elementary school libraries where there is a need for a detailed, scholarly atlas.

The Times Atlas of the World: Comprehensive Edition. Produced and published by the Times of London in collaboration with John Bartholomew & Son. 4th ed. Boston: Houghton Mifflin, 1972. 556p. $65.00.

Based on the famous five-volume Mid-Century Edition of the Times Atlas of the World, the Comprehensive Edition is an updated and scholarly work. Preceding the main plates are a table of states, territories, and islands of the world; tables of geographical comparisons; an essay on resources in relation to man's needs; and a series of special maps showing world minerals, energy, food, climate, the solar system, and the moon. The main map section is very well balanced with coverage quite equitably divided among political units. Following a series of thematic maps showing population, vegetation, climatology, oceanography, physiography, politics, and air routes, the atlas proceeds with maps of various countries and regions, beginning with islands of the orient and Australasia and south-west Pacific. Maps of Eurasia, Arctica, Europe, Africa, North America, South America, the Pacific Ocean, and Antarctica follow. The maps themselves are accurate and legible; however, they may be difficult for children, for the place names all bear the spelling officially used in the region involved.

An outstanding feature of the Comprehensive Edition is the index-gazetteer which contains more than 200,000 entries representing nearly all of the place names appearing on the maps. For each entry there is identification, latitude, longitude, map number, and location reference. An international glossary precedes the index-gazetteer. The Times Atlas of the World, Comprehensive Edition, considered to be one of the most outstanding atlases available, is recommended for junior high schools that can afford it, and for elementary schools where both need and funds exist.

SPECIAL PURPOSE ATLASES

Atlas Moderno Universal. Edicion Nuevamente Revisada. Maplewood, N.J.: Hammond Inc., 1973. 47p. $1.25.

An inexpensive paperback atlas printed entirely in Spanish, Atlas Moderno Universal is a collection of political maps. Included are the solar system, the Antarctic, South America, North America, Europe, Asia, Oceania, Africa, and the World. A gazetteer lists population, page numbers, and reference symbols. An index of principal cities locates names on the maps. This Spanish language atlas is a good choice to supplement the expensive and comprehensive Britannica Atlas or The International Atlas.

Atlases 73

Large Type Hammond-Jennison World Atlas. New York: Watts, 1969. 144p. $12.95.

Designed for use by the partially-sighted, the Large Type Hammond-Jennison World Atlas is printed in large, bold, print. Containing 100 maps, it is arranged by continent: The World, North America, South America, Europe, Asia, Australia and New Zealand, Africa, and Antarctica. The maps themselves are very bare, four-color political maps; although they accomplish their purpose of providing easy to read type, they are not attractive in appearance. Preceding the map section is the 2,000-entry Gazetteer-index of the World, which lists continents, countries, states, colonial posessions and other major geographical terms. Following the maps is the "Index of the World." While the atlas is in need of updating, it is recommended for schools needing a map collection for partially-sighted students.

Hammond Comparative World Atlas. New Rev. ed. Maplewood, N.J.: Hammond Inc., 1973. 48p. $1.28 paper.

This valuable and inexpensive atlas consists of a series of comparative maps for each continent. Shown for each are political and physical features, vegetation, population, temperature and rainfall. World distribution and resource maps show such information as major religions of the world, languages of the world, accessibility, agricultural regions of the world, climates of the world, natural vegetation of the world, etc. A special section, called "Landtypes of the World," incorporates a paragraph and a color photograph to describe each of the twelve landtypes. On the inside of the front and back covers is an "Index of the World" listing major cities and physical features. A gazetteer-index of the world alphabetically gives the grand divisions, countries, states, colonial possessions, and so forth, noting for each the area in square miles, the population, the capital or chief town, the index reference, and the plate number. Packed full of important material, this atlas will be helpful for both upper elementary and junior high school students.

Hammond International World Atlas. Maplewood, N.J.: Hammond Inc., 1973. 192p. $6.95.

Designed primarily for foreign use, this atlas has both advantages and disadvantages for student use. Containing the same maps as pages one to 192 of the Ambassador and Medallion atlases, the International World Atlas presents each continent or country as a complete unit on consecutive pages, making it more self-contained for reluctant users. Special maps showing transportation, population, vegetation, temperature, and rainfall appear for each continent. For each country there is a political map plus a classified index of its administrative divisions, cities and towns, and physical features. The major disadvantage of this work is the lack of any combined index of the world as in the larger atlases; instead there are only the regional indexes and the gazetteer-index. This particular atlas contains a mere five pages of maps on the United States, rendering it unsuitable as an all-purpose atlas. However, for students needing only maps of foreign countries, it is fine, for most atlases contain a preponderance of United States maps. This work is recommended for upper elementary and junior high school libraries if they need an atlas with intended limitations.

HISTORICAL ATLASES

World History Atlases

Muir's Historical Atlas; Ancient, Medieval, and Modern. 10th ed. Ed. by R. F. Treharne and Harold Fullard. New York: Barnes & Noble, 1964. 166p. $8.50.

Actually two volumes in one, Muir's Historical Atlas contains Muir's Atlas of Ancient and Classical History and Muir's Historical Atlas--Medieval and Modern. The map section for the first part is preceded by an introduction giving a narrative description of each plate and the history involved. In the second part the narrative descriptions are replaced by an alphabetically arranged classified list of maps and subjects. Each of the atlases contains its own index. This atlas will serve junior high students who have need for historical maps.

Rand McNally Atlas of World History. R. R. Palmer, ed. Chicago: Rand McNally, 1970, c1965. 216p. $8.95.

The Rand McNally Atlas of World History, prepared by authorities in the field of history, traces world history through maps from ancient times to the end of World War II. Arranged chronologically, a brief text aids in covering the political, economic, social, military, and religious aspects of history. Given more detailed treatment are the histories of Europe and the United States. A comprehensive index and a short bibliography are also included.

McEvedy, Colin and Sarah McEvedy. The Atlas of World History: The Classical World. New York: Macmillan, 1973. 64p. $7.95.

Incorporating more than 50 historical maps and many illustrations, this atlas describes the destruction of the Alexandrian Empire and traces history through the development and downfall of the Roman Empire in the West and the Chinese Han dynasty in the East. In general it spans the years from 300 B.C. to A.D. 400. Readable and attractive, it should appeal to junior high students.

Shepherd, William Robert. Shepherd's Historical Atlas. 9th rev. ed. New York: Harper & Row, 1973 (c1964). 341p. $15.00.

A long established historical atlas, Shepherd's Historical

Atlases 75

Atlas is one of the best general ones and is currently in its ninth revised edition. It covers the period of history from 2000 B.C. to the present. Concise and convenient, it shows developments of commerce, war campaigns, and treaty adjustments. An extensive index of 115 pages provides location dates.

Hammond Atlas of World History. Maplewood, N.J.: Hammond Inc., 1972. 48p. $2.50, $1.28 paper.

The Hammond Atlas of World History is a collection of attractive colored maps covering history from 3000 B.C. to the Cold War. The subtitle reads, "A collection of maps illustrating geographically the most significant periods and events in the development of Western Civilization." An index identifies the plate number and specific location. The book is also published under the title Hammond's Historical Atlas.

American History Atlases

Adams, James Truslow, ed. Atlas of American History. New York: Scribner, 1943. 360p. $20.00.

Chronologically arranged, the Atlas of American History is a collection of 147 black and white historical maps and is designed as a companion to the Dictionary of American History, and the Dictionary of American Biography. It is arranged chronologically from the discovery of America to 1912. Edited by 64 historians, it contains clearly drawn maps which are easy to use and authoritative. Its index numbers 10,000 entries.

The American Heritage Pictorial Atlas of United States History. New York: American Heritage, 1966. 424p. $16.50.

An excellent collection of maps, the American Heritage Pictorial Atlas of United States History covers from prehistory to the present time. Divided into nine chronologically arranged chapters, it includes the following divisions: Prehistoric North America, Discoveries and Possessors, Struggle for the Continent, Revolution and a New Nation, The National Era, The Nation Divided, Expansion and Immigration, A World Power, and The World--Divided Yet United. Special portfolios of pictorial maps and prints are entitled Battles of the Revolution, City Views, Battles of the Civil War, and National parks of the U.S. The text which accompanies the maps is interestingly written and readable. The exhaustive index fills over fifty pages.

Hammond Atlas of United States History. Maplewood, N.J.: Hammond Inc., 1973. 64p. $2.50, $1.60 paper.

In the Hammond Atlas of United States History, political, physical, and special purpose maps trace the story of America from its discovery to the present time. The special maps show such diverse information as growth of industry and cities, foreign trade, sources of immigration, conservation of natural resources, presidential electoral vote by states and parties, and many others. A detailed table of contents lists the maps in chronological order. An index lists important places, areas, events, and geographical features appearing on the maps. The book is also published as Hammond's United States History Atlas.

History Atlas of America. Maplewood, N.J.: Hammond Inc., 1969. 32p. $.80 paper.

This very simple historical atlas is designed for use in elementary schools and is coordinated with the Hammond American History transparencies. Chronologically arranged, the 24 maps trace American history from the voyages of discovery to post-World War II. The maps are basic political maps using bold colors and few words in large type print. The gazetteer of states precedes the maps and the index follows them. Small and inexpensive, this book should definitely be valuable for neophytes needing a historical atlas.

BIOGRAPHICAL REFERENCE BOOKS

Biographical reference books often form one of the most frequently used sections of the reference collection. Whatever subject is being studied, important names come to the fore. Using biographical indexes, many persons can be located in biography collections or in periodicals. For the researcher seeking persons omitted from these sources or brief identification of individuals, a biographical dictionary may provide the answer.

To determine the usefulness of biographical indexes, one should examine not only the index but also the library collection. Only if the library owns or will acquire a large portion of the books and/or periodicals analyzed in the index will the index serve any real purpose for the students.

In evaluating biographical dictionaries, one should examine the books in the light of specific criteria. In addition to the general questions asked while evaluating reference books, the following should be considered. Is the biographical dictionary prepared under the auspices of a significant organization? What are the sources of data and how complete is it? Is it universal or national in scope, or possibly limited to a particular subject? Is it selective or comprehensive? Is it current or retrospective, and in either case what period of time is covered? On what basis are the biographees selected? Are the entries descriptive or critical? Does the style take the form of narration, outline, or tabulation? How current and accurate is the information? Is the arrangement alphabetical, regional, chronological, or classified? How extensive is the index? Are bibliographies included?

Although children must to a great extent utilize adult biographical reference tools, most of the ones included in this chapter are simple to use and can be mastered by upper elementary school students. They are arranged under the following subheadings: biographical indexes, general biographical dictionaries, American biographical dictionaries, British biographical dictionaries, biographical dictionaries of authors and illustrators, biographical dictionaries of political figures, biographical dictionaries of scientists, and biographical dictionaries of composers and musicians. Some titles containing biographical information are listed in chapters treating a specific subject; e.g., Who's Who in the Middle Ages appears in the history section and Who's Who in Jewish History is listed in the chapter dealing with ethnic groups in America.

BIOGRAPHICAL INDEXES

<u>Biography Index: A Cumulative Index to Biographical Material in Books and Magazines, 1946--   . New York: Wilson, 1947-   </u>. Quarterly (August issue is bound annual cumulation); three-year cumulations. $25.00/year; $50.00 each three-year cumulation.

A standard Wilson index, <u>Biography Index</u> is a guide to biographical information appearing in about 1,900 periodicals, current books of individual and collective biography in English, obituaries (including those of national interest published in the <u>New York Times</u>), and incidental biographical material in otherwise nonbiographical books. It is arranged by name in the main alphabet and has an index of professions and occupations. Works of collective biography are marked by a star and juvenile books by a pyramid. A checklist of composite books analyzed is included. This tool should be considered for junior high libraries owning enough of the books and periodicals to justify the price of the index.

Silverman, Judith. <u>An Index to Young Readers' Collective Biographies; Elementary and Junior High School Level</u>. 2nd ed. New York: Bowker, 1975. 322p. $14.95.

A much needed tool, this book indexes approximately 5,833 people representing the contents of 720 collective biographies. The first section lists people alphabetically, giving dates of birth and death, nationality, field or activity for which they are best known, and the collective biographies which contain information about them. Part II consists of an alphabetical list of fields of activity and national groupings. This section also gives names, dates, and books containing biographical material. In the back of the book are two valuable sections entitled "Index to Subject Headings" and "Indexed Books by Title." All school libraries will benefit from this book.

Stanius, Ellen J. <u>Index to Short Biographies; for Elementary and Junior High Grades</u>. Metuchen, N.J.: Scarecrow Press, 1971. 348p. $7.50.

Arranged alphabetically by surnames, this index has gleaned the biographical information included in more than 450 books. Entries include the person's name with a short identifying description, then the author's last name, short title of the book, and the pages in the book. A "Title List" gives the author, title, place, publisher, date, and grade designation for each of the books indexed. Although this index is similar to Silverman's <u>An Index to Young Reader's Collective Biographies</u>, there is enough significant difference in content to justify purchasing both titles. Both will make easier the tasks of elementary and junior high school librarians.

Ireland, Norma Olin. <u>Index to Women of the World, from Ancient to Modern Times: Biographies and Portraits</u>. Westwood, Mass.: Faxon, 1970. 573p. $16.00.

Biographical Reference Books

About 13,000 women are indexed in this valuable source. Their biographies and in some cases portraits appeared in 945 collective biographies; Current Biography, 1940-68; New Yorker's Profiles, 1925-68; Time's cover stories, 1924-68; and Bulletin of Bibliography's special features on librarians and authors. Books indexed include all levels from juvenile to adult. For each entry the index gives dates, nationality, and vocation, thus identifying the subject as well as providing sources of additional information about her. School libraries will find this tool useful in tracking down much requested material on women.

Nicholsen, Margaret E. People in Books; a Selective Guide to Biographical Literature Arranged by Vocations and Other Fields of Reader Interest. New York: Wilson, 1969. 498p. $12.00.

Alphabetically arranged by vocation or activity, People in Books indexes biographies for children, young adults, and adults. In addition to the main text, the book features a country-century appendix which indexes first by country and then by century the persons appearing in the main section. A second appendix lists autobiographies, letters, and personal accounts. An index and a directory of publishers round out this unique and useful tool. It will serve well in both elementary and in junior high school libraries.

Ireland, Norma Olin. Index to Scientists of the World from Ancient to Modern Times: Biographies and Portraits. Boston, Mass.: Faxon, 1962. 662p. $13.00.

More than 7,475 scientists whose biographies appeared in 338 collections have been indexed in this alphabetical volume. Covering all areas of science except social science, the book lists each scientist with his dates and some identification followed by the sources of information. Many juvenile titles are among those indexed and they are indicated with asterisks.

GENERAL BIOGRAPHICAL DICTIONARIES

Current Biography Yearbook. Charles Moritz, ed. New York: Wilson, 1940- . $10.00 each.

Issued monthly in periodical format, Current Biography consists of three- to four-column biographical sketches and photographs of persons who appear in the news. A list of additional references is included for each entry. The year's monthly issues are bound in a cumulated volume which includes about 300 to 350 biographies. Names are arranged in one alphabet with cross references. Each yearbook contains indexes by names and by professions, a necrology, and a cumulated index to all previous volumes. The bound volumes provide source material on contemporary persons who may not be included in other biographical dictionaries.

Who Did That? Gerald Howat, gen. ed. New York: Crown, 1974. 383p. $12.95.

The subtitle of this biographical dictionary reads: "the lives and achievements of the 5000 men and women--leaders of nations, saints and sinners, artists and scientists--who shaped our world." Comprehensive in scope, it covers all time periods and all countries. Included are such diverse persons as Cyrus of fifth century Persia and Mohammed Ali, contemporary boxer. Entries are short, giving full name, dates, and a brief biographical sketch. About 450 illustrations, including 150 in color, appear in this book. It will be useful for upper elementary and junior high school students.

Webster's Biographical Dictionary; A Dictionary of Noteworthy Persons with Pronunciation and Concise Biographies. Rev. ed. Springfield, Mass.: Merriam, 1972. 1697p. $12.95.

Alphabetically arranged, Webster's Biographical Dictionary identifies over 40,000 persons from all periods of time and all countries with emphasis on British and American subjects. Length of entries, which includes pronunciation, varies from a few lines to a full page. Concise and clearly written, the sketches are unsigned but considered trustworthy and adequate. Liberal cross references aid the user in locating information. Also included are tables of popes, American government officials, and rulers of various countries.

Chambers's Biographical Dictionary. Rev. ed. J. O. Thorne, ed. New York: St. Martin's, 1968. 1432p. $22.50.

This British publication lists over 15,000 short biographies of famous persons living in all periods of time and from all different countries. A brief supplement, including such names as Spiro Agnew and Dr. Benjamin Spock, precedes the main body of text. Alphabetically arranged, the dictionary lists the main entry in bold type and gives the pronunciation, dates, and a biographical sketch. The subject index further aids in locating material.

Who's Who in the World. Chicago: Marquis, 1970- . Biennial. $44.95.

The second edition of Who's Who in the World (1973-74) attempts to present a balanced picture of prominent world figures. To be included in the work an individual must be of world-wide reference value because of (1) a position of responsibility held, or (2) level of achievement. Entries include name, profession, personal data, education, positions held, written works, memberships, and home address. Although the type used is small, it is clear and is printed on good paper. The book should be considered for junior high school libraries.

Biographical Reference Books 81

Who Was When? A Dictionary of Contemporaries. 2nd ed. By Miriam A. Deford. New York: Wilson, 1950. unp. $8.00.

Arranged in tabular form under such subject headings as Literature, Painting and Sculpture, Government and Law, Science and Medicine, Travel and Exploration, Who Was When shows the contemporaries of famous people from 500 B.C. to the date of publication. It indicates, for example, that William Shakespeare was born the same year in which Michelangelo died, or that Woodrow Wilson and Joseph Conrad died in the same year. A unique source that points out horizontal history at a glance, the book includes an alphabetical index to assist users in locating information.

The McGraw-Hill Encyclopedia of World Biography. New York: McGraw-Hill, 1973. 12 vols. $250.00.

Attractive, easy to use, and recent, this multi-volume set lists 880 contributors. Alphabetically arranged, it contains biographies of 5,000 distinguished women and men of all times, all countries, and all vocations. Entries are especially interesting and well written. Two of its strong features are the inclusion of 5,500 illustrations and the bibliographies which follow each essay. Volume 12 of the set is a 100,000-entry index which lists persons, places, battles, institutions, books, paintings, ideas, philosophies, styles, and movements. Since there is no comparable biographical source, school librarians should examine this set and seriously consider for purchase this extensive reference tool.

AMERICAN BIOGRAPHICAL DICTIONARIES

Dictionary of American Biography. Prepared under the auspices of the American Council of Learned Societies. Ed. by Allen Johnson and Dumas Malone. New York: Scribner, 1927-1974. 10 vols plus 4 supplements. $336.00.

For the more affluent library with demanding junior high school students, the Dictionary of American Biography might well be considered for purchase. Traditionally authoritative, it contains 14,870 signed articles describing persons from all walks of life who lived in America's past. The entries range from 500 to 10,000 words according to the importance of the subject; articles about some very prominent persons have as many as 16,500 words. The first ten volumes are arranged alphabetically and have a subject index. The supplements contain biographies of persons who have died since the publication of the original set.

Concise Dictionary of American Biography. Joseph G. E. Hopkins, ed. New York: Scribner, 1964. 1273p. $25.00.

An abridgment of the comprehensive Dictionary of American Biography, the concise edition summarizes into brief notations all of the 14,870 biographies in the original set. Length of entries varies from a few lines to several pages. This handy volume includes only Americans who died before 1940. Because of its broad scope and brevity, it is useful for quick identification. For a small library that cannot afford the original, the abridgment will provide needed information.

Encyclopedia of American Biography. John A. Garraty, ed. New York: Harper, 1974. 1241p. $22.50.

More than a thousand notable Americans from the time of Columbus to the present are included in this alphabetical encyclopedia. A very usable tool, it divides each entry into two sections. The first part consists of a chronology of facts pertaining to the person's life. The second part is a subjective interpretation of the total career of the subject. The combined sections provide an interesting collection of information which will be useful to students of all ages.

Who's Who in America: with World Notables; A Biographical Dictionary of Notable Living Men and Women. Chicago: Marquis, 1899- . $69.50.

Primarily made up of Americans, Who's Who in America also includes persons from other countries who are associated with American interests. Approximately three per 10,000 Americans are selected on the basis of the best known men and women. Information covers pertinent facts about the person's life, his writings, and his present address. Revised and reissued biennially, the 1972-1973 edition, Volume 37, has been expanded to list 80,000 names, 15,000 of them for the first time.

Who Was Who in America. Chicago: Marquis, 1943-1973. 6 vols. $195.30 set. Vols. 1-5, $34.50 each. Vol. 6, $44.50.

A collection of sketches having appeared in Who's Who in America, Who Was Who In America represents important persons who are deceased. Volumes have been published covering the periods 1897-1942, 1943-1950, 1951-1960, 1961-1968, and 1969-1973. Who Was Who In America: Historical Volume, 1607-1896 includes people famous in the early development of the country.

BRITISH BIOGRAPHICAL DICTIONARIES

The Concise Dictionary of National Biography. London: Oxford University Press, 1971. 2 vols. plus supplement.

While most junior high schools would have little need for the definitive Dictionary of National Biography, most should consider owning the concise edition which is a summary of the parent set. Alphabetically arranged, it lists signed articles on deceased noteworthy persons who lived in the British Isles and the colonies. Part I covers from the beginnings to 1900; Part II covers 1901-1950;

Biographical Reference Books 83

and the supplement covers 1951-1960. Progressively, the three volumes become easier to read, easier to use, and contain longer articles. The supplement features a cumulative index.

Who's Who, An Annual Biographical Dictionary. New York: St. Martin's, 1849- . 1974-75. $52.50.

A handbook of prominent, living persons, Who's Who principally lists British but also includes noteworthy names of other countries. Concise, accurate, up-to-date entries provide full name, degrees, titles, occupation, birth date, parentage, marriage, children, education, offices, publications, recreations, addresses, and clubs. A large amount of information is contained in this volume.

Who Was Who, A Companion to Who's Who. New York: St. Martin's, 1935- . $52.50.

For the most part the contents of Who Was Who are reprints of sketches which had appeared in Who's Who. Death dates have been added. The first volume covers 1897 through 1915 ($17.00), the second 1916 through 1928 ($17.00), the third 1929 through 1940 ($17.00), the fourth 1941 through 1950 ($16.00), the fifth 1951 through 1960 ($17.00), and the sixth 1961 through 1970 ($17.00).

AUTHORS AND ILLUSTRATORS

Commire, Anne. Something about the Author; Facts and Pictures about Contemporary Authors and Illustrators of Books for Young People. Detroit: Gale Research, 1971- . 7 vols. $18.00 per vol.

One of the most appealing reference books for young people, Something about the Author not only provides valuable information on contemporary authors of children's books but is also intriguing to browse through. Packed with illustrations, it contains portraits of authors and numerous illustrations from their works. Arrangement is alphabetical giving with the main entry the author's name and dates plus pseudonyms, if any. Format of entries is data style: Personal (birth place, date, family, education, etc.), Career; Writings; Work in Progress; and Sidelights. Most entries are quite long and contain the types of information of interest to children. In general, usefulness and attractiveness have joined in this set in a happy combination, making it a necessary purchase for school libraries. Forthcoming volumes will indeed be watched for.

Ward, Martha E. and Dorothy A. Marquardt. Authors of Books for Young People. 2nd ed. Metuchen, N.J.: Scarecrow Press, 1971. 579p. $15.00.

An alphabetical dictionary, this helpful book contains 2,161 biographies plus cross-reference for all pseudonyms. Entries are very brief, giving only the barest sketch of the author's life and naming some of the more important writings. Included are both old stand-by authors and contemporary; in fact, many of the contemporary ones have not yet been listed in another source.

Kunitz, Stanley J. and Howard Haycraft. The Junior Book of Authors. 2nd rev. ed. New York: Wilson, 1951. 309p. $8.00.

Over 280 authors and illustrators of children's books are listed alphabetically in this essential dictionary. Rather long, interesting life stories with photographs and the biographee's works make up each entry. It is first purchase for elementary and junior high school libraries.

Fuller, Muriel, ed. More Junior Authors. New York: Wilson, 1963. 235p. $8.00.

A supplement to Junior Book of Authors, More Junior Authors includes autobiographical material on 268 authors and illustrators of children's and young adult books. Those covered in More Junior Authors have been writing within the past thirty years. Similar in format to the first volume, it comprises information which often cannot be located elsewhere. It is a must for school libraries.

DeMontreville, Doris and Donna Hill, eds. Third Book of Junior Authors. New York: Wilson, 1972. 320p. $10.50.

The latest addition to the familiar Junior Authors series, the Third Book of Junior Authors alphabetically lists 255 biographical and autobiographical sketches of authors and illustrators. As in the previous volumes, entries are informally written and depict the authors first of all as people. This standard title should be in both elementary and junior high school collections.

Hopkins, Lee Bennett. Books Are By People; Interviews with 104 Authors and Illustrators of Books for Young Children. New York: Citation, 1969. 349p. $6.95. $4.50 paper.
Hopkins, Lee Bennett. More Books By More People; Interviews with 65 Authors of Books for Children. New York: Citation Press, 1974. 432p. $8.95. $4.95 paper.

These companion volumes attempt, as their titles indicate, to show that authors are people doing interesting things as they live their lives. The first book lists, alphabetically, rather long entries for 104 authors and illustrators; the second includes 65 biographies. Many current names are included such as Betsy Byars, William Armstrong, Isaac Bashevis Singer, Symeon Shimin, Arnold Lobel, Blair Lent and Brinton Turkle.

Biographical Reference Books

Hoffman, Miriam and Eva Samuels. Authors and Illustrators of Children's Books; Writings on Their Lives and Works. New York: Bowker, 1972. 471p. $13.95.

A collection of reprints of articles about 50 authors and author-illustrators from Ardizonne to Yates, this book was designed to aid children's literature classes but could also be useful to good students who are younger. Following each reprinted article is a page of editors' notes which update the biographical data as well as writings and awards.

Ward, Martha E. and Dorothy A. Marquardt. Illustrators of Books for Young People. 2nd ed. Metuchen, N.J.: Scarecrow Press, 1975. 229p. $9.00.

Similar to the writers' Authors of Books for Young People, this title provides short biographical sketches for 750 illustrators of books for children. Preference for inclusion is given to contemporary illustrators about whose lives little is available. A list of Caldecott Medal winners and a title index are also included.

Magill, Frank N., ed. Cyclopedia of World Authors. New York: Harper, 1958. 1198p. $12.95.

Cyclopedia of World Authors is a collection of critical biographical sketches of 753 authors whose works are included in Masterpieces of World Literature in Digest Form. Entries, which range from Hans Christian Andersen to Dante, E. E. Cummings to Shakespeare, and Cotton Mather to Karl Marx, present a detailed picture of the author's life, a critical discussion of his works, a list of his principal works, and bibliographical references. A cross reference index aids in location of names and pseudonyms.

Kunitz, Stanley J. and Howard Haycraft. Twentieth Century Authors; A Biographical Dictionary of Modern Literature. New York: Wilson, 1942. 1577p. $22.00.

Based on two out-of-print titles, Living Authors and Authors of Today and Yesterday, this reference book attempts to provide biographical data on world writers of this century whose works are familiar to readers of English. The rather long sketches are often accompanied by photographs.

Kunitz, Stanley J. and Vineta Colby. Twentieth Century Authors: First Supplement; A Biographical Dictionary of Modern Literature. New York: Wilson, 1955. 1123p. $18.00.

The First Supplement, consisting of about 2,550 names, updates the information and bibliographies in the original work. It also contains some 700 new entries of which 670 include photographs. Most of the authors listed have come into prominence since 1942.

Kunitz, Stanley J. and Howard Haycraft. American Authors, 1600-1900: A Biographical Dictionary of American Literature. New York: Wilson, 1938. 846p. $12.00.

About 1,300 authors of both major and minor significance are incorporated in this biographical dictionary. American writers from the Jamestown settlement to the end of the nineteenth century are included. The relatively long entries, many with photographs, are readable and informative.

Kunitz, Stanley J. and Howard Haycraft. British Authors Before 1800; A Biographical Dictionary. New York: Wilson, 1952. 584p. $10.00.

Concise and factual, British Authors Before 1800 combines pertinent biographical and critical information for the literary persons of Britain before the nineteenth century.

Kunitz, Stanley J. and Howard Haycraft. British Authors of the Nineteenth Century. New York: Wilson, 1936. 677p. $12.00.

Major and minor nineteenth century British writers appear alphabetically in this reference book. Featuring brief, readable biographical entries, it was prepared with the student of English literature in mind.

Kunitz, Stanley J. and Vineta Colby. European Authors, 1000-1900; A Biographical Dictionary of European Literature. New York: Wilson, 1967. 1016p. $24.00.

This most recent volume edited by Kunitz covers continental European authors born after the year 1000 and dead before 1925. 967 biographies, of which 309 are accompanied by photographs, represent thirty-one different literatures. Writers included range from mystics to troubadors. The importance of the biographee is usually indicated by the proportionate length of the entry. Bibliographies follow each sketch.

Kinsman, Clare D. and Mary Ann Tennenhouse, eds. Contemporary Authors; A Bio-bibliographical Guide to Current Authors and Their Works. Detroit: Gale Research, 1962-   . Vols. 1-32 (1962-1972). Semiannual volume 1972 to date. Available in 4-vol. units at $25.00 per unit; annual subscription $25.00.

More than 28,000 of today's active writers (excluding scientific, medical, and technical authors) are included in this biobibliographic tool. Many of these are difficult to find elsewhere, as 75% are not in major biographical reference works. Information for the set was obtained from questionnaires and personal correspondence with the biographee. Alphabetically arranged, the entries contain brief biographical data, work in progress, and sidelights of

Biographical Reference Books   87

special interest. The annual indexes are cumulated from volume 1 to the present and appear in the latest bound 4-volume unit. Before purchasing, junior high school librarians should assess carefully the needs of their students. If there is considerable demand for biographical information on contemporary writers, then the expense of this set is justified. Otherwise, the cost may be greater than the service it affords to youngsters.

POLITICAL FIGURES

Who's Who in American Politics. New York: Bowker, 1967- . $40.00.

Edited by Paul A. Theis and Edmund L. Henshaw, Jr., this biennial Who's Who gives comprehensive coverage of contemporary politicians living in the United States. In alphabetical format it includes for each entry data, such as, birthplace and date, party affiliation, present political position, education, memberships, military service, religion, and books and articles published. Information is gathered primarily by direct questionnaire.

Coy, Harold. Presidents. Rev. ed. (A First Book). New York: Watts, 1973. 66p. $3.95.

Providing information on the office of the Presidency as well as information on the Presidents, this first book includes such topics as: Why we have a President; Who can be President; What does the job pay? The President's Cabinet; etc. The bulk of the text, however is devoted to one- or two-page biographies of each President, with a photograph and pertinent information at the beginning of each entry. On the whole much less sophisticated than Cooke, Atlas of the Presidents, the book is good for younger students but will not insult poor-reading junior high people.

Cooke, Donald E. Atlas of the Presidents. Maplewood, N.J.: Hammond, 1967. 93p. $4.50.

A slim but important reference book for young students, Atlas of the Presidents is arranged chronologically and features two pages per entry. For each President the entry includes a color photograph, illustrations, a map and a concise, to-the-point biographical sketch. An alphabetical index aids in locating material. Appended to the text is the Constitution of the United States of America (Articles Pertaining to the Office of the President).

Kane, Joseph Nathan. Facts about the Presidents; A Compilation of Biographical and Historical Data. 3rd ed. New York: Wilson, 1974. 416p. $15.00.

This dictionary is divided into two sections. The first contains a chapter for each President from Washington through Nixon. In statistical form, it concisely presents the family histories, elections, congressional sessions, vice-presidents and cabinets, and highlights in their lives. The second section is a tabulation of comparative data concerning the Presidents. The extensive information included and the index make this a valuable tool. The third edition incorporates two new sections: an alphabetical list of Presidential and Vice-Presidential candidates and a chronological list of the State of the Union messages.

Feerick, John D. and Emalie P. Feerick. The Vice-Presidents of the United States. Rev. ed. (A First Book). New York: Franklin Watts, 1973. 91p. $3.95.

This treatise is on the oft-forgotten man in American politics, the Vice-President of the United States. Arranged chronologically, the book features two-page biographies and photographs of each Vice-President. Information includes pertinent data and also interesting anecdotes. The introduction describes the office of the Vice-President, the duties of the Vice-President, the compensation he receives, etc. An index aids in locating the valuable information contained in this volume. Although it is more difficult than Coy's Presidents, it will still be useful to elementary and junior high school youngsters.

Merlick, Arden Davis. Wives of the Presidents. Ed. by Ernest Dupuy. Maplewood, N.J.: Hammond, 1972. 93p. $4.39.

A chronologically arranged sourcebook listing the wives of United States Presidents from Martha Washington to Patricia Nixon, this title contains entries varying in length from one to five pages depending upon the prominence of the First Lady in question. An interesting chart, "Comparative Data on Wives of the Presidents," depicts each First Lady by name, birth place, birth date, marriage date, death date, age, sons, and daughters. An index and a short bibliography are included.

SCIENTISTS

American Men and Women of Science: Social and Behavioral Sciences--12th Edition. Ed. by the Jaques Cattell Press. New York: Bowker, 1973. 2 vols. $42.50 per vol.

More than 34,000 biographies of active United States and Canadian scientists representing the fields of psychology, political sciences, sociology, economics, anthropology, geography, and statistics are included in this directory. Alphabetically arranged, the books, which are sponsored by the Social Science Research Council, list a distinguished advisory committee.

American Men and Women of Science: Physical and Biological Sciences-12th Edition. Edited by the Jaques Cattell Press. 12th ed. New York: Bowker, 1971-74. 6 vols. $37.50 per vol.

Biographical Reference Books

Brief sketches of nearly 138,500 persons in the fields of agriculture, astronomy, biochemistry, botany, chemistry, engineering, genetics, geology, medicine, nucleonics, physics, and zoology appear in this alphabetical directory. Included are contemporary United States and Canadian scientists with a necrology list appended.

Asimov, Isaac. Asimov's Biographical Encyclopedia of Science and Technology. New rev. ed. Garden City, N.Y.: Doubleday, 1972. 805p. $12.95.

Asimov has subtitled this book: "The living stories of more than 1,000 great scientists from the Age of Greece to the Space Age chronologically arranged." For each entry, the name in bold type is followed by the pronunciation and a nationality-profession note (e.g., Egyptian scholar, American astronomer), and dates. Each entry is consecutively numbered; items in the index refer to the entry number rather than the page number.

McGraw-Hill Modern Men of Science: Leading Contemporary Scientists. 2 vols. New York: McGraw-Hill, 1966-   . $22.50 per vol.

Designed as a supplement to the McGraw-Hill Encyclopedia of Science and Technology, which contains no biographies, Modern Men of Science is alphabetically arranged and has an analytical and classified index. Volume I, published in 1966, and Volume II, published in 1968, together contain 846 entries of international scope but stressing scientists of the United States and Great Britain. Most entries are autobiographical and tell how the subject solved the problems of his research and how he assessed the results.

COMPOSERS AND MUSICIANS

Ewen, David, ed. Great Composers 1300-1900; A Biographical and Critical Guide. New York: Wilson, 1966. 429p. $12.00.

Nearly 200 composers are included in this biographical dictionary. Entries, varying in length from one to several pages, are arranged alphabetically and contain complete and detailed biographical, historical, and critical information plus listings of principal works and bibliographies. About 150 of the sketches are accompanied by portraits. Appended are "Chronological Listing of Composers" and "Composers Grouped by Nationality."

Ewen, David, ed. Composers Since 1900; A Biographical and Critical Guide. New York: Wilson, 1969. 639p. $17.00.

A dictionary replacing Composers of Today, American Composers Today, and European Composers Today, this source lists 70 North and South Americans, 147 Europeans, and 3 Australians. Each entry consists of biographical information, critical evaluations of music; and a list of major works arranged by type of composition. Most have portraits; pronunciation of names is at the bottom of the page. Two appendixes include: Major Schools of Composers and Specific Techniques, Idioms, and Styles; and A Select Bibliography.

Ewen, David, ed. <u>Popular American Composers; from Revolutionary Times to the Present.</u> New York: Wilson, 1962. 217p. $8.00.

Ewen, David, ed. <u>Popular American Composers; from Revolutionary Times to the Present, First Supplement.</u> New York: Wilson, 1972. 121p. $6.00.

America's foremost popular composers are listed in this alphabetical dictionary. In the parent volume are 130 biographies, approximately one third of them of living persons. The supplement updates some biographies included in the first volume and adds 31 new composers who have achieved prominence since 1962. Portraits are provided for most entries.

<u>Baker's Biographical Dictionary of Musicians.</u> Completely rev. by Nicolas Slonimsky. 5th ed. New York: G. Schirmer, 1958. 1855, 262p. $35.00 with 1971 supplement. $7.50 separate supplement.

Universal in scope and including both living and deceased musicians, Baker's 5th edition contains concise biographies filled with factual data. In this edition special attention has been given to stars of popular modern music ranging from the Beatles to folk singers.

FOREIGN LANGUAGE DICTIONARIES

In most schools today foreign languages form an integral part of the curriculum, often as early as kindergarten. Wherever a foreign language is taught, it is essential that a variety of dictionaries representing the language be available for reference. Reasonably, these materials would serve to enhance and stimulate the neophytes in their first encounters with a language other than their own. Equally important on the reference shelf are dictionaries of languages NOT studied in the school. Foreign words found in fiction, in geography classes, or in magazines will send a curious youngster to find out their meanings.

Particular attention should be given to maintaining adequate dictionaries in the mother tongue of students not speaking English. For example, Mi Primer Diccionario is a good choice for young Spanish-speaking children. Bilingual dictionaries should be available, however, when the student is learning English as a second language.

With increased emphasis being placed on teaching languages at the elementary level, good juvenile dictionaries are being published. For the most part, however, the gap between picture dictionaries and adult bilingual dictionaries remains unspanned.

The books included in this chapter are arranged by level of difficulty, simplest first, under each of the alphabetically arranged languages.

FRENCH

Geisel, T. S. and P. D. Eastman. Cat in the Hat Beginner Book Dictionary in French. New York: Random, 1964. 133p. $4.95.

Adapted into elementary French by Odette Filloux of the Department of Linguistics, University of California at San Diego, this picture dictionary is based on the original Cat in the Hat Beginner Book Dictionary. Featuring cheerful cartoon drawings in full color, it is arranged alphabetically by the English words with illustrative sentences in French for each entry. More than 1,000 French words are introduced.

Fonteneau, Marthe and Helene Poirie. Mon Larousse en Images.
   Paris: Librairie Larousse, 1956. 97p. $3.95.

   A picture dictionary with a color illustration for each entry,
this book defines about 2,000 words. It is written entirely in
French and would be usable only by a student who was fluent enough
in the language to think in it. It provides illustrative sentences for
each entry and conjugations for verbs.

Fonteneau, Marthe and S. Theureau. Mon Premier Larousse en
   Couleurs. Paris: Larousse, 1953. Dist.: New York:
   World. 171p. $11.50.

   Nearly 4,000 words are defined in this French dictionary.
Pictures and words are effectively used to aid the student in understanding meanings. This dictionary is not bilingual but is written
entirely in French with no English equivalents. Designed for children aged 5 to 8, it includes conjugations of verbs, and sentences
for definitions and plurals.

Fonteneau, Marthe, Claude Gauvin, and Margaret Melrose. Larousse Illustrated French-English/English-French Dictionary
   for Young Readers. New York: Larousse, 1969. Dist.:
   New York: World. 60, 60, viiip. $7.95.

   Intended for students in their first and second years of a
foreign language, this bilingual dictionary is divided into two complete dictionaries, the first in French giving English equivalents
and the second in English listing corresponding French words.
About 1,700 entries appear in each part. Each entry contains the
entry word in bold type, the pronunciation according to the International Phonetic Alphabet, the translated word in the other language,
and one or more sentences illustrating the definition. An eight-page appendix shows abbreviations, sounds in both French and English, French verbs, English contractions, and indexes for vocabulary tables.

Pillet, Roger, ed. Mon Premier Dictionnaire. New York: World,
   1963. 457p. $5.95.

   Mon Premier Dictionnaire uses sentences, quotations, and
pictures to define 2,400 words selected from both the speaking and
reading vocabularies of American children. The colorful illustrations entice browsing in this book. It is based on The Rainbow
Dictionary by Wright.

Cassell's New French Dictionary (French-English, English-French).
   Completely rev. by Denis Girard. New York: Funk &
   Wagnalls, 1967. 762, 655p. 2 vols. in 1. $8.95.

   In this bilingual dictionary are 40,000 entries in the French-English section and 35,000 in the English-French part. In addition
to the usual vocabulary, the dictionary includes hundreds of recent

Foreign Language Dictionaries 93

scientific, economic, political and cultural words and phrases plus many new colloquialisms. Its value for American students is increased because it also covers French-Canadian terms. It contains a key to pronunciation, tables of irregular and defective verbs, weights and measures, and abbreviations.

Larousse Modern French-English, English-French Dictionary. Marguerite-Marie Dubois, ed. New York: Tudor, 1965. 2 vols. in 1. $9.95. $.75 paper. Washington Square Press.

Containing dictionaries of both French-English and English-French, the Larousse is comprehensive and clearly arranged. It distinguishes between American and British usage, shows correct usage, and lists synonyms. It includes a section called "Essentials of French Grammar," a table of French sounds, and French currency, weights and measures.

Levieux, Michel and Eleanor Levieux. Cassell's Beyond the Dictionary in French. New York: Funk & Wagnalls, 1967. 156p. $2.95.

This inexpensive little book attempts to show many words and phrases frequently used in everyday speech in order to assist the student to express himself freely in the language of the native Frenchman. Besides the main body of the text, the book contains a number of special vocabulary lists such as banking, telling time, numbers, housing, the post office, telephone, cars, etc. An English-French cross reference index completes the work.

GERMAN

Cassell's New German Dictionary: German-English, English-German. Completely rev. and re-edited by Harold T. Betteridge. Based on the eds. by Karl Breul. New York: Funk & Wagnalls, 1971. 2 vols. in 1. 632p. $8.95.

Emphasizing modern German, this bilingual dictionary covers terms that have become accepted in contemporary literary, practical, and colloquial German. It includes words in science, politics, technology, etc. This edition is set in clear Roman type rather than in Gothic, making its use easier for American students. In addition to the two dictionaries, the book contains sections entitled Advice to the User, Abbreviations, Key to Pronunciation, Index of German Names, Chemical Elements, German Irregular Verbs, German Weights and Measures, Index of English Names, and English Strong and Anomalous Verbs.

ITALIAN

Joslin, Sesyle. Spaghetti for Breakfast: Spaghetti per Prima Colazione, and Other Useful Phrases in Italian and English for

Young Ladies and Gentlemen Going Abroad or Staying at Home. New York: Harcourt, 1965. unp. $2.95.

Illustrated with charming pen-and-ink drawings, this little word book contains a number of pertinent phrases in both Italian and English with pronunciation given for the Italian. Typical phrases include "A ticket to Rome, please," "Is this seat taken?" "Good night, miss," and "Do you speak English?" While this book is not a reference book per se, it will be useful for learning basic Italian sentences.

Cassell's Italian Dictionary: Italian-English, English-Italian. Comp. Piero Ribora. New York: Funk & Wagnalls, 1967. 1096p. $8.95.

This dictionary is new and up-to-date in that it contains colloquialisms and words brought into use by World War II, by recent political and social developments, and by industrial and technological growth. Although geared to the modern, it does include obsolete words used by classic Italian writers. It has special sections featuring the Italian alphabet and an outline of Italian verbs.

LATIN

Cassell's New Latin Dictionary: Latin-English, English-Latin. D. P. Simpson, ed. A completely new revision. New York: Funk & Wagnalls, 1960. 883p. $8.95.

The author of this bilingual dictionary has attempted to combine the "fashions of the present day" with the classical Latin. He has used modern English idioms and Latin spelling and has incorporated new material from various sources. At the same time he has followed the traditional principle that "classical" Latin be of prime concern. The book begins with a section called "Advice to the User," and contains a list of Latin authors, a list of abbreviations, and the Roman calendar.

RUSSIAN

Parker, Fan. The Russian Alphabet Book. New York: Coward-McCann, 1966. 40p. $3.39.

Unlimited possibilities present themselves in this unique book which shows the complete Russian alphabet. Each letter is given in both capital and lower case with pronunciation. The entirety of Russia is shown on a double-page map which cites many cities, regions, mountains, seas, rivers, and plains. Each letter is given the name of a geographical locale along with the proper pronunciation, the location in Russia, a description of its people, and its relationship to the country's economy. Obviously, this book would introduce children to the Russian language but would also be invaluable in many other areas of the curriculum.

Foreign Language Dictionaries 95

Dictionary of Spoken Russian; Russian-English, English-Russian.
New York: Dover, 1958. 573p. $4.50 paper.

Following the premise that the basic unit of communication is the phrase or sentence, this dictionary indexes these fundamentals of language activity by word entries. Each entry has illustrative sentences in both English and Russian for each meaning of the word. While most of the illustrative sentences are on a standard colloquial level, some are slang and some are formal, literary usage. In addition to the 400 English entries and the 7,700 Russian entries, the book contains the following appendixes: Gazetteer; Weights and Measures; Money; Territorial and Administrative Structure of the U.S.S.R.; Glossary of Special Soviet Terms; Names of the Days and Months; National Holidays; Russian Foods; Military Ranks and Grades; Abbreviations; Important Signs; Given Names; and Numerals. This edition is an unabridged republication of the War Department Technical Manual TM 30-944, Dictionary of Spoken Russian.

SPANISH

Geisel, T. S. and Philip D. Eastman. The Cat in the Hat Beginner Book Dictionary in Spanish. New York: Random, 1966. 133p. $4.95.

Robert R. Nardelli adapted into Spanish the original Beginner Book Dictionary by T. S. Geisel. A basic vocabulary of more than 100 Spanish words is defined in Spanish with cartoon-type illustrations by P. D. Eastman. Designed for beginners learning Spanish, the book is bright, colorful, and attractive. A guide to Spanish pronunciation appears at the back of the book.

Aquino-Bermudex, Frederico and others. Mi Diccionario Illustrado. Ed. Bilingue. My Pictionary by Marion Monroe and others. Bilingual ed. New York: Lothrop, 1972. 96p. $4.59.

Following the same format as My Pictionary, Mi Diccionario Illustrado classifies words by subjects. Each Spanish word is followed by the English word in parentheses. Variations of Spanish used by Spanish speaking children in America are given. Both Spanish and English language indexes are included.

Daroqui, Julia. Mi Primer Diccionario. Buenos Aires: Editorial Sigmar, 1953. 59p. $2.95.

A picture dictionary written entirely in Spanish with no English translation, Mi Primer Diccionario contains about 500 entries. Each entry word appears in large, bold print and is illustrated by a color picture and a sentence. It is simple to use and contains only a minimum of text.

Fonteneau, M. and S. Theureau. Mi Primer Larousse en Colores. Paris: Editorial Larousse, 1958. 189p. $3.95.

Translated and adapted from the French version by Elena Urquiljo and Maria Lucia Curora, Mi Primer Larousse en Colores lists 4,000 words. All entries are defined in one or more illustrative sentences, and many have a color picture. Verb conjugations are given when appropriate. A single language dictionary, this one contains no translations into English.

Cassell's Spanish Dictionary: Spanish-English, English-Spanish. Edited by Edgar Allison Peers and others. New York: Funk & Wagnalls, 1966. 1477p. $8.95.

Up-to-date and broad in scope, Cassell's Spanish Dictionary includes modern Spanish and literary Spanish, and Latin American Spanish. Somewhat longer than the English section, the Spanish section shows the part of speech and the field to which the word belongs. It has the following appendixes: conjugation of Spanish verbs, irregular English verbs, common Spanish abbreviations, common English abbreviations, English geographical names, and weights and measures.

Cuyas, Arturo. Appleton's New Cuyas English-Spanish, Spanish-English Dictionary. Rev. and enl. by Lewis E. Brett (Part I) and Helen S. Eaton (Part II). 5th ed. rev. New York: Appleton-Century-Crofts, 1972. 2 vols. in 1. 698, 589p. $7.95.

This bilingual dictionary gives equivalents of more than 130,000 principal and subsidiary terms. It includes irregular verb forms, idioms and technical usages, and appendixes of proper names, abbreviations, pronunciation guide, verb tables, monetary units, tables of weights and measures, thermometer, geographical names and colloquial pet names. The clear print and good paper make this dictionary attractive.

Gerrand, A. Bryson. Cassell's Beyond the Dictionary in Spanish; A Handbook of Everyday Usage. 2nd ed., rev. and enl. New York: Funk & Wagnalls, 1972. 226p. $5.95.

A handbook for assisting the student of Spanish to speak the language as natives do, this dictionary covers Spanish as spoken in the Americas as well as in Spain. In the main text entry words are discussed in one to several paragraphs. Included are groups of appendixes and special vocabularies covering such topics as cars, courtesy, food, household words, telephones, etc. The final section consists of an English-Spanish cross-reference index.

ENGLISH AND LANGUAGE ARTS

The English and language arts segments of the school curriculum include a wide span of vital subjects. The entire spectrum of communications is included, ranging from grammar mechanics to dramatic interpretations.

Beginning with the preschool years, children are introduced to stories and poetry. Gradually, as the students grow older, they emerge into junior high school demanding more mature literary fare, in many cases serious adult works. Commensurately, libraries must provide literature reference materials, whether it be deAngeli's Book of Nursery and Mother Goose Rhymes for the primary library or Thrall and Hibbard's Handbook to Literature for junior high collections.

This chapter discusses a broad range of reference books. The first section, "General Works," includes titles covering a variety of literary genres and is arranged alphabetically since most are of a similar level of difficulty. The remaining sections include drama, fiction, folklore and mythology, poetry, quotations, spelling and grammar, and word books. In each of these alphabetical topics, titles are arranged by level of difficulty with simplest materials listed first. Thus, in the "Word Books" section, In Other Words will precede Webster's New World Thesaurus. An attempt has been made, based upon available and appropriate materials, to incorporate reference works suitable for primary children as well as for ninth graders. Although there is still a need for language arts reference books for elementary school children, a number of good titles have been published recently. Until all of the gaps are filled, however, youngsters must continue to rely upon adult resources to meet some of their reference needs.

GENERAL WORKS

Barnhart, Clarence L., ed. New Century Handbook of English Literature. Rev. ed. New York: Appleton, 1956. 1167p. $15.75.

More than 14,000 articles on British authors, literary works, ficticious characters, and allusions are arranged alphabetically in this handbook. Based in part upon the New Century Cyclopedia of Names, it identifies entries without offering judgments. Since entries are concise and generally only one paragraph long, the book lends itself to checking facts quickly, and will be useful for junior high students.

Benet, William Rose. The Reader's Encyclopedia. 2nd ed. New York: Crowell, 1965. 1118p. $10.00.

Broad in scope, The Reader's Encyclopedia explains briefly allusions from art, music, history, and geography in addition to all facets of literature. It contains mostly adult material but does include such entries as "Alice in Wonderland," "Arthur of Britain," "Hans Christian Andersen," and "Felix Salten." Illustrations are old posters, programs, caricatures, and drawings of literary objects. This is a good adult title for children to begin on.

Brewer's Dictionary of Phrase and Fable. Centenary ed. Rev. by Ivor H. Evans. New York: Harper, 1970. 1175p. $10.00.

This handbook contains a massive collection of 20,000 terms, phrases, names of persons and ficticious characters found in world literature, figures from mythologies, slang, superstitions, and etymological information. The latest edition is much larger, listing new material, primarily recent and current phrases. Consistently consulted, this work can provide untold assistance in answering reference questions.

Cassell's Encyclopaedia of World Literature. New York: Funk and Wagnalls, 1954. 2 vols. $25.00.

Edited by S. H. Steinberg, this handbook in dictionary form covers all periods of time and both western and Oriental literature. It contains signed entries on various literary topics such as movements, style, and genre; on individual authors; on anonymous works, and on the literatures of the world. Parts II and III consist of biographies of individual authors, each giving a sketch of a person's life, a list of the author's publications, and suggested secondary works. This title is particularly useful because of the breadth of its scope.

Eagle, Dorothy, ed. Concise Oxford Companion to English Literature. 2nd ed. New York: Oxford University Press, 1970. 628p. $8.00.

Based on the standard title, the Oxford Companion to English Literature by Sir Paul Harvey, the concise edition contains entries on English authors and their works, mythological and historical subjects related to English literature, literary terms and topics, and references to characters in books and plays. The short articles identify subjects quickly and easily and are usually a

English and Language Arts

paragraph in length. Beowulf, David Copperfield, and Frankenstein are samples of the items included which are of particular interest to junior high youngsters.

Feder, Lillian. Crowell's Handbook of Classical Literature. New York: Crowell, 1964. 448p. $7.95.

This Crowell handbook deals solely with Greek and Roman literature. It lists terms, persons, gods, places, and historical background; analyzes famous books and plays, and contains extensive cross-references. Its dictionary arrangement facilitates ease of use.

Freeman, William. Dictionary of Fictional Characters. Rev. ed. New York: The Writer, 1974. 579p. $8.95.

In a clear readable format, this dictionary lists and identifies nearly 20,000 characters appearing in some 2,000 literary works. The works of some 500 authors spanning six centuries have been analyzed.

Hammond, N. G. L. and H. H. Scullard, eds. Oxford Classical Dictionary. 2nd ed. New York: Oxford University Press, 1970. 1176p. $35.00.

As alphabetically arranged dictionary, this work is filled with short signed articles on biography, literature, mythology, philosophy, religions, science, geography, etc., of Greece and Rome. It also contains longer survey articles showing the evolution of classical literature. Bibliographies of outstanding works on each subject are appended to most articles.

Hart, James D. Oxford Companion to American Literature. 4th ed. New York: Oxford University Press, 1965. 991p. $15.00.

Arranged for providing ready reference, this alphabetical handbook includes articles on American authors; summaries of more than one thousand important novels, stories, poems, plays, and essays; definitions; information on literary prizes and awards, and so forth. Information included is basically factual rather than critical and should be usable by most junior high students.

Harvey, Sir Paul. The Oxford Companion to Classical Literature. New York: Oxford University Press, 1966 (c. 1937) 468p. $5.75.

This Oxford Companion brings together principal authors and their chief works in tracing the evolution of classical literature. In a simple alphabetical arrangement, it depicts historical, political, social, and religious background as well as defining many terms. Plates, maps, and charts illustrate the book.

Herzberg, Max J. Reader's Encyclopedia of American Literature.
    New York: Crowell, 1962. 1280p. $15.00.

    Covering American and Canadian writing and writers from colonial times to 1962, this comprehensive one-volume reference book covers all aspects of literature. Articles include information on authors, novels, plays, poems, stories, literary groups, newspapers and places and terms associated with literature.

The Lincoln Library of Language Arts. 2nd ed. Columbus, Ohio:
    Frontier Press, 1972. 2 vols. $49.95.

    Based on the general reference work Lincoln Library of Essential Information, this set is limited to the language arts and is intended for home and student use. Arranged in three sections, the work includes the English Language, Literature, and Biography. The first section covers usage, grammar, spelling, writing, speaking. Its entries are concise and easy to understand. The literature section includes subdivisions for the literatures of many nations from English to Czech. The entire second volume is devoted to biographical sketches, incorporating 3,600 entries for such diverse persons as Leonardo da Vinci, Virgil, Wernher von Braun, and Davy Crockett. The master index is printed in both volumes to facilitate ease of use. The bibliographies, test questions, and the varieties of dictionaries will make this a useful work for junior high students.

Magill, Frank N. Cyclopedia of Literary Characters. New York:
    Harper, 1964. 1280p. $11.95.

    More than 1,300 novels, dramas, and epics are arranged alphabetically by title in this work. Each entry gives the author, time of action, first presented or published, and description of principal characters. More than 16,000 world literature characters are identified in the text. Completing the book are the author index and the alphabetical character index.

Seymour-Smith, Martin. Funk and Wagnalls Guide to Modern World
    Literature. New York: Funk and Wagnalls, 1973. 1206p.
    $13.95.

    A criticism of modern literature, the author has arranged this work alphabetically by country and chronologically within each country. This arrangement deceptively simplifies this rather scholarly volume. Individual authors must be located through the lengthy index; each receives the barest biographical sketch with primary emphasis on a critical evaluation of his writings. This reference book is not for every junior high school library; for those having a need for sophisticated material, however, it should definitely be considered.

Shaw, Harry. Dictionary of Literary Terms. New York: Mc-
    Graw-Hill, 1972. 402p. $12.50.

English and Language Arts 101

More than 2,000 literary terms, references, and allusions are listed in the alphabetical sequence of this book. Broad in scope, it covers books, magazines, newspapers, films, plays, television programs, and speeches. Its clear inviting format will encourage youngsters who may be frightened off by tiny print and crowded pages.

Shipley, Joseph. A Dictionary of World Literary Terms; Forms, Technique, Criticism. Completely rev. and enl. ed. Boston: The Writer, 1970. 466p. $12.95.

This alphabetically arranged work was first published in 1943 by Philosophical Library with the title, Dictionary of World Literature. In the first of three parts, the dictionary contains entries covering topics such as definitions, genres, techniques, terms, and forms and types. Part II consists of critical surveys of criticism of the various literatures, e.g., American, English, Greek, Medieval, Russian. Included in Part III are bibliographies for the literatures of 25 different countries.

Thrall, William Flint and Addison Hibbard. A Handbook to Literature. 3rd ed. Ed. by C. Hugh Holman. New York: Odyssey Press, 1972. 646p. $6.00. $3.50 paper.

Arranged alphabetically, this handbook includes relatively brief explanations of the words and phrases peculiar to literary study. While many of the entries are too difficult for children, the book does define such terms as "title," "slang," "simile," "short story," "Dark Ages," "comedy," etc. The Thrall and Hibbard Handbook should definitely be available to junior high students, especially ninth-graders.

DRAMA

Kreider, Barbara. Index to Children's Plays in Collections. Metuchen, N.J.: Scarecrow Press, 1972. 138p. $5.00.

A much-needed source of information, this book indexes over 500 children's one-act plays and skits which were published in the United States between 1965 and 1969. Twenty-five collections were indexed according to 340 subjects. Each play is indexed by author, title, and subject, with the author being the main entry. Also included is a cast analysis, a directory of publishers, a bibliography of collections indexed, and professional aids used in choosing plays.

The Chicorel Theater Index to Children's Plays in Periodicals, Anthologies, Discs, and Tapes. Marietta Chicorel, ed. New York: Chicorel Library Publishing Corp., 1974. 490p. $49.50. (Chicorel Index Series, vol. 9)

Over 5,000 plays for young people from kindergarten through high school are indexed in this volume. The 15,000 entries are arranged in one alphabet. Additional information includes the play title list, author list, list of anthologies and collections, list of periodicals indexed, and directory of publishers. A subject list is, unfortunately, not included. While teachers, librarians, and drama coaches will find this computer-produced index helpful, its high cost will force librarians to examine their needs carefully before purchasing it.

Play Index, 1949-52; An Index to 2616 Plays in 1138 vols. Comp. by Dorothy Herbert West and Dorothy Margaret Peake. New York: Wilson, 1953. 239p. $8.00.
Play Index, 1953-60; An Index to 4592 Plays in 1735 vols. Ed. by Estelle A. Fidell and D. M. Peake. New York: Wilson, 1963. 404p. $11.00.
Play Index, 1961-1967. Ed. by Estelle A. Fidell. New York: Wilson, 1968. 464p. $16.00.
Play Index, 1968-1972; An Index to 3848 Plays. Ed. by Estelle A. Fidell. New York: Wilson, 1973. 403p. $20.00.

This useful tool indexes plays for both children and adults, including, according to the preface, "plays in collections and single plays, one-act plays and full-length plays, radio plays and those written for television, trade editions of Broadway plays and paperbound plays for amateur production." Part I contains author, title and subject entries arranged alphabetically; Part II lists the collections of plays indexed; Part III is cast analysis; and Part IV is the directory of publishers.

Salem, James M. Drury's Guide to Best Plays. 2nd ed. Metuchen, N.J.: Scarecrow Press, 1969. 512p. $15.00.

This helpful list, first published in 1953, indexes plays most frequently performed by school and amateur theater groups. More than 1,500 plays are arranged by the author with entries giving bibliographic data, a synopsis, number of acts, number of men and women characters, holder of the play, and the royalty fee. Appended indexes include the cast index; index of selected subjects; plays requiring no scenery; award winning plays; most popular plays for amateur groups; plays recommended for "All Groups"; popular plays for high school productions, 1967-68; frequently produced plays (high school theater); addresses of play publishers represented; abbreviations used for citing collections; index of co-authors, original authors, and adaptors; and index of titles. Drury's Guide to Best Plays will be most valuable to any junior high school having an active drama department.

Connor, John M. and Billie M. Connor. Ottemiller's Index to Plays in Collections: An Author and Title Index to Plays Appearing in Collections Between 1900 and Mid-1970. 5th ed. Rev. & enl. Metuchen, N.J.: Scarecrow Press, 1971. 452p. $11.00.

Ottemiller's Index to Plays in Collections was first published

English and Language Arts 103

in 1953 and has been revised to include 8,912 copies of 3,049 different plays by 1,644 different authors in 1,947 collections. The fifth edition adds plays published from 1963 through mid-1970. For junior high schools incorporating plays into the curriculum, this index will greatly simplify locating copies of specific titles.

Gassner, John and Edward Quinn, ed. Reader's Encyclopedia of World Drama. New York: Crowell, 1969. 1030p. $15.00.

Covering drama for five centuries from its ritual origins to the present, this book has fairly long, readable entries emphasizing plays, their authors, and their historical background. Basically, the entries include national drama, playwrights, plays, and genres. The book features many photographs and illustrations.

Hartnoll, Phyllis, ed. Oxford Companion to the Theatre. 3rd ed. London: Oxford University Press, 1967. 1088p. $17.50.

An alphabetical dictionary that is international in scope, the Oxford Companion to the Theatre emphasizes the non-literary aspects of the theater such as the actors, the playhouse, and popular works and writers. It does not cover television and motion pictures and includes very little of opera and ballet. It contains a bibliography of more than 1,000 books on the theater and related subjects.

McGraw-Hill Encyclopedia of World Drama, An International Reference Work in Four Volumes. New York: McGraw-Hill, 1972. 4 vols. $119.50.

This easy to use, four-volume set features an excellent format: heavy paper, large clear type, and many photographs including shots from productions. The text itself consists of mostly biographical entries with abbreviated nonbiographical entries for dramatic terms, theater movement and styles, and anonymous plays. For all major dramatists the entries include a complete biography, a critical section on his work, a group of selected synopses, a play list, and two bibliographical sections, one listing editions and the other critical material. In volume 4 is the index of play titles which includes every title listed in the set. This comprehensive work is a fine choice for junior high schools needing extensive information in the field of drama.

FICTION

Subject and Title Index to Short Stories for Children. Chicago: American Library Association, 1955. 333p. $6.50.

Although limited by its 1955 imprint date and therefore not including the many fine recent story collections, this index is still quite valuable to a library containing anthologies of an earlier vintage, particularly some out-of-print ones. Planned to cover material from third grade through junior high school, it is especially useful for identifying short stories on specific subjects and for locating them in specific anthologies. It indexes some 5,000 stories from 372 books and anthologies under more than 2,000 subject headings.

Gillespie, John and Diana Lembo. Introducing Books; A Guide for the Middle Grades. New York: Bowker, 1970. 318p. $10.95.

Arranged by developmental goals of childhood, this book is designed to help teachers and librarians who are giving reading guidance and book talks to children and young people between the ages of 9 and 14 years. Information included for each book discussed is plot analysis, thematic material, book talk material, additional suggestions (other books and media on the theme). Both an author and title index and a subject index appear at the end of the book. Although the book is actually aimed at adults, it can certainly be useful to students by aiding them in selecting reading material as well as analyzing and reviewing it.

Gillespie, John and Diana Lembo. Juniorplots; A Book Talk Manual for Teachers and Librarians. New York: Bowker, 1967. 222p. $9.95.

Similar in goals and arrangement to the authors' Introducing Books, Juniorplots analyzes books, according to the authors, for youngsters 9 to 16. However, a close look at the material included reveals very few titles appealing to either the 9 or the 16 year old, for most seem geared to the middle school level. The choices, however, are good, and can be easily located in either the author-title index or the subject index.

Cook, Dorothy Elizabeth and Isabel S. Monro. Short Story Index: An Index to 60,000 Stories in 4320 Collections. New York: Wilson, 1953. 1553p. $20.00.
Cook, Dorothy E. and Estelle A. Fidell. Short Story Index, Supplement 1950-1954. New York: Wilson, 1956. 394p. $10.00.
Fidell, Estelle A. and Esther V. Flory. Short Story Index, Supplement 1955-1958. New York: Wilson, 1960. 341p. $10.00.
Fidell, Estelle A. Short Story Index; Supplement 1959-1963. New York: H. W. Wilson, 1965. 487p. $13.00.
Fidell, Estelle A. Short Story Index, Supplement 1964-1968. New York: Wilson, 1969. 599p. $16.00.

This series of indexes is an author, title, and subject index to collections of short stories. The main volume indexes some 60,000 stories in 4,320 collections; the 1950-1954 supplement 9,575 stories in 549 collections; the 1955-1958 supplement 6,392 stories in 376 collections; the 1959-1963 supplement 9,068 stories in 582 collections; the 1964-1968 supplement 11,301 stories in 793

FOLKLORE AND MYTHOLOGY

Palmer, Robin. Dragons, Unicorns, and Other Magical Beasts; A Dictionary of Fabulous Creatures with Old Tales and Verses about Them. New York: Walck, 1966. 95p. $5.00.

A slim, well-illustrated volume, this book begins with a dictionary listing 68 alphabetical entries of magical beasts, e.g., Anansi, griffin, etc. For each entry there is an illustration, the geographic locale, and one to several paragraphs describing the beast and its activities. Following the dictionary section are 12 stories and poems featuring these magical creatures.

Palmer, Robin and Pelagie Doane. Fairy Elves: A Dictionary of the Little People with Some Old Tales and Verses about Them. New York: Walck, 1964. 92p. $4.50.

Similar to Palmer, Dragons, Unicorns, and Other Magical Beasts, this dictionary lists over 40 entries alphabetically arranged from Boggart to Witch. For each entry the author gives an illustration, a geographical location, and a description of the fairy in 3 to 15 lines. The remainder of the book consists of 12 stories, folk tales, and poems about fairies of various kinds throughout the world.

Asimov, Isaac. Words from the Myths. New York: Houghton Mifflin, 1961. 225p. $4.50.

Delving into the Greek myths to find the roots of hundreds of words that appear in daily usage, Mr. Asimov has geared his work to upper elementary and junior high students. Not actually a reference book, Words from the Myths certainly can be used as one because of the inclusion of the index of mythological terms and the index of modern words deriving from them.

White, Anne Terry. The Golden Treasury of Myths and Legends. New York: Golden Press, 1959. 164p. $5.95.

To supplement the various ready reference sources for mythology, the reference shelf should contain at least one good collection of myths. While several fine collections are available, this one illustrated by Alice and Martin Provensen is attractive in format, style, and illustrations. Selections come from varied sources, including Greek, German, British, Norse, etc.

Eastman, Mary Huse, comp. Index to Fairy Tales, Myths, and Legends. 2nd ed. rev. and enl. Westwood, Mass.: Faxon, 1926. 610p. $11.00.

Eastman, Mary Huse, comp. Index to Fairy Tales, Myths, and
  Legends, Supplement. Westwood, Mass.: Faxon, 1937.
  566p. $11.00.
Eastman, Mary Huse, comp. Index to Fairy Tales, Myths and
  Legends, Second Supplement. Westwood, Mass.: Faxon,
  1952. 370p. $11.00.
Ireland, Norma Olin, comp. Index to Fairy Tales, 1949-1972, Including Folklore, Legends and Myths in Collections. Westwood, Mass.: Faxon, 1973. 741p. $18.00.

An invaluable reference source for locating specific tales in collections, these indexes together analyze nearly 2,000 volumes. Libraries owning early editions of fairy tale collections will find all four volumes helpful. However, since the first three index only those books published before 1952, libraries should purchase them only if their collections are old enough to merit it. All elementary and junior high school libraries, though, will wish to purchase the most recent index by Ireland. It analyzes over 400 collections published in the twenty-three year span beginning where the 1952 edition left off. Since there has been a recent up-surge in the publishing of juvenile books of folklore of all types, this volume will be extremely useful. Its 3,000 subject headings, interfiled alphabetically with title entries, should make the book even easier to use than its predecessors.

Ziegler, Elsie B. Folklore: An Annotated Bibliography and Index
  to Single Editions. Westwood, Mass.: Faxon, 1973. 203p.
  $12.00.

Another valuable source in locating folklore for story hours, reading units, social studies units, voluntary reading and analysis, the Ziegler index is a guide to folklore in single editions. Part 1 consists of an annotated bibliography arranged alphabetically by title of all the books listed and includes cross-references to variants. Parts 2-6 are respectively a subject index, motif index, country index, type of folklore index, and illustrator index.

Ullom, Judith C. comp. Folklore of the North American Indians;
  An Annotated Bibliography. Washington, D.C.: Library of
  Congress, 1969. 126p. $2.25.

The Children's Book Section of Library of Congress compiled this selective bibliography for the compiler or reteller of these folktales, for the storyteller or librarian serving children, and for the child's own reading. Stories included were chosen on the basis of the following criteria: (1) a statement of sources and faithfulness to them; (2) a true reflection of Indian cosmology, and (3) a written style that retains the spirit and poetry of the Indian's native manner of telling. Entries are arranged by geographic locale and alphabetically by author in each section. In addition to the rather detailed annotations, each entry lists complete bibliographical data.

English and Language Arts 107

Tripp, Edward. Crowell's Handbook of Classical Mythology. New York: Crowell, 1970. 631p. $10.00.

Another comprehensive alphabetical guide to Greek and Roman mythology, the Crowell handbook covers characters, events, places, the constellations named for mythological personages, and brief descriptions of the principal classical works in which the myths are found. It also includes five maps of the classical world, genealogical charts of great royal lines, and a pronouncing index giving both English pronunciations and transliterated Greek spellings of all names of persons and places in entry titles. Easy to use, this book will provide a fine reference source for upper elementary and junior high school students.

Oswalt, Sabine G. Concise Encyclopedia of Greek and Roman Mythology. Chicago: Follett, 1969. 313p. $3.95. $2.95 paper.

Alphabetically arranged, this book includes entries on Greek and Roman mythology ranging in length from a few lines to a page. Many black and white reproductions of paintings, sculpture, ceramics, etc., enhance the text. A rather complicated series of genealogy charts show the descendants of the original gods, Prometheus, Io, Cadmus, and Tantalus. This useful little volume is marred only by its small size, which gives the entire format a cramped appearance. For the money, however, it is still a good buy.

Zimmerman, John E. Dictionary of Classical Mythology. New York: Harper, 1964. 300p. $5.95.

Limited only to Greek and Roman mythology, Zimmerman's dictionary includes nearly 2,100 personal and place names. It gives pronunciation, brief identification, and in some instances, citations to classical sources. As an inexpensive mythological dictionary, this one is well worth the cost.

Evans, Bergen. Dictionary of Mythology; Mainly Classical. Lincoln, Neb.: Centennial, 1970. 292p. $6.95.

Although the title of this alphabetically arranged dictionary claims to be "mainly classical," the book does also cover Norse, Egyptian, and Babylonian mythology as well as the Arthurian legends. Entries, ranging from a few lines to several paragraphs in length, identify gods, people, places, events, and things relating to mythology. It includes a comparative list of most prominent Greek and Roman figures. It also contains a comprehensive index and a bibliography.

Funk and Wagnalls Standard Dictionary of Folklore, Mythology and Legend. New York: Funk and Wagnalls, 1972. 1236p. $17.95.

Edited by Maria Leach and Jerome Fried and written by authorities in the fields of anthropology and folklore, this mammoth work includes definitions of terms, survey articles, brief biographies, accounts of museums, etc. It explains allusions to legendary characters; folk tale heroes; the mythology of the world's gods; the significance of plants, animals, and rocks in folklore; and folk dances and songs. The new edition features a key to the 2,405 countries, regions, culture areas, peoples, tribes, and ethnic groups discussed.

New Larousse Encyclopedia of Mythology. Rev. ed. New York: Putnam, 1969. (c1959) 500p. $17.95.

Translated by Richard Addington and Delano Ames, the New Larousse Encyclopedia of Mythology is elegantly illustrated with photographs of artifacts and works of art. It is a comprehensive survey arranged by countries, such as prehistoric, Egyptian, Assyro-Babylonian, Greek, Roman, Celtic, Teutonic, Persian, Indian, Chinese, Japanese, Slavonic, African, and American. An extensive index of names facilitates easy location of specific information.

POETRY

DeAngeli, Marguerite. Marguerite DeAngeli's Book of Nursery and Mother Goose Rhymes. Garden City, N.Y.: Doubleday, 1954. 192p. $6.95.

This oversized book contains a comprehensive collection of nursery and Mother Goose rhymes. One of the largest collections available, it is filled with lovely black and white and color drawings by the author-illustrator. A rather long index of first lines and familiar titles aids in locating selections within the text. This volume is a must for all primary libraries.

Arbuthnot, May Hill and Shelton L. Root, Jr. Time for Poetry. 3rd ed. Glenview, Ill.: Scott, Foresman, 1968. 277p. $7.95.

Indexed in Index to Poetry for Children and Young People, Time for Poetry is an excellent anthology especially for young children. Although its contents range from Mother Goose to Walt Whitman, its emphasis is on the so-called children's poets, especially contemporary ones, e.g. Rachel Field, Harry Behn, Dorothy Aldis, Ailene Fisher, etc.

Sechrist, Elizabeth Hough. One Thousand Poems for Children. Rev. ed. Philadelphia: Macrae-Smith, 1946. 601p. $8.50.

A comprehensive collection of poetry which includes a wide range of titles from nursery rhymes to William Wordsworth, Alfred Tennyson, and Robert Browning. It is subject arranged with

English and Language Arts

author, title, and first line indexes. It is a good title to complement Arbuthnot's Time for Poetry which contains more poems by the "children's poets" while Sechrist lists more works which were not written for children but have been adopted by them. Both are indexed in Brewtons' Index to Children's Poetry.

Subject Index to Poetry for Children and Young People. Comp. by Violet Sell and others. Chicago: American Library Association, 1957. 582p. $9.00.

Poems in 157 anthologies plus selected works by individual poets are indexed in this reference book. Arranged by subjects, it provides a guide for the location and grade levels for all entries. Useful for the period covered, it needs to be updated either by revision or supplements. Librarians should check their holdings carefully before purchasing this one.

Brewton, John E. and Sara W. Brewton, comps. Index to Children's Poetry. New York: Wilson, 1942. 966p. $16.00.
Brewton, John E. and Sara W. Brewton, comps. Index to Children's Poetry, First Supplement. New York: Wilson, 1954. 405p. $10.00.
Brewton, John E. and Sara W. Brewton, comps. Index to Children's Poetry, Second Supplement. New York: Wilson, 1965. 453p. $12.00.

Index to Children's Poetry and its two supplements provide a key by author, title, subject and first line to poems in collections for children and young people. The main volume indexes 15,000 poems by 2,500 authors found in 130 different poetry collections. The First Supplement indexes 7,000 poems by 1,300 authors appearing in 66 collections published between 1938 and 1951. The Second Supplement indexes 8,000 poems by 1,400 poets in 85 collections published between 1949 and 1963. Approximate grade levels between one and twelve, as well as location, accompanies each entry. This tool is an invaluable reference source.

Brewton, John E., Sarah W. Brewton, and G. Meredith Blackburn, III. Index to Poetry for Children and Young People: 1964-1969. New York: Wilson, 1972. 574p. $20.00.

This reference book, an extension to the three previous Brewton indexes, bears the subtitle: A Title, Subject, Author, and First Line Index to Poetry in Collections. It analyzes 11,000 poems by about 2,000 authors representing 117 collections. More than 2,000 subjects are used. This volume because of its timeliness will probably be used frequently.

Granger's Index to Poetry. 6th ed. Completely rev. and enl. indexing anthologies published through Dec. 31, 1970. Ed. by William James Smith. New York: Columbia University Press, 1973. 2223p. $80.00.

First published in 1904 with the title Index to Poetry and Recitations, Granger's, in its sixth edition, indexes poetry anthologies under nearly 5,000 subject entries. Prose selections are omitted entirely. It includes a combined title and first line index and author index. The sixth edition indexes 114 new works and deletes out of print titles listed in the fifth edition and the 1967 supplement.

Deutsch, Babette. Poetry Handbook; A Dictionary of Terms. 4th ed. New York: Funk and Wagnalls, 1974. 203p. $5.95.

A useful dictionary for junior high students, the Poetry Handbook consists of entries describing types and forms of poetry and poetic imagery. Most entries include quotations to illustrate the term defined.

QUOTATIONS

Cohen, John Michael and Mark J. Cohen. The Golden Book of Quotations; from the Penguin Dictionary of Quotations. Adapted by Ann Reit. New York: Golden, 1964. 176p. $3.99.

Based on the Penguin Dictionary of Quotations, the Golden Book of Quotations is adapted for children by Ann Reit and illustrated in color by James Spanfeller. It contains famous quotations arranged alphabetically by the author and has an index of key words and phrases. The attractive format and appealing selections combine to make this an essential introduction to quotation dictionaries.

Bartlett, John. Familiar Quotations: A Collection of Passages, Phrases and Proverbs Traced to Their Sources in Ancient and Modern Literature. 14th ed. Boston: Little, Brown, 1968. 1750p. $15.00.

Originally published in 1855, the fourteenth edition has been revised, updated, and enlarged to include more than 20,000 quotations and the index is the most thorough in its history. Chronologically arranged by author and indexed by key words, Familiar Quotations is an index for identification of memorable quotations, including such recent writers as J. D. Salinger, John F. Kennedy, and Mao Tse-Tung.

Stevenson, Burton, ed. Home Book of Quotations, Classical and Modern. 10th ed. New York: Dodd, Mead, 1967. 2816p. $35.00.

Arranged alphabetically by subjects, e.g., Home, Wanderlust, Individuality, the Home Book of Quotations includes approximately 73,000 quotations. It contains an index of authors which gives the full name, identifying phrase, dates of birth and death, and references to all quotations cited. In addition, a word index

English and Language Arts   111

lists the quotation by leading words, usually nouns but occasionally verbs and adjectives. The tenth edition was revised by Bruce Bohle who updated it to include such recent persons as Lyndon B. Johnson, John F. Kennedy, and Nikita Khrushchev.

Bohle, Bruce, comp. Home Book of American Quotations. New York: Dodd, Mead, 1967. 512p. $10.00.

Alphabetically arranged by subject with a good index, this volume is patterned on Stevenson's Home Book of Quotations but is unique unto itself. Outstanding for its contemporary quotations, it concentrates on America but includes items of foreign source provided they deal specifically with America. Selections included were written by such authors as Adlai Stevenson, Robert Frost, George Santayana, Abraham Lincoln, Albert Einstein, and Will Rogers.

Oxford Dictionary of Quotations. 2nd ed. New York: Oxford University Press, 1953. 1003p. $14.00.

Entries, totaling over 40,000, are included on the basis of popularity rather than merit. Arranged alphabetically by the authors, and indexed by key words, the Oxford Dictionary of Quotations contains liberal amounts of Doyle, Keats, Kipling, Stevenson, and others who might appeal to children.

SPELLING AND GRAMMAR

Semmelmeyer, Madeline and Donald O. Bolander. Instant English Handbook; An Authoritative Guide and Reference on Grammar, Correct Usage, and Punctuation. Mundelein, Ill.: Career Institute, 1968. 320p. $2.65.

This small volume is part of the Career Institute's Instant Reference Library, which provides practical information in a pocket-sized format. The Instant English Handbook certainly fills a need, being an easy to use guide to grammar and usage. Using simple explanations and many illustrations the text is easy to follow. Arranged from the most simple to the most complex usage, the book features a comprehensive index and a glossary of terms. This small sized, low-priced handbook could be considered also for classroom quantity purchase as well as personal copies for individual students.

Wittels, Harriet and Joan Greisman. The Perfect Speller. New York: Grosset and Dunlap, 1973. 330p. $6.49.

Designed as a reference book specifically for spelling, The Perfect Speller contains about 30,000 entries in a single alphabet. Arranged with three double columns per page, the book lists every entry, both correct and incorrect spellings of words, in the left-hand column. All correct spellings are printed in red and all incorrect ones in black. In the right-hand column adjacent to any incorrect spellings are the correct ones, also printed in red type. The simple, uncluttered text, printed in large readable type, combined with the single purpose of the book make it a valuable and practical tool for students in elementary and junior high schools.

Norback, Peter and Craig Norback. The Misspeller's Dictionary. New York: Quadrangle/The New York Times Book Co., 1974. unp. $6.95.

Over 20,000 words are listed in one alphabet, including both correct and incorrect spellings. If the student looks up a word as it sounds, he will find it. Correct spellings are in black type; incorrect spellings are in red type with the correct spellings in black type in the adjacent right hand column. All homonyms are defined and cross-referenced. This book provides the perfect answer for the poor speller who cannot use a standard dictionary which lists only properly spelled words. An introduction, "Basic Rules of Spelling," precedes the alphabetic master list.

Dougherty, Margaret M. and others. Instant Spelling Dictionary. New 3rd ed. Mundelein, Ill.: Career Institute, 1967. 320p. $2.65.

A pocket-sized volume, the Instant Spelling Dictionary contains 25,000 words which are spelled, divided and accented. In addition, it has the complete rules for spelling, word division, punctuation, capitalization, abbreviating, word compounding, forms of address, and proof-reader's marks. It is a useful tool for individual libraries as well as for school libraries.

Webster's Instant Word Guide. Springfield, Mass.: Merriam, 1972. 369p. $2.95.

More than 35,000 words and 1,500 abbreviations are listed in this small volume. It provides a ready reference tool for word division, spelling, and often-confused words. Following the main word list are sections of proofreaders' symbols, punctuation rules, and tables of weights and measures.

WORD BOOKS

Hanson, Joan. Antonyms; Hot and Cold and Other Words that are Different as Night and Day. Minneapolis: Lerner, 1972. unp. $3.95.
Hanson, Joan. More Antonyms: Wild & Tame & Other Words That Are as Different in Meaning as Work & Play. Minneapolis: Lerner, 1973. unp. $3.95.
Hanson, Joan. Homographs; Bow and Bow and Other Words That Look the Same But Sound as Different as Sow and Sow. Minneapolis: Lerner, 1972. unp. $3.95.
Hanson, Joan. Homographic Homophones: Fly & Fly & Other

English and Language Arts 113

Hanson, Joan. Words That Look & Sound the Same But Are as Different in Meaning as Bat & Bat. Minneapolis: Lerner, 1973. unp. $3.95.

Hanson, Joan. Homonyms; Hair and Hare and Other Words that Sound the Same But Look as Different as Bear and Bare. Minneapolis: Lerner, 1972. unp. $3.95.

Hanson, Joan. More Homonyms: Steak & Stake & Other Words That Sound the Same but Look as Different as Chili & Chilly. Minneapolis: Lerner, 1973. unp. $3.95.

Hanson, Joan. Synonyms: French Fries and Chips and Other Words that Mean the Same Thing But Look and Sound as as Different as Truck and Lorry. Minneapolis: Lerner, 1972. unp. $3.95.

Hanson, Joan. More Synonyms: Shout & Yell & Other Words That Mean the Same Thing But Look as Different as Loud & Noisy. Minneapolis: Lerner, 1973. unp. $3.95.

While none of these small volumes could qualify as a reference book per se, they should be considered for the reference shelf in primary collections. Even though they contain few words, have no location device nor ready reference arrangement, and are unpaged, they do introduce the beginner to the concept of word books and show how such word books can help in developing one's vocabulary.

Greet, W. Cabell, William A. Jenkins, and Andrew Schiller. In Other Words; A Beginning Thesaurus. Glenview, Ill.: Scott, Foresman, 1969. 240p. $5.50.

A thesaurus designed specifically for children in elementary school, In Other Words is a simple-to-use introduction to word books other than dictionaries. Part I, "How to Use This Book," consists of sections about the book itself, about synonyms and antonyms, about entries, about choosing synonyms, and about cross references. Part II, "Synonyms and Antonyms," comprises the main body of text. Arranged alphabetically, 100 entry words are followed by lengthy definitions, many illustrations of use, synonyms with shades of meanings, and antonyms. Part III, "Sets," has a narrative text with pictorial examples of terms; for instance, in the category of "Things" are bunch, clump, cluster, bale, bundle, etc. Numerous cross references throughout the book are clear and easy to follow, e.g., "'Race'--look up 'Run'". This colorfully illustrated thesaurus is an essential addition to elementary school libraries.

Greet, W. Cabell, William A. Jenkins, and Andrew Schiller. Junior Thesaurus; In Other Words II. Glenview, Ill.: Scott, Foresman, 1970. 448p. $5.50.

According to the preface, Junior Thesaurus is a book of words listing over 300 words commonly known and overused and also more than 2,000 very good words. Actually, this volume is a proper sequel to In Other Words and directs the student one step closer to using an adult thesaurus. While the approach is similar to the introductory volume, Junior Thesaurus offers more information in a more sophisticated format. Part I describes what the book is all about and how to use it; Part 2 is the main body including all of the entries; and Part 3 is the index which lists every word used in the text. For each entry, the entry word is in capital letters followed by a paragraph or more explaining the word and using it in a sentence, and sometimes giving the history of the word. Synonyms are in bold type and each is described with shades of meaning explained and many illustrative sentences used. Antonyms are underlined in blue. This reference book is a must for all elementary school libraries and probably should be considered for some junior high school libraries having students not ready for adult thesauri.

Wittels, Harriet and Joan Greisman. The Young People's Thesaurus Dictionary. New York: Grosset and Dunlap, 1971. 319p. $5.95.

Edited by William Morris, Editor-in-chief of the American Heritage Dictionary, this thesaurus can effectively follow in sequence behind In Other Words and Junior Thesaurus, and definitely should receive a place in the reference collections of both upper elementary and junior high school libraries. Its introduction explains how to find the right word. In the section on how to use the book the authors note that entry words are in bold type, that synonyms and antonyms are listed--not definitions; that antonyms are in red; that slang terms are indicated; that other forms of root words are indicated in capital letters. Unlike the other two juvenile thesauri, entries are not long, but comprise succinct brief notes from one to five lines and averaging 14 to 18 entries per page. It contains no cross references for each word has a full entry in its alphabetical location.

Laird, Charlton. Webster's New World Thesaurus. New York: World, 1971. 677p. $4.95.

Listing nearly 30,000 entries, Webster's New World Thesaurus uses as its main entry the most common synonym. It is arranged alphabetically in two columns and unfortunately is printed in small, pale print on very thin paper. Despite these drawbacks, this thesaurus is useful and usable. Its main entry is in bold type and gives a part of speech label, followed by numbered meanings. Synonyms are listed first and then antonyms. Some "see" references aid in locating similar information.

Webster's New Dictionary of Synonyms; A Dictionary of Discriminated Synonyms; With Antonyms and Analogies and Contrasted Words. Springfield, Mass.: Merriam, 1968. 909p. $7.95.

Designed to discriminate carefully the shades of meaning of synonyms, Webster's New Dictionary of Synonyms provides precise definitions and numerous examples taken from both classical and

English and Language Arts   115

contemporary writers from Jonathon Swift to Norman Cousins.
Thorough and extensive, it includes besides the main body, lists of
analogous words, antonyms and contrasted words. The 1968 edition is based on the old Webster's Dictionary of Synonyms, first published in 1942 and revised in 1951.

Funk and Wagnalls Modern Guide to Synonyms and Related Words.
Comp. by S. I. Hayakawa and the Funk and Wagnalls Dictionary Staff. New York: Funk and Wagnalls, 1968. 726p. $8.95.

Compiled by the well-known linguist, S. I. Hayakawa, this up-to-date, well-organized, and legible synonym dictionary was new in 1968. Easy to use with key words in the margin, this dictionary contains over 1,000 essays between one half page and a page in length which define, compare, and contrast 6,000 synonyms and related words. It also lists antonyms, has numerous cross references, and has an alphabetical index. Comprehensive in content including idiomatic and slang terms, it features illustrative sentences and phrases to aid in indicating shades of meaning for each word.

Whitford, Harold Crandall. A Dictionary of American Homophones and Homographs. New York: Teachers College Press, Columbia University, 1966. 83p. $2.75 paper.

Over 2,000 entries make up this unique handbook which is helpful for young people and especially for foreign students learning English. With illustrative examples it lists homophones, words identical in pronunciation but differing in spelling and meaning, and homographs, words spelled alike but differing in meaning and usually in pronunciation.

New Roget's Thesaurus of the English Language in Dictionary Form. Rev. and greatly enl. ed. Norman Lewis, ed. New York: Putnam, 1965. 552p. $3.75.

Although several publishing houses have produced Roget thesauri, Putnam's is a recognized edition. It is based on C. O. Sylvester Mawson's alphabetical arrangement of Roget's famous word classification. Approximately 17,000 entries make up this volume which includes, in addition to the traditional words, modern slang and colloquial uses, and terms from psychology, atomic science, space engineering, and television. The dictionary form facilitates easier use by neophytes, but experienced students should also be introduced to the original Roget classification system.

New American Roget's College Thesaurus in Dictionary Form. Albert H. Morehead, ed. New York: Grosset and Dunlap, 1958. 433p. $3.95.

The New American Roget's College Thesaurus is similar to the Putnam edition by Norman Lewis, but it is based on American rather than British usage. Although it is arranged alphabetically, Roget's original categories appear in the back of the book and are keyed to the main body of text. This edition provides synonyms, antonyms, and words related in some way.

Roget's International Thesaurus: the Complete Book of Synonyms and Antonyms in American and British Usage. 3rd ed. New York: Crowell, 1962. 1258p. $5.95.

Roget, an English physician and scholar, worked for fifty years and first published his thesaurus in 1852. Arranged by classification of ideas, it provides words for meanings as opposed to a general language dictionary which gives definitions to words. The third edition of Roget's International Thesaurus represents a complete revision and has been expanded to 240,000 entries plus 45,000 additional words particularly in the area of science and technology and a glossary of foreign words and phrases. The alphabetical index has been both simplified and enlarged.

Shipley, Joseph T. Dictionary of Word Origins. Paterson, N.J.: Littlefield, Adams, 1970. $2.95 paper.

Dictionary of Word Origins traces the history of American speech and shows fascinating sources for common words in the language. From "A-1" to "zymurge" the book provides interesting browsing material as well as sound facts. It was first published in 1945 by Philosophical Library.

Wood, Clement, ed. The Complete Rhyming Dictionary and Poet's Craft Book. Garden City, N.Y.: Doubleday, 1936. 607p. $5.50.

Divided into two major parts, "The Poet's Craft Book" and "The Dictionary of Rhyming Words," this book has been a long-time standard reference tool. "The Poet's Craft Book" contains chapters discussing poetry and versification, rhythm and meter, rhyme, stanza patterns, and types of poetry. "The Dictionary of Rhyming Words," arranged alphabetically by the position of the accent and by vowel sounds, lists over 66,000 rhyming words, including proper nouns.

Berrey, Lester V. and Melvin Van Den Bark. The American Thesaurus of Slang; A Complete Book of Colloquial Speech. 2nd ed. rev., reset, and enl. New York: Crowell, 1953. 1272p. $19.50.

Arranged by the dominant idea e.g., mankind, shape, geography, conditions etc., this thesaurus contains over 100,000 expressions of general slang such as radio, bowling, occupation, military, etc. It provides long lists of synonyms for each entry. An alphabetical word index facilitates ease of use.

Wentworth, Harold and Stuart Berg Flexner, eds. Dictionary of American Slang; Includes Etymologies and Quotations and Is Cross Referenced. New York: Crowell, 1967. 718p. $7.95.

Although briefer than the American Thesaurus of Slang, the Dictionary of American Slang gives full definitions with illustrative quotations and often the date of first use and citation of the printed sources. Over 1,000 new terms serve to update the 1960 edition. Arrangement is alphabetical.

MUSIC AND ART

The fine arts of music and art are generally an integral part of the curriculum for both elementary and junior high schools. In some cases these areas are taught as separate, unique courses and incorporate appreciation and history as well as the applied aspects of both subjects. In other instances, art and music are approached through the social studies with music and art history taking their appropriate places in the story of man and his achievements. In still other situations music and art are taught as part of a general humanities program, while yet other schools include topics such as opera and folk songs in the language arts classes.

Regardless of how music and art are presented in elementary and junior high schools, the school library should have an adequate selection of reference books available on the subjects. Materials available cover a wide range of sophistication. For example, the picture dictionary, Music Dictionary by Davis and Broido, provides simple definitions in elementary terminology. By way of contrast, Grove's Dictionary of Music and Musicians is a scholarly comprehensive work to be used by serious students of music. Similarly, Famous Paintings by Chase is a basic elementary title for helping children appreciate art, while the McGraw-Hill Encyclopedia of World Art is a definitive work filled with long scholarly essays. Each librarian must determine the demands the school's curriculum will make in the fields of art and music in order to build a reference collection to meet the needs of the students and faculty. The selections included in this chapter are chosen to represent fine materials available on a variety of academic levels.

MUSIC

Buchanan, Fannie R. and Charles L. Luchenbill. How Man Made Music. Rev. ed. Chicago: Follett, 1959. 224p. $4.95.

Standard for elementary school libraries, this interesting history of music traces each segment of music within a separate chapter. Some chapter titles, for example, are: From shouting to song; From hollow stump to drum; From ram's horn to trumpet; From bards to bands; From church to theater; From tribal song to symphony, etc. Each section contains factual information, and most tell a story of how the instrument probably was discovered.

Music and Art   119

Besides a glossary of terms and an index, the book contains a
time line of great composers and charts showing the seating arrangements of a concert band and a symphony orchestra.

Lang, Paul Henry and Otto Bettman. A Pictorial History of Music.
      New York: Norton, 1960. 242p. $15.00.

    Adapted from the author's Music in Western Civilization
(1941), A Pictorial History of Music gives brief but important information on each period and artist. Its outstanding feature is the
lavish illustrative material consisting of mosaics, vase painting,
medieval manuscripts, drawings, and photographs.

Scholes, Percy A. The Oxford Junior Companion to Music. Fairlawn, N. J. : Oxford University Press, 1966. 435p.
      $10.95.

    Written by a distinguished authority, this reference book
consists of brief articles on composers, instruments, musical
terms and expressions, and church music. Although it leans heavily towards British topics, it is a valuable source book for children from 8 to 16 years old. Profusely illustrated, it contains
sections entitled "Some Suggestions on How to Use This Book,"
"Music the Reader May Like to Play," and "Tables of Notation"
as well as a lengthy pronouncing glossary.

The Golden Encyclopedia of Music. By Norman Lloyd. New York:
      Golden Press, 1968. 720p. $14.95.

    Comprehensive in scope, the Golden Encyclopedia of Music
covers almost every aspect of music. The main body of text includes stories of operas, analyses of symphonies, biographies of
composers, and explanations of technical terms. Over 800 illustrations depict people, instruments, stage scenes, and musical passages. Additional materials incorporated are tables of signs and
symbols, glossaries of abbreviations and foreign terms, and an
extensive index.

Davis, Marilyn Kornreich and A. Broido. Music Dictionary.
      Garden City, N. Y. : Doubleday, 1956. 63p. $4.25.

    One of the most elementary of the music reference books,
Music Dictionary is attractive and readable. In picture book format, profusely illustrated with black and white drawings by Winifred
Greene, it features short definitions of musical terms from "A" to
"Zither." Tables of musical signs and musical abbreviations are
also useful.

Watson, Jack M. and Corinne Watson. A Concise Dictionary of
      Music; An Introductory Reference Book. New York: Dodd,
      Mead, 1965. 332p. $6.95. Woodbridge, Conn. : Apollo
      Bks. $2.75 paper.

This music dictionary, considerably more detailed and extensive than Davis' dictionary, defines in simple language many technical musical terms. It also describes various instruments, and includes half-page biographies of composers most likely to be encountered by beginners. Small black and white drawings and musical examples illustrate the book.

Ammer, Christine. Harper's Dictionary of Music. New York: Harper and Row, 1972. 414p. $10.00. $2.95 paper.

This music dictionary, of probable value to junior high school students, emphasizes a historical approach. Its entries include the most commonly used musical terms, music history, biographies and compositions of composers. Nearly 100 pictures and 150 musical terms illustrate the book. Pronunciation is given for names and foreign terms.

Apel, Willi. Harvard Dictionary of Music. 2nd ed. Rev. and enl. Cambridge, Mass.: The Belknap Press of Harvard University Press, 1969. 935p. $20.00.

This authoritative dictionary of music was first published in 1944. Omitting biography which is covered in so many other sources, it includes entries on music history, theory, aesthetics, forms, instruments, notation, and performance. This well-illustrated work contains bibliographies for each article.

Larousse Encyclopedia of Music. Ed. by Geoffrey Hindley. New York: World, 1971. 576p. $19.95.

Illustrated with over 700 pictures, many in color, the Larousse Encyclopedia of Music is based upon a work published in 1965 in France. Divided into six broad categories, the work includes music of the oral traditions, monody and rhythm, age of polyphony, age of harmony, romantics, and music in the modern world. Historically, it traces the development of Western music from the chants of the early Church to the electronic age. This comprehensive work will appeal to upper elementary students for browsing and to junior high students for research.

Grove, Sir George. Dictionary of Music and Musicians. 5th ed. Ed. by Eric Blom. New York: St. Martin's, 1970 (c1954). 9 vols. plus supplement. $69.50 paper.

The fifth edition of this standard encyclopedia of music in English was published in nine volumes in 1954 with a supplement issued in 1961. Comprehensive in scope, it includes entries on music history, theory, terms, instruments, biographies of composers and musicians, songs and operas, and individual composers. Because the use of this scholarly work in junior high schools will probably be limited, librarians should consider adding the paperback edition, which costs about one third as much as the hardcover set. Students would then have access to valuable material at a reasonable expenditure.

Cross, Milton and David Ewen. The Milton Cross New Encyclopedia of the Great Composers and Their Music. Rev. and expanded. Garden City, N.Y.: Doubleday, 1969. 2 vols. 1284p. $14.95.

Alphabetically arranged by composer, The Milton Cross New Encyclopedia of the Great Composers and Their Music provides sketches of 100 composers of both past and present. Each entry includes sections entitled Major Works, His Life, His Music, and Analytical Notes. Both renowned and secondary persons are included. In addition to the main body of text, the work contains the history of music before Bach, the history of music since Bach, basic works for the record library, the anatomy of the symphony orchestra, a dictionary of musical forms, a glossary of musical terms, and a selected bibliography. A lengthy index facilitates easy use of the two-volume set.

Thompson, Oscar. International Cyclopedia of Music and Musicians. 9th ed. Robert Sabin, ed. New York: Dodd, Mead, 1964. $35.00.

In its ninth edition the International Cyclopedia of Music and Musicians remains a useful alphabetical reference tool. Its signed articles cover such topics as public school music, music criticism, Negro music, libraries of music, individual compositions, biographies, folk music, opera and history. American music and musicians receive quite full treatment. Names and titles with pronunciation are given in an appendix.

Bulla, Clyde Robert. Stories of Favorite Operas. New York: Crowell, 1959. 277p. $4.95.
Bulla, Clyde Robert. More Stories of Favorite Operas. New York: Crowell, 1965. 309p. $4.50.

Clearly written in direct, simple language, these attractively illustrated books present the stories of favorite operas. Twenty-three are described in the first volume and 22 in the second. Preceding the scene-by-scene telling of each opera is information concerning the opera's origin and first performance. In the appendix are the cast of characters for each opera and biographical sketches of the composers. The simplicity of style makes these two books readable and enjoyable even for third and fourth graders. Designed specifically for young readers, they are valuable reference sources.

Rosenthal, Harold and John Warrack. Concise Oxford Dictionary of Opera. Fairlawn, N.J.: Oxford University Press, 1964. 446p. $7.20.

The Concise Oxford Dictionary of Opera presents material on operas, composers, librettists, conductors, and singers. Capsule summaries of opera plots, identification of characters in many operas, and biographical sketches make up this valuable work. The list of operas based on the works of literary authors constitutes an important feature.

Ewen, David. The New Encyclopedia of the Opera. New York:
Hill and Wang, 1971. 759p. $15.00.

Alphabetically arranged, this encyclopedia contains more than 5,000 entries covering some aspect of opera. Included are stories of more than 100 operas; characters of operas; biographies (including composers, librettists, singers, conductors, stage directors, impresarios, teachers, critics, and musicologists); history of opera; opera in performance; literary sources; special articles; and terms. Written in popular style, the entries are concise, rarely being a full page.

Kobbe, Gustav. Kobbe's Complete Opera Book. Ed. and rev. by
the Earl of Harewood. New York: Putnam, 1972. 1262p. $12.95.

Arranged by centuries and subdivided into countries with all of the works of each composer grouped together, this book contains the plots of operas with some critical comments and musical notation for leading airs and motives. About 100 photographs show stars in costume and scenes from the operas. Although the arrangement of the book is rather complicated, the index aids in locating material.

Goulden, Shirley. The Royal Book of Ballet. Chicago: Follett, 1962. 74p. $4.95.

This lovely book provides plot summaries for six famous ballets. Included are Swan Lake, Sleeping Beauty, Giselle, the Nutcracker, Petrushka, and Coppelia. Each story is told in detail and is illustrated with lovely color paintings by Maraja. This book will effectively serve students in upper elementary and junior high schools.

Gaden, Francis and Robert Maillard, gen. eds. Selma Jeanne
Cohen, Am. ed. Dictionary of Modern Ballet. New York:
Tudor Publishing Co., 1959. 360p. $7.95.

Alphabetically arranged with rather short entries, this dictionary covers many aspects of ballet. Included are synopses of ballet plots, dance companies, dancers, composers, and artists, such as costume and set designers. Many drawings and photographs, some in color, fill this book.

Wessells, Katharine Tyler. The Golden Song Book. New York:
Golden Press, 1945. 69p. $2.95.

Included in this book are more than 50 songs with words, piano accompaniment, and illustrations which preschool and primary level children like to sing. Besides many Mother Goose rhymes, there are singing games with suggestions for playing them, lullabies, a few religious songs, and miscellaneous titles such as "Jingle Bells," "The Star-Spangled Banner," and "Yankee Doodle." The table of contents doubles as an index, for it is arranged alphabetically by title.

The American Heritage Songbook. New York: American Heritage, 1969. 223p. $7.95.

This valuable collection of songs contains a brief history, the piano accompaniment, the guitar chords, and the words for 120 songs including hymns, sea chanteys, martial airs, ballads, novelty tunes, and love songs. Covering the historical developments of America with sections on early America, the frontier, the Civil War, etc., this book is an essential supplement to the social studies program for upper elementary and junior high schools. It lists a subject index and an index of titles and first lines.

Haywood, Charles. Folk Songs of the World. New York: Day, 1966. 320p. $10.95.

The subtitle of Folk Songs of the World reads as follows: "Gathered from more than one hundred countries, selected and edited, with commentary on their musical cultures and descriptive notes on each song; in the original languages with English translations, and with chord suggestions for instrumental accompaniment." The notes and commentary preceding the songs for each country are so relevant that this book should be used in supplementing the geography curriculum as well as the music one. An index of first lines appears in the back of the book.

Roxon, Lillian. Rock Encyclopedia. New York: Grosset and Dunlap, 1969. 611p. $9.95.

Alphabetically arranged from "acid rock" to "Zombies," this book includes terms, composers, singers, performers, etc. Entries for individuals include one paragraph to three pages of narration plus lists of albums and single records with release dates and song titles. Included are such diverse persons as Chet Atkins, Joan Baez, Mick Jagger, and Janis Joplin. Although this book is much too old to list the current rock personalities, it is valuable for its coverage up to the publication date.

ART

Chase, Alice Elizabeth. Famous Paintings; An Introduction to Art. Rev. ed. New York: Platt and Munk, 1962. 120p. $6.95.

The author of this standard title for elementary schools offers interpretations of famous paintings designed to help children understand and appreciate what the artist is doing. The interesting text is complemented by 184 plates, including 54 in full color. There is also an index of pictures, artists, and owners.

Chase, Alice Elizabeth. Famous Artists of the Past. New York: Platt and Munk, 1964. 120p. $6.99.

Containing somewhat more text than the author's Famous Paintings, this book covers 27 painters and sculptors. Using the same interesting style as in the earlier volume, the author tells the story of the life, ambitions, struggles, and triumphs of each of the artists and relates it to the works and themes. This book, too, has an index to artists, pictures, and owners.

Kainz, Luise C. and Olive L. Riley. Portraits and Personalities; An Introduction to the World's Great Art. New York: Abrams, 1967. 127p. $7.50.

This fine volume discusses specific examples from each of the major historical periods from ancient Egypt, Greece, China, and Byzantium to Picasso and Klee in the modern period. The text is brief and to the point with the illustrations making up its bulk. A list of artists, a glossary, and an index follow.

Janson, H. W. and Dora Jane Janson. The Story of Painting for Young People, from Cave Painting to Modern Times. Textbook ed. New York: Abrams, 1962. 259p. $6.75. $3.95 paper.

Restricted to the history of painting, this attractive volume in a readable style is illustrated with 245 reproductions. Covered in the text are: How painting began; The Middle Ages; Explorers and discoverers; The age of genius; The triumph of light; Toward revolution; The age of machines; and Painting in our times. It is indexed and is designed for elementary and junior high school students.

Janson, H. W., with Samuel Cauman. History of Art for Young People. New York: Abrams, 1971. 412p. $15.00.

Rewritten from Janson's college text, History of Art, this book surveys the history of Western art. Included are how art began, the Middle Ages, the Renaissance, and the modern world. The text is illustrated with 434 reproductions. Additional features include a bibliography, a glossary, with chronological tables of events from B.C. 4000 to 1950 A.D. This art history, written especially for young people, will enhance any school reference shelf.

Kainz, Luise C. and Olive L. Riley. Understanding Art: People, Things, and Ideas. New York: Abrams, 1966. 135p. $7.50.

This unique volume attempts to teach art appreciation to children. Through the history of art ("from ancient Egypt to Chagall and Picasso"), the authors show the ability of an artist to reveal character, to dramatize moods, and also to express his own individuality as he approaches various subjects and ideas. Biographical

Music and Art 125

sketches are given for thirty great painters. A list of artists giving pronunciation, nationality, and dates; a glossary; and an index are included.

Ruskin, Ariane. Pantheon Story of Art for Young People. New York: Pantheon, 1964. 157p. $6.95.

In 157 pages the Pantheon Story of Art provides an introduction to art history. Basically following a chronological arrangement, the book presents art and artists from prehistory to the present. Extremely well illustrated, it contains many fine reproductions in both color and black and white. The usefulness of the book as a reference tool, however, is drastically reduced because it contains no index, nor does it contain a list of artists and illustrations. Despite these unfortunate omissions, the Pantheon Story of Art is a valuable book and merits examination for elementary and junior high libraries.

Craven, Thomas. The Rainbow Book of Art. New York: World, 1956. 256p. $4.95.

Written especially for children, The Rainbow Book of Art covers the history of art from prehistoric times to the present. Illustrated with numerous black and white reproductions and 32 color plates, it is readable and filled with facts. Painting and architecture receive the most attention with whole chapters being devoted to the masters. A rather detailed index locates paintings, artists, and subjects. This source is a valuable addition to elementary and junior high libraries.

Munro, Eleanor C. The Encyclopedia of Art: With a Glossary of Artists and Art Terms. Rev. ed. New York: Western, 1964. 300p. $14.95.

The Encyclopedia of Art, according to its title page, covers painting, sculpture, architecture, and ornament, from prehistoric times to the twentieth century. Arranged by historical periods, the book is beautifully illustrated with over 650 plates, more than 300 of which are in color. Illustrations include reproductions of paintings, sculpture, architecture, frescoes, mosaics, tapestries, and other works of art. A glossary of art terms contains long, full explanations of terms from "abstract art" to "woodcut." The glossary of artists presents brief biographies. Another valuable feature is the three-page chart called "Comparative Chronology of Periods of Art." The book contains an index in a somewhat abbreviated form.

Gardner, Helen. Art Through the Ages. 5th ed. Rev. by Horst dela Croix and Richard G. Tansey. New York: Harcourt, 1970. 801p. $12.95.

A comprehensive survey of world art, Art Through the Ages covers the historical development from prehistoric times to the twentieth century. Each section treats painting, sculpture, architecture, and the various minor arts, and culminates with an information summary and an extensive bibliography. Liberally illustrated in black and white, the book is attractive and readable. A glossary of technical terms and a 50-page pronouncing index further the value of the book. As a general survey of art history, Art Through the Ages represents a worthwhile addition to any reference collection.

The Praeger Picture Encyclopedia of Art: A Comprehensive Survey of Painting, Sculpture, Architecture and Crafts, Their Methods, Styles and Technical Terms, from the Earliest Times to the Present Day. New York: Praeger, 1958. 584p. $13.95.

This one-volume alphabetically arranged work is divided into the following parts: A general introduction; Antiquity; The Middle Ages; The Renaissance, Baroque and Rococo; The 19th and 20th centuries; and art outside of Europe. Each section begins with a survey of the period, the historical background, and a glossary of technical terms, artists and their works, and movements. Extensively indexed, the encyclopedia contains 192 color plates and 416 illustrations in monochrome. This book is particularly good for small school libraries that cannot afford one of the more expensive, comprehensive sets.

The Book of Art: A Pictorial Encyclopedia of Painting, Drawing, and Sculpture. Sir Herbert Read, ed. New York: Grolier, 1965. 10 vols. $150.00.

Less grandiose and less expensive than the Encyclopedia of World Art, The Book of Art claims to "survey the history of art in text and pictures." Arranged with one broad topic per volume, the set includes: vol. 1, Origins of Western Art; vol. 2, Italian Art to 1850; vol. 3, Flemish and Dutch Art; vol. 4, German and Spanish Art to 1900; vol. 5, French Art from 1350-1850; vol. 6, British and North American Art to 1900; vol. 7, Impressionists and the Post-Impressionists; vol. 8, Modern Art; vol. 9, Chinese and Japanese Art; and vol. 10, How to Look at Art. The general index is an accurate location guide for artists, places, styles and groups, but it omits titles of works of art. Nearly 5,000 illustrations appear in the set, and over 850 are in color. This inclusion of over 600 biographies, bibliographies of related material, and a glossary of terms adds to the usefulness of the set. While The Book of Art has limitations, it is one of the more comprehensive works in the field of art for young people. Where it is not feasible to buy the scholarly and costly Encyclopedia of World Art, elementary and junior high libraries should consider The Book of Art, which will provide adequate material for neophytes in this field.

The Britannica Encyclopedia of American Art. Chicago: Encyclopaedia Britannica, 1973. 669p. $29.95.

This alphabetically arranged one-volume encyclopedia covers

Music and Art   127

all areas of American art including painting, sculpture, architecture, prints, photography, folk and decorative arts, and contemporary handicrafts. The signed articles vary in length from a paragraph to several pages. The 1,100 entries and 800 illustrations (350 in full color) provide information on art from early colonial days to the present. The fine text is further amplified by the appendixes: A guide to the entries arranged by broad art terms; A guide to museums and public collections; A glossary; and an extensive bibliography. The attractive format and easy to read style will make this popular with young students. It should be available to supplement American history as well as art programs in both elementary and junior high schools.

New International Illustrated Encyclopedia of Art. New York: Greystone, 1967-1972. 24 vols. $144.00.

Written for the student or layman with no previous knowledge of the subject, the New International Illustrated Encyclopedia of Art, edited by Sir John Rothenstein, provides a good basic survey of the visual arts. Entries cover definitions, techniques, biography, and history, some of the general articles being almost book-length. An 80-page index facilitates easy use of the text. Although the articles are unsigned and there are no bibliographies, this well-illustrated set written in non-technical terms will be a fine purchase for both elementary and junior high schools.

McGraw-Hill Dictionary of Art. Ed. by Bernard S. Myers. New York: McGraw-Hill, 1969. 5 vols. $159.50.

This most complete art dictionary contains 15,000 entries, 1,700,000 words, 2,300 illustrations, and 2,900 double-column pages and was prepared by 125 contributors. Alphabetically arranged, the set includes articles on the art of the Near East, the Far East, and the world's primitive cultures including Africa, Oceania, and the American Indian. Specific entries include biographies, terms, art history, museums, works of art, archaeological sites, etc. Entries range in length from 25 words or less to major articles of 4,000 words. Extensively cross-referenced, the set lists bibliographies wherever they are appropriate and useful. Utilizing an attractive, inviting format and written in a popular readable style, this set should be considered for first purchase for elementary and junior high school reference collections.

Praeger Encyclopedia of Art. New York, Praeger, 1971. 5 vols. $150.00.

Based upon the French encyclopedia Dictionnaire Universel de l'Art et des Artistes, this reference book purports to provide within limits of space a comprehensive and authoritative reference guide for students and general readers. Alphabetically arranged, it contains some 4,000 entries on periods, styles, schools, and movements (including 1,000 survey articles); and 3,000 entries on individual artists. Nearly 5,000 pictures including 1,700 in color illustrate the five volume text. This set should be considered for junior high school libraries where the need exists.

Encyclopedia of World Art. New York: McGraw-Hill, 1959-1968. 15 vols. $597.00. Each vol. $50.00.

The most definitive reference work in the field of art, Encyclopedia of World Art is a mammoth set representing the work of many outstanding authorities. Containing about 1,000 articles, it covers architecture, painting, sculpture, and all other man-made objects entering the realm of aesthetic judgment. Alphabetically arranged by long essays rather than dictionary type entries, it includes an extensive analytical index and useful bibliographies. The outstanding collection of illustrations, both black and white and full color plates, is extremely valuable. Also useful are the 550 biographies of artists. Up to date and scholarly, the Encyclopedia of World Art would make a fine addition to those elementary and junior high libraries that could afford the set.

PHILOSOPHY AND RELIGION

Since it is virtually impossible to study history, art or music appreciation, or literature without encountering philosophy and religion, the school library should maintain a collection of reference books in these areas, even if religion is not taught as a formal course in the curriculum. Reference books on philosophy are few, indeed, and those written for young students are nonexistent. Two scholarly adult works are included in this chapter and can be used by junior high students who are seriously pursuing the subject. Books on religion are considerably more abundant. Those included in this section cover the major religions of the world; The Bible; atlases of Biblical lands; the history of the Biblical period; Bible dictionaries, commentaries, concordances, and quotation books; and biographical dictionaries. Books covering the classical religions are included in the mythology section of the chapter on English and language arts. An adequate collection of materials covering the areas of religion and philosophy will greatly improve the reference service offered by the school library.

PHILOSOPHY

Encyclopedia of Philosophy. Paul Edwards, ed. New York: Macmillan, 1973. 4 vols. $99.50.

This comprehensive set contains nearly 1,500 signed articles written by over 500 scholars. Authoritative and well-edited, it covers the entire field of philosophy from Eastern and Western religions to mathematics and other disciplines which have influenced philosophy. It includes excellent biographies. An exhaustive index of 38,000 entries and annotated bibliographies following articles add to the set's value. A major adult work first published in eight volumes in 1967 and costing $219.50, The Encyclopedia of Philosophy can now be a valuable addition to junior high libraries at a reasonable price.

Runes, Dagobert D., ed. Dictionary of Philosophy. 15th ed., rev. New York: Philosophical Library, 1960. $2.95 paper.

According to the editor's preface, the Dictionary of Philosophy aims "to provide ... clear, concise, and correct definitions and descriptions of the philosophical terms, throughout the range of philosophic thought." The alphabetically arranged entries range in length from a few lines to two pages, and are all signed by one of the 72 contributors. While much of the material is too difficult for children, many of the terms will be encountered by junior high students. If the curriculum is sufficiently sophisticated, faculty and students could benefit from this relatively inexpensive work.

RELIGION

The World's Great Religions. By the editors of Life, Time, Inc. Abr. ed. New York: Golden Press, 1958. 192p. $5.95. $3.95 paper.

Based on the parent version bearing the same title, the abridged edition discusses the major religious philosophies throughout the world. With a narrative text and hundreds of illustrations, it covers the history, beliefs, and customs of Hinduism, Buddhism, Islam, Taoism, Confucianism, Judaism, and Christianity. Although Christianity is emphasized, it provides a valuable introduction to the other religions.

Fitch, Florence Mary. Their Search for God: Ways of Worship in the Orient. New York: Lothrop, 1947. 160p. $5.75.

This attractive standard work for intermediate level children covers the major religions of the East including Hinduism, Confucianism, Taoism, Shinto, and Buddhism. The text describes the belief, ceremonies, and festivals, and the thoughts of the philosophers and saints for each religion. The black and white photographs fill nearly every other page. At the back of the book is a helpful index glossary.

Seeger, Elizabeth. Eastern Religions. New York: Crowell, 1973. 213p. $4.95.

Focusing on five major religions, the author introduces Hinduism and Buddhism from India, Confucianism and Taoism from China, and Shinto from Japan. For each she gives the history and origin, leaders, traditions, moral and ethical ideals, shrines, festivals, and communal celebrations. A bibliography and an index follow the text. This fine book should be available for upper elementary and junior high students.

Gaer, Joseph. How the Great Religions Began. Rev. ed. New York: Dodd, Mead, 1957. 424p. $6.00.

Providing a "glimpse of how the living religions of the world arose, how they differ, and what they have basically in common one with another," this book is divided into three sections: Religions of India; Religions of China and Japan; and The advance of the One God. For each of the eleven chapters there is a preliminary summary listing the date the religion was founded, the founder, the

Philosophy and Religion 131

place, the sacred books, the number of adherents, the distribution, the sects, and the number of members in the United States.

Zehavi, A. M., ed. Handbook of the World's Religions. New York: Franklin Watts, 1973. 203p. $8.95.

This well organized and much needed handbook for upper elementary and junior high school students includes sections on Christianity, Judaism, Buddhism, Hinduism, other religions, and religion: a summary. Taken directly from the Encyclopedia International, the material is authoritative and well-written and has been placed under a single cover in a useful format. For each religion there is alphabetically arranged information under each of the following sub-sections: denominations, personalities, and terms; some of the religions also include holidays and literature. Illustrated throughout with photographs and reproductions, this indispensable volume contains a rather full index for reaching the masses of detail in the text.

National Geographic Society. Great Religions of the World. Washington, D.C.: The Society, 1971. 420p. $11.95.

Utilizing a lavish format typical of the National Geographic books, Great Religions of the World treats historically the growth, beliefs, customs, and adaptations of Hinduism, Buddhism, Judaism, Islam, and Christianity. To enhance the text are 350 full color photographs and a reference chart. Although this book is probably not a first choice as a reference work for elementary and junior high students, it should definitely be considered for purchase as a luxury item sure to instill an interest in the subject.

Parrinder, Geoffrey. Dictionary of Non-Christian Religions. Philadelphia: Westminster, 1973. 320p. $10.95.

Scholarly definitions and over 300 drawings and photographs fill this dictionary of non-Christian religions. Emphasizing the Eastern religions, e.g., Islam, Buddhism, and Hinduism, it includes information on all non-Christian religions including primitive and classical.

Altman, Addie Richman. The Jewish Child's Bible Stories. New York: Bloch, 1969. 138p. $2.95.

This small illustrated volume contains eighteen Old Testament stories which have been written in an easy to read, semi-folktale style. Stories included are Adam and Eve, Cain and Abel, Noah, Abraham, Isaac, Esau and Jacob, Joseph, Moses, Deborah, Ruth, Samuel, David, Solomon, Daniel, Queen Esther, and Judah Maccabee (The Story of Chanukah).

Ish-Kishor, Sulamith. Pathways Through the Jewish Holidays. New York: Ktav, 1967. 144p. $4.50.

Explaining how each holiday was celebrated historically and is celebrated now in different geographical areas, this book includes chapters on twelve major Jewish holidays. The Jewish calendar, black and white photographs, and an extensive index provide additional help for the user of this book.

Terrien, Samuel. The Golden Bible Atlas. New York: Golden, 1957. 97p. $3.95.

Also published by Simon and Schuster as Lands of the Bible, this easy to read volume will help to make ancient history come alive. Arranged chronologically from "The Beginnings" to "The Holy Land of Three Faiths," the book tells the various Bible stories from a historical viewpoint and also from a geographical one with maps on nearly every other page. A chronology of Bible history and an index are useful aids.

Atlas of the Bible Lands. Maplewood, N.J.: Hammond, 1959. 32p. $2.50.

A series of 31 full-color maps trace Biblical history from 2000 B.C. to the Holy Land today. In addition there are many photographs and reproductions of art works. Containing a maximum amount of information in a simple format, this atlas is good for upper elementary and junior high level students.

Kotker, Norman. The Holy Land in the Time of Jesus. New York: American Heritage, 1967. Dist. by Harper. 151p. $5.89.

Prepared by the editors of Horizon Magazine, this book is a historical treatment of the period of two centuries at the time of Jesus, the Rome-in-Palestine period. Filled with reproductions of outstanding art, mostly in color, the book includes a bibliography and an index. Contents consist of sections entitled: A kingdom for Herod; Faith of the Jews; Voices in the wilderness; Jesus of Nazareth; Paul, the first Christian; Jerusalem beseiged; and Struggle to survive.

Heaton, E. W. Everyday Life in Old Testament Times. New York: Scribner, 1956. 240p. $8.95.

Provides a broad view of Israelite life as ordinary families knew it from 1250 to 586 B.C. Sample topics include family relations, children, food and drink, dress, recreation, mourning, crops, cattle breeding, industrial workers, military life, law and order, taxation, education, music, medicine, art, and religious life. Well illustrated and containing an index, the book is suitable for both upper elementary and junior high school students.

Bouquet, A. C. Everyday Life in New Testament Times. New York: Scribner, 1953. 236p. $8.95.

Philosophy and Religion 133

A companion volume to Everyday Life in Old Testament Times which tells how people lived in the Mediterranean world in the first century of the Christian era. Historically accurate and based on contemporary sources, this work covers practically the same topics as mentioned for the Old Testament volume.

The Old Testament. Arranged and illus. by Marguerite de Angeli. Garden City, N.Y.: Doubleday, 1960. 256p. $6.95.

Containing selections from the King James Version of the Old Testament of The Bible, this lovely book has a de Angeli illustration on every page. In addition to the attractive paintings and drawings, the text appears in such excellent large type that it seems to be much easier to read.

The Common Bible with the Apocrypha/Deuterocanonical Books. New York: Collins, 1973. 1 vol. $6.36.

Resulting from long years of ecumenical scholarship and cooperation, the Revised Standard Version Common Bible contains a text approved by Protestant, Catholic, and Greek Orthodox authorities. This universal Bible should be available in every library.

The Holy Scriptures According to the Masoretic Text; A New Translation with the Aid of Previous Versions and with Constant Consultation of Jewish Authorities. New ed. Philadelphia: Jewish Publication Society of America, 1961 (c1955). 1270p. $8.50.

Max L. Margolis is editor-in-chief of this Jewish version of The Bible. This translation, prepared by a board of editors, is a necessary item for all libraries.

Northcott, Cecil. Bible Encyclopedia for Children. Philadelphia: Westminster, 1964. 176p. $5.95.

To provide basic Bible knowledge for children and to guide them towards finding out more through reading The Bible for themselves is the purpose of this easy to read and use dictionary. Arranged alphabetically, the 850 entries ranging from Aaron to Zorah are relatively brief, with most averaging three or four sentences and some nearly a page. Names of people, places, and events found in both Old and New Testaments are included.

Miller, Madeleine S. and J. Lane Miller. Harper's Bible Dictionary. 8th ed. New York: Harper, 1973. 853p. $12.50.

First published in 1952, this popular dictionary of alphabetical entries ranging in length from one paragraph to several pages, is now in its eighth edition. Included are people, places, events, archaeology, theology, and other topics. Some entries consist of short subdictionaries, e.g., under the entry "Flowers" is an alphabetical checklist of all flowers mentioned in The Bible with the

Latin name and a scripture reference complete with quote. In the back of the book is a set of color maps by Hammond and a map index. In addition 500 illustrations appear throughout the text. Accurate and readable, this dictionary is recommended for junior highs and for elementary schools where the need exists.

Jacobus, Melancthon W., Elbert C. Lane and Andrew C. Zenos. <u>Funk and Wagnalls New "Standard" Bible Dictionary.</u> 3rd rev. ed. New York: Funk and Wagnalls, 1936. 965p. $8.50.

Bearing the subtitle "Designed as a comprehensive help to the study of the scriptures, their languages, literary problems, history, biography, manners and customs, and their religious teachings," the <u>New Standard Bible Dictionary</u> is readable and useful for elementary and junior high school students from a historical viewpoint as well as from a religious one. Covering such important topics as food, houses, hunting, education, etc., the book provides a Biblical reference for each entry. The alphabetically arranged, signed articles comprise the main body of text which is illustrated with drawings and photographs.

<u>Abingdon Bible Commentary.</u> Ed. by F. C. Eiselen, E. Lewis, and D. G. Downey. New York: Abingdon, 1929. 1452p. $10.00.

This standard Bible commentary is fairly easy to read and suitable for junior high students where the need exists. The work is divided into five parts: articles on the Bible as a whole; articles on the Old Testament; commentary of the Books of the Old Testament; articles on the New Testament; and commentary on the Books of the New Testament. A small collection of maps and a long, full index complete this volume.

Young, Robert. <u>Young's Analytical Concordance to the Bible.</u> 22nd rev. ed. New York: Funk and Wagnalls, 1955. 1090p. $13.75.

This concordance to <u>The Bible</u> contains a huge list of 311,000 entries. Although the print is small and not too easy to read, the book is still usable by serious junior high students. In addition to providing Biblical references to quotes alphabetically arranged by topic, the entries have the original Hebrew or Greek for the word, a literal meaning, a definition or identification, and parallel passages. In the back of the work are index-lexicons for both the Old and New Testaments and a list of scripture proper names.

Cruden, Alexander. <u>Cruden's Complete Concordance to the Old and New Testaments.</u> Grand Rapids, Mich.: Zondervan, 1949. 800p. $4.95.

Included in this standard work are more than 220,000 references to both the King James Version and the Revised Version of

Philosophy and Religion   135

1881 of The Bible. Arranged in one alphabet, the entries list quotes from scripture followed by location (Book, chapter, verse). Two helpful supplementary lists are "A list of proper names, seldom mentioned in Scripture and not included in the body of the concordance" and "A list of proper names in the Old and New Testaments with the meaning or significance of the words in their original languages."

Nelson's Complete Concordance of the Revised Standard Version Bible. Ed. by John W. Ellison. New York: Nelson, 1957. 2157p. $29.50.

This alphabetically arranged work is a concordance to the Revised Standard Version of The Bible. Listed by principal words, the entries give the quote, the Book, the chapter, and the verse. The easy to use format features two column arrangement and clear readable type.

Complete Concordance to the Bible. Ed. by Newton Thompson. St. Louis: Herder, 1945. 1914p. $17.00.

Based on the Douay version of The Bible, this concordance is a useful one, especially for Catholic students. Containing 280,000 lines of references, the book utilizes a simple two-column format. Under each term in tabular form is the Book, the chapter, the verse, and the scripture reference.

Usherwood, Stephen. The Bible Book by Book. New York: Norton, 1962. 93p. $3.95.

This unusual reference book is an indispensable tool for teaching Sunday school classes, for teaching The Bible as literature, or for teaching ancient history. Arranged book by book, it generally contains one page of text and one of illustration for each entry. For each book the author tells something about the book and then gives the authorship, contents, history, geography, and language. The interesting pictures include murals of flowers, animals, birds, and trees of The Bible, as well as drawings showing trades, costumes, buildings, and Bible stories.

Daves, Michael. Young Readers Book of Christian Symbolism. Nashville, Abingdon, 1967. 128p. $3.95.

In this slim volume, the author traces Christian symbols and their relationship to the church and its history and traditions from the Creation down through the Apostles. Included are the cross, the symbols of Holy Week, the fish, the lamb of God, the Good Shepherd, the crown, the dove, the candle and torch, etc. Well indexed and illustrated with muted red and blue drawings, the book is designed for elementary school children.

Stevenson, Burton, ed. Home Book of Bible Quotations. New York: Harper, 1949. 645p. $13.50.

Confined strictly to Bible quotations, this book is alphabetically arranged by topic. It contains many cross references within the main body of text, and also has a very large index consisting of more than 100 pages of entries.

Comay, Joan. Who's Who in the Old Testament, Together with the Apocrypha. New York: Holt, 1971. 448p. $14.95.

More than 3,000 entries are included in this Who's Who. According to the publisher, "most of the text is devoted to the important characters, but not one person in the Old Testament is omitted." A special section for persons in the Apocrypha follows the main part of the work. A clear attractive format and 450 black and white illustrations and maps help make this a valuable reference source.

Brownrigg, Ronald. Who's Who in the New Testament. New York: Holt, 1971. 448p. $14.95.

This alphabetically arranged text is a "guide to named and unnamed personalities who shared the earthly life of Jesus." Although the book has rather long articles, ranging in length from a paragraph to several pages, it has an appealing format utilizing clear print and 450 black and white illustrations and maps.

The Book of Saints; A Dictionary of Persons Canonized or Beatified by the Catholic Church. Comp. by the Benedictine monks of St. Augustine's Abbey, Ramsgate. 5th ed. entirely rev. and reset. New York: Crowell, 1966. 740p. $10.00.

This alphabetical listing of saints provides for each entry the following: the name of the holy person, the canonical rank, the liturgical rank, the religious order, the status of the cult--approved or popular, the feast date, birth and death dates, and a brief biographical sketch.

GEOGRAPHY

Geography as a subject in the curriculum begins very early in elementary school and pervades the social studies program thereafter. Unfortunately, this is a rather neglected area as far as beginning reference tools are concerned. While geographical reference works for students in the middle grades are practically nonexistent, trade books in this field are not adequate to meet the needs. Many of them are sadly out of date; a 1970 book describing the countries of Africa will hardly be applicable today. Revision policies for series books on countries usually leave the old edition with wrong information to remain in print too long before the new edition is published. Since providing wrong information is worse than providing no information at all, geography is an area in which the library's collection should be carefully monitored and weeded frequently by the librarian. It is imperative that the school library acquire reference sources that are revised annually or at least frequently to include the latest world developments.

The titles included in this chapter are sources either recently published or subject to frequent revision. While many of them are in fact designed for adult use, most are easily used by children. The specific titles chosen for the library's reference shelf will depend upon the curriculum demands of a particular school. The books listed here include a number of general works covering the entire world, and a variety of sources dealing with specific geographical locales. Related material can be found in the chapter on atlases.

Webster's New Geographical Dictionary; A Dictionary of Names of Places with Geographical and Historical Information and Pronunciations. Springfield, Mass.: Merriam, 1972. 1370p. $14.95.

First published in 1949 and revised periodically to bring it up to date, Webster's New Geographical Dictionary includes over 47,000 entries. Listing both ancient and modern place names, it gives a brief statement of geographical and historical information and the pronunciation for each entry. It contains special sections on signs and symbols, geographical terms, and maps and map projection. It includes 217 small maps prepared by Hammond. Concisely written and easy to understand, it is an indispensable tool for elementary and junior high libraries.

Monkhouse, F. J. A Dictionary of Geography. 2nd ed. Chicago: Aldine, 1970. 378p. $7.95.

Nearly 4,000 terms are defined in this dictionary. Types of entries include items related to landforms, oceanography, climate and weather, cartography and surveying, the earth as a spheroid, units and dimensions, soil, vegetation and biogeography, political economic and cultural geography, archaeology, and geographical theory. Important statistical data are included in some entries, e.g., under "lake" are largest lakes in each continent. This book will be helpful for advanced elementary and for junior high school students.

The Times Index-Gazetteer of the World. John Bartholomew, ed. Boston: Houghton Mifflin, 1966. 959p. $50.00.

The Times Index-Gazetteer of the World, containing 345,000 entries, is an index to place names throughout the world. Serving as an index to the famed Times Atlas of the World, it lists over 194,000 entries for locating material in the giant atlas. Included in the main alphabet are towns, villages, mountains, rivers, etc., with a reference to where or in which country the feature belongs and the latitude and the longitude to the nearest minute. Extremely comprehensive, it cannot replace the Columbia Lippincott Gazetteer since it omits such information as pronunciation and population. It is recommended, however, even for libraries not owning the Times Atlas because of its scope.

Columbia Lippincott Gazetteer of the World. With 1961 Supplement. L. E. Seltzer, ed. New York: Columbia University Press, 1962. 2148p. $85.00.

Containing over 1,300 entries, the Columbia Lippincott Gazetteer of the World is a geographical dictionary listing names of places and geographical features. Entries include pronunciation, variant spellings, population, location, altitude, trade, industry, natural resources, history, and cultural institutions. In its main alphabet it incorporates every place of importance, i.e., cities (including the smallest villages), mountains, passes, volcanoes, bodies of water, deserts, and islands. Even though the 1962 printing included a supplement, the dictionary is somewhat out of date. Nevertheless, it is accurate and authoritative for facts not subject to rapid change, and therefore is still a valuable reference source.

Standard Encyclopedia of the World's Mountains. Anthony Huxley, ed. New York: Putnam, 1962. 383p. $15.00.

Alphabetically arranged, this encyclopedia contains over 300 articles on the most important mountain peaks, ranges, glaciers, and passes throughout the world. Information included for each entry covers the geological formation, historical importance, the flora and fauna, the inhabitants, and who first discovered or claimed it. An extensive gazetteer gives information on 500 peaks and ranges of lesser importance. A glossary of technical, geological, and geographical terms; capsule biographies of mountaineering pioneers; and an essay on mountain formation and the history of mountaineering complete the work. Reference maps in two colors and over 100 illustrations further implement the book's use. A comprehensive index aids in locating information.

Standard Encyclopedia of the World's Oceans and Islands. Anthony Huxley, ed. New York: Putnam, 1969. 383p. $15.00.

More than 350 articles in alphabetical sequence describe the oceans, seas, islands, bays, straits, and capes of the world. Information included in the entries includes the historical importance, the explorers who discovered them, the creatures of the seas and the flora and fauna of the islands, the primitive cultures of lonely isles, and the development of populous island nations. Nearly 100 illustrations, 10 of which are in full color, and a gazetteer of some 2,000 oceanic features round out this special reference work. An index is also provided.

Standard Encyclopedia of the World's Rivers and Lakes. R. Kay Gresswell and Anthony Huxley, eds. New York: Putnam, 1966. $15.00.

More than 450 alphabetically arranged articles discuss in detail the major rivers and lakes of the world. Ranging in length from one half column to two or more pages, the entries cover geographical features, explorers who discovered the river or lake, the commercial and industrial importance, the scenic splendors, and the bridges and dams associated with each. A large gazetteer, it provides brief entries for over 2,000 lesser lakes and rivers. Over 100 illustrations, including 16 color plates, and location maps add to the work. A detailed index further facilitates the book's use.

Encyclopedia of World Geography; Man and His World Today. London: Octopus Books, 1974. 400p. $12.98. Dist. by Quality Books.

Beautifully illustrated with full color photographs, the Encyclopedia of World Geography is an outstanding one volume reference book for elementary and junior high school students. Carefully balanced in its coverage, it includes the following sections: Aspects of geography, Europe, Asia, Africa, North America, South America, Oceania, and Antarctica. The first section covers physical geography and man's impact on it, such as pollution and conservation, iron and steel, and transportation and industry. The sections arranged by continents are subdivided by countries; for each country there is a small location map; the flag; data including area, population, population growth rate, capital, language, religion, and currency; and a readable text describing all the major aspects of each country, e.g., climate, vegetation, the people, agriculture, industry, transport and communications, etc. Attractive and easy to use, this book should be a first purchase item.

Lands and Peoples. Martha Glauber Shapp, ed. in chief. New
      York: Grolier, 1973. 7 vols. $89.50.

   This is a completely new set, published in 1972, and bearing
only the name of the old set. Both authoritative and easy to read,
Lands and Peoples is the story of all the nations of the world.
The seven volumes are entitled: Vol. 1, Africa; Vol. 2, Asia,
Australia, New Zealand, Oceania; Vol. 3, Europe; Vol. 4, Europe;
Vol. 5, North America; Vol. 6, South and Central America; Vol. 7,
The World, Facts and Figures, Index. Using all four-color pictures and maps (over 1,800 color illustrations in all), and a well-
written text, the set provides the history and geography of each
country, as well as information about the government, religion,
economy, food, clothing, manners, and customs. Volume 7 contains articles of special interest, such as "Religions of the World,"
"Peoples of the World," "Languages of the World," as well as 27
tables of facts and figures, a reading guide, and a complete index.
Lands and Peoples is subject to continuous revision. It is an attractive and useful reference work for students from the intermediate grades up.

   National Education Association of the United States. Committee on
      International Relations. Other Lands, Other Peoples; A
      Country-by-Country Fact Book. 5th ed. Washington, D. C.:
      National Education Association, 1969. 309p. $2.00 paper.

   Arranged by continent, Other Lands, Other Peoples describes
141 independent and quasi-independent nations. The following topics
are covered for each country: location and size; geographical features; cities, people, language, religion; political background; government; economy; education; holidays; relations with communist
states; relations with western states; food; national holiday; cultural
note; and historical data. Although there is no index, the table of
contents combined with the simple-to-use format facilitates ease in
locating information. Appended are the calendar of national holidays, United Nations members, and notes on Hinduism, Buddhism
and Islam. This convenient, concise, and inexpensive source book
should be in all elementary and junior high school reference collections.

   Peoples of the Earth. Danbury, Conn.: Danbury, 1973. 20 vols.
      $119.50.

   An anthropological survey of the peoples living throughout the
earth, this 20 volume set attempts with text and pictures to depict
the various societies of mankind. Both highly civilized and primitive cultures are presented in this work which describes the people
themselves rather than the country in which they live. Prepared by
journalists, anthropologists, sociologists, archaeologists and explorers, the set will provide added depth for geography students studying the various countries of the world. Included in the set are the
following volume titles: Australia and Melanesia (including New
Guinea); Africa from the Sahara to the Zambesi; Europe (including

Geography

USSR west of the Urals); Mexico and Central America; Islands of the Atlantic (including the Caribbean); Amazonia, Orinoco and Pampas; Andes; The Pacific--Polynesia and Micronesia; Southern Africa and Madagascar; Indonesia, Philippines and Malaysia; South-East Asia; The Indian subcontinent (including Ceylon); China (including Tibet), Japan and Korea; USSR east of the Urals; Western and Central Asia; The Arctic; The Arab World; North America; Man the Craftsman; and The Future of Mankind. Volume 20 also contains the general index for the set and is essential for its use since individual volumes have no indexes. Written in a rather sophisticated style, Peoples of the Earth is recommended for junior high school libraries as a supplementary reference source for studies in anthropology and geography.

Encyclopedia of World Travel. Nelson Doubleday and C. Earl Colley, ed. 2nd rev. ed. Garden City, New York: Doubleday, 1973. 2 vols. $12.95.

Written by twenty authorities, the Encyclopedia of World Travel covers generalities as well as details of interest to the traveler for each of the countries included. Information is provided on the physical features, climate, people, industry, farming, towns, history, and cultural aspects, including sights and diversions on such specific topics as food, sports, and shopping. Volume 1 includes the United States, Canada, Mexico, Central America, the Caribbean, and South America; Volume 2 covers Europe, Africa, the Middle East, Asia, and the Pacific. Black and white photographs and outline maps are distributed throughout the set. A detailed index in each volume locates specific place names. A tremendous amount of material can be found in this two-volume world travelogue.

Worldmark Encyclopedia of Nations; A Practical Guide to the Geographical, Historical, Political, Social, and Economic Status of all Nations, Their International Relationships, and the United Nations System. 4th ed. Moshe Y. Sachs, ed. New York: Worldmark Press, 1971. 5 vols. $69.95.

A comprehensive, authoritative set, Worldmark Encyclopedia of Nations covers geographical, historical, political, social, and economic information for 146 countries. The contents of the five volumes include: vol. 1, United Nations; vol. 2, Africa; vol. 3, the Americas; vol. 4, Asia and Australia; and vol. 5, Europe. Material is arranged under 50 topical headings for each nation with a bibliography appended for each. An index arranged by country is useful in locating information. All in all, the Worldmark Encyclopedia supplies valuable information to support the elementary and junior high school curriculum and should be available in the library.

Fact Book of the Countries of the World. New York: Crown, 1970. 792p. $7.95. $5.95 paper.

Arranged alphabetically by the popular or generally known

name of the country, this book consists of "Background Notes Reprinted from Materials Published by the United States Department of State." Each entry contains information on any or all of the following topics: population, capital, the people, history and government, economy, foreign relations, reading list, political conditions, trade, principal government officials, and current issues. The clear readable format and well-organized entries compensate for the lack of an index and make this a tool easily used by intermediate and junior high students. Appended to the main body of text is a section called International Organizations Series which includes the Central Treaty Organization, the Organization of African Unity; the North Atlantic Treaty Organization; the Organization for Economic Cooperation and Development; and the European Communities.

Europa Yearbook. London: Europa, 1946- . 2 vols. $70.00.

A fine and expensive two-volume annual, Europa first appeared in loose-leaf form but is now published in two sturdily bound volumes. Volume I covers international organizations, including extensive information on the United Nations and Europe. Volume II extends over Africa, the Americas, Asia, and Australia. Arrangement is alphabetical by country within each continent. Up-to-date, accurate, and comprehensive, Europa Yearbook provides for each country economic and statistical data, details of the constitution, government, political parties, legal system, education, newspapers, periodicals, publishers, radio and television stations, banks and insurance companies, chambers of commerce, trade associations and unions, transport companies, learned societies, research institutes, libraries, museums, and universities. This important reference source supplies such extensive information that all but the tiniest libraries could easily justify its expense.

Pearcy, G. Etzel and Elvyn A. Stoneman. A Handbook of New Nations. New York: Crowell, 1968. $8.95.

A Handbook of New Nations contains information on the 61 nations emerging since World War II. Alotting one chapter per country, the handbook provides for each a physical description, the population, history, government, economic and social conditions, and a black and white map. The appendix has charts showing the chronology, date of independence, form of government, short and long form names, former states, populations, areas and capital. A glossary and the index assist the user in locating specific information.

The Book of Europe: Your Guide to the Best Things to See and Do. Chicago: Rand McNally, 1973. 256p. $19.95.

Designed as a vacation guide, this book is sure to answer numerous upper grade geography questions. Filled with timely facts and 300 color and black and white illustrations, it offers tourist guidance to over 4,500 different places in Europe and North Africa.

Geography

Pertinent human interest information of special concern to intermediate level students includes for each country sections on the people, food, resorts and sports, places to see, festivals, etc. Created just for this book, the 109 maps in the atlas section are marked with symbols for diverse cultural and recreational highlights. A series of special maps, e.g., the gourmet's guide which shows food indigenous to particular locales, not only provides specific facts but also invites browsing for pleasure. Appended is the Vacation Information Pack listing the festivals by month for each country, a mileage chart, and a climate chart by month. A gazetteer aids in locating details and rounds out this fine volume.

The Far East and Australasia 1973: A Survey and Directory of Asia and the Pacific. 6th ed. London: Europa, 1974. $42.00.

Part one of this excellent source of information is entitled "General Introduction" and consists of general essays. Sample titles include "The Religions of Asia," "Agrarian Issues in Asia," and "Major Commodities of Asia and the Pacific." In the second part is a listing of regional organizations with descriptions of each. The following sections, "South Asia," "South-East Asia," "East Asia," and "Australasia and the Pacific Islands," are country-by-country listings of specific facts. For each country there is the physical and social geography, history, an economic survey, a statistical survey, the constitution, the government, diplomatic representation, etc. The final section, "Other Reference Material," contains chapters on weights and measures, calendars and time reckoning, research institutes, biographies of important persons, and a selected bibliography.

Concise Encyclopedia of the Middle East. Mehdi Heravi, ed. Washington, D.C.: Public Affairs Press, 1973. 336p. $12.00.

Arranged alphabetically, this book attempts to provide accessible information concerning the nations, the institutions, the problems, and the key personalities of the Middle East. Particular emphasis is placed upon current issues. Although the entries are relatively short, ranging in length from a brief paragraph to a page, all are signed with initials which are identified in the list of contributors. Readable and easy to use, this encyclopedia will be useful for elementary schools and essential for junior highs.

The Middle East and North Africa 1974-75. 21st ed. London: Europa, 1974. $36.00.

Accurate and up to date, The Middle East and North Africa is an authoritative compendium of hard-to-locate information. In the first section are essays of a general nature covering such topics as, "The Religions of the Middle East and North Africa," "The Arab-Israeli Confrontation 1967-73," "Oil in the Middle East and North Africa," and "The Suez Canal." Part two is a listing of the regional organizations. Part three, arranged alphabetically by country, provides specific facts for specific nations from Afghanistan to Yemen. For each is provided the physical and social geography, an economic survey, the constitution, the government, the diplomatic representation, etc. A statistical survey indicates area and population, agriculture, industry, forestry, fishing, finance, external trade, transport, tourism, communications media, and education. The fourth part, entitled "Other Reference Materials," includes "Who's Who in the Middle East and North Africa" consisting of brief biographies of important personalities; "Calendars, Time Reckoning and Weights and Measures"; "Bibliographies"; and "Research Institutes."

Africa South of the Sahara 1974. 4th ed. London: Europa, 1974. 1119p. $42.00.

This reference source surveys the countries in Africa south of the Sahara Desert. Organized similarly to the other fine Europa reference books, this one begins with a series of general essays. Typical titles include "Africa in Historical Perspective," "Political and Social Problems of Development," and "Problems of Educational Development." Part II, "Regional Organizations," lists organizations giving pertinent information for each. Part III is the "Country Survey," arranged alphabetically by country from Angola to Zambia. For each country there is included the physical and social geography, recent history, the economy, statistics, a select bibliography, and a directory giving the constitution, the government, the diplomatic representation, parliament, political parties, defense, judicial system, religion, the press, publishers, radio and television, finance, trade and industry, transport, power, tourism, and education. Part IV consists of calendars, time reckoning, weights and measures; primary commodities of Africa; research institutes; a bibliography; and an important listing of key personalities in the form of a "Who's Who."

Veliz, Claudio, ed. Latin America and the Caribbean; a Handbook. New York: Frederick A. Praeger, 1968. 434p. $25.00.

Latin America and the Caribbean consists of a combination of statistics and scholarly essays. Part I is arranged alphabetically by country with each entry written by a specialist. Each includes an historical narrative; an economic summary; and statistics for climate, population, the constitutional system, defense, international relations, economy, transport and communications, social welfare, and mass media. The remainder of the articles are of a general nature and are divided as follows: Part II, Latin American Political Affairs; Part III, Latin American Economic Affairs; Part IV, Latin American Social Background, and Part V, Contemporary Arts of Latin America and the Caribbean. Sixteen plates, outline maps, and a good index add to the reference value of the book.

American Heritage New Pictorial Encyclopedic Guide to the United

Geography

States. Created and designed by the editors of American Heritage Magazine. New York: Dell, 1965. 2 vols.

Arranged alphabetically by state, this reference work provides a variety of information in a short space. Included for each state are a map, the flora and fauna, legends and lore, places of interest, and the information roundup. Under the latter topic the following material is listed: topography, rivers, lakes, mountains, climate, major cities, national forests, national parks, national monuments, state parks, universities and colleges, nickname, motto, origin of name, area, population, capital, date admitted to the Union, finance, number of United States representatives, flower, tree, bird, and so on. A time line of historical events, a thumbnail history, and surveys of the government and politics, economy, transportation, communications, industry, agriculture, and personal income by type of work all add to the value of the work. Written in a simple, readable style and illustrated with color pictures on every page, the New Pictorial Guide to the United States contains a vast amount of hard-to-find information needed by intermediate level students.

Jordan, Emil Leopold. Pictorial Travel Atlas of Scenic America. Bicentennial ed. Maplewood, N.J.: Hammond, 1973. 288p. $14.95.

Lavishly illustrated, this book purports to offer pages of practical travel information and to dramatize America as a unique travel land. It is arranged by geographical regions: Northeast, Southeast, North Central, South Central, Northwest, and Southwest, with special sections on Mexico and the Caribbean. Each two-page spread constitutes one full subheading and includes a small map, a full-color photograph, and interesting descriptive narration. A special sight-seeing guide for each region contains detailed information. Sections on transcontinental highways, national parks, highway mileage chart, climate data, and vacation travel by air and train are appended. An additional bonus is the specially numbered section entitled "1776 Revisited" consisting of maps, illustrations, and guidance for seeing and reliving the American Revolution by way of visiting historic sites.

Frome, Michael. National Park Guide. 8th ed. New York: Rand, 1974. 209p. $7.95.

An attractive and useful guide, this book provides much information on national parks. Arranged alphabetically by state and then alphabetically by park, the book covers for each park spots of interest, seasons, hiking, boating, photography, recreation, and where to write for further information. Filled with color plates and black and white photographs, it includes a special section on Washington D.C., including historical areas, archaeological areas, etc. National Park Guide will be valuable in both elementary and junior high schools.

Colby, C. B. America's Natural Wonders. New York: Coward-McCann, 1956. 48p. $3.86.

Bearing the subtitle: "Strange forests, mysterious caverns, and amazing formations," this slim Colby book describes about 40 natural wonders of America. In one or two pages each it contains entries on such features as the Grand Canyon, Old Faithful Geyser, Carlsbad Caverns, Florida Everglades, Crater Lake, etc. Each is accompanied with black and white photographs. This volume will suffice for those students unable to handle the sophisticated American Heritage Book of Natural Wonders.

American Heritage Book of Natural Wonders. Alvin M. Josephy, Jr., ed. New York: American Heritage; distributed by McGraw-Hill. 1972. 384p. $16.50.

The American Heritage Book of Natural Wonders describes the United States in a brief text and in elaborate photographs over 100 of which are in full color. Showing the land as it was in the early days as well as depicting it as it is now, the book tours the favorite vacation spots of America by means of beautiful photography. Written by eight well-known men, e.g., William O. Douglas and Bruce Catton, it is divided in the following sections: The Atlantic Coast, The Eastern Forests, The Southern Lowlands, The Prairie and Plains, The Great Mountains, The Basins and Deserts, and The Pacific Coast.

America's Historylands; Touring Our Landmarks of Liberty. New ed. Melville Bell, ed. Washington, D.C.: National Geographic Society, 1967. 576p. $9.95.

America's Historylands describes in text and pictures the most important landmarks in the history of the country. Using excellent photographs, mostly in color, the editors offer a tour of famous places in the nation. The book is divided into the following parts: Freedom's Capitol, The New Land, the Colonials, the Revolution, the Surge of Freedom, Manifest Destiny, the House Divided, the Great American War, the Lusty West, the Growing Giant, and New Frontiers. An index locates information by places, people, and events. This volume is valuable in both history and geography classes for elementary and junior high schools.

Goetz, Delia. State Capital Cities. New York: Morrow, 1971. 159p. $4.81.

Alphabetically arranged by state, this book contains information sometimes difficult to locate on the capital cities of all states. Each entry is about three pages in length and describes the capital with some historical background, the city as it is today, and current events, such as a calendar of activities. Ninety-two photographs illustrate the work. No index is included, but none is needed. Intermediate level youngsters studying United States geography will find this a valuable resource.

Geography

Kane, Joseph Nathan. The American Counties. 3rd ed. Metuchen, N.J.: Scarecrow Press, 1972. 608p. $15.00.

This informative book bears the subtitle: "Origins of names, dates of creation and organization, area, population, historical data, and published sources." In addition to the information described in the subtitle, the 3,000 plus alphabetical entries give the county seat and origin of its name, county nicknames, and population figures for three decades (1950, 1960, and 1970). The citations for additional information sources are new in the revised and expanded third edition. Other sections in the book include a list of counties by state and date, a list of counties whose names have changed, a list of persons for whom counties have been named, and a list of independent cities.

Kane, Joseph Nathan and Gerald L. Alexander. Nicknames and Sobriquets of U.S. Cities and States. 2nd ed. Metuchen, N.J.: Scarecrow Press, 1970. 456p. $10.00.

This unusual index lists the nicknames and sobriquets of American states, cities, and towns and contains more than 10,000 entries. The first section is arranged alphabetically by state with cities in one column and nicknames adjacent in another. The nicknames index follows, arranged alphabetically by nickname. The geographical index of states, also alphabetical, provides state nicknames in paragraph form. This section also has a nicknames index.

HISTORY

History constitutes an important area of the curriculum for upper elementary and junior high schools. Included in the instructional program are ancient and medieval history, modern world history, United States history, and history of individual states. Children at this level are concerned with specific details which aid them in reconstructing a living past. Coordinately, they seek information in related subjects to assist in determining how those in the past felt, thought, worked, and played. To expedite students' search for historical data, the library should provide a combination of adult and juvenile reference works. Materials ranging from mature specific entry works such as Langer's Encyclopedia of World History to narrative surveys such as Carpenter's Everyday Life in Ancient Times should be included in the collection.

In this chapter the titles included are arranged under the following subheadings: world history--bibliographies; world history --general works; ancient and medieval history; modern world history; American history--bibliographies; American history--general works; American history--specific topics; American history--documents; American history--names, symbols, and stories; and flags. Enrichment and supplementary materials can also be found in the chapters on biography, art and music, atlases, social sciences, geography, recreation and hobbies, philosophy and religion, and ethnic groups in America. In other words, a subject as broad as history cannot be confined to generalized works, but must encompass all aspects of the story of mankind. Children should be encouraged to seek information from the array of related topics.

WORLD HISTORY--Bibliographies

Hotchkiss, Jeanette. European Historical Fiction and Biography for Children and Young People. 2nd ed. Metuchen, N. J.: Scarecrow, 1972. 272p. $7.50.

Selected on the basis of historical accuracy, literary merit, readability, and good taste, the titles in this bibliography are arranged alphabetically by geographical unit and then chronologically by centuries. Entries contain author, title, publisher, date, a brief annotation, and a suggested age level. Titles included are all related to countries located in Europe.

Irwin, Leonard B. A Guide to Historical Reading: Nonfiction; For the Use of Schools, Libraries, and the General Reader. 9th rev. ed. Philadelphia: McKinley, 1970. 276p. $10.00.

This book list replaces an older work, Historical Nonfiction by Hannah Logasa. Arranged by geographical areas and historical periods, this edition contains fewer titles than in previous editions but is more selective. In addition to the bibliographic data provided, the entries give brief annotations and symbols to indicate age levels.

Irwin, Leonard B. A Guide to Historical Fiction; For the Use of Schools, Libraries, and the General Reader. 10th ed. new and rev. Philadelphia: McKinley, 1971. 255p. $10.00.

Formerly Historical Fiction by Hannah Logasa, A Guide to Historical Fiction contains 2,000 titles published in the past 35 years. It is arranged by broad time periods and by geographical areas. Each entry has a brief annotation which follows the bibliographic data. Some juvenile novels are included in each chronological division and are so indicated. Author and title indexes follow the main text.

Logasa, Hannah. World Culture, A Selected Annotated Bibliography. Philadelphia: McKinley, 1963. 384p. $12.00.

A companion volume to Guide to Historical Fiction and Guide to Historical Reading: Nonfiction, this bibliography is concerned mainly with world culture, civilization, environment, ideas, science, and religion of mankind. Arranged alphabetically by topic, the book list contains complete bibliographic data plus brief annotations. It also has an author and title index.

Metzner, Seymour. World History in Juvenile Books; A Geographical and Chronological Guide. New York: Wilson, 1973. 356p. $12.00.

Suitable for use by elementary and junior high school students themselves, this bibliography lists more than 2,700 titles of fiction and nonfiction relating to world history. Entries give author, title, grade level, publisher, date, and pagination. Very brief annotations appear if the title does not adequately indicate its relevance to world history. Other useful features are an author index, a biographical subject index, a title index, and a directory of publishers.

Sutherland, Zena, comp. History in Children's Books, An Annotated Bibliography for Schools and Libraries. Brooklawn, N.J.: McKinley, 1967. 248p. $8.50.

Covering all of the world in all time periods, this bibliography is arranged by geographical locale and then chronologically within each section. Bibliographic data is followed by a brief but critical, well-written annotation. An author-title index aids in locating material on a specific subject.

WORLD HISTORY--General Works

Man and History. Maplewood, N.J.: Hammond, 1971. 192p. $12.95.

To cover briefly all periods of history, Man and History is arranged chronologically. The brief entries are placed on a page with a simple map. About 80 pages of the chronology cover basic world history followed by another sixty-plus pages on American history. A number of special sections, e.g., man's family tree, his distribution, languages, and religions, provide interesting and helpful information. Both entries and maps are so clear and easy to read that upper elementary and junior high school students will enjoy using this tool.

Mirkin, Stanford M. What Happened When; a Noted Researcher's Almanac of Yesterdays. Rev. ed. New York: Washburn, 1966. 442p. $7.95.

Based on When Did It Happen? (1957), What Happened When is a completely new, revised and enlarged edition of the popular dictionary of dates. Arranged chronologically by days throughout the year, it lists under each day facts, events, trends, and human interest items in the news. For example, the following information appears under the entry August 18: 1587--Virginia Dare born in Roanoke Island, N.C.; 1914--Germany declares war on Russia in World War I; and 1963--James Meredith is graduated from the University of Mississippi (the first Negro to graduate there). A lengthy alphabetical index aids the user in locating information.

Langer, William L., ed. An Encyclopedia of World History; Ancient, Medieval, and Modern, Chronologically Arranged. 5th ed. Boston: Houghton Mifflin, 1972. 1569p. $17.50.

An Encyclopedia of World History is chronologically arranged from prehistory through 1970 and is subdivided by periods and by regions and countries. Included in this comprehensive reference work are historical events, such as the development of the Greek civilization, the settlement of the Americas, the two world wars, the history of Africa, and a special section, "The Recent Period," which includes the exploration of space and scientific and technological advances. Historical maps and royal genealogies are distributed throughout the book. In addition to the main text the appendices list genealogical tables of the major ruling houses of Europe and Asia, tables of Popes, members of the United Nations, etc. An extensive 190-page index provides a key to the text. Up to date and reliable, this reference book provides in brief outline form information for all historical periods on a world-wide scale.

History 151

Purnell's History of the 20th Century. A. J. P. Taylor, ed. in chief. New York: Purnell, 1971, 1972. 10 vols. $179.50.

Prepared in England by a panel of 242 international contributors, the majority of which are British, Purnell's History of the 20th Century attempts to cover the "history of all the world in the 20th century." Emphasizing political and social developments, the set is extremely well illustrated with 5,000 illustrations, mostly in color. Stating that "no other century possesses such an abundant visual record of history in the making," the editors have devoted about one half of the page space to illustrations. Reasonably well balanced and unbiased, the set is arranged predominantly in chronological order. In the last volume is the bibliography, a thematic index, an illustration index, and a general subject index. Junior high school students studying twentieth century history will find this pictorial history a valuable aid.

ANCIENT AND MEDIEVAL HISTORY

Falls, C. B. The First 3000 Years: Ancient Civilizations of the Tigris, Euphrates, and Nile River Valleys and the Mediterranean Sea. New York: Viking, 1960. 220p. $5.95.

The well-written, narrative text of this book stretches from the beginning of civilization in 4000 B.C. to the fall of Rome. Defining "civilization" as "an advanced state of human society in which a high level of art, science, religion, and government has been reached," the author relates each of the early societies to Western culture as it is today. Preceding the text is a series of ten two-page maps each depicting the development of a particular civilization. A reading list and an index conclude the book.

Carpenter, Rhys and others. Everyday Life in Ancient Times; Highlights of the Beginnings of Western Civilization in Mesopotamia, Egypt, Greece, and Rome. Washington, D.C.: National Geographic Society, 1964. 368p. $6.00.

Written by five authorities on ancient history, this book uses an intriguing text, paintings, photographs and maps to provide the researcher with a glimpse of life in ancient times. Beginning in 4500 B.C. in Mesopotamia, the book describes that civilization plus those of Egypt, Greece, and Rome. The authors attempt to portray the fundamentals of the lives of both the elite and the humble of each culture. A rather full index helps in locating details in this interesting book. It is recommended for upper elementary and junior high school libraries.

Radice, Betty. Who's Who in the Ancient World. New York: Stein and Day, 1971. 225p. $12.50.

This biographical dictionary consists of an alphabetical listing of historical and mythological personae of the ancient world.

Each entry contains a concise identification of the person followed by references to painting, sculpture, music and literature. A very full index lists every subject mentioned in the main text. A helpful "Table of Main Dates" is appended.

McEvedy, Colin and Sarah McEvedy. The Atlas of World History: From the Beginning to Alexander the Great. New York: Macmillan, 1971. 62p. $5.95.

Beginning with the most primitive men, the authors trace the evolution of man up to the death of Alexander the Great in 323 B.C. Using text, maps, photographs, and drawings, the book shows how agriculture, metalworking, and writing formed the basis of the great early civilizations. The ancient cultures of Egypt, Greece, India, China, and others are included.

The New Century Classical Handbook. Catherine B. Avery, ed. New York: Appleton-Century-Crofts, 1962. 1162p. $18.90.

The New Century Classical Handbook consists of 6,000 alphabetically arranged entries dealing with the personalities, ideas, and accomplishments of classical Greece and Rome. Entries cover archaeology, architecture, art, geography, history, literature, mythology, philosophy, religion, and science. Biographies of statesmen, generals, artists, sculptors, dramatists, poets, philosophers, historians, potters, and painters are included as well as synopses of famous epics and dramas. Over 100 photographs and 114 line drawings appear throughout the text. Clear print and readable entries make this a usable reference source.

Bray, Warwick and David H. Trump. The American Heritage Guide to Archaeology. New York: American Heritage, 1970. 269p. $6.95.

More than 1,600 alphabetically arranged entries in this book cover the whole field of archaeology. Ranging from human evolution and the prehistoric period to the civilizations of Egypt, the Near East, Europe, and the Americas, the entries contain lucid, clear definitions. The small but clear drawings and black and white plates show artifacts and sites of excavation throughout the world. Appended are a regional index and maps of important archaeological locations in various countries.

Larousse Encyclopedia of Archaeology. New York: Putnam, 1972. 432p. $25.00.

Edited by Gilbert Charles-Picard and translated from the French by Anne Ward, the Larousse Encyclopedia of Archaeology is a comprehensive treatise filled with color and black and white illustrations. Covered in the text are western Asia; the Nile Valley; the Aegean World; classical Greece, the Etruscans; the Romans; Europe in the Bronze and Iron Age; the Americas; India, Pakistan, and Afghanistan; and the Far East. An extensive index renders the unconventional encyclopedia format easy to use.

History

Banks, Arthur. A World Atlas of Military History, vol. 1, to 1485. New York: Hippocrene Books, 1973. 154p. $12.95.

This British atlas spans the period from about 2350 B.C. to 1485 A.D. Included in it are maps of military history in the Middle East, India, China, Italy, and Greece. The maps depict the development of cities and empires, and show how the course of battles changed European and Asian history.

Dunan, Marcel, ed. Larousse Encyclopedia of Ancient and Medieval History. New York: Harper, 1963. 413p. $25.00. New York: Crown, 1972. $6.95 paper.

A typical Larousse, scholarly but readable and attractive, this encyclopedia covers from prehistory through the Middle Ages. Contents by topics include: Man before history, Eastern peoples and empires, Supremacy of the Eastern Mediterranean, Great empires of antiquity, The barbarian invasion, The rise of Europe, The fourteenth and fifteenth centuries, and Medieval retrospect. Over 500 illustrations, maps, and photographs enhance this book. Although this encyclopedia is not arranged in the traditional alphabetical style, the very detailed index is the key to the text.

Williams, Jay. Life in the Middle Ages. New York: Random House, 1966. 160p. $4.95.

Employing a rather sophisticated narrative style, the author describes all aspects of life in the middle ages. He touches upon feudalism, the medieval village, town, castle, war camp, and so forth. This book offers some insight into the lives of the people living during the period. Where such information is needed, it should serve elementary and junior high students quite well.

Fines, John. Who's Who in the Middle Ages. New York: Stein and Day, 1971. 218p. $12.50.

Scholarly, but easy to use, this biographical dictionary includes sketches of influential people in the Western world from the collapse of the Roman Empire to the Renaissance. The long readable entries include diverse people from all areas of society, e.g., St. Francis, Attila, Macbeth, and Joan of Arc. An index of proper names follows the main text. Junior high students will benefit from this tool, as will good students in elementary school.

Uden, Grant, A Dictionary of Chivalry. New York: Crowell, 1968. 352p. $10.00.

A Dictionary of Chivalry defines nearly all terms needed for a study of medieval history, specifically the era of chivalry. Entries included in the book tell all about the knight: his education and training; the complex code he followed; his weapons, armor, horses; his stories, enterprises, and leisure time activities. Proper names such as Caxton, Charlemagne, and Chaucer are also identified in the single alphabet. A subject index follows the main text. A truly beautiful book with a very readable text, this reference book belongs in any elementary and junior high school library where the students are studying the Middle Ages.

Storey, R. L. Chronology of the Medieval World 800 to 1491. New York: McKay, 1973. $15.95.

Covering the period of history from 800 to 1491, this book is arranged chronologically by dates. On the left-hand page appears dates and events, primarily political and military. On the corresponding right-hand page is listed much information under the topics: law and politics; religion and education; art, architecture, and music. The chronology is obviously dominated by the history of Western Europe, since few records remain for the rest of the world during this time period. A long index is helpful.

McEvedy, Colin and Sarah McEvedy. The Atlas of World History: The Dark Ages. New York: Macmillan, 1972. 64p. $6.95.

Covering the period of the Dark Ages (approximately 400 to 1000 A.D.), this atlas utilizes an interesting text, maps, drawings, and photographs to tell the story of this era of history. Attractive and appealing, it will be a fine supplement for the study of the Byzantine, Persian, Indian, and Chinese empires as well as the rise of Islam, the Viking voyages, the evolution of England from Britain, and the exploits of Charlemagne.

MODERN WORLD HISTORY

Gail, Marzieh. Life in the Renaissance. New York: Random House, 1968. 160p. $4.95.

Written in an interesting narrative style, Life in the Renaissance covers numerous details of living which are often omitted from reference sources. Information important to upper elementary students is included, such as how people earned a living, what they did in their leisure time, what type of educational system they had, how they traveled, etc.

Williams, Neville. Chronology of the Expanding World 1492 to 1762. New York: McKay, 1969. 700p. $12.50.

This chronologically arranged reference work is a companion to the author's Chronology of the Modern World. Arranged by year and by specific date when known, the left-hand page contains the chief events of the year. On the right-hand page adjacent to the event is listed corresponding information under the following headings: politics, economics, law and education; philosophy, religion, and scholarship; art, sculpture, fine arts, and architecture; music; literature including drama; births and deaths of notabilities. A long index lists persons, places, subjects, and titles of books.

History

Atlas of Discovery. Text by Gail Roberts; maps by Geographical Projects. New York: Crown, 1973. 192p. $9.95.

Printed and bound in Spain, the atlas is filled with historical, relief, and political maps produced by Geographical Projects Limited of London. The maps, aided by the text by Gail Roberts, attempt to trace the story of exploration from the earliest days to the present. This volume is attractive enough to invite browsing and provides valuable information on exploration.

Riverain, Jean. Concise Encyclopedia of Explorations. Chicago: Follett, 1969 (English language edition). 279p. $3.95, $2.95 paper.

This alphabetically arranged volume attempts to provide a large amount of information about explorers and explorations in one source. For each explorer included, the entry gives his name, an identification both with country and occupation, home, dates, the place explored, and a paragraph describing his exploration. Entries for places explored include location, discoverer, settler, and a paragraph description of the history and circumstances. A small book illustrated with many black and white pictures, the dictionary suffers somewhat from the slightly small, cramped format, but is still usable.

The Encyclopedia of Discovery and Exploration. 18 vols. London: Aldus Books Limited, 1971. $93.50. (Dist. by Grolier, New York).

Lavishly illustrated with more than 3,750 illustrations, 1,600 of which are in full color, The Encyclopedia of Discovery and Exploration covers the entire span of history including the moon explorations. Volume titles include: The first explorers; Beyond the horizon; The great age of exploration; God, gold and glory; Lands of spice and treasure; Rivers of destiny; Charting the vast Pacific; Bridging a continent; Jungle rivers and mountain peaks; Lands of the southern cross; Seas of sand; The challenge of Africa; The heartland of Asia; The frozen world; Secrets of the sea; The roof of the world; The moon and beyond; and Guide and index. Each volume is signed; all contain four parts: an introduction; the story or main body of text; an appendix describing the major changes brought about by the discoveries; and biographical sketches of explorers, a glossary, and an index. Volume 18 merits special attention, for it not only contains the master index for the set but also an alphabetical collection of brief encyclopedic articles on explorers and specific subjects. This attractive set should be available to both elementary and junior high school students.

Duncan, Marcel, ed. Larousse Encyclopedia of Modern History; from 1500 to the Present Day. New York: Harper, 1964. 405p. $25.00.

Including sections on each century in modern history, the

Larousse Encyclopedia of Modern History is a beautifully illustrated reference work which is extensively indexed. It covers the dissolution of the fifteenth century European feudal aristocracies and proceeds up through the twentieth century ideological Cold War. It also traces the rise of nations through warfare, conquest, and peaceful colonization.

Williams, Neville. Chronology of the Modern World; 1763 to the Present Time. Rev. ed. New York: McKay, 1969. 923p. $12.50.

Arranged by year, then month, then date, the left-hand pages of this chronology cover the political, military events of each month of each year under the exact calendar dates. On the corresponding right-hand pages, arranged by subject, are sections dealing with politics, law, economics, science, technology, discovery, philosophy, religion, scholarship, art, sculpture, architecture, music, literature, the press, drama, entertainment, sport, births and deaths of notables, and others. Nearly one-third of this interesting volume is an encyclopedic index of cross references.

Morris, Richard B. and Graham W. Irwin. Harper Encyclopedia of the Modern World; A Concise Reference History from 1760 to the Present. New York: Harper, 1970. 1271p. $17.50.

Divided into two parts, the chronological and the topical, this companion to the Encyclopedia of American History is a summary of modern history. In the first section is the political, military, and diplomatic history of the various parts of the world. The second or topical section covers technological, economic, social, and cultural developments on a worldwide scale during the modern period of history. Although much information is packed into a small space, it is clearly presented in concise entries. The valuable detailed index makes this a fine ready reference tool.

AMERICAN HISTORY--Bibliographies

Coughlan, Margaret N., comp. Creating Independence, 1763-1789; A Selected Annotated Bibliography. Washington, D.C.: Library of Congress, 1972. 62p. $.75.

This alphabetically arranged book list was prepared by the Children's Book Section of the Library of Congress as a guide in the selection of background reading in connection with the Bicentennial of the American Revolution. Entries, which give title, place, publisher, date, and pagination, contain annotations ranging from three lines to one-half page in length.

Hotchkiss, Jeanette. American Historical Fiction and Biography for Children and Young People. Metuchen, N.J.: Scarecrow, 1973. $7.50.

History 157

An annotated bibliography of 1,600 titles, designed to aid teachers, librarians, and students themselves in locating authentic and exciting novels and biographies concerning the history of both Americas. Arranged chronologically in the first section and topically in the second one, the list contains symbols indicating reader ability and interest levels from kindergarten through high school.

Metzner, Seymour. American History in Juvenile Books: A Chronological Guide. New York: Wilson, 1966. 329p. $8.00.

More than 2,000 trade books, both fiction and non-fiction, relating to American history, are arranged chronologically with topical subheadings. A comprehensive list for elementary and junior high school students, it includes for each entry the full bibliographical information, the suggested grade level span, and a brief annotation if the title does not indicate the book's subject. This guide is invaluable for enriching the social studies program.

AMERICAN HISTORY--General Works

Miers, Earl Schenk. The Golden History of the United States. New York: Golden Press, 1970. 320p. $6.21.

To provide a broad, general survey of United States history, the author has included material covering from the early explorers through Richard Nixon's first election and the first astronauts on the moon. Written in an interesting narrative style, the book is illustrated with drawings or color paintings on nearly every page. It is suitable for middle elementary grades and up.

The Record of America. Joseph F. X. McCarthy, ed. New York: Scribner, 1974. 10 vols. $175.00.

Based on the curriculum needs of middle and high school students, The Record of America is a comprehensive ready-reference set covering all phases of colonial and national history of the United States. The editors of this work have attempted to combine in one set adapted for student use all of the features of the publisher's well-known and authoritative reference works including Dictionary of American Biography, the Dictionary of American History, the Atlas of American History, and the Album of American History. Articles in volumes one through eight are arranged alphabetically by topic and are cross-referenced. Volumes nine and ten consist of documentary material, in the forms of text, graphics, and pictures. This material is organized in resource units with each unit providing information for the study of a theme, an idea, an event, or a problem in American history. Over 3,000 illustrations throughout the set aid in explaining concepts. Authoritative and readable, this set will be essential for both elementary and junior high school students.

Webster's Guide to American History; A Chronological, Geographical, and Biographical Survey and Compendium. Springfield, Mass.: Merriam, 1971. 1428p. $14.95.

Part I, some of which is adapted from The Annals of America (Encyclopaedia Britannica, 1969), consists of a comprehensive survey of American history from 1492 to the 1970's. Arranged chronologically year-by-year and day-by-day, it contains the chronology in the left-hand column of each page. In the right-hand column adjacent to the appropriate date is a quotation from a primary source relating to an event sited on the other side of the page. More than 700 illustrations accompany this text. In Part II are 125 maps, many in color, which trace the nation's growth and development. Also included are clear, easy-to-read tables covering topics from Presidential elections and cabinets to popular songs and books, Academy Award winners, and leading magazines. Alphabetically arranged in Part III are concise biographical sketches of more than 1,025 key figures in American history. An index of 11,000 entries offers ready access to the wealth of information in this readable, easy-to-use reference book.

Johnson, Thomas H. The Oxford Companion to American History. New York: Oxford University Press, 1966. 906p. $17.50.

This standard dictionary, suitable for use in junior high schools, contains 4,710 entries, including 1,835 biographical sketches, on the history of America from colonial times to the present. Exceedingly well cross-referenced, the alphabetical source concludes with the text of the United States Constitution.

Morris, Richard B., ed. Encyclopedia of American History. Updated and rev. New York: Harper, 1970. 850p. $12.50.

First published in 1953, the Encyclopedia of American History provides historical facts about American life and institutions. It is divided into three sections, "Basic Chronology," "Topical Chronology," and "400 Notable Americans." The "Basic Chronology" covers history from the original peopling of the Americas 50,000-8000 B.C. through the mid-1960's. The "Topical Chronology" covers such subjects as science, culture, economics, and population. Part III consists of brief biographical sketches of 400 people who made important contributions to American history. Well written in a narrative style, it contains a valuable index and many maps and charts.

Carruth, Gordon, ed. Encyclopedia of American Facts and Dates. 6th ed. with a supplement of the 1970's. New York: Crowell, 1972. 922p. $8.95.

Arranged chronologically from 986 A.D. through 1971, the Encyclopedia of American Facts and Dates provides a vast array of information concerning America's past. Each page is divided into four parallel columns so that events in various areas of interest are indicated with each date. The first column shows politics, government, war, disasters, and vital statistics; the second shows books, painting, drama, architecture, and sculpture; the third lists science, industry, economics, education, religion, and philosophy; and the fourth, sports, fashions, popular entertainment, folklore, and society. This unusual reference book, which shows in a glance all aspects of American life for any given year, contains an index which refers back to the appropriate year and column, rather than to page numbers.

Colonial America; From the First Settlements to the Close of the American Revolution. By the Editors of the Album of American History. New York: Scribner, 1972. 449p. $19.20.

Colonial America, the first volume of the Album of American History, is now published separately from the set. Having a detailed index, this pictorial chronology is a suitable supplement for American history students of any age. Reproductions of sketches, maps, and drawings and photographs of real objects illustrate nearly every aspect of colonial life.

Adams, James Truslow, ed. Album of American History. New York: Scribner, 1944-1969. 6 vols. $120.00.

This indispensable set attempts to tell the history of America through pictures made at the time the history was being made. The text seeks merely to identify the time, place, and subjects together with the minimum requirement of explanatory narration. The magnificent collection of 6,300 photographs, portraits, and facsimiles of contemporary prints was selected for inclusion according to the following criteria: "Is the picture authentic; was it made during the period it represents; and does it illustrate some significant aspect of the life of the times?" The index contains over 10,000 entries with more than 20,000 references and cross-references. This excellent album was designed as a companion to the Dictionary of American History, Atlas of American History, and Dictionary of American Biography.

Concise Dictionary of American History. Thomas Cochran, advisory ed.; Wayne Andrews, ed. New York: Scribner, 1962. 1156p. $25.00.

Based on the six-volume Dictionary of American History by James Truslow Adams, the Concise Dictionary of American History contains 2,000 articles from the original, some condensed and some printed in their complete form. Covering social, cultural, and economic forces as well as major historical events, it provides capsule summaries of items from 1492 to 1961. Well indexed, it offers a wealth of concise information at a relatively low cost. The condensed version was prepared by a large staff, many of whom assisted in preparation of the complete set.

Adams, James Truslow, ed. Dictionary of American History. New York: Scribner, 1940-1963. 6 vols. $120.00.

The Dictionary of American History, a six-volume set plus an index volume, consists of 6,425 articles dealing with the political, economic, social, industrial, and cultural history of the United States. Alphabetically arranged and averaging one fourth to one half page in length, the entries are written by over 1,000 historians. Numerous cross references appear in the work, and selected bibliographies accompany each article. The detailed index, revised in 1963, locates obscure subjects, names, and illustrations. Since the dictionary is a companion to the Dictionary of American Biography, it omits all biographical sketches. This excellent source is authoritative and comprehensive.

AMERICAN HISTORY--Specific Topics

Randel, William Peirce. The American Revolution: Mirror of a People. Maplewood, N.J.: Hammond Inc., 1973. 256p. $14.95.

This superior volume treats in narrative style life as it was during the American Revolutionary War times. Using the text and excellent color plates, portraits, reproductions of paintings, sketches, advertisements, maps, etc., the author details the most minute specifics of colonial life. All the kinds of information that interest upper elementary school children are included, e.g., schooling, food, holidays, diversions and entertainments, and so on. This beautiful volume is lovely to look at but also has potential as a useful reference source.

Boatner, Mark Mayo, III. Encyclopedia of the American Revolution. Bicentennial ed., rev. and expanded. New York: McKay, 1974. 1290p. $17.50.

Alphabetically arranged, the Encyclopedia of the American Revolution is a highly accurate source book covering the years 1763 to 1783. Nearly 2,000 entries discuss fifteen major campaigns including land actions, naval actions, political issues and events, and personalities. The biographies, which form a valuable portion of the encyclopedia, describe patriot army and navy officers and statesmen; Loyalists; British statesmen; British, French, and German officers; medical men; jurists; and clergymen. Over 50 black and white maps and diagrams and a bibliography of 400 entries add to the book. Well-written and concise, the volume provides summary information of men and events during the Revolutionary period.

Boatner, Mark Mayo. The Civil War Dictionary. 3rd ed. New York: McKay, 1959. 974p. $15.00.

Alphabetically arranged, The Civil War Dictionary briefly covers a maximum number of important topics rather than providing detailed information on fewer ones. Over one-half of the 4,000 entries are biographical, with material provided for generals on both sides, prominent civilian leaders, and famous women. Other entries include military operations, military organizations, weapons, tactics and strategy, military terms, naval matters, and political issues. Maps and diagrams are prepared by Allen C. Northrop and Lowell I. Miller. Although the material tends to be scholarly, the book could be used by interested elementary and junior high school students.

Grant, Bruce. The Cowboy Encyclopedia; The Old and the New West from the Open Range to the Dude Ranch. New York: Rand McNally, 1951. 160p. $2.65.

This alphabetically arranged dictionary covers all aspects of western range life. Entries vary in length from a few lines to two pages; entry words appear in bold type and many have pronunciations. The many illustrations and bibliography make this book more useful.

Grant, Bruce. American Forts: Yesterday and Today. New York: Dutton, 1965. 381p. $6.95.

Arranged by geographical regions, this book gives the location, history, and interesting features of forts throughout the United States. A sectional map at the beginning of each region lists the forts in that locale. A glossary, a selected bibliography, and an index to forts and states follow the main text.

Freedom Encyclopedia; American Liberties in the Making. By Frances Cavanah in collaboration with Elizabeth L. Crandall. New York: Rand McNally, 1968. 205p. $4.95.

This fine reference book, designed for intermediate level children, is an alphabetically arranged collection of influences on rights and liberties throughout America's history. From Abigail Adams to John Peter Zenger and including twentieth century leaders such as Martin Luther King and John F. Kennedy, Freedom Encyclopedia incorporates biographies and appropriate quotations, documents and books, landmarks that have been the scene of important events, terms used in discussions of liberty and human rights, and historical events involving liberty and human rights. Preceding the main body of text is the "Guide to Freedom Encyclopedia," which classifies all main entries according to the following categories: colonial quest for freedom and a new nation; documents and declarations; fundamental rights of Americans; government, law, and politics; heritage of liberty from the Old World; landmarks and museums; organizations; problems and progress in an expanding America; songs, poems, creeds, and speeches; responsibilities of freedom; the United States in war and peace; leaders in liberty; and definition of terms. A bibliography is divided into sections called "Of General Interest," and "Leaders in Liberty." An easy to use and accurate index aids in locating specific terms. Tasteful illustrations, large readable print, and an attractive format make this book invaluable.

Colby, C. B. Historical American Landmarks; From the Old North Church to the Santa Fe Trail. New York: Coward-McCann, 1968. 48p. $3.49.

Using a very brief and simple text, Colby relies heavily on photographs to describe 28 various American historical landmarks. Included are such well-known places as Plymouth Rock, Jamestown, the Statue of Liberty, etc. Although there is no index, the book is easy to use, for each entry is only one or two pages long.

Landmarks of Liberty. Maplewood, N.J.: Hammond Inc., 1970. 93p. $4.50.

Contents of this slim but useful book include the Lincoln Birthplace, Jamestown, the Mesa Verde Cliff Dwellings, the Statue of Liberty, and eighteen other shrines and monuments. It is nicely arranged, easy to use, and full of pictures. Although it duplicates some of the information in Colby's Historical American Landmarks, its treatment is much more detailed and sophisticated.

Sloane, Eric. ABC Book of Early Americana. Garden City, N.Y.: Doubleday, 1973 (c1963). unp. $4.95.

An encyclopedia in the format of an alphabet book, the ABC Book of Early Americana provides definitions and illustrations of items originating in America. Allowing two pages for each letter, the book includes such topics as almanacs, hornbooks, hex signs, cornhusk dolls, cigar-store Indians, and zig-zag fences. This valuable book offers in print and pictures information concerning old-time objects. It is appealing to older students despite the picture book format.

AMERICAN HISTORY--Documents

Reuben, Gabriel H. How Documents Preserve Freedom. Chicago: Benefic Press, 1964. 96p. $3.20.

Covered in this middle elementary level book are the Mayflower Compact, the Declaration of Independence, the Northwest Ordinance, the Constitution of the United States, the Emancipation Proclamation, and the Universal Declaration of Human Rights. For each document the author tells the events leading to it and who wrote it, gives the complete text and the location of the original text.

Morris, Richard B. and James Woodress, eds. Voices from America's Past. New York: Dutton, 1962. 3 vols. $12.95.

Providing a documentary history of America, Voices from America's Past consists of diaries, letters, biographies, memoirs, essays, and narratives by those people who were living at the time. Volume 1, "The Colonies and the New Nation," covers the period from 1607, the founding of Jamestown, to 1829, the inauguration as

History 163

President of Andrew Jackson. Volume 2, "Backwoods Democracy to World Power," extends from 1820 to the outbreak of World War I in 1914. Volume 3, "The Twentieth Century," includes documents appearing from 1914 to the 1960's; it incorporates material on World Wars I and II, the Cold War, and the Great Depression. The editors have used modern spelling and punctuation for seventeenth century writings but otherwise have not tampered with selections. Whenever possible complete texts for documents have been supplied, but occasionally cuts have been necessary. Attractive in format, this set may likely have more appeal for younger students than Commager's famous Documents of American History.

Cooke, Donald E. Our Nation's Great Heritage; The Story of the Declaration of Independence and the Constitution. Maplewood, N.J.: Hammond Inc., 1972. 223p. $14.95.

Written as living history, Our Nation's Great Heritage creates the individuals included as real, live people. Part I is a narrative description of the signing of the Declaration of Independence, the events precipitating it, and the aftermath. Part II encompasses the same sequence of events concerning the United States Constitution. Beautifully illustrated and indexed, this luxury item will probably not be a first purchase except by affluent libraries; however, it should definitely be considered for the elementary or junior high school library that can afford it.

Commager, Henry Steele, ed. Documents of American History. 9th ed. New York: Appleton-Century-Crofts, 1973. 2 vols. $14.95 text ed.

A collection of documents appearing throughout America's past, Documents of American History is a standard reference source for reprints of primary sources. Chronologically arranged, it includes the colonial charters, state charters, speeches of the Presidents, laws, important acts such as the Stamp Act, and proclamations. Helpful notes by the editor, a well-known authority, accompany the documents. Although it contains no illustrations, it is well indexed. This valuable tool is necessary for all libraries.

The Annals of America. Chicago: Encyclopaedia Britannica, 1968-71. 21 vols. $174.50.

A massive collection of original source material, The Annals of America is a chronologically arranged history of American life, action and thought from 1793 to 1968. A total of 2,202 selections includes articles, speeches, letters, songs, poems, official documents, etc. More than 5,000 illustrations and nearly 100 maps appear throughout the set, adding pictorial authenticity to the portrayal of American history. Editing this fine set are Mortimer J. Adler and Charles Van Doren, assisted by a number of staff editors and well-known historians. A special feature of the set is the two-volume Conspectus which arranges information according to "25 Great Issues in American Life." For each of the chapters there is an introduction, an overview, an outline of topics, references to all passages, cross references, and a bibliography. The final volume of the set is the Index, which contains a chronological listing of all sections in the text volumes, an alphabetical proper name index, and an author and source index. A set of transparencies accompanying Annals of America demonstrates to students how to locate material in the main text. Although smaller collections of documents may suffice for some junior high school libraries, this set is definitely recommended for those schools needing a more comprehensive compilation of original source material. Its attractive format will appeal to young teenagers.

AMERICAN HISTORY--Names, Symbols, and Stories

Krythe, Maymie R. What So Proudly We Hail. New York: Harper, 1968. 278p. $5.95.

Written in narrative style, What So Proudly We Hail is a collection of facts about American symbols and national monuments. Some of the items treated are the flag, the Great Seal, Uncle Sam, the Liberty Bell, the eagle, the Statue of Liberty, and the National Capitol. The history of each item is given as well as a complete description. The table of contents and the extensive index are necessary to locate information. A bibliography of books, magazines, booklets, and brochures is also included. Unfortunately, much-needed illustrations are omitted.

Lehner, Ernst, comp. American Symbols, A Pictorial History. New York: William Penn, 1966. 96p. $3.95. $1.95 paper.

This handy little book includes illustrations of the following symbols: seals of the colonies, homes of the leaders, costume, hope and hex signs, cattle brands, transportation signs, trademarks, social and civic organizations, colleges and universities, baseball, politics, elected leaders, the fifty states, etc. Even though the material is in black and white instead of color, it will be helpful.

Ross, Frank, Jr. Stories of the States; A Reference Guide to the 50 States and the U.S. Territories. New York: Crowell, 1969. 327p. $5.95.

An essential reference source for elementary schools, Stories of the States is alphabetically arranged by state. For each entry it gives the origin of the state name, motto, nickname, flag, song, tree, flower, bird, fish, area, climate, population, natural resources, agriculture, manufacturing, and major cities, plus approximately four pages of history. For each state there are black and white drawings of a location map, the tree, bird, flag, etc.

Arnold, Pauline and Percival White. How We Named Our States. New York: Criterion, 1965. 192p. $5.50.

History 165

Written in narrative style, How We Named Our States describes the means by which each state received its name, nickname, and capital. Also included for each state is a brief early history, including prominent persons directly related, the date of independence, and an anecdote. Arranged by regional sections from New England to the west coast, it has an adequate index to assist the user.

Shankle, George Earlie. State Names, Flags, Seals, Songs, Birds, Flowers, and Other Symbols. Rev. ed. St. Clair, Mich.: Scholarly, 1971 (reprint of 1938 ed.). 524p. $22.00.

This book is best described by its lengthy subtitle: "A study based on historical documents giving the origin and significance of the state names, nicknames, mottoes, seals, flags, flowers, birds, songs, and descriptive comments on the capitol buildings and on some of the leading state histories with facsimiles of the state flags and seals." Each topic is covered in a separate chapter and most chapters are arranged alphabetically by state. An extensive detailed index helps to locate minute facts in this interesting volume.

Earle, Olive L. State Trees. Rev. ed. New York: Morrow, 1973. unp. $4.14.

This thin book is arranged alphabetically by the names of trees serving as state symbols. Brief descriptions of the trees with legends about most of them make up the entries. Also included are the physical appearance, growing habits, and the uses of each. Detailed drawings show the seed, leaf, flower, bark, and shape of each tree. A brief index in the front of the book locates material by state.

Earle, Olive L. State Birds and Flowers. New York: Morrow, 1961. 64p. $4.14.

Alphabetically arranged by state, State Birds and Flowers shows in brief text and illustrations the symbols chosen by each state. The text explains the nesting habits and food of the various birds, and the growth habits and reproductive processes of the flowers. An outline map and the capitol of each state is drawn as well as the bird and flower. A short index in the front of the book aids in location of birds and flowers.

FLAGS

Barraclough, E. M. C. Flags of the World. Rev... with 340 flags in color and over 400 text drawings. New York: Warner, 1969. 352p. $14.95.

First published in England in 1897 under the authorship of F. E. Hulme, Flags of the World has undergone many revisions. Although it emphasizes information on Great Britain, it includes flags of the United States, Latin America, Asia, Africa, and Europe, and also international flags. Obscure flags are given, e.g., house flags of shipping companies, yacht flags, signal flags, and flags of corporations and public institutions. The book contains a bibliography and an index.

Smith, Whitney. The Flag Book of the United States. New York: Morrow, 1970. 306p. $12.95.

Utilizing both text and 270 illustrations, this book covers the history of the American flag, flags of all fifty states, state seals, important flags of the United States government and Armed Forces, and flag etiquette. A glossary and an index further its usefulness.

Crouthers, David D. Flags of American History. Maplewood, N.J.: Hammond Inc., 1973. 96p. $4.50.

Flags of American History describes in text and illustration 89 flags which have played an important role in the history of America from the European settlements to the present time. Illustrated with four-color paintings, the book contains drawings of all 50 state flags plus the historical ones. The book follows a chronological arrangement and has no index. Additional material includes the "Pledge of Allegiance," the American credo, instructions for displaying the flag, and a glossary of terms. Altogether, it is an outstanding book of great value.

THE SOCIAL SCIENCES

Social sciences in elementary and junior high schools are geared to provide an understanding of the American way of life. Beginning with home, school, and community, the curriculum expands to incorporate food, clothing, shelter, customs, holidays, etiquette, vocations, politics, transportation, communication, economics, and so forth. In some of these areas reference books for children are sparse or nonexistent. In others an abundant supply of material is available. The librarian will probably have to supplement the reference collection for these areas with trade books from the general collection.

In this chapter titles are arranged by level of difficulty, with the simplest first, under the following subheadings: general works, citizenship, costume, economics, etiquette, festivals and holidays, international relations, parliamentary procedure, political science, transportation, and vocations and careers. Particular attention has been paid to primary level material for some of these topics which are customarily taught in kindergarten and primary grades. For instance, to correlate with the study of community helpers, two titles (Richard Scarry's What Do People Do All Day? and Now You Know About People at Work) of interest to young children are included. At the opposite end of the scale are the Encyclopedia of Careers and Vocational Guidance and the NICEM Index to Vocational and Technical Education--Multimedia, different enough to challenge the brightest junior high student. In selecting material for the social sciences, the librarian should carefully examine the titles and choose only those appropriate for the age and maturity level of the students in her school.

GENERAL WORKS

Gould, Julius and W. L. Kolb, eds. A Dictionary of the Social Sciences. New York: Free Press, 1964. 761p. $19.95.

A Dictionary of the Social Sciences, compiled under the auspices of UNESCO, is an alphabetical listing of terms. For each entry the history of the term is given and its usage in the fields of political science, social anthropology, economics, social psychology, and sociology. Definitions are quite long, usually about one page. About 270 social scientists from the United Kingdom and the United States contributed to the dictionary.

Lincoln Library of the Social Sciences. 4th ed. Columbus, Ohio: Frontier Press, 1971. 3 vols. $57.95.

Patterned after the famous Lincoln Library of Essential Information, this reference work is designed to answer all questions of social studies students. It is divided into six distinct parts: history, government and politics, geography and travel, economics and useful arts, biography, and miscellany. Under these topics are a variety of specific items, e.g., commerce; communication; mining; popular superstitutions; festivals and holidays; air and water pollution; dictionaries of American history, world history, and American geography; a Hammond atlas; etc. The master index appears complete in each of the three volumes, a most useful convenience. Although some of the statistics are dated, the set will nonetheless be useful to upper elementary and junior high school students.

International Encyclopedia of the Social Sciences. David L. Sills, ed. New York: Macmillan, 1968. 17 vols. $495.00.

A monumental work produced by over 1,500 scholarly contributors, the International Encyclopedia of the Social Sciences contains 1,716 signed articles on the philosophy, conceptual problems, and major fields of anthropology, economics, nonphysical geography, psychology, sociology, and statistics. Also incorporated are biographies of 600 persons. Alphabetically arranged, the set contains numerous cross references, a good index, and bibliographies for each article. Although this set is scholarly and mature and is designed for college and adult use, many junior high school students could easily benefit from it. Where the level of difficulty is no problem, and where the expense of the set can be justified, school librarians should seriously consider the purchase of this outstanding reference set.

CITIZENSHIP

Brown, Harriett M. and Joseph F. Guadagnolo. America Is My Country; The Heritage of a Free People. New York: Houghton Mifflin, 1961. 268p. $6.50.

Despite a rather "text-bookish" format, America Is My Country is a valuable source on Americanism. Included is information on the symbols of democracy, documents of freedom, the United States capitol, patriotic landmarks and monuments, great Americans, patriotic songs and poems, and patriotic holidays. Following each chapter are sections which include vocabulary, bibliographies, and check tests. Although most of this information is available elsewhere, it is handily assembled here in one volume.

Morgan, Joy Elmer. The American Citizens Handbook. Rev. ed. Washington, D.C.: National Council for the Social Studies, 1968. 640p. $6.00.

An unbelievably large amount of information is contained in this handbook on citizenship: important documents of American history and of the United Nations; creeds, pledges and codes (for Girl Scouts, Boy Scouts, 4-H Clubs, Future Farmers of America, Future Teachers of America, etc.); information on the fifty states; the Hall of Fame; the Statue of Liberty, and considerably more. Although it was originally designed for young citizens as they reached the voting age, it is easily usable as a reference tool by upper elementary and junior high students.

COSTUME

Leeming, Joseph. The Costume Book. Philadelphia: Lippincott, 1966. 123p. $4.95.

The Costume Book presents the folk costumes of 27 different nations, fanciful and fairy tale costumes, and costumes of nine historical periods, e.g., ancient Greece, medieval Europe, and American colonial. Clear simple directions for making the costumes are included. Directions on how to cut and use a pattern, and hints on inexpensive, but effective materials are shown. Clear black and white outline drawings depict each example.

Snook, Barbara. Costumes for School Plays. Newton, Mass.: Branford, 1965. 96p. $3.75.

A useful source for instructions in all phases of costuming for school plays, this book includes simple construction notes for making medieval, Elizabethan, ancient, eighteenth century, fantasy, and peasant costumes as well as armor, accessories, properties, etc. A bibliography and an index follow the main body of text.

Purdy, Susan. Costumes for You to Make. Philadelphia: Lippincott, 1971. 121p. $4.95.

This costume book, extensively illustrated, successfully shows how to make costumes for plays, pantomines, Halloween, or costume parties. Patterns are scaled for the average ten-year-old. Every facet of costuming is included from basic costume parts to trimmings and accessories to hats, to headbands, to masks and quick disguises. Every item listed is also illustrated and has simple instructions for construction.

Hansen, Henny Harald. Costumes and Styles; 689 Examples of Historic Costume in Color. New, rev. ed. New York, Dutton, 1972. 160p. $10.00.

A beautiful book illustrated with color plates, Costumes and Styles traces the development of costume from ancient Egypt to the present. The author likens clothing styles to architectural styles and throughout the book describes clothing in terms of history. The book is intriguing for the browser as well as useful for the student searching for specific fashions of a particular period in history.

Wilcox, R. Turner. Five Centuries of American Costume. New
York: Scribner, 1963. 207p. $12.95.

Clothing worn in both North and South America is described
and illustrated in Five Centuries of American Costume. Costumes
of American Indians, military dress from the sixteenth century on,
and children's clothing from the sixteenth century through the twentieth are all included. In each chapter, the text is followed by approximately ten pages of drawings.

Gorsline, Douglas. What People Wore; A Visual History of Dress
From Ancient Times to Twentieth Century America. New
York: Viking, 1952. 266p. $12.95.

Comprehensive in scope, What People Wore traces with text
and illustrations costumes on a world-wide scale from ancient times
to the twentieth century. It is divided into three parts: the Ancient
World, European costume, and American costume. Over 1,800 line
drawings and color paintings are sketched from tapestries, paintings, and other art sources. Extensive bibliographies are included.
The author throughout attempts to portray the people who wore the
costumes. For example, he shows that the American way of life
created variations in clothing.

Wilcox, R. Turner. The Dictionary of Costume. New York:
Scribner, 1969. 406p. $15.00.

This excellent reference book contains more than 3,200 alphabetically arranged entries pertaining to costume. Broad in
scope, it covers all periods of history throughout the whole world.
Entries include items of clothing, fabrics, accessories, styling,
tools, terms, and brief biographies. Numerous drawings illustrate
the text. The brief, concise entries are cross-referenced throughout the work. A rather long bibliography is appended. This volume
is a first purchase item for junior high schools and should be considered where needed for upper elementary schools.

ECONOMICS

Saunders, Rubie. Smart Shopping and Consumerism. New York:
Watts, 1973. 63p. $3.95.

This handy, readable guide to consumerism suggests practical tips on money, buying, bank accounts, and credit. It also offers wise words on shopping manners as well as buying clothes,
gifts, restaurant meals, groceries, cosmetics and other items. It
even discusses shoplifting, mail order buying, book and record
clubs, and provides sample budgets.

Paradis, Adrian A. The Economics Reference Book. New York:
Chilton, 1970. 191p. $5.95.

The Social Sciences   171

Utilizing a dictionary arrangement with many cross references, and an index, The Economics Reference Book provides junior high students with easy access to information on economics. It defines common terms in economics, identifies prominent economists, and describes the various agencies, institutions, and organizations concerned with economics. Appended is an extensive bibliography arranged by subject.

Paradis, Adrian A. The Labor Reference Book. New York: Chilton, 1972. 234p. $5.95.

Prepared as a companion volume to The Economics Reference Book, The Labor Reference Book is also alphabetically arranged. Entries include brief biographies of labor leaders and information on the United States labor movement. A good bibliography is appended.

ETIQUETTE

Hoke, Helen. Etiquette: Your Ticket to Good Times. New York: Watts, 1970. 66p. $3.95.

This First Book is designed for children in middle elementary grades. It covers the usual aspects of etiquette--table manners, parties, letter writing, telephone etiquette--but is simply written and utilizes many quizzes and illustrations.

Young, Marjabelle and Ann Buchwald. Stand Up, Shake Hands, Say "How Do You Do." New York: McKay, 1969. 134p. $5.95.

Subtitled "What boys need to know about today's manners," this book is so precise and interestingly written that even reluctant boys may pick it up. An intriguing foreword by humorist Art Buchwald is followed by chapters on such topics as good sportsmanship, locker room manners, spectator sports, parties, grooming, table manners, traveling, and so on. Young men in both elementary and junior high schools will use this guide.

Post, Elizabeth L. The Emily Post Book of Etiquette for Young People. New York: Funk and Wagnalls, 1967. 238p. $6.95.

This etiquette book contains several chapters on each of the following topics: Etiquette begins at home, When you're in public, Your personal appearance, The art of conversation, Correspondence, Everyday manners, Dating data, Travel talk, Tipping at a glance, Entertaining and being entertained. Not readily outdated, this book is a good choice for junior high schools.

Haupt, Enid A. The New Seventeen Book of Etiquette and Young Living. New York: McKay, 1970. 325p. $7.95.

This rather sophisticated work is carefully written so as not to be easily outdated. It covers topics such as boys and dates, telephone etiquette, clubs, travel, college, work, and weddings. A thorough index helps in locating specific information. This guide will be especially popular in junior high schools.

FESTIVALS AND HOLIDAYS

Reck, Alma Kehoe. The First Book of Festivals Around the World. New York: Watts, 1957. 60p. $3.95.

Following the usual format of the First Book series, The First Book of Festivals tells how people celebrate their special festivals in Italy, Peru, Japan, England, Finland, Turkey, China, Mexico, and the United States. Illustrated by Helen Borton, the book contains an index to assist the user. A special feature is the explanation of the word "festival."

Meyer, Robert. Festivals U.S.A. and Canada. Rev. ed. New York: Washburn, 1970. 280p. $5.95.

An extremely valuable reference tool, Festivals U.S.A. and Canada describes annual events, festivals, special exhibits and contests. Arranged first by category then by state and province, it includes not only the festivals with their special features, inauguration dates, and average attendance, but reports on special attractions and gives historic landmarks, national parks, and the state's flower and bird. Broad in scope, the book encompasses all activities related to festivals, such as art exhibits and fishing derbies.

Krythe, Maymie R. All About American Holidays. New York: Harper, 1962. 275p. $5.95.

Arranged chronologically by the calendar, this book presents the history of more than fifty holidays. For each the author tells how it originated and how it is observed today. Whenever applicable, entries describe specific customs, e.g., for Christmas there is the history of caroling, trees, gifts, decorations, Yule log, etc. Long bibliographies and an index are also included.

Sechrist, Elizabeth Hough. Red Letter Days; A Book of Holiday Customs. Rev. ed. Philadelphia: Macrae Smith, 1965. 253p. $5.95.

From New Year's Day to Christmas, each of 21 major holidays is covered in a chapter. Twenty-eight lesser holidays receive brief, one- or two-paragraph treatment. The most valuable material included in the entries is probably the history and origin of customs for each holiday. The source is a must for elementary schools.

The Social Sciences 173

Dobler, Lavinia. National Holidays Around the World. New York: Fleet, 1968. 234p. $6.50.

This book is arranged by month, with each country arranged chronologically according to the date of its national holiday. In each entry is a description of the holiday and a brief history of it. The unfortunate inclusion of a description of each country's anthem without the words and flag without illustration detracts slightly from the book's usefulness. Nevertheless, it should be of assistance in upper elementary school students' study of nations around the world.

Dobler, Lavinia. Customs and Holidays Around the World. Written under the supervision of Howard V. Harper. New York: Fleet, 1962. 234p. $6.00.

Arranged according to the four seasons, Customs and Holidays Around the World discusses holidays, primarily religious, celebrated in many countries. Although it emphasizes Christian holidays, it also includes those of Judaism, Islam, Buddhism, and other religions. A selective bibliography, a comprehensive index, and a pronunciation key are all helpful. Many three-color illustrations add to the book.

Lipkind, William. Days to Remember, An Almanac. New York: Obolensky, 1961. unp. $3.95.

Arranged chronologically according to the days of the calendar, Days to Remember provides brief entries describing the importance of special days, such as birthdays, dates of events, holidays, and seasons. Information explains how these days came to be celebrated, how they are celebrated, and shows items of special interest about the four seasons. Illustrations by Jerome Snyder appear throughout the book. An index locates names of persons and events.

Hazeltine, Mary Emogene. Anniversaries and Holidays; A Calendar of Days and How to Observe Them. 2nd ed. completely rev. with the editorial assistance of Judith K. Sollenberger. Chicago: American Library Association, 1944. 316p. $7.00.

This book shows in calendar form the names of important people and memorable events and how to celebrate each anniversary and holiday. Following the main text are bibliographies about the holidays, special days and seasons, and about the people referred to in the calendar. An index is available to aid in finding information.

Douglas, George William. American Book of Days. Rev. by Helen Douglas Compton. 2nd ed. New York: Wilson, 1948. 697p. $10.00.

American Book of Days bears the subtitle "A Compendium of

Information About Holidays, Festivals, Notable Anniversaries and Christian and Jewish Holy Days with Notes on Other American Anniversaries Worthy of Remembrance." Arranged chronologically according to the days on the calendar, it contains an extensive index to aid in location of material. Special features of this book are the Zodiac signs and rhymes of the days and the seasons.

INTERNATIONAL RELATIONS

Epstein, Edna. The United Nations. Rev. ed. 8th ed. New York: Watts, 1973. 88p. $3.95.

This "First Book" provides brief, easy to read material on the United Nations. It includes the Preamble to the Charter, a list of commissions, a list of specialized agencies, a chronology of the United Nations, special terms, and a list of member nations. Much information is packed into this small, simple-to-use volume.

Chamberlin, Waldo and others. A Chronology and Fact Book of the United Nations, 1941-1969. 3rd rev. ed. Dobbs Ferry, N.Y.: Oceana, 1970. 234p. $7.50.

Rather difficult to use and printed in very small type, this book is nonetheless a valuable source for identifying matters pertaining to the United Nations. In addition to the chronology, it contains the complete text of the United Nations Charter and the rules of procedure.

Plano, Jack C. and Roy Olten. International Relations Dictionary. New York: Holt, 1969. 337p. $4.50.

To cover all aspects of international relations, this dictionary is divided into twelve topics, such as geography and population, international economics, war and military policy, ideology and communication, American foreign policy, etc. Within each category the terms are alphabetically arranged. The simple attractive format somewhat compensates for the difficulty of the content. This book should be considered for junior high schools where information of this nature is needed.

PARLIAMENTARY PROCEDURE

Powers, David Guy. First Book of How to Run a Meeting. New York: Watts, 1967. 62p. $3.95. $.95 paper.

An introduction to parliamentary procedure, the First Book of How to Run a Meeting is written for the intermediate level student. The basics are included, e.g., how to run a meeting, how to make a motion, how to take a vote, how to make committee reports, and how to conduct an election. In the appendix are a sample constitution, a simplified chart of motions, and a glossary.

The Social Sciences 175

Bailard, Virginia and Harry C. McKnown. So You Were Elected! 3rd ed. New York: McGraw-Hill, 1966. 264p. $4.72.

Designed for upper elementary and junior high students, So You Were Elected! provides readable information on all aspects of club work. Using outlines, charts, photographs, and dialogs, it discusses topics from parliamentary procedure to being a successful committee member. Also covered are the duties of the officers, how to handle and account for funds, how to be a leader, and how to be a helper. A helpful index and a bibliography are included.

Robert, Henry M. Robert's Rules of Order, Newly Revised. New & enl. ed. by Sarah Corbin Robert & others. Glenview, Ill.: Scott, Foresman, 1970. 594p. $6.75. N.Y: Morrow, 1970. $1.45 paper.

First published in 1876, Robert's Rules of Order presents the standard rules for conducting meetings. Part I of the book consists of the rules of order, a compendium of parliamentary law based upon the rules and practices of Congress. Part II is the organization and conduct of business, an explanation of the methods of organizing and conducting the business of societies, conventions, and other assemblies. Although it is somewhat difficult, it can be used by elementary and junior high school students.

POLITICAL SCIENCE

Alvarez, Joseph A. Politics in America. Mankato, Minn.: Creative Education, 1971. 95p. $5.95.

A rather elementary dissertation on the subject of American politics, this book discusses the party system, leaders and images, lobbies, state power, political power and the new politics. Filled with drawings, cartoons, and photography, it explains and defines in context all important italicized terms. In a special section called "Useful Information," it contains three pages of definitions, a page of recommended books, and a page of recommended booklets. Its interesting text and appealing format make this a usable book for upper elementary children.

Johnson, Gerald W. The Presidency. New York: Morrow, 1962. 128p. $4.75.

Although this book is somewhat out of date, written with John F. Kennedy as the current President of the United States, it provides important information about what the President does. It lists and expounds upon the five duties listed in the Constitution, tells how the Presidency has changed and developed over the years, and describes how the office expanded under six specific Presidents.

Johnson, Gerald W. The Supreme Court. New York: Morrow,
    1962. 127p. $5.11.

    This readable book describes how the Supreme Court functions, how the Justices are chosen, and what they do. It also provides a narrative history of the Supreme Court including special attention to outstanding Chief Justices. Appended is a list of the Justices of the United States Supreme Court.

Johnson, Gerald W. The Cabinet. New York: Morrow, 1966.
    160p. $4.95.

    A very readable book, The Cabinet contains a concise description of each of the departments of the United States President's Cabinet and tells the duties and responsibilities of the incumbant. It also narrates the history of the Cabinet's development from George Washington to 1966, and discusses the future of the Cabinet.

Johnson, Gerald W. The Congress. New York: Morrow, 1963.
    128p. $4.95.

    Chapter I of The Congress comprises a full fifty pages of fact-by-fact details on how Congress works. It gives the size of Congress, how numbers of members are determined and elected and their qualifications, the kinds of committees, etc. The lengthy chapters cover the history of Congress and are followed by lists of Speakers of the House of Representatives, Vice Presidents of the United States, and Standing Committees of the Senate and the House of Representatives.

Dunner, Joseph. Dictionary of Political Science. Totowa, N.J.:
    Littlefield, Adams, 1970 (c1964). 585p. $3.95 paper.

    The Dictionary of Political Science is prepared by over 100 contributors and defines terms, events, and personalities involved in political science. Varying from brief definitions to entries of several pages in length, the dictionary is clearly written and is usable by junior high school students who have need of such material.

Smith, Edward C. and Arnold J. Zurcher. Dictionary of American
    Politics. 2nd ed. New York: Barnes and Noble, 1968.
    434p. $5.50. $2.95 paper.

    More than 3,800 terms are listed in alphabetical order and defined in this dictionary. For each entry the authors give the definition, a clause showing the application of the word to a specific subject, a usage clause, and an etymological clause. Terms included are similar to the following: Good Neighbor Policy, Mayflower Compact, Cuba Missile Confrontation, Creeping Socialism, Scottsboro Cases, etc. Covered in the work are the fields of comparative government, political theory, constitutional law, international law, public administration, and social welfare. The appendix includes information for each state, the Presidents of the United States, and the Constitution of the United States.

The Social Sciences   177

Plano, Jack C. and Milton Greenberg. American Political Dictionary. 3rd ed. New York: Holt, 1972. 462p. $7.95.

    The American Political Dictionary is arranged by eighteen broad topics, e.g., United States Constitution, civil liberties, finance and taxation, foreign policy, the legislative process, etc. Over 1,100 terms, agencies, court cases, and statutes are listed under these topics and clearly and concisely defined. A complete index compensates for the topical arrangement and aids ready reference. Considerably more complete but less easy to use than the Dictionary of American Politics, it should be available as a complementary reference work.

Barone, Michael and others. The Almanac of American Politics: The Senators, the Representatives--Their Records, States and Districts. 1974. 2d. ed. Boston: Gambit, 1974. 1240p. $15.00. $6.95 paper.

    Arranged alphabetically by state, The Almanac of American Politics describes each state and district and gives a biographical sketch and photograph of each Senator and Representative. An important appendix lists Senate Committees, House Committees, national outlays, defense contractors, and outline maps alphabetically arranged of each state depicting its districts.

The Book of the States. Lexington, Ky.: The Council of State
    Governments, 1935-   . Biennial. $13.50. $19.50 with supplements.

    Published every two years, the Book of the States provides detailed information on the structures, working methods, financing, and functional activities of the state governments. Major divisions include Constitutions and Elections, Legislatures and Legislation, The Judiciary, Administrative Organization, Finance, Inter-governmental Relations, Major State Services, and The State Pages. The latter section, arranged alphabetically by state, gives major officers, supreme court members, and other vital statistics. Packed with facts, this book affords access to much hard-to-locate material.

United States Congress. Official Congressional Directory. 92nd
    Congress, 2d session. Washington, D.C.: U.S. Government Printing Office, 1809-   . Annual. $6.80. $5.05 paper.

    Members of the Senate and the House of Representatives are listed in this directory. Also included are members of committees, and officers of governmental departments as well as diagrams of the Capitol Building and maps of each Congressional district.

U.S. National Archives & Records Service. Office of the Federal
    Register. United States Government Organizational Manual. Washington, D.C.: Government Printing Office, 1935-   . Annual. $3.00 paper.

Revised annually, the United States Government Organization Manual is an authoritative source of information concerning the nation's government. Covering the executive, legislative, and judicial branches of the federal government, it lists for each department the officials, organization, activities, and responsibilities. It includes the text of the Constitution and a directory of 5,000 key government officials, including members of Congress. Charts showing the organization of the various agencies are appended. An extensive index is incorporated.

TRANSPORTATION

Zaffo, George. Giant Nursery Book of Things That Go; Fire Engines, Trains, Boats, Trucks, Airplanes. Garden City, N.Y.: Doubleday, 1959. 189p. $5.95.

Using large, bold illustrations of fire engines, trains, boats, trucks, and airplanes, this book has only one small line of text per page. It is a valuable source book for all primary students and teachers who are seeking material on transportation. Much information is readily available for the non-reading child in the full page or 2-page spread drawings.

Scarry, Richard. Richard Scarry's Hop Aboard: Here We Go! Racine, Wis.: Western, 1972. 48p. $2.95.

Written and illustrated by the popular Richard Scarry, this book contains a fine collection of material suited to the kindergarten teacher's unit on transportation. Divided into four parts, it includes cars, buses, and trucks; airplanes, aircraft, and spacecraft; trains and locomotives; and ships and boats. For each topic there is an illustration with a one line description. While the book is not designed as a reference book, it certainly can be used profitably by preschool and primary students.

Zehavi, A. M., ed. The Complete Junior Encyclopedia of Transportation. New York: Watts, 1973. 280p. $8.95.

This handy encyclopedia is arranged alphabetically from aerodynamics to wheels, and covers just about all areas of transportation, including such diverse topics as the Suez Canal, jet propulsion, driver education, and gyroscopes. The signed articles are either lifted completely or abridged somewhat from the New Book of Knowledge and therefore are authoritative and accurate. The long entries fully resemble the encyclopedia entries with numerous subheadings, boxes of special information, and illustrations and photographs. A lengthy index aids in tracking down detailed facts. An outstanding volume, this reference book collects all the information on a popular elementary school subject and places it in one easy to use source. It successfully utilizes the research done for a major juvenile encyclopedia to form a reliable work on a specific topic.

The Social Sciences 179

Georgano, G. N., ed. Complete Encyclopedia of Motorcars, 1885 to the Present. Rev. ed. New York: Dutton, 1973. 640p. $30.00.

Alphabetically arranged by the name of the automobile, the Complete Encyclopedia of Motorcars 1885 to the Present describes 4,100 different cars. The editor claims that every car ever made is included. More than 2,000 photographs are incorporated in the book. Glossaries and indexes are available to assist the user.

Bucknall, Rixon. Trains. New York: Grosset and Dunlap, 1971. 46p. $1.95.

A history of trains from the steam engine pioneers to the futuristic hovertrains, this book is filled with illustrations, both black and white and color. Easy to read and attractive, Trains will be a fine supplement to the study of American history by upper elementary school students.

Ellis, Hamilton. The Pictorial Encyclopedia of Railways. New York: Crown, 1968. $10.00.

The 150-year history of the railroad is portrayed in this encyclopedia. The book contains 830 photographs which depict viaducts, stations, carriage interiors, signal systems, steam elevateds, subways, monorails, and inclined railways. Steam, electric, and diesel engines are all shown.

Munson, Kenneth. Aircraft. New York: Grosset and Dunlap, 1971. 46p. $1.95.

Covering the history of aircraft from the beginning to the present time, this book touches upon the history, technology, aerodynamics, navigation, and the problems of supersonic transport. Illustrated with both black and white and color pictures, this attractive volume will be useful for upper elementary school students.

Ahnstrom, D. N. The Complete Book of Jets and Rockets. Rev. and enl. new ed. New York: World, 1970. 184p. $6.50.

A narrative history illustrated with black and white photographs and drawings, this volume covers a variety of topics related to jets and rockets, e.g., discovery of jet propulsion, problems of propulsion, protection for the pilot, filling stations in the sky, how to become a jet pilot, and the age of rockets. Appended is a glossary of aerospace age terms.

Air Facts and Feats. John W. R. Taylor, Michael J. H. Taylor, and David Mondey, eds. 2nd ed. New York: Two Continents, 1974 (c1973). 288p. $8.95.

A fascinating volume, Air Facts and Feats contains a vast amount of information relating to aviation. Facts are organized under the following chapter titles: pioneers of the air, military aviation, maritime aviation, route-proving and commercial aviation, lighter-than-air, rotorcraft, flying for sport and competition, and rocketry and spaceflight. Material included appears in short paragraphs with bold headings or in tabular form. Illustrated with 200 photographs, the book includes 16 pages in full color. Appendices include air speed records, and aviation's worst diasters. A bibliography and index complete this book which will be interesting browsing as well as ready reference for upper elementary and junior high school students.

Benson, Brian. Ships. New York: Grosset and Dunlap, 1971. 46p. $1.95.

This well-illustrated book covers the history of ships from the first boats made by man to present day pleasure boats. Ships of various types are clearly drawn with their parts labeled and are carefully described in the easy to read text. Somewhat simpler than Knight's Ships, this attractive title will appeal especially to upper elementary school students.

Knight, Frank. Ships. New York: Crowell-Collier, 1969. 64p. $3.95.

A history of ships in reverse chronological order, this book contains chapters on ships of the nuclear age, the cargo ship--present day, the Atlantic wonder ships 1906-66, modern passenger ships, the warship--the present day, times of change 1900-1950, the windjammers 1870-1920, the steamer grows up 1800-1900, iron ships, the great days of sail 1800-1870, the ocean-conquering ship 1450-1750, round ships and long ships, and in the beginning. Illustrated with excellent photographs, over fifty in full color, Ships will enhance the study of history for upper elementary and junior high students.

VOCATIONS AND CAREERS

NICEM Index to Vocational and Technical Education--Multimedia. 2nd ed. Los Angeles: National Information Center for Educational Media. $26.50 paper. $18.50 microfiche. (18,000 entries).

In this NICEM index are more than 18,000 titles in a variety of non-book formats dealing with both general and specific aspects of vocational and technical education. Entries give title, series, release date, technical description, LC card number, producer/distributor code, and an annotation. The subject index and directory of producers/distributors will prove helpful. While this book is rather expensive for individual school libraries to purchase, it should be available to them from the district media center.

The Social Sciences   181

Scarry, Richard. Richard Scarry's What Do People Do All Day?
   New York: Random, 1968. 95p. $4.99.

    Huckle, Lowly Worm and the entire Richard Scarry gang appear in this popular book on vocations. Preschool and primary children will enjoy studying community helpers with the aid of this delightful picture book. This is an essential title for the primary library.

Now You Know About People at Work. Chicago: Encyclopaedia
   Britannica, 1974. 5 books, 5 records or cassettes. $52.50.

    Designed as a career orientation program for early childhood, Now You Know About People at Work consists of a series of five books accompanied by five records or cassettes on which the text has been recorded. Included in the set are the following titles: Who Works, Where People Work, When People Work, Why People Work, and Work You Can Do. Well organized and presented, the set provides excellent information for primary level students who cannot read well enough to glean factual information on their own. Although the books are not designed as reference books per se, each is short enough for the user to locate material by browsing. The entire set is also available in a Spanish edition.

Ferguson, J. G., ed. Concise Handbook of Occupations. Rev. ed.
   Garden City, N.Y.: Doubleday, 1974. $11.95.

    This alphabetically arranged source lists 305 jobs ranging in educational requirements from an eighth grade certificate to a Ph.D. Each one-page, alphabetically arranged entry gives the type of work done, necessary personal qualities, educational requirements, average earnings, working conditions, advancement possibilities, and long-range employment outlook. It certainly fulfills its purpose of providing extensive information in a concise format.

The Encyclopedia of Careers and Vocational Guidance. William E.
   Hopke, ed. Chicago: J. G. Ferguson, 1972. 2 vols.
   $39.50. (Dist. by Doubleday & Co.)

    A unique and indispensable set, The Encyclopedia of Careers and Vocational Guidance brings together a wealth of varied information. Vol. 1, "Planning Your Career," consists of broad articles written by different specialists, and describing opportunities in the major fields. Vol. 2, "Careers and Occupations," describes specific occupations, jobs, trades, specialities, and professions. For each is given a definition, the history, the nature of the work, the requirements, opportunities for experience and exploration, methods of entering, advancement, employment outlook, earnings, conditions of work, and the social and psychological factors. Altogether, the book includes descriptions of about 650 career opportunities. Attractive in format, it contains about 600 black and white illustrations. It is simply written in an appealing style. Usable by students, teachers, parents and guidance counselors, The Encyclopedia of Careers and Vocational Guidance is a must for elementary and junior high school libraries.

United States Bureau of Labor Statistics. Occupational Outlook Handbook. Washington, D. C. : U. S. Government Printing Office. 1949- . Biennial. $6.25.

Published biennially, this valuable guide shows the trends and prospects for all major occupations. For each it gives the potential earnings, qualifications, working conditions, outlook for the future and sources for further information. It is arranged alphabetically by type of occupation.

Splaver, Sarah. Your Career If You're Not Going to College. Rev. ed. New York: Messner, 1971. 224p. $4.79.

Treating each major job classification in a separate chapter, this book covers occupations that require varying amounts of training and apprenticeship. For each specific vocation, the author indicates the qualifications, duties, training, and the future outlook. Sources of further information are appended.

Lovejoy, Clarence E. Lovejoy's Career and Vocational School Guide; A Source Book, Clue Book and Directory of Job Training Opportunities. 4th enl. rev. ed. New York: Simon & Schuster, 1973. 184p. $7.95. $3.95 paper.

This valuable source book brings together much information on vocational training institutions for a wide variety of occupations such as airline jobs, health services work, truck driving, and so on. It is arranged alphabetically by vocation, then alphabetically by state, and then alphabetically by institution. The guide also lists a capsule description of the schools including the type of training offered, fees, length of course, and admission requirements.

Lovejoy, Clarence E. Lovejoy's College Guide, A Complete Reference Book to about 3500 American Colleges & Universities. New York: Simon and Schuster, 1974. 406p. $8.95.

Lovejoy's College Guide discusses pertinent topics, such as costs, scholarships, loans, admissions, selecting a college and college religious groups. It also contains a section arranged alphabetically by state with the colleges in each state alphabetized, and vital statistics for each college to assist the user in evaluating and choosing.

Cass, James and Max Birnbaum. Comparative Guide to Junior and Two-Year Community Colleges. New York: Harper, 1972. 396p. $10.00. $3.95 paper.

Providing concise information on all types of two-year colleges, this guide contains descriptive entries covering admissions policies, academic environment, religious orientation, and campus

The Social Sciences

life for each school listed. The series of indexes include the State Index, the Religious Index, Institutions conferring the largest number of associate degrees, and others.

Cass, James and Max Birnbaum. <u>Comparative Guide to American Colleges</u>; general ed. for students and parents. 6th ed. New York: Harper, 1973. 916p. $5.95 paper.

Concise, evaluative information is provided for American colleges and universities in this alphabetical guide. Topics covered include the character of the school, admission policies, academic environment, campus life, regulations regarding student conduct, graduation requirements, and so on. Among the useful indexes are the State Index, Selectivity Index, Religious Index, and Institutions Conferring the largest number of baccalaureate degrees in selected fields.

ETHNIC GROUPS IN AMERICA

With emphasis today on understanding the many cultural and ethnic groups in America, the school library must do its part by providing a collection of reference materials about the various groups. Fortunately, in the last few years a number of books have been published dealing with minority groups. While many of these are trade books rather than reference books, at least there is now material available at the elementary school level. The books range in sophistication from the primary source material included in Makers of America to narrative descriptions such as Manana Is Now. Bibliographies of information in both print and non-print formats have been published by a number of presses.

Titles in this chapter have been arranged under the following subheadings: general works, series, American Indians, Asian Americans, Black Americans, Jewish Americans, and Spanish-speaking Americans. The general works consist of sources covering a number of ethnic groups. The books in series are not reference books in the strictest sense; but they are included because they discuss minority and ethnic groups not covered in other sources, e.g., The Czechs and Slavaks in America. Unevenness in the quantity of materials listed for specific groups indicates unevenness in the published output. On the whole, however, enough material is available to develop an adequate reference collection.

GENERAL WORKS

Carlson, Ruth Kearney. Emerging Humanity; Multi-Ethnic Literature for Children and Adolescents. Dubuque, Iowa: Brown, 1972. 246p. $3.95 paper.

This book consists of eight chapters in which the author describes and interprets literature available about various ethnic groups. Although the text itself is thought-provoking for librarians and teachers, the most valuable part of the book is probably the extensive graded bibliographies following each chapter.

Jackson, Anne, ed. Contributions of Ethnic Groups. Little Rock, Ark.: Arkansas State Dept. of Educ., 1970. 153p. $1.00.

This list of books, films and recordings is arranged by the

following ethnic groups: American Indians, Black Americans, Mexican Americans, and Oriental Americans. Each group is further subdivided into elementary and high school levels. Entries, arranged by Dewey number, give author, title, publisher, date, pagination, price, and annotation. An author-title index aids in locating items in the classified arrangement.

Johnson, Harry A. Guide to Media and Materials on Ethnic American Minorities. New York: Bowker, 1975. 375p.

Similar to the author's Multimedia Materials for Afro-American Studies, this bibliography lists materials for American Indians, Spanish-Americans, Asian-Americans, and Afro-Americans, plus a special section for other ethnic and economic groups such as the Appalachians, Jews, Eskimos, Migrants, etc. Films, audio tapes, video tapes, slides, transparencies, and recordings are included. Bibliographic and ordering data and an annotation accompany each entry.

Keating, Charlotte Matthews. Building Bridges of Understanding Between Cultures. Tucson, Ariz.: Palo Verde, 1971. 233p. $7.95.

An excellent bibliography listing titles to aid young people in understanding other ethnic groups and cultures, Bridges of Understanding is arranged first by ethnic group and then by three reading levels: Preschool and primary, upper elementary, and junior and senior high. Entries are presented alphabetically by author in each category and give title, publisher, date, age level, and rather long critical annotations. Titles suited for Adult Basic Education are so indicated. Section titles include Black Americans, Indians and Eskimos, Spanish-Speaking Americans, Asian Americans, Nationality groups and religious minorities, Selections with multi-ethnic representation, Books for bilingual/bicultural children, Books that belong but don't fit, Africa, Asia, Caribbean, and Mexico. This valuable source will serve as a checklist and will also aid librarians in reader guidance.

Makers of America. Wayne Moquin, ed. Chicago: Encyclopaedia Britannica, 1971. 10 vols. $83.50.

Chronologically arranged, Makers of America is a documentary history of ethnic pluralism in America. Using more than 700 selections from original source materials, the ten-volume set represents more than 85 different ethnic, national, and religious groups. Printed in large, clear print, the set contains over 1,000 illustrations. Volume titles include: The firstcomers: 1536-1800; Builders of a new nation: 1801-1848; Seekers after freedom: 1849-1870; Seekers after wealth: 1871-1890; Natives and aliens: 1891-1903; The new immigrants: 1904-1913; Hyphenated Americans: 1914-1924; Children of the melting pot: 1925-1938; Refugees and victims: 1939-1954; and Emergent minorities: 1955-1970. Incorporated in volume 10 are the bibliography of recommended readings;

the ethnic index; the proper name index; the topical index; the author-source index; and the illustration index. Pulling together more documentary material on minorities than any other current reference book, this set contains original material in the form of diaries, letters, readings, newspaper editorials, speeches, and congressional debates. Attractive and readable, Makers of America is definitely recommended for junior high schools and for upper elementary schools where such sophisticated source material is needed.

Nichols, Margaret S. and Margaret N. O'Neill. Multicultural Bibliography for Preschool Through Second Grade: in the Areas of Black, Spanish-Speaking, Asian American, and Native American Cultures. Available from Multicultural Resources, P. O. Box 2945, Stanford, Calif. 94305. 40p. $2.00.

According to the Foreword, this bibliography "lists the early childhood sections of a widely recognized collection of multicultural materials for all ages and reading abilities." Its contents include Black culture, Spanish-speaking cultures, Asian American cultures, native American cultures, multicultural, pictures and posters, materials for teachers and parents, multiethnic bibliographies, directory of publishers, and title index. Entries, arranged alphabetically by author, give title, publisher, date, and price. This useful little book will be a valuable checklist for librarians in elementary schools.

Spache, George D. Good Reading for the Disadvantaged Reader: Multi-Ethnic Resources. Champaign, Ill.: Garrard, 1970. 201p. $4.25 paper.

Emphasizing the need for an individual's positive self-concept, this book presents guidelines for aiding a minority child in developing one. Lists of books and other resources ranging from primary to secondary levels in all subject areas are presented. Minority groups receiving special attention are Black Americans, American Indians, Mexican Americans, Oriental Americans, and Puerto Ricans.

SERIES

America Is Also Series (Putnam)

Goldhurst, Richard. America Is Also Jewish. New York: Putnam, 1973. 128p. $3.89.
Malmberg, Carl. America Is Also Scandinavian. New York: Putnam, 1970, 126p. $3.89.
Mangione, Jerre. America Is Also Italian. New York: Putnam, 1969. 126p. $3.89.
Webb, Robert N. America Is Also Irish. New York: Putnam, 1973. 128p. $3.89.

Ethnic Groups in America

Designed for junior high school students but usable by younger ones, this series attempts to show why various groups emigrated from their native lands to America and how they fared in the new country. How the people arrived in America, where and how they settled, and the skills and trades they brought with them make up the bulk of each volume. This series is somewhat different from either the Messner or the Lerner series on ethnic groups.

Helped Build America Series (Messner)

Dowdell, Dorothy and Joseph Dowdell. The Japanese Helped Build America. New York: Messner, 1970. 96p. $4.50.
Gay, Kathlyn. The Germans Helped Build America. New York: Messner, 1971. 96p. $4.50.
Kurtis, Arlene Harris. The Jews Helped Build America. New York: Messner, 1970. 95p. $4.50.
McDonnell, Virginia B. The Irish Helped Build America. New York: Messner, 1969. 96p. $4.50.

This series of books deals with specific ethnic groups which immigrated to America. Each of the slim volumes tells about the homeland of the group, how they arrived in America, where they settled, what types of work they did, and how they kept their customs and holidays. In each book, the author tells of the group's struggles and accomplishments in its adopted land. The series is best suited for use with upper elementary school children.

In America Series (Lerner)

Bagai, Leona B. The East Indians and Pakistanis in America. Minneapolis: Lerner, 1967. 61p. $3.95.
Butwin, Frances. The Jews in America. Minneapolis: Lerner, 1969. 107p. $3.95.
Cates, Edwin H. The English in America. Minneapolis: Lerner, 1966. 70p. $3.95.
Eubank, Nancy. The Russians in America. Minneapolis: Lerner, 1973. 94p. $3.95.
Gracza, Rezsoe and Margaret Gracza. The Hungarians in America. Minneapolis: Lerner, 1969. 76p. $3.95.
Grossman, Ronald. The Italians in America. Minneapolis: Lerner, 1966. 62p. $3.95.
Hillbrand, Percie V. The Norwegians in America. Minneapolis: Lerner, 1967. 79p. $3.95.
Hillbrand, Percie V. The Swedes in America. Minneapolis: Lerner, 1966. 79p. $3.95.
Johnson, James E. The Irish in America. Minneapolis: Lerner, 1966. 78p. $3.95.
Johnson, James E. The Scots and Scotch-Irish in America. Minneapolis: Lerner, 1966. 86p. $3.95.
Jones, Claire. The Chinese in America. Minneapolis: Lerner, 1972. 95p. $3.95.
Jones, Jayne C. The Greeks in America. Minneapolis: Lerner, 1969. 78p. $3.95.

Jones, Jayne Clark. The American Indian in America. Minneapolis: Lerner, 1973. 2 vols. $3.95 each vol.
Kunz, Virginia B. The French in America. Minneapolis: Lerner, 1966. 94p. $3.95.
Kunz, Virginia Brainard. The Germans in America. Minneapolis: Lerner, 1966. 85p. $3.95.
Kuropas, Myron B. The Ukrainians in America. Minneapolis: Lerner, 1972. 86p. $3.95.
Larsen, Ronald J. The Puerto Ricans in America. Minneapolis: Lerner, 1973. 87p. $3.95.
Leathers, Noel L. The Japanese in America. Minneapolis: Lerner, 1967. 70p. $3.95.
Pinchot, Jane. The Mexicans in America. Minneapolis: Lerner, 1973. 99p. $3.95.
Roucek, Joseph S. The Czechs and Slovaks in America. Minneapolis: Lerner, 1967. 70p. $3.95.
Spangler, Earl. The Negro in America. Minneapolis: Lerner, 1966. 93p. $3.95.
tenZythoff, Gerrit. The Dutch in America. Minneapolis: Lerner, 1969. 98p. $3.95.
Wytrwal, Joseph. The Poles in America. Minneapolis: Lerner, 1969. 84p. $3.95.

The most complete series on ethnic groups in America, the Lerner "In America Books" is aimed at grades five to eleven. Each volume begins with a history of the "old country" including the present time. Each describes the immigration to America and the problems involved in adjusting into American life. Each title concludes with a list of achievements and contributions by individual members of the ethnic group. Although this series is not designed for reference use per se, it provides enough accessible material to function in that role.

Picture Album Series (Watts)

Brahs, Stuart. An Album of Puerto Ricans in the United States. New York: Franklin Watts, 1973. 84p. $4.95.
LaGumina, John. An Album of the Italian-American. New York: Franklin Watts, 1972. 96p. $4.95.
Murphy, Eugene and Timothy Driscoll. An Album of the Irish Americans. New York: Franklin Watts, 1974. 96p. $4.95.
Suhl, Yuri. An Album of Jews in America. New York: Franklin Watts, 1972. 96p. $4.95.
Yellow Robe, Rosebud. An Album of the American Indian. New York: Franklin Watts, 1969. 87p. $4.95.

In this series of books, the history of various ethnic groups is traced from their beginnings in this country to the present time. While the text is informative and interesting, perhaps the most valuable feature of these books is the illustrations. Drawings and photographs appear on every page of each title. For this reason, this series complements rather than duplicates other juvenile series on ethnic minorities.

AMERICAN INDIANS

Grant, Bruce. American Indians, Yesterday and Today; A Profusely Illustrated Encyclopedia of the American Indian. Rev. ed. New York: Dutton, 1960. 352p. $6.95.

American Indians, Yesterday and Today is an alphabetically arranged resource book giving information about Indian tribes, customs, beliefs, tools, food, homes, leaders, garments, games, animals, important events in Indian history, and Indian words in the American language. Easy to read and filled with black and white drawings, the book is useful for elementary children in spite of slight errors. Appendices include a bibliography, a list of museums, Indian population on reservations, and an Indian family tree.

Jacobson, Daniel. Great Indian Tribes. Maplewood, N.J.: Hammond, 1970. 93p. $4.50.

A slim volume discussing 25 American Indian tribes, this book is arranged geographically: the Southern tribes, the Eastern tribes, the Western tribes, and the Northern tribes. In concise, easy-to-read style it traces the history of each tribe to the present time and is particularly useful because of the information on twentieth century Indians. In addition, it contains an introduction, and epilogue, a bibliography, and an index.

LaFarge, Oliver. A Pictorial History of the American Indian. New York: Crown, 1956. 272p. $7.50. $3.95 paper.

A standard treatise on the American Indian, this history covers from prehistoric times to the 1950's. The readable text is filled with 350 illustrations including many full color plates. The lengthy detailed index provides easy access to specific information.

Stoutenburgh, John L., Jr. Dictionary of the American Indian. New York: Philosophical Library, 1960. 462p. $10.00.

Arranged alphabetically, the Dictionary of the American Indian lists brief definition-type entries giving information about the American Indian. Entries include tribes and clans, place names, plants, animals, objects, and biographies of important persons. Although this book is easy to use and will be valuable for the advanced student, it will probably not be as useful to children as Grant's American Indians, Yesterday and Today. The material is considerably more difficult.

Thompson, Hildegard. Getting to Know American Indians Today. New York: Coward-McCann, 1965. 64p. $3.49.

Written for students in the intermediate grades, this title treats American Indians as they live today rather than their history. Although very little information is provided, the book attempts to show American Indians as individual persons who are very much a part of today's United States. It is neither as complete nor as successful as The American Indian in America, vol. 2, by Jayne Clark Jones (Lerner, 1973).

ASIAN AMERICANS

Chu, Daniel and Samuel Chu. Passage to the Golden Gate; A History of the Chinese in America to 1910. Garden City, N.Y.: Doubleday, 1967. 117p. $3.75. $1.45 paper.

This small readable book traces the history of the Chinese in America from the first known immigrations to 1910. It serves as a needed history but unfortunately stops short of providing any current information on the Chinese and their contributions to modern society.

BLACK AMERICANS

Rollock, Barbara. The Black Experience in Children's Books. New York: New York Public Library, 1974. 122p. $2.50 paper.

A revision of Augusta Baker's 1971 edition of the same title, this booklist contains selected stories portraying Black life for children from preschool to age twelve. Arranged geographically (United States, South and Central America, the Caribbean, Africa, and England), the list is further subdivided by subjects with titles alphabetically arranged under each heading. Subjects include picture books, readers, stories for younger children, stories for older boys and girls, folklore, poetry and verse, music and art, sports, science, Civil Rights, Frederick Douglass, Dr. Martin Luther King, Jr., biography, history, the way it is, references, and periodicals. Each entry gives the title, author, illustrator, publisher, date, price, and brief annotation.

Black Experience in Children's Audio Visual Materials. New York: New York Public Library, 1973. 32p. $1.00 paper.

Designed as a supplement to The Black Experience in Children's Books, this bibliography is a well organized list of audiovisual materials depicting Black life. It is divided into the following sections: records and cassettes, films, filmstrips, and multimedia kits. It also contains a directory of sources. Each section lists materials held by the North Manhattan and Countee Cullen branch libraries which have proved popular with children and which are still available for purchase.

Davis, John Preston, ed. American Negro Reference Book. New York: Prentice-Hall, 1966. 969p. $24.95.

Covering every aspect of Negro life in America from Colonial

Ethnic Groups in America 191

times to the present, this extensive reference work was compiled
by 126 experts. Each chapter was written by a different author,
each an authority in the specific field. Topics covered include
Negro history, culture, politics, economics, prejudice, etc. Most
chapters contain bibliographies and tables. Well-indexed, this book
is a valuable source for names, dates, and data.

Ebony Pictorial History of Black America. By the Editors of
Ebony. Nashville, Tenn.: Southwestern, 1971, 1973. 4
vols. $10.00 each.

 Utilizing the vast collection of pictures of African-Americans
accumulated by Ebony magazine, Ebony Pictorial History of Black
Americans combines pictures and a readable text to trace the history of American Blacks from the Golden Age of Africa through
1972. Volume I of the set is called "African Past to the Civil
War"; volume II is "Reconstruction to Supreme Court Decision
1954"; volume III is "Civil Rights Movement to Black Revolution";
and volume IV is "The 1973 Year Book." Indexes to the first three
volumes are listed in volume III, while volume IV contains its own
index. Attractively presented and interesting to read, the set will
be much used by students at all levels and should be available in
all libraries.

The Ebony Success Library. By the Editors of Ebony. Nashville,
Tenn.: Johnson, 1973. 3 vols. $27.50.

 This outstanding three-volume set uses text and photographs
to tell the stories of achievements of more than 1,100 black men
and women. Volume I, "1,000 Successful Blacks," consists of alphabetically arranged biographical sketches of one paragraph in
length plus photographs which depict the lives of 1,000 Blacks in
business, industry, arts, sciences, sports, entertainment, and government. Volume II, named "Famous Blacks Give Secrets of Success," contains 72 in-depth articles on black persons who have
achieved success in various areas of employment from entertainment to management. Entitled "Career Guide: Opportunities and
Resources for You," Volume III is composed of information on
careers and career planning. Divided into two parts, the volume
begins with "Careers and People." This section, consisting of two
pages per entry, is an alphabetical listing of successfully employed
persons. On the left-hand page is a photograph and biographical
sketch of the person and on the right-hand page is related career
information including training and job outlook. The second section,
"Careers and Resources," provides sources and addresses for
scholarships and financial aid of various types. Volume three also
contains the indexes for each of the three volumes in the set. The
interesting text and attractive format make The Ebony Success Library an essential item for both elementary and junior high school
libraries.

Goodman, Morris C. A Junior History of the American Negro. 2
vols. New York: Fleet, 1969, 1970. 124p. $5.00 each.

This juvenile history of the American Negro covers from the discovery of America to the Civil War in volume 1, and from the Civil War to the Civil Rights War in volume 2. The first volume is primarily a catalog of sketches of famous and obscure Blacks who made accomplishments, while volume 2 is a rather complete history. Indexes of both volumes consist primarily of names. Although this set is not especially well-written, it is probably the only one of its kind written for upper elementary school children and will be a valuable purchase.

Hopkins, Lee Bennett. Important Dates in Afro-American History. New York: Franklin Watts, 1969. 188p. $4.95.

Arranged in calendar fashion starting with January 1 and ending with December 25, there is for each day a listing of important Afro-American events. Included are such incidents as January 1--Lincoln issues Emancipation Proclamation; January 3--News note 1966--Robert Henry is first mayor of Ohio; January 5--Death of George Washington Carver (1864-1943); etc. Considerable biographical data is included. Almost every page contains photographs. An index locates details.

Jackson, Miles, M., Jr. A Bibliography of Negro History and Culture for Young Readers. Pittsburgh: Published for Atlanta University by the University of Pittsburgh Press, 1968. 134p. $2.50 paper.

This bibliography, keyed to elementary, junior high, and high schools, is arranged according to the following sections: picture books, fiction, the arts, literature, religion, science, social science, sports, reference books, magazines and newspapers, audiovisual materials (phonograph records, films and filmstrips, and pictures). Each of the nearly 550 entries, arranged alphabetically by the author within each section, gives the title, publisher, date, price, grade level, and an annotation. Two appendixes give a list of biographies and sources used in selecting materials. The author index and title and subject index locate specific information within the book.

Johnson, Harry A. ed. Multimedia Materials for Afro-American Studies; A Curriculum Orientation and Annotated Bibliography of Resources. New York: Bowker, 1971. 353p. $19.95.

This rather expensive work presents about 1,400 titles on Afro-American studies for elementary through university use. The first of three parts consists of four position papers concerning the education of Blacks. Part II is an annotated bibliography on the Afro-American, his culture, heritage, and contributions to the growth and development of the United States. Part III lists multimedia materials on the peoples of Africa, their cultures, and contributions to mankind. Parts II and III list 8mm and 16mm films, audiotapes, silent and sound filmstrips, multimedia kits, disc recordings, slides, study prints, transparencies, and video tapes.

Ethnic Groups in America

In Part II is a selected list of paperback books. Entries provide title, producer/distributor, grade level, number in series or description of items, price, and annotation. A directory of producers and distributors and a list of publishers of paperback books precedes the index.

The Negro in American History. Rev. ed. Chicago: Encyclopaedia Britannica, 1972. 3 vols. $26.95.

Edited by Charles Van Doren, George Ducas, and Mortimer J. Adler, The Negro in American History is a collection of original source material drawn from the much larger Annals of America. Written by 144 different authors, the text contains 195 selections including letters, diaries, interviews, court decisions, articles, speeches, and other items. Arranged in reverse chronological order, the set contains Volume I, Black Americans 1928-1971; Volume II, A Taste of Freedom, 1854-1927; and Volume III, Slaves and Masters, 1567-1854. This valuable set will be useful in school libraries, especially those which do not own the Annals of America.

NICEM Index to Black History and Studies--Multimedia. 2nd ed. Los Angeles: National Information Center for Educational Media, 1971. $19.50 paper. (10,000 entries).

Listed in this multimedia sourcebook are over 10,000 non-book titles dealing with the history and contributions of Blacks in America. This typical NICEM index gives title, series, release date, technical description, LC card number, producer/distributor code, and a brief annotation. A subject index and a producers/distributors directory are included. This volume in most instances should be purchased by the district media center for use in individual school libraries.

Ploski, Harry A. and Ernest Kaiser. The Negro Almanac. 2nd ed. New York: Bellwether, 1971. 1100p. $27.95.

An essential compendium of facts about the Negro, The Negro Almanac provides information on almost every phase of life. Some representative chapters include a chronology of history in review; significant documents in American history; historical landmarks of Black America; Civil Rights organizations and their leadership; legal status of Black Americans; Black writers, scholars, poets; The Black artist; Black inventors and scientists; Black entertainers in the performing arts; Black women; and soul food. The extensive bibliography is a valuable asset to the book. Altogether, it is a necessary volume for all libraries.

JEWISH AMERICANS

Ben-Asher, Naomi and Hayim Leaf, eds. The Junior Jewish Encyclopedia, 7th rev. ed. New York: Shengold, 1970. 350p. $8.95.

Seeking to provide a dependable and accurate guide for the young Jew to the past and present of his people, this alphabetically arranged dictionary covers a wide range of topics including history, customs, communal life, biography, literature, legal structure, and religious backgrounds. The articles, most of which are signed, range in length from brief definitions to lengthy treatises. Many photographs, drawings, and maps appear throughout the text.

Comay, Joan. Who's Who in Jewish History After the Period of the Old Testament. New York: McKay, 1974. 448p. $16.95.

An alphabetically arranged work, Who's Who in Jewish History contains information about the lives of more than a thousand persons spanning twenty centuries. Entries relate to Jews who have made a significant contribution to the history and thought of their own people; individual Jews who have been eminent in the general life and culture of their time; and non-Jews who have had a special impact on Jewish history. Preceding the main text is a glossary and a chronology covering from 134 B.C. to the present. The 450 black and white illustrations and maps add to the attractiveness of this readable book.

SPANISH-SPEAKING AMERICANS

Conwell, Mary K. and Pura Belpré. Libros en Espanol; An Annotated List of Children's Books in Spanish. New York: Office of Children's Services, New York Public Library, 1971. $.50 paper (prepaid).

This very useful bibliography of children's books in Spanish is divided into nine categories. These are picture books; young readers; books for the middle age; books for older boys and girls; folklore, myths, and legends; songs and games; bilingual books; books for learning Spanish; and anthologies. Titles are alphabetically arranged under each heading, with entries supplying author, illustrator, publisher, date, price, and brief annotations in both languages. A list of sources and an index are appended. This list, sponsored by the South Bronx Project of the New York Public Library is essential for any library serving Spanish-speaking children.

Dobrin, Arnold. The New Life--La Vida Nueva; The Mexican Americans Today. New York: Dodd, Mead, 1971. 109p. $3.95.

A treatise on the Chicano today, The New Life--La Vida Nueva describes all phases of life among the Mexican-American today, including prejudice and discrimination. Interviews with many people including a social worker, a priest, a teacher, and an artist offer insight into feelings about education, political action, and prejudices. Illustrated with numerous fine black and white photographs, the book offers a positive viewpoint.

Eiseman, Alberta. Mañana Is Now: The Spanish-Speaking in the United States. New York: Atheneum, 1973. 184p. $6.25.

Describing the lives of the Spanish-speaking people in the United States, the author includes Puerto Ricans, Cubans, Chicanos, and groups from other Latin American countries. While the discussion of each group is prefaced by a historical background, the bulk of the text concerns the Spanish-speaking people in America today. A brief chronology and a bibliography follow the text.

Lamb, Ruth S. Mexican Americans: Sons of the Southwest. Claremont, Calif.: Ocelot, 1970. 198p. $5.95.

A history of Mexican Americans going back as far as 4000 B.C. and tracing their story to the present day. The Treaty of Guadalupe Hidalgo is presented both in English and Spanish as well as the Gadsden Treaty. Two final chapters are "Civil Rights and Political Activity" and "Mexican Americans Today." An extensive 47-page bibliography is one of the strong points of this book. Most elementary school students will find this book difficult; junior high students, however, should be able to use it profitably.

THE NATURAL SCIENCES AND MATHEMATICS

Science is an area of the curriculum which receives much emphasis in elementary and junior high schools, and since it is a subject which lends itself to independent study and experimentation, science reference books should be plentiful in quantity and excellent in quality. Dictionaries and encyclopedias which cover science in general are valuable as well as those which deal only with specific topics. Ready reference works for locating brief simple explanations are necessary companions for works that are exhaustive and scholarly. Children need access to many varied reference sources in this field.

Included in this chapter is a variety of types of reference books representing different levels of difficulty. Subheadings used are bibliographies, general works, biological sciences, zoology, botany, mathematics, physical sciences, astronomy, chemistry and physics, geology, and oceanography. Additional materials can be located in the chapters on applied science and recreation and hobbies; both will contain titles which relate to the sciences.

BIBLIOGRAPHIES

Logasa, Hannah. Science for Youth; An Annotated Bibliography for Children and Young Adults. Brooklawn, N.J.: McKinley, 1967. 159p. $7.50.

This bibliography of science books covers all aspects of the subject with the exceptions of invention, technology, machinery, and automation. Alphabetically arranged by subject and then by author, the book list includes for each entry the author, title, publisher, date, and a brief descriptive annotation. An author and title index aids in finding information. Perhaps one of the strong points of this bibliography is that it includes nonfiction, fiction, poetry, and biography. Its usefulness is further enhanced by the use of two symbols: a dagger to indicate material for younger readers and an asterisk to denote especially useful material. Despite the age of the book, it can be valuable as an extension of the card catalog in locating science materials by subject.

Deason, Hilary J., comp. The A. A. A. S. Science Book List for Children. 3rd ed. Washington, D. C.: American Association for the Advancement of Science, 1972. 253p. $8.95.

The subtitle of this bibliography is: "a selected and annotated list of science and mathematics books for children in elementary schools, and for children's collections in public libraries." Arranged by Dewey classification number, it lists 1,530 titles. For each it gives the author, title, publisher, date, pagination, illustrations, price, L. C. card number, level of difficulty designation; and a succinct annotation ranging from two to eight or more lines. The book also includes an author index, a subject and title index, and a directory of publishers. It is updated by the fine periodical, Science Books: A Quarterly Review. An essential checklist for building library collections, it also can be of great value for locating books on specific subjects.

Deason, Hilary J., comp. The A. A. A. S. Science Book List: A Selected and Annotated List of Science and Mathematics Books for Secondary School Students, College Undergraduates, and Nonspecialists. 3rd ed. Washington, D. C.: American Association for the Advancement of Science, 1970. 439p. $9.00.

An outstanding, authoritative booklist, this bibliography contains 2,441 titles covering all areas of pure and applied science. Arranged by Dewey classification, it includes materials for secondary school and college. Updated by the quarterly periodical, Science Books, it is a comprehensive, well annotated list which will help immensely in building junior high school science collections.

GENERAL WORKS

Adventures in Discovery. New York: Western, 1970. 12 vols. $39.25. Dist. by Encyclopaedia Britannica.

Although this set contains more than science information, it is incorporated with the science reference books because science is heavily emphasized. Designed for the very young, Adventures in Discovery consists of 12 volumes filled with information expounding upon the important concepts that are learned in preschool and primary school years. Volume titles are: Listening for sounds, Adventures with color, Nature wonderland, The wonders of science, Understanding numbers, Time and measuring, Discovering shapes, Learning about sizes, Adventures with words, The thinking book, All kinds of signs, and The magic of everyday things. While these books are not arranged for ready reference, they will serve admirably for the child with very limited reading skills.

Asimov, Isaac. Words of Science; And the History Behind Them. Boston: Houghton Mifflin, 1959. 266p. $5.95.
Asimov, Isaac. More Words of Science. Boston: Houghton Mifflin, 1972. 267p. $5.95.

Arranged alphabetically from "Absolute zero" to "Zodiac," Words of Science lists 250 words explained in full page entries. Each word provides the basis for histories and derivations of other related words. An interesting book for both the science student and the language student, it is well balanced and comprehensive, although the choice of words is somewhat arbitrary. A fine index locates material not in the main alphabet. Written to cover new words developed as science developed, and to take up where Words of Science left off, More Words of Science has the same format including 250 one-page explanations and derivations. It also has a rather long 17-page index.

Britannica Yearbook of Science and the Future. Chicago: Encyclopaedia Britannica, 1969- . $12.50.

An annual first published in 1969, this yearbook, according to the publisher, has been designed to provide those who have little or no background in science with authoritative, up-to-date comprehensive information about current scientific and technological efforts and achievements. Written by authorities, it has numerous photographs and illustrations which extend the text and further the editor's purpose of making science appealing to non-scientists.

Science Year; the World Book Science Annual. Chicago: Field Enterprises, 1965- . $6.95.

Issued annually since 1965 by the publishers of World Book Encyclopedia, Science Year is an attempt by scientists to communicate the progress of science to the general reader. It contains approximately a dozen signed depth-study articles on recent achievements in science. An additional section, "Science File," lists many short articles arranged alphabetically by subject. Sections on biography and awards and prizes are also included. The annual is exceptionally well illustrated with color plates, black and white drawings, maps, charts, diagrams, and transparent acetate overlays. An excellent index with many cross references locates specific details. All in all, Science Year is a valuable record of scientific progress in the preceding year.

Young People's Science Encyclopedia. Edited by the staff of National College of Education. Evanston, Illinois: Children's Press, 1970. 20 vols. $79.95.

Prepared specifically for children in elementary and junior high schools, the Young People's Science Encyclopedia is a 20-volume set covering the natural and physical science with emphasis on the plant and animal kingdoms. Alphabetically arranged, it contains over 4,000 entries with more than 2,500 colored illustrations, maps, and charts. Its primary purposes are to provide interest through convenience, help with school work, learn by doing experiences, and a wide vocabulary for different ages. Nearly 200 "Things To Do" are incorporated into the text. Volume 20 contains a general index and a bibliography. Also in the last volume is the

Parents' and Teachers' Guide which suggests ways of working with young people as individuals and presents detailed science units for grades three through eight. Simple to use and published in slim, easy to handle volumes, the Young People's Science Encyclopedia provides in ready reference format scientific information not easily located for children in this age bracket.

The Book of Popular Science. Herbert Kondo, ed. in chief. New York: Grolier, $89.50.

Bearing a long list of contributing specialists and recommended by the American Association for the Advancement of Science, The Book of Popular Science is an authoritative, ten-volume, classified encyclopedia. First published in 1924, it is revised and updated annually. According to the editors, its purpose is: "to provide the learner with knowledge about the boundless universe; about the planet on which he lives; about man, master of the earth; about maintenance of health; about the diverse forms of energy; about man's industries; about transportation and communication; about the study of science through the ages; about the problems of society; about science; about science in the home." Well illustrated and well indexed, the set contains a lengthy annotated bibliography, "Selected Readings in Science." Appended is useful scientific data under the heading "Scientific Facts and Figures." An extensive index in Volume 10 can also be obtained in separate paperback format. A favorite with children, this set is a must for elementary and junior high school libraries. The major science stories of each year are covered in an annual supplement, The Encyclopedia Science Supplement.

Van Nostrand's Scientific Encyclopedia. 4th ed. New York: Van Nostrand Reinhold, 1968. 2008p. $42.75.

Van Nostrand's Scientific Encyclopedia, according to its title page, covers aeronautics, astronomy, botany, chemical engineering, chemistry, civil engineering, electronics, geology, guided missiles, mathematics, mechanical engineering, medicine, metalurgy, meteorology, mineralogy, navigation, nuclear science and engineering, photography, physics, radio and television, statistics, and zoology. The 16,500 articles vary from simple definitions to long, complex explanations. Basically accurate and authoritative, the alphabetically arranged encyclopedia contains over 200 graphs and line drawings. Up to date and comprehensive, it is a worthwhile addition to the science reference collection.

Harper Encyclopedia of Science. James R. Newman, ed. Rev. ed. New York: Harper, 1967. 1379p. $40.00.

A one-volume revision of the four-volume set published in 1963, this contains nearly 4,000 articles covering the facts and theories of technology, the physical sciences, mathematics, logic, the history and philosophy of science, and the lives of nearly 1,000 scientists. Approximately 450 scientists and engineers contributed to the work. Arranged alphabetically by subject, all entries are signed. The concise, accurate articles are well illustrated, many with color plates. Bibliographies are included for all of the ten major scientific disciplines. An accurate general index and many cross references locate information within the text.

McGraw-Hill Encyclopedia of Science and Technology. 3rd ed. New York: McGraw-Hill, 1971. 15 vols. $360.00. $24.00 each vol.

Extremely comprehensive as well as expensive, the McGraw-Hill Encyclopedia of Science and Technology is designed for the student, intelligent layman, and specialists in fields other than their own. Articles cover the natural sciences and their applications in engineering, agriculture, forestry, industrial biology, food, and other technologies. Alphabetically arranged, the entries are written by over 2,100 contributing authorities. Two indexes are included in Volume 15; one is a topical index and the other is a comprehensive general index. Updated by annual volumes, it is further supplemented by the McGraw-Hill Modern Men of Science and the McGraw-Hill Bibliography of Science and Technology. Although this set is costly and is relatively mature in nature, it should seriously be considered for elementary and junior high school libraries where extensive, authoritative science materials are needed.

BIOLOGICAL SCIENCES

Chinery, Michael. Concise Color Encyclopedia of Nature. New York: Crowell, 1972. 254p. $7.95.

A valuable volume, especially for the price, The Concise Color Encyclopedia of Nature doubles as a fine reference tool and a browser's delight. Containing over 150,000 words of text and more than 1,000 pictures, both color and black and white, it is a readable introduction to all facets of nature. Contents include Part I - Living organism; Part II - Plant physiology; Part III - Animal physiology; and Part IV - Ecology. At the end of Part II is a section called "Dictionary of Flower Families," arranged alphabetically with one paragraph of information for each entry. At the end of Part III is the "Dictionary of Animals," another alphabetical section containing one-paragraph definitions for each entry. Copies of this book should be in both the reference and circulating collections, for while it can admirably answer ready-reference questions, it will also be carried home by devotees for further perusal.

Comstock, Anna Botsford. Handbook of Nature-Study. 24th ed. Ithaca, New York: Comstock; a division of Cornell University Press, 1939. 937p. $15.00.

A comprehensive source book covering many areas of nature study, the handbook is divided into four parts: The Teaching of nature-study, Animals, plants, and Earth and sky. Perhaps one of the most unique and valuable features of this book is that the author combines wildlife and domesticated animals, wild flowers and garden flowers, weeds and cultivated crop plants, soil formation and soil conservation. The information concerning plants man has cultivated and animals that man has domesticated is particularly difficult to locate in specific reference books. An extensive bibliography, many titles of which are standard juvenile resources despite their age, covers topics including poetry, history and biography, plant life, animal life, earth and sky, textbooks and readers, etc.

Klinge, Paul., ed. Discovering Natural Science, An Introductory Dictionary. Chicago: Encyclopaedia Britannica, 1971. 568p. $14.45.

Superseding Compton's Dictionary of the Natural Sciences, this dictionary has been rewritten using language and sentence patterns familiar to youngsters in the early elementary grades. Over 1,000 alphabetical definitions describe plants, animals, and earth subjects while 1,000 more words are entered in the "Illustrated Index and Glossary of Terms." For each entry in the main text there is a clearly written, easy to read, and succinct article; most have pronunciations and color illustrations. A number of the same charts and tables appearing in the Dictionary of the Natural Sciences have been reproduced in this volume. This interesting book is a basic selection for elementary schools and should be considered for junior highs where easy reading material is needed.

Reid, George K. Pond Life; A Guide to Common Plants and Animals of North American Ponds and Lakes. New York: Golden Press, 1967. 160p. $4.95. $1.50 paper.

A volume in the Golden Nature Guide series, Pond Life explains the dynamics of a pond or lake and shows numerous examples of the plants, animals, insects, and fishes which will be located near it. It also tells how to collect specimens. Accurate illustrations in full color accompany the text.

Audubon Nature Encyclopedia. 2nd ed. John D. Terres, ed. Sponsored by the National Audubon Society. New York: Curtis, 1973. 16 vols. $68.00.

Alphabetically arranged by specific entry, the Audubon Nature Encyclopedia is a twelve-volume set covering all areas of nature. Entries are easy to read and understand and are enhanced by numerous beautiful plates, many of which are in full color. The information included in the encyclopedia is of prime importance to students in the intermediate grades. Relatively small and easy to handle, the volumes are sturdily bound and feature large, clear type on good paper. Volume 16 contains a bibliography and the index which lists both scientific and common names.

Clement, Roland C. Hammond Nature Atlas of America. Maplewood, N.J.: Hammond, 1973. 255p. $17.95.

A beautiful book filled with full color photographs, the Nature Atlas of America is a luxurious volume which should be considered for all libraries. Divided into the areas of Rocks and minerals, Trees, Wildflowers, Mammals, Birds, Reptiles and amphibians, Fishes, and Insects, each chapter title appears on a two-page spread color photograph followed by a two-page range map. Specific entries, uniform in length, describe topics for identification. Each entry has a full color photograph. A one-page glossary, a list of suggested reading, and an index add to the book's usefulness.

Gray, Peter. Student Dictionary of Biology. New York: Van Nostrand, 1972. 194p. $7.95.

Designed specifically for students, this dictionary of biology contains about 8,000 entries, including both terms and roots. Each entry contains the pronunciation and a definition. Numerous cross-references connect information throughout the book. Written in a scholarly style and using a rather difficult vocabulary, this work will be valuable to accelerated junior high school students.

Gray, Peter. Encyclopedia of the Biological Sciences. 2nd ed. New York: Van Nostrand, 1970. 1027p. $24.95.

Alphabetically arranged, the Encyclopedia of the Biological Sciences lists terms and topics in all areas of the biological sciences but with emphasis upon developmental, ecological, functional, genetic, structural, and taxonomic aspects. Intended to be used by the biologist, teacher, and student, it could be utilized by interested students in junior high classes.

Henderson, Isabella and William D. Henderson. A Dictionary of Biological Terms. 8th ed. John H. Kenneth. Princeton, N.J.: Van Nostrand, 1963. $16.95. British Book Center, $2.95.

First published in 1920, A Dictionary of Biological Terms has been revised periodically with those revisions since 1939 edited by J. H. Kenneth. A standard and respected reference work, it provides the pronunciation, derivation, and definitions for terms in biology, botany, zoology, anatomy, cytology, genetics, embryology, and physiology.

The International Wildlife Encyclopedia. Maurice Burton and Robert Burton, eds.-in-chief. New York: Purnell, 1971, (c. 1969). 20 vols. $179.50.

Edited by two English zoologists who gathered information from all over the world, The International Wildlife Encyclopedia attempts to cover all species in all geographical regions. The

Natural Sciences and Mathematics 203

alphabetically arranged articles include over 1,200 entries. Lavishly illustrated with more than 2,500 full color illustrations, the set is intriguing to browse through as well as helpful as a reference source. It contains three indexes: the animal index, the subject index, and the systematic index.

ZOOLOGY

Gersh, Harry. Animals Next Door; A Guide to Zoos and Aquariums of the Americas. New York: Fleet, 1971. 170p. $6.95.

Published in cooperation with the National Recreation and Park Association in Washington, D.C., this book is divided into three major parts. Part one tells the purpose of zoos and aquariums, particularly in saving some animal and fish species from becoming extinct. Part two contains a thorough listing of the zoos and aquariums throughout the world. In Part three is a list of the various endangered species.

Hoffmeister, Donald F. Zoo Animals. New York: Golden Press, 1967. 160p. $4.95.

Specific species of mammals, birds, and reptiles and amphibians living in zoos are described in text and illustrations in this Golden Nature Guide. For each animal there is a picture, the name, height, description, food and special qualities.

Burnett, R. Will, Harvey I. Fisher, and Herbert S. Zim. Zoology, An Introduction to the Animal Kingdom. New York: Golden Press, 1958. 160p. $4.95.

The first volume in the Golden Nature Guide series, Zoology provides an introduction to the animal kingdom both past and present. Briefly surveyed in the text are the processes of reproduction, the science of genetics, the physiology of animals, evolution, migration, adaptation to changing environmental conditions, and geographical distribution of animals. Breaking the animal kingdom into its largest subdivisions, the authors include a simple and accurate illustration for each category--450 illustrations in all.

Now You Know About Animals. Chicago: Encyclopaedia Britannica, 1972. 5 books and 5 records or cassettes. $52.50.

The simplest of the "Now You Know Series," this set provides the preschool and primary level child with an insight into the animal kingdom and an introduction to ecology. Using large, bold color pictures, a very easy text, and correlated read-along records, Now You Know About Animals is a simple, appealing source of information for young children, especially non-readers. Titles in the set include "Many Animals," "Where Animals Live," "Animal Coverings," "Animal Homes," and "How Animals Stay Alive." Throughout the set the information is presented in a style that invites the reader/listener to observe and compare.

Zim, Herbert S. and Donald F. Hoffmeister. Mammals; A Guide to Familiar American Species. New York: Golden Press, 1955. 160p. $4.95. $1.50 paper.

Over 200 of the 350 species of mammals found in the United States and southern Canada are described according to appearance and distinguishing characteristics. Full color pictures of each mammal included are drawn by James Gordon Irving. Supplementary material includes a list of museums and zoos to visit, a list of scientific names, and bibliography for further study. Mammals is a volume in the Golden Nature Guide series.

Sanderson, Ivan T. Living Mammals of the World. Garden City, N.Y.: Doubleday, 1955. 303p. $15.95.

This colorful and comprehensive volume gives detailed information on the history, habits, appearance, and location of all living mammals. Thousands of varieties of mammals are included. Beautiful photographs, 330 altogether, including 190 in color, are done by John Markham and others.

Jordan, E. L. Animal Atlas of the World. Maplewood, N.J.: Hammond, 1969. 224p. $16.95.

A beautiful volume that invites browsing as well as ready reference, Animal Atlas of the World discusses various mammals arranged according to similarity. For each entry there is a brief history or some interesting facts as well as physical description. The 182 full-color illustrations, the distribution maps showing the ranges of the species, the climate and vegetation maps, geological time chart of all orders, and the zoological breakdown of the orders of mammals combine to make this book a most appealing tool.

Chinery, Michael. A Science Dictionary of the Animal World; an Illustrated Demonstration of Terms Used in Animal Biology. New York: Franklin Watts, 1969. 288p. $4.95.

Over 1,000 alphabetically arranged terms fill this rather mature little dictionary. Entries are generally brief but may be more than a page in length. "See" references and cross references help to link related material. Separate from the corresponding text but clearly marked in bold type with a subject heading are the 128 pages of more than 500 color plates.

Wild Animals of North America. Washington, D.C.: National Geographic Society, 1960. 400p. $7.75.

An excellent guide to animals on the North American continent, Wild Animals of North America is divided into the following categories: Animals in fur, The hoofed mammals, The meat eaters, Gnawing mammals, Survivors of ancient orders, and Ocean dwellers. Outstandingly illustrated, it contains 409 illustrations, 258 in full color. Attractive and authoritative, this book will serve students at any age level.

Jarman, Catherine. Atlas of Animal Migration. New York: Day, 1972. 124p. $10.00.

Covering all types of animals in separate chapters, including birds, mammals, fish, reptiles and amphibians, and insects, this book is devoted entirely to the topic of animal migration. It tells why animals migrate, where they go, and how they get there. Colored maps prepared by Geographical Projects in London depict the various migration routes. This attractively illustrated volume should answer many questions of inquiring young people.

Nayman, Jacqueline. Atlas of Wildlife. New York: Day, 1972. 124p. $10.00.

An interesting book illustrated with color paintings, Atlas of Wildlife aims at explaining the distribution of animals around the world. Maps made by Geographical Products of London show by animal symbols the distribution throughout the six zoogeographical regions. The book will be interesting browsing for intermediate and junior high level students.

The Illustrated Encyclopedia of the Animal Kingdom. 2nd ed. New York: Danbury Press, 1972. 20 vols. 237p. $108.50.

Intended for use by elementary and secondary school students, The Illustrated Encyclopedia of the Animal Kingdom is an outstanding set emphasizing the principles of zoology. Contents are as follows: vol. 1--Introduction to vertebrates; vols. 2-6--Mammals; vols. 7-8--Birds; vols. 9-10--Reptiles/amphibians; vol. 11--Fishes; vols. 12-13--Arthropods; vols. 14-16--Arthropods: insects; vol. 17--Mollusks; vols. 18-19--Lesser invertebrates; and vol. 20--Endangered species/index. Each volume contains its own index, and vol. 20 has the combined index for the entire set. The illustrations are perhaps the most valuable portion of the set and indeed make up about 60 percent of it. Illustrations include approximately 5,000 photographs, black-and-white drawings, maps, charts, and diagrams. Nearly 3,000 of the photographs are in color. Checked for accuracy by authorities at the American Museum of Natural History, the set is useful, attractive, and readable for young students.

The Rand McNally Atlas of World Wildlife. New York: Rand McNally, 1973. 208p. $25.00.

A beautiful "coffee table" book, the Atlas of World Wildlife, according to the publisher, was "produced in consultation with the Zoological Society of London and with contributions from leading zoologists throughout the world." Arranged geographically by region, the book contains chapters entitled: The living earth, North America, Central and South America, Africa, Europe, Northern Asia, Southeast Asia, Australia and New Zealand, Arctic, Antarctic, the great oceans, Island habitats, and Man and wildlife. Each chapter contains maps, text, and many color plates to depict the wildlife inhabiting the various locales of each region. The last timely chapter discusses man's impact upon wildlife, covering such topics as conservation, pollution, and endangered species. Although this lovely book is somewhat expensive, it should be considered for purchase in all libraries as a reference source and as browsing material.

Kieran, John. An Introduction to Birds. Garden City, N.Y.: Doubleday, 1965. 77p. $5.95.

An identification book for beginners, this volume describes 99 birds and tells how to recognize them by sight or sound, when and where to find them, and what to expect of them. According to the author, the species are "presented as nearly as possible in order of their abundance in our fields, woods, and dooryards."

Gilliard, E. Thomas. Living Birds of the World. Garden City, N.Y.: Doubleday, 1958. 400p. $14.95.

A volume in the World of Nature series, this book describes over 1,500 species of birds. The text presents much information on the various species' habits and habitats. Illustrated with over 400 photographs, over half in color, the book is extremely attractive.

Sprint, Alexander and Herbert S. Zim. Gamebirds; A Guide to North American Species and Their Habits. New York: Golden Press, 1961. 160p. $4.95. $1.50 paper.

This guide book contains a vast amount of information on gamebirds, including the classification of gamebirds, extinct and threatened species, waterfowl, rails, shorebirds, pigeons, doves, gallinaceous gamebirds, habitat improvement, and flyways and migration routes. A part of the Golden Nature Guide series, Gamebirds is illustrated with 266 pictures in full color.

Wetmore, Alexander and others. Song and Garden Birds of North America. Washington, D.C.: National Geographic Society, 1964. 400p. $11.95.

Beautifully illustrated with 555 pictures, Song and Garden Birds of North America portrays 327 species of birds that breed north of Mexico. Included for each is information on the life history, breeding, winter ranges, and characteristics. An alphabetical index locates specific information in the text. A special feature is a small album of records presenting songs of 70 species.

Zim, Herbert S. and Ira N. Gabrielson. Birds; A Guide to the Most Familiar American Birds. New York: Golden Press, 1964. 160p. $4.95. $1.50 paper.

Over 120 American birds are identified, described, and illustrated in full color in this handbook. Additional information

Natural Sciences and Mathematics

includes material on migration, eggs, nests, food, parts of birds, history of birds, photography of birds, bird watching and collecting. Birds is issued as part of the Golden Nature Guide series.

Ivins, Ann. The Beginning Knowledge Book of Turtles. New York: Macmillan, 1965. unp. $4.95.

Designed for the youngest inquirer, this book describes and identifies 18 different turtles. After a brief introduction to turtles in general, the text provides one- to two-page entries for each turtle. Simple text and clear illustrations will make this useful for primary children.

Lowndes, Marion. The Beginning Knowledge Book of Snakes. New York: Macmillan, 1965. unp. $4.95.

An introductory identification book for the youngest student, this title tells about 19 common snakes. For each the author includes a large illustration, a description, its habitat, its food, and its young. The simple text and large uncluttered illustrations make this a good book for beginners.

Bevans, Michael H. The Book of Reptiles and Amphibians. Garden City, N.Y.: Doubleday, 1956. 87p. $4.95.

Nearly 100 different reptiles and amphibians are described and identified in this fieldbook. Each entry, generally one paragraph, includes the common name, the scientific name, the length, the food, the habitat, the range, and a color illustration. Appended is "Reptiles and Amphibians as Pets."

Cochran, Doris M. Living Amphibians of the World. Garden City, N.Y.: Doubleday, 1961. 199p. $16.95.

This volume in the World of Nature series is divided into the following sections: the caecilians; the salamanders; the frogs, toads, and their relatives; some biological aspects of amphibians; and how to keep amphibians as pets. Beautiful in format, it contains 220 illustrations, 77 in full color. A bibliography and a general index are appended to the text.

Zim, Herbert S. and Hobart M. Smith. Reptiles and Amphibians; A Guide to Familiar American Species. New York: Golden Press, 1957. 160p. $4.95. $1.50 paper.

A handbook devoting about one page to each of 100 common reptiles and amphibians, this book is published in the Golden Nature Guide series. It depicts over 200 species in full color illustrations by James Gordon Irving.

Cochran, Doris M. and Coleman J. Goin. The New Field Book of Reptiles and Amphibians. New York: Putnam, 1970. 359p. $5.95.

This guide is an introduction to the salamanders, frogs and toads, turtles, crocodilians, lizards, and snakes now known to occur in the United States, including Alaska and Hawaii, according to the preface. Definitely not for beginners, this book describes and illustrates each subdivision in general, then provides one-paragraph descriptions of individual species. While most illustrations are black and white, a section of color plates appears in the middle of the book. An index lists both common names and Latin names of all species included.

Zim, Herbert S. and Hurst H. Shoemaker. Fishes; A Guide to Fresh and Salt-water Species. New York: Golden Press, 1956. 160p. $4.95. $1.50 paper.

An identification guide, Fishes depicts 278 species of freshwater and salt-water fishes. All are illustrated in beautiful full color drawings. A special feature of Fishes is a list of public aquaria where the specimens may be seen. Similar in format to the rest of the series, Fishes is a Golden Nature Guide book.

Herald, Earl S. Living Fishes of the World. Rev. ed. Garden City, N.Y.: Doubleday, 1962. 303p. $16.95.

Living Fishes of the World is a survey of the principal varieties of the world's fishes including life cycle, feeding, range, and habits. Depicting fishes of the ocean, the deep sea, lake, and stream, it discusses economic aspects, edibility, and sporting qualities of the many types. Lavishly illustrated, it contains 145 color plates and many black and white photographs. A glossary, a bibliography, and an index add to the book's value as a reference source. It is part of the World of Nature series.

Hervey, George and Jack Hems. Illustrated Encyclopedia of Freshwater Fishes. Garden City, N.Y.: Doubleday, 1973. 176p. $14.95.

This rather specialized volume is designed to aid in setting up and maintaining an aquarium and describes the range of fishes and aquatic plants. According to the preface, the authors "believe that an aquarium consists of no more than a glass tank of adequate size, water to fill it, fishes to swim in the water, aquatic plants to keep the water healthy, and a planting medium for the plants to take root in." Although the subject appeals to all ages, the rather difficult text will render this book most useful at the junior high school level.

Abbott, R. Tucker. Sea Shells of the World; A Guide to the Better Known Species. New York: Golden Press, 1962. 160p. $4.95. $1.50 paper.

A guide for collecting seashells, Sea Shells of the World tells how to find shells and how to prepare them for study. The main body of text of this Golden Nature Guide, however, contains 790 color illustrations of the various species of shells with identifying descriptions of each.

Zim, Herbert S. and Lester Ingle. Seashores; A Guide to Animals and Plants Along the Beaches. New York: Golden Press, 1955. 160p. $4.95. $1.50 paper.

In addition to general information about the sea, tides, and waves, Seashores provides detailed description of shells, marine plants, and sea animals. Over 450 species are illustrated in full color. Seashores belongs to the Golden Nature Guide series.

Swain, Su Zan Noguchi. The Doubleday First Guide to Insects. Garden City, N.Y.: Doubleday, 1964. 32p. $1.95.

An introduction to insects designed for the primary school child, the First Guide to Insects identifies and describes more than 40 insects. Preliminary material provides considerable information of a general nature. Each entry consists of a paragraph of easy-to-read text and a color illustration. Although there is no index, the table of contents is arranged alphabetically and lists page numbers.

Zim, Herbert S. and Clarence Cottam. Insects; A Guide to Familiar American Insects. New York: Golden Press, 1956. 160p. $4.95. $1.50 paper.

Typical of the Golden Nature series, Insects discusses only the more common important and showy insects. Over 220 species are described and illustrated in full color.

Mitchell, Robert T. and Herbert S. Zim. Butterflies and Moths; A Guide to the More Common American Species. New York: Golden Press, 1964. 160p. $4.95. $1.50 paper.

Using 423 illustrations in full color, this Golden Nature Guide identifies butterflies and moths common to America. Brief descriptive entries each accompanied by a color painting make this book easy to use. Its value is further enhanced by a list of scientific names, an index, and a selected bibliography.

Klots, Alexander B. and Elsie B. Klots. Living Insects of the World. Garden City, N.Y.: Doubleday, 1959. 304p. $14.95.

Covering the behavior and life cycles of insects from primitive springtails to mantids, locusts, thrips, dragonflies, bugs, beetles, lacewings, moths, butterflies, mosquitoes, flies, wasps, ants, and bees, Living Insects of the World is a valuable reference book. Extremely well illustrated with photographs and drawings, many in color, the book is part of the World of Nature series.

Fichter, George S. Insect Pests. New York: Golden Press, 1966. 160p. $4.95. $1.50 paper.

In this typical Golden Nature Guide, more than 350 pests found in middle North America are identified and described. Of particular interest is the section on pesticides. The color illustrations and the helpful index are important facets of this handbook.

Holland, W. J. The Butterfly Book. Rev. ed. Garden City, N.Y.: Doubleday, 1931. 424p. $12.50.

First published in 1898 and enlarged and revised in 1931, The Butterfly Book is a reputable authoritative guide to the study of butterflies. Its subtitle states it to be "a popular and scientific manual, describing all the butterflies of the United States and Canada." Illustrations, mostly in color, and text describe nearly 1,800 butterflies, caterpillars, and chrysalids.

Klots, Alexander B. A Field Guide to the Butterflies of North America, East of the Great Plains. Boston: Houghton Mifflin, 1951. 349p. $5.95.

A volume in the Peterson Field Guide series, A Field Guide to the Butterflies identifies and locates butterflies from Greenland to Mexico (east of the Great Plains). It also discusses the habits, the range, and the food plant of the caterpillar. The 247 color paintings by Marjorie Statham and the 232 photographs by Florence Longworth illustrate the book. A bibliography and a checklist of butterflies are appended.

Fenton, Carroll Lane and Mildred Adams Fenton. The Fossil Book; A Record of Prehistoric Life. Garden City, N.Y.: Doubleday, 1959. 482p. $17.95.

Covering fossils from the earliest animals to those that lived only a few centuries ago, The Fossil Book is arranged in chapters by specific subjects and contains an alphabetical index and a glossary. Excellent photographs and illustrations are included in the book.

Rhodes, Frank H. T., Herbert S. Zim, and Paul R. Shaffer. Fossils; A Guide to Prehistoric Life. New York: Golden Press, 1962. 160p. $4.95. $1.50 paper.

Another book in the Golden Nature Guide series, Fossils provides information on fossil collecting and on the geological periods. Various animal fossils, both vertebrate and invertebrate, and plant fossils are discussed individually and illustrated with accurate colored pictures. The book lists much needed material on a popular subject.

Glut, Donald F. The Dinosaur Dictionary. Secaucus, N.J.: Citadel, 1972. 218p. $12.50.

Natural Sciences and Mathematics 211

Every known genus of dinosaur is listed alphabetically in this dictionary. For each is listed the suborder, family, a description, and the skeletal evidence on which the classification is based. Over 400 black and white illustrations enhance the text.

BOTANY

Now You Know About Plants. Chicago: Encyclopaedia Britannica, 1973. 5 books and 5 records or cassettes. $52.50.

Designed for use by pre-primary and primary level students, Now You Know About Plants consists of five books and five correlated records or cassettes describing plants. Included in the series are "Many Plants," "Where Plants Live," "How Plants Grow," "Plants and Their Seeds," and "Plants We Need." Written in a simple vocabulary which most second and third graders can read independently, the set provides a pleasant read-along recording. The open-ended text aims at encouraging children to think and compare as they proceed from one concept to another. Available also in a Spanish edition, the set is excellent, especially for the nonreading child.

Alexander, Taylor R., R. Will Burnett, and Herbert S. Zim. Botany. New York: Golden Press, 1970. 160p. $3.95.

This Golden Science Guide contains the following sections: The plant world; Thallophytes--simple plants; Embroyophytes; Anatomy of seed plants; Plant nutrition; Sensitivity and reactions; Reproductions; Inheritance; Evolution; and Plants and their environment. It is indexed and lists a small bibliography. An easy to use reference book on a popular subject, this book should join the other popular Golden Guides in the reference collection.

Chinery, Michael. A Science Dictionary of the Plant World; An Illustrated Demonstration of Terms in Plant Biology. New York: Franklin Watts, 1969. 264p. $4.95.

Nearly 1,000 botanical terms alphabetically arranged are defined in this reference book. Entries range in length from one sentence to more than a page. "See" references and cross references connect related material, and over 400 color pictures illustrate the text. Although the small print and rather sophisticated approach may frighten some students, the book should be considered for upper elementary and junior high school libraries.

Edlin, Herbert Leeson. Atlas of Plant Life. New York: Day, 1973. 128p. $10.00.

Similar to the Atlas of Wildlife by Nayman and the Atlas of Animal Migration by Jarman, the Atlas of Plant Life surveys region by region the various wild and cultivated plants of the world. Relief maps showing plant distribution, diagrams, and color paintings illustrate the interesting text. A list of scientific names of principal plants is appended.

Watts, May Theilgaard. Doubleday First Guide to Trees. Garden City, N.Y.: Doubleday, 1964. 32p. $1.95.

 Twenty-five trees are presented in this introductory handbook. For each tree the book gives a brief description and colored illustrations of the bark, trunk, bud, leaf, flower, and fruit. Easy to use and small in size, it is a fine reference source for the very young.

Zim, Herbert S. and Alexander C. Martin. Trees; A Guide to Familiar American Trees. New York: Golden Press, 1956. 160p. $4.95. $1.50 paper.

 A guide book with outstanding color illustrations, Trees provides identification for 140 species. Each tree with its leaf and fruit is shown in pictures. Distribution maps locate the many varieties in the United States. Trees is a Golden Nature Guide.

Kieran, John. An Introduction to Trees. Garden City, N.Y.: Hanover House, 1966. 77p. $5.95.

 One hundred common trees are identified by both the common name and scientific name plus one half to one page of descriptive text. Color pictures by Michael H. Bevans show the leaf, the fruit or cone, as well as the tree itself.

Brockman, C. Frank. Trees of North America. New York: Golden Press, 1968. 280p. $5.95.

 A Golden Guide identifying 594 species of trees native to North America north of Mexico, this little book also lists important foreign species that have become naturalized or that are grown commercially as ornamentals. The format of the book consistently has the descriptive text on the left hand page while the right hand page bears the illustrations. By way of comparison, the volume Trees in the Golden Nature Guide series lists 143 species, is more elementary in text and format, and has larger, clearer plates.

Parker, Bertha Morris. Leaves. New York: Harper, 1959. 36p. $.60.

 This reference book for beginners is a guide for identifying leaves of the most common trees. Simple text and large color pictures make this a useful guide for the very youngest.

Hathaway, Polly. The Beginning Knowledge Book of Backyard Flowers. New York: Macmillan, 1965. unp. $4.95.

 Designed for the student in primary grades, this identification book uses very simple text to describe 18 cultivated flowers. The large clear pictures blend compatibly with the text.

Natural Sciences and Mathematics 213

Selsam, Millicent. The Doubleday First Guide to Wild Flowers. Garden City, N.Y.: Doubleday, 1964. 32p. $1.95.

Grouped according to color, The Doubleday First Guide to Wild Flowers describes and identifies 60 species. For each the book designates the season when it is in full bloom and whether it is found in the backyard, meadow, or woods. Large, clear print and full color drawings make this an attractive handbook for even the youngest student.

Zim, Herbert S. and Alexander C. Martin. Flowers; A Guide to Familiar American Wildflowers. New York: Golden Press, 1950. 160p. $4.95. $1.50 paper.

Arranged by color, Flowers provides the common name, habitat, flowering time, and other special characteristics for some 200 kinds of flowers. Included are 134 full color paintings by Rudolf Freund illustrating varieties of wild flowers. A Golden Nature Guide, Flowers is easily usable as a field guide.

Shuttleworth, Floyd S. and Herbert S. Zim. Non-Flowering Plants. New York: Golden Press, 1967. 160p. $4.95. $1.50 paper.

Non-Flowering Plants, in text and full color illustrations, describes over 400 species of non-flowering plants, such as algae, fungi, lichens, mosses, liverworts and hornworts, ferns and fern allies, and gymnosperms. A Golden Nature Guide, it provides a list of scientific names and an alphabetical index.

Kieran, John. An Introduction to Wild Flowers. Garden City, N.Y.: Doubleday, 1965. 77p. $5.95.

Arranged approximately in the order that the flowers are found blooming in spring, summer, and winter, this book identifies 100 common flowers found largely in the northeast section of the United States. In the one-half to one-page entries, the author gives the name, the scientific name and a description of the wild flowers. Color paintings illustrate the text.

Hylander, Clarence J. The Macmillan Wild Flower Book. New York: Macmillan, 1954. 480p. $12.95.

Arranged by families, The Macmillan Wild Flower Book describes 500 flowers according to appearance, structure, and habitat. Edith F. Johnston illustrates 425 flowers in beautiful plates, mostly color. An attractive, large book, it is more suitable for browsing or indoor reference work than it is as a field guide.

Hausman, Ethel Hindkley. Beginner's Guide to Wild Flowers. New York: Putnam, 1948. 376p. $4.95.

Designed to be used by amateurs, the Beginner's Guide to

Wild Flowers is arranged by color. The 1,080 individual species described are mostly found east of the Mississippi River, with some located in the West. Each entry has illustrations of the flower, leaf, and stem, and gives information such as the common and scientific names, the color, size, period of bloom, and geographic range.

MATHEMATICS

Hardgrove, Clarence Ethel and Herbert F. Miller. Mathematics Library--Elementary and Junior High School. Reston, Va.: National Council of Teachers of Mathematics, 1973. 70p. paper. Apply.

Arranged alphabetically by author, Mathematics Library suggests books to enrich the mathematics program in the primary, intermediate, and junior high levels. Each entry contains a good annotation, complete bibliographical information, and possible grade levels.

Bendick, Jeanne and Marcia Levin. Mathematics Illustrated Dictionary; Facts, Figures, and People Including the New Math. New York: McGraw-Hill, 1965. 223p. $4.50.

Prepared especially for elementary school children, Mathematics Illustrated Dictionary is an alphabetical list of terms from "abacus" to "zero." Covering mathematics from ancient times through the new math, the dictionary also includes portraits and biographical sketches of mathematicians. Particularly appealing to children with its vast array of illustrations, it should be accessible to children both in the library and the math classroom.

James, Glenn and Robert C. James, eds. Mathematics Dictionary. 3rd ed. New York: Van Nostrand, 1968. 446p. $14.50. $18.50 multilingual ed.

Comprehensive in scope, Mathematics Dictionary defines terms beginning with simple arithmetic and extending through calculus. Appended to the main body of text are many useful tables and a list of mathematical symbols. Because of its extensive scope, this reference work could be valuable for both elementary and junior high school students.

Bendick, Jeanne. How Much and How Many; The Story of Weights and Measures. McGraw-Hill, 1960. 192p. $3.95.

Easy to read and understand, this book discusses the history of weights and measures, defines terms, and describes the metric system. It includes numerous tables of weights and measures including conversion tables of metric to imperial and imperial to metric. With the current interest in the metric system, How Much and How Many might well provide quick information for both elementary and junior high school students.

Natural Sciences and Mathematics

Kelly, Gerard W. Metric System Simplified. New York: Sterling, 1974. 80p. $3.95.

A timely little reference book, Metric System Simplified, begins with essays on both the United States System of Weights and Measures and Metric System of Weights and Measures. For each there is a table of the system as well as conversion tables and formulas. Special chapters cover Fahrenheit and Celsius (Centigrade) temperature, metric in the kitchen, and metric in the car. An index aids in quick location. This easy to use volume should be in every library.

PHYSICAL SCIENCES

Ackner, Joseph. Pocket Encyclopedia of Physical Science. New York: Golden Press, 1968. $5.95. $2.95 paper.

The Pocket Encyclopedia of Physical Science consists of 400 articles concerning the major concepts of astronomy, chemistry, geology, meteorology, and physics. Illustrated with 300 colored drawings and diagrams, it is clear and easily understood by young students.

Earth and Space. Rev. ed. Maplewood, N.J.: Hammond, 1970. 192p. $12.95.

Divided into four major areas, this graphic encyclopedia contains sections on astronomy, earth science, oceanography, and meteorology. Packed with illustrations, diagrams, charts, maps, and photographs, it contains an interesting narration written in simple everyday language that is easy to understand but does not talk down. Claiming to be a guide to ecology, the book could indeed have an entire curriculum developed from it. The glossary of terms and rather detailed index increase the value of a good book.

ASTRONOMY

Ivins, Ann. The Beginning Knowledge Book of Stars and Constellations. New York: Crowell-Collier, 1969. unp. $3.95.

Nineteen constellations are described in simple text and large illustrations. Although slightly more difficult than some of the titles in the Beginning Knowledge Book Series, this book is nonetheless valuable to primary levels and could be useful for poor readers in the upper grades. Its simplicity and clarity are its strongest features.

Zim, Herbert S. and Robert H. Baker. Stars; A Guide to the Constellations, Sun, Moon, Planets, and Other Features of the Heavens. Rev. ed. New York: Golden Press, 1956. 160p. $4.95. $1.50 paper.

A Golden Nature Guide, this authoritative handbook is divided into three sections: stars, constellations, and the solar system. Extremely well illustrated, it contains 150 paintings in color. Appended is a list of 88 constellations. Stars tells why, how, and when to observe the skies and the equipment necessary for the amateur astronomer.

Gallant, Roy A. The ABC's of Astronomy. Garden City, N.Y.: Doubleday, 1962. 121p. $4.50.

Designed to be used both by the beginning and advanced student, The ABC's of Astronomy is divided into four parts. Part I is a dictionary of over 500 terms; Part II consists of 18 reference tables, e.g., centigrade and fahrenheit temperatures, occurrence of meteor showers, comets, etc.; Part III provides detailed maps of the stars, constellations, and planets; and Part IV gives descriptions of the various types of telescopes. Clearly written and well illustrated, the book is useful in elementary and junior high school libraries.

Jackson, Joseph Hollister. Pictorial Guide to the Planets. 2nd ed. New York: Crowell, 1973. 248p. $10.00.

Designed for the general reader, this survey of the solar system includes new scientific data gathered from the Apollo astronauts' space flights and the unmanned probes of Venus and Mars. The color and black and white illustrations include maps, graphs, tables, and diagrams.

Howard, Neal E. The Telescope Handbook and Star Atlas. New York: Crowell, 1967. 226p. $12.00.

An amateur observer's manual, The Telescope Handbook and Star Atlas is a clearly written, well illustrated source book for the beginning astronomer. It describes planets, comets, meteorites, galaxies, nebulae, and other phenomena. Also included is a textual discussion along with diagrams and photographs of telescopes and other astronomical instruments. A star atlas and gazetteer locates and identifies over 230 stars.

CHEMISTRY AND PHYSICS

Gallant, Roy A. The ABC's of Chemistry. Garden City, N.Y.: Doubleday, 1963. 88p. $4.50.

Prepared in a picture book format, The ABC's of Chemistry consists of an alphabetically arranged dictionary listing over 500 basic chemical terms and concepts with concise definitions. A second section contains a series of additional tables, including those dealing with acids, food, plastics, and synthetic fibers. Drawings and diagrams in color add to the appeal of the book.

Handbook of Chemistry and Physics. Robert C. Wease, ed. Cleveland: Chemical Rubber Co. Annual. $24.95.

First published in 1914 and frequently revised since then, the Handbook of Chemistry and Physics contains a vast amount of data. It is divided into the following sections: mathematical tables, inorganic compounds, organic compounds, general chemical terms, general physical constants, and miscellaneous. This technical handbook should be in all junior high schools teaching chemistry or physics.

GEOLOGY

Shuttlesworth, Dorothy. The Doubleday First Guide to Rocks. Garden City, N.Y.: Doubleday, 1963. 30p. $1.95.

An identification book, The Doubleday First Guide to Rocks describes the characteristics of various rocks, how they are formed, and where they are found. Color pictures illustrate each rock included. A glossary provides scientific names, pronunciations, and definitions.

Zim, Herbert S. and Paul R. Shaffer. Rocks and Minerals; A Guide to Familiar Minerals, Gems, Ores, and Rocks. New York: Western, 1957. 160p. $4.95. $1.50 paper.

Over 400 specimens of rocks and minerals are described in text and with color illustrations in this Golden Nature Guide. Information on the formation, structure, use, and importance of each is included. Basic geological information and activities such as collecting and identifying specimen are also included.

Deeson, A. F. L., ed. Collector's Encyclopedia of Rocks and Minerals. New York: Clarkson N. Potter, 1973. 288p. $12.50. (Dist. by Crown).

Over 2,000 types of rocks and minerals are alphabetically arranged in this encyclopedia with over 1,000 color photographs integrated in the text. Each entry deals with a particular mineral and provides information such as composition, crystal formation, color, streak, luster, physical properties, distinguishing characteristics, methods of identification, environment, geographical occurrence, and variety. Alternate names are cross-referenced. This lovely volume is quite sophisticated and will meet the demands of the serious student.

Bertin, Leon. Larousse Encyclopedia of the Earth. Rev. ed. New York: Crown, 1972. 416p. $6.95 paper.

An up-to-date version of a well-known French publication, the revision was completed by a panel of British and American consultants. It is divided into three major parts: the present;

Earth in the service of man; and the past. Included are such timely topics as petroleum, hydro-electric power, and future sources of energy. A typical scholarly, readable, attractive Larousse, it will entice students to read it. The more than 500 illustrations and the detailed index add to this appealing selection.

Adams, George F. and Jerome Wyckoff. Landforms. New York: Golden Press, 1971. 160p. $4.95.

Designed to help the reader identify and understand common kinds of natural rock scenery, this Golden Science Guide bears the appealing simplicity typical of the Golden Guides. Covering such topics as the Earth's crust; rock; work of weathering; features of mass wasting; scenery shaped by streams, mountains, plains and plateaus, glaciers and glaciated lands; the book is illustrated with fine color plates on each page.

Rhodes, Frank Harold Trevor. Geology. New York: Golden Press, 1971. 160p. $4.95.

With a minimum of text and with many color photographs, maps, and diagrams, Geology, a Golden Science Guide, describes such topics as igneous rocks, ores, mountains, earthquakes, volcanoes, and oceans. Somewhat more difficult in concept than the Golden Nature Guide series, this volume will appeal to more mature students.

OCEANOGRAPHY

Voss, Gilbert L. Oceanography. New York: Western, 1973. 160p. $4.95.

A Golden Guide, Oceanography describes the field and its various branches. Included are marine, physical, chemical, meteorological, biological, and fisheries oceanography as well as ocean engineering. The book is an attractive one with color illustrations covering a current topic.

The Ocean World of Jacques Cousteau. Danbury, Conn.: Danbury, 1973. 20 vols. $104.50.

Beautifully illustrated with more than 3,500 full color pictures, The Ocean World of Jacques Cousteau is a fascinating 20-volume set which will appeal to all ages. Written in a readable, easy-to-understand style, the set is printed in large clear type. Utilizing the undersea exploration and research of Jacques Cousteau, the text presents the sea as a living organism. Volume titles include: Oasis in space; The act of life; Quest for food; Window in the sea; Invisible messages; Instinct and intelligence; Attack and defense; Propulsion; Migrations; Pharaohs of the sea; Oddities-fantastics of the sea; The margins of the continents; Mammals return to the sea; The abyss; Social manners; Man invades the sea;

Natural Sciences and Mathematics

Treasures from the sea; Legends and truth; and The sea in danger. Volume 20 contains a comprehensive, cross-referenced index to the entire set, including the indexes to the individual volumes. Although not a first purchase reference set, this work is recommended for school libraries with need and funds for a specialized set on ocean life.

APPLIED SCIENCE

Technology and applied science are areas of particular interest to children; however, few reference books in this fields are prepared specifically for them. This may be because youngsters tend to regard the applied sciences as hobbies rather than serious applications of the natural sciences to improve man's existence.

The lack of suitable materials results in this chapter being less than complete. The topics covered depend upon two factors: the availability of materials and the interests of elementary and junior high school students. Subheadings listed are general works, child care, cooking, gardening, health and medicine, home repairs and tools, mechanics, pets, sewing, and space. Titles relating to this subject can also be located in the chapters on science and recreation and hobbies.

GENERAL WORKS

Bronowski, J. Doubleday Pictorial Library of Technology: Man Remakes His World. Garden City, N.Y.: Doubleday, 1963. 367p.

Encyclopedic in scope but arranged with one subject leading to another, this important reference covers the following areas of technology: measurement; power; riches of the earth; chemical technology; metals; ceramics and glass; food and agriculture; textiles and leather; building; land, water, and air transport; military technology; and communications. A scholarly work which lists contributors and the pages of their contributions, it is nonetheless readable and attractive. Each entry or topic covers two facing pages and has at least one photograph, graph, or drawing. Since this book has gone out of print, elementary and junior high school libraries owning copies should keep them as long as possible, for there is nothing comparable for this level of student.

Crispin, Frederic Swing. Dictionary of Technical Terms. Rev. ed. New York: Macmillan, 1970. 455p. $6.95.

Included in this dictionary are terms used in modern trades, technical procedures, industry, shopwork, and occupations of mass production. Designed for students as well as draftsmen, mechanics, builders, electricians, and workmen in general, it may be too technical for ordinary junior high school students, but should be considered if the need is present.

Gerrish, Howard H. Gerrish's Technical Dictionary; "Technical Terms Simplified." 11th ed. Homewood, Ill.: Goodheart-Willcox, 1970. 455p. $6.95.

This dictionary attempts to "clarify definitions and obscure meanings of technical words and phrases that form our vast technical vocabulary." Entry words appear in large type followed by the pronunciation and a very simple definition. For each entry the word is identified with the trade or craft in which it is used. This book is both easy to read and easy to use; it will be valuable to junior high students.

CHILD CARE

Saunders, Rubie. The Franklin Watts Concise Guide to Baby-Sitting. New York: Franklin Watts, 1972. 63p. $4.50.

This well-written manual gives specifics on baby-sitting, e.g., why baby-sit, how to prepare to sit, finding a job, getting to and from your job, feeding, etc. The author's section on know your duties and responsibilities is particularly good for neophyte sitters. The text of the guide is arranged in an appealing format with many sub-headings listed under major topics. The only questionable part of the book is the last chapter, "How to organize a summer play school," which seems somewhat sophisticated for a beginner. An index, a checklist for baby-sitters, and a sample play-school schedule are appended.

Lowndes, Marion. A Manual for Baby Sitters. 2d rev. ed. Boston: Little, Brown, 1974. 144p. $4.95.

A standard manual for baby-sitting, this book begins with twelve requirements for sitters, from being prompt to being properly introduced to family pets. Separate chapters offer suggestions for sitting with babies, two to five year olds, and six and seven year olds. Another section describes potentially dangerous situations and how to avoid them, plus how to handle emergencies. Especially valuable is the final chapter listing stories, games, and menus suitable for sitters to use with small children.

The New Encyclopedia of Child Care and Guidance. Sidonie Matsner Gruenberg, ed. Garden City, N.Y.: Doubleday, 1968. 1016p. $12.95.

Alphabetically arranged by topic, the first part of the New Encyclopedia of Child Care and Guidance consists of some 1,000 entries of varying lengths. Emphasized in this section are the practical aspects of day to day living. Part II of the book includes

31 basic chapters covering the fundamental background of how children develop at different stages and of the interlocking influence of the home, school, church, and community upon the child. Authors of these chapters include such authorities as Margaret Mead, Josette Frank, and Benjamin Spock. Covering child development from the prenatal period through adolescence, this encyclopedia will be a useful source in any junior high school offering courses in child development.

COOKING

Crocker, Betty. Betty Crocker's New Boys and Girls Cookbook. Rev. ed. New York: Golden, 1965. 156p. $2.95.

The recipes included in this cook book were selected and tested by a panel of 25 boys and girls. Selections cover a wide variety of foods, such as beverages, breads and sandwiches, salads and vegetables, meats and main dishes, and various desserts. The book also features special information, e.g., a dictionary of cooking terms, kitchen safety, utensils, how to measure, setting the table, and table manners. Although the book is aimed at upper elementary children, young teenagers will also find its succinct instructions easy to follow.

Better Homes and Gardens Junior Cook Book for the Hostess and Host of Tomorrow. Rev. ed. New York: Meredith, 1973. 77p. $4.95.

Containing recipes for all the usual foods, e.g., beverages, main dishes, salads and vegetables, breads and sandwiches, and desserts, The Better Homes and Gardens Junior Cook Book has excellent instructions for the beginning chef. For each recipe (each recipe is on a separate page) the authors state "You'll need ... " the following ingredients and "Take out ... " the following utensils. Each step of the recipe is simple and illustrated with a drawing. The book contains a glossary of cooking terms and an illustrated section on how to measure. Upper elementary students will find this book most appealing, as will junior high students who are not offended by the basic and simple approach to cooking.

Rombauer, Irma S. A Cookbook for Girls and Boys. New York: Bobbs-Merrill, 1952. 243p. $4.50.

Written by the author of The Joy of Cooking, this cookbook for girls and boys provides instructions for preparing all the regular foods, from sandwiches to outdoor cookery. In addition to recipes, the book contains such thorough explanations and descriptions that it can be read as well as consulted. Special features of this juvenile cook book are: a nutrition chart, a history of food, how to cook a meal, measurements, the stove/the oven, utensils, definitions of cooking terms and processes, and serving food. Both elementary and junior high school people will enjoy this book.

Kohn, Bernice. The Organic Living Book. New York: Viking, 1972. 91p. $4.50.

The Organic Living Book introduces youngsters to raising and preparing food without the aid of chemicals. In addition to instructions in organic gardening, growing bean sprouts, and checking food labels for additives, it includes a number of recipes. Examples are yogurt, whole wheat bread, soybean snacks, and granola. A bibliography and an index complete this book.

Better Homes and Gardens New Cook Book. Rev. ed. New York: Meredith, 1968. 400p. $6.95.

A popular, standard cook book, The Better Homes and Gardens New Cook Book contains over 1,500 triple-tested recipes, 182 cooking tips, a meal-planning guide and menus, new methods and techniques, and entertaining ideas. Arranged alphabetically by broad subjects, from appetizers to vegetables, the recipe section is filled with full color, two-page spread photographs and small black and white ones. A full index completes the book, which should be available for all junior high home economics students.

De Sola, Ralph and Dorothy De Sola, comps. A Dictionary of Cooking. Des Moines, Iowa: Meredith, 1969. 246p. $7.95.

Containing an introduction by Peg Bracken, A Dictionary of Cooking lists 8,000 terms on the subject, giving concise, easy to understand definitions. Included are ingredients, methods, techniques, utensils, equipment, and cooking terminology. While this tool is unnecessary for most junior high school libraries, it will be a nice addition to the reference collection for those schools needing specialized material for home economic studies.

ECOLOGY

Miles, Betty. Save the Earth! An Ecology Handbook for Kids. New York: Knopf, 1974. 91p. $5.57.

Listing a variety of experiments and practical ways for individuals to change their consumption habits, Save the Earth! contains considerable information on pollution and what to do about it. Illustrated with drawings and photographs, it has a list of ecology organizations and a bibliography of background reading.

Durrenberger, Robert W., comp. Dictionary of the Environmental Sciences. Palo Alto, Calif.: National Press Books, 1973. 282p. $7.95. $4.95 paper.

Compiled as an environmental science aid for students from junior high through college, this dictionary features short succinct entries. Terms included relate to a number of academic disciplines, e.g., economics, engineering, geology, geography, anthropology, archaeology, botany, zoology, agriculture, etc. Two appendixes follow the text: Geologic Time Scale and Measures (equivalents and conversions).

> Nobile, Philip and John Deedy, eds. The Complete Ecology Fact Book. Garden City, N.Y.: Doubleday, 1972. 472p. $10.00.

A very useful compendium of facts on a popular subject, this book attempts to bring together hard-to-find information in a comprehensive compilation of ecology statistics. Covered in the text are such topics as population, endangered species, pollution, detergents, food: a crisis in supply, pesticides, non-renewable mineral wastes, and solid wastes. Each section contains a narrative interpretation and easy to use tables, charts, and other statistical data, followed by a bibliography. A glossary of terms and an index increase the usefulness of the book. This book will answer many questions for ecology-minded young people.

> NICEM Index to Ecology--Multimedia. 2nd ed. Los Angeles: National Information Center for Educational Media, 1971. 212p. $19.50 paper. (11,000 entries).

Over 11,000 entries for non-book materials dealing with the preservation of the environment are included in this NICEM index. Main entries are alphabetical by title and give series, release date, technical description, LC card number, producer/distributor code, and a brief annotation. The book also contains a subject index and directory of producers/distributors. This sourcebook is probably best owned by district media centers and borrowed by individual school libraries.

GARDENING

> Paul, Aileen. Kids Gardening; A First Indoor Gardening Book for Children. Garden City, N.Y.: Doubleday, 1972. 96p. $4.50.

This easy to read guidebook gives step-by-step instructions for all types of indoor gardening. Written for elementary school children, it covers flowering plants, foliage plants, plants growing in water, plants grown from bulbs, desert gardens, rock gardens, terrariums, the arrangement of plants, starting new plants, and artificial light for plants. An important section tells where to get additional information and lists the addresses of agricultural colleges and extension services for all states. Attractive in format, the book contains a useful index.

> Bush-Brown, Louise. Young America's Garden Book. New York: Scribner, 1962. 280p. $4.37.

Applied Science 225

In this rather comprehensive book the author discusses the art, the craft, and the science of gardening. The bulk of the text is divided into five sections: flower projects, fruit projects, vegetable projects, general projects, and experimental projects. Throughout, there are outlines of chores that the young gardener should perform. Well illustrated with pictures, charts, and tables, Young America's Garden Book features important tabulated lists giving such information as the common name, the scientific name and degree of hardiness, the height in inches, the distance apart in inches, whether to sow indoors or outdoors, the color, and special remarks. This guide is suitable for both elementary and junior high school students.

Taylor, Norman. The Guide to Garden Flowers; Their Identity and Culture with 324 Species Illustrated in Color and 88 in Black and White. Boston: Houghton, 1958. 315p. $4.95.

The goal of this book is twofold: to make the identification of garden flowers as painless as possible, and to provide such cultural notes that growing them will be easy for all. Arranged by families, each entry gives a brief history and derivation; color; height; flowering date; varieties; culture: annual, biennial, or perennial; with brief growing instructions. A number of finding lists identify garden flowers by a variety of approaches: arranged by preferred habitat, arranged by height; arranged by season of bloom; especially fragrant flowers; perennial ground covers; fifteen plants difficult enough to grow to require patient or expert care; and annual plants, or best grown as such. Containing many cross references, the index lists both the Latin names in italic type and the English names in Roman type. This book is suitable for all ages.

HEALTH AND MEDICINE

American Red Cross. Standard First Aid and Personal Safety. Garden City, N.Y.: Doubleday, 1973. 268p. $3.50. $1.95 paper.

Prepared by the American National Red Cross, this volume is intended for the instruction of first aid classes. Included in it are wounds; specific injuries; respiratory emergencies and artificial respiration; swallowed objects and choking; poisoning; drugs and their abuse; burns, frostbite and cold exposure; heat stroke, heat cramps, and heat exhaustion; sudden illness; dressings and bandages; bone and joint injuries; emergency rescue and short-distance transfer. Each item begins with a clear definition and outlines the treatment step by step in easy to follow and understand instructions. An extensive index aids the user to locate information rapidly. This up to date handbook is a must for all school libraries.

Morrison, Thomas F., Frederick D. Cornett and J. Edward Tether. Human Physiology. Rev. ed. New York: Holt, 1972. $8.64.

Although Human Physiology is designed as an introductory college textbook, it is also useful as a reference book. Written in clear readable style with all important words defined and in bold type, it is easily utilized by upper elementary and junior high school students. Contents include the body as a whole; bones and muscles; the nervous system; the digestive system; the respiratory system; the circulatory system; the skin; metabolism and excretion; the endocrine system; and genetics. Special features are the transparencies with overlays to depict the various organs and systems. A glossary of terms and an index follow the text.

Smith, Jeanne and Isadore Rossman. Instant Medical Advisor. Mundelein, Ill.: Career Institute, 1970. 319p. $1.65.

An inexpensive little handbook, the Instant Medical Advisor provides alphabetically arranged information about more than 300 medical problems, diseases, and emergencies. Printed in rather small but clear dark type, the book provides a concise understandable description of each disease and in some instances suggests treatment. A brief first aid chart appears on the end papers in both the front and back of the book. An extensive index locates specific subjects not listed in the main alphabetical sequence.

Brown, J. A. C. The Stein and Day International Medical Encyclopedia. New York: Stein, 1971. 464p. $17.50.

Designed as a home reference book, this medical encyclopedia is written in simple layman's terms. Arranged in a dictionary format, it has entries ranging in length from one line to one page. Nearly 200 black and white photographs, drawings, and diagrams illustrate this book. One of its strong features is a series of color transparency overlays showing the organs and structure of the body. The clear format and popular style will render this book usable by junior high and advanced elementary school students.

Anthony, Catherine Parker. Structure and Function of the Body. 4th ed. St. Louis: C. V. Mosby, 1972. 175p. $5.65.

This book was written to "help teachers teach, and practical nursing students and others learn basic information about the human body in an effective, efficient, and enjoyable manner." Although much of the text is written directly to student nurses and is somewhat distracting, it is readable and to the point. It is divided into the following units: The body as a whole; Systems that form the framework of the body and move it; Systems that control body functions; Systems that process and distribute foods and eliminate wastes; and Systems that reproduce the body. More than 100 illustrations, a glossary, and an index are included. As a whole the book will be useful to junior high students.

Lingeman, Richard R. Drugs From A to Z; A Dictionary. 2nd rev. ed. New York: McGraw-Hill, 1974. 320p. $6.95. $3.50 paper.

Applied Science   227

This is an alphabetical listing of the drugs of abuse such as hallucinogens, opiates, barbiturates and other central nervous system depressants. Also included are 1,100 slang terms and expressions dealing with the drug addict and with the pharmacist. In clear terms it defines and explains such common terms as glue sniffing, heroin, marijuana, etc.

NICEM Index to Health and Safety Education--Multimedia. 2nd ed. Los Angeles: National Information Center for Educational Media. $26.50 paper. $18.50 microfiche. (18,000 entries).

Over 18,000 entries list non-book titles dealing with both general and very specific areas of health and safety education. Typical of the NICEM indexes, this volume also gives title, series, release date, technical description, LC card number, producer/ distributor code, and an annotation. A helpful subject index and directory of producers/distributors also appears in the volume. This book should be purchased by district media centers to loan to individual school libraries.

HOME REPAIRS AND TOOLS

Moore, William and Robert Cynar. Fun with Tools. New York: Random, 1957. 64p. $1.95.

A slim book illustrated with black and white photographs and drawings, Fun with Tools describes in two pages each the most common tools, i.e., rulers and tape measures, hammers and screwdrivers, saws, tin snips, square, block plane, and hand drill. In two additional sections the authors offer specific instructions for making objects from wood and from metal or metal foil. A glossary of workshop terms appears at the back of the book. This volume, because it describes each tool, its use, and its proper care, will be valuable for upper elementary and junior high school collections.

Symons, Arthur. 101 Things a Boy Can Do Around the House. New York: Sterling, 1961. 128p. $2.50.

Written in a comfortable, conversational style, this guide offers specific instructions for performing a number of necessary chores around the home. Divided into a number of broad subjects, it includes painting, knowing tools, easy creative projects, taking care of the family car, taking care of the lawn, garden and house plants; tricks for easier home maintenance; taking care of the plumbing and heating; household electricity; and safety in the home. Under each topic there are several specific tasks, e.g., unplugging drains, replacing broken plugs, changing a tire, driving a nail correctly, etc. Although this book is somewhat old, the information is still valid; it should be available in both elementary and junior high school libraries.

Demske, Dick. The Instant Home Repair Handbook. Mundelein, Ill.: Career Institute, 1973. 308p. $2.65.

A quick reference guide for the home handyman, this book covers everything from home insurance to planning a regular maintenance program. Included are specifics primarily related to the home itself, such as replacing a wall switch, repairing walks and driveways, mending screens. Much more sophisticated in approach than Symons' book, The Instant Home Repair Handbook is an inexpensive addition for junior high school libraries which need slightly more advanced material.

Hand, Jackson. Complete Book of Home Repairs and Maintenance. New York: Popular Science/Harper, 1971. 358p. (A Popular Science Book). $8.95.

Well illustrated with black and white photographs and drawings, this guide to home repair is divided into three parts: Tools and working facilities; Keeping utility systems in repair; and Repairs to the structure of your home. Particularly helpful to upper elementary and junior high students will be the first section describing tools and how to use them. The last two sections are filled with instructions for specific repairs, from fixing a leaking faucet to patching concrete.

MECHANICS

Darby, Gene. What Is a Simple Machine. Chicago: Benefic, 1961. 48p. $2.40.

A book for the youngest primary level students, What Is a Simple Machine utilizes a vocabulary of 120 words to explain the six basic simple machines: levers, wheels, pulleys, inclined plane, screws, and wedge. Each of the six is identified, described, explained, and demonstrated in the text. Illustrated throughout, the book has a brief vocabulary list which doubles as a rudimentary index.

Kaufman, Joe. Joe Kaufman's What Makes It Go? What Makes It Work? What Makes It Fly? What Makes It Float? New York: Golden, 1971. 93p. $3.95.

Designed primarily for children aged six to ten, this fascinating book is simple to understand and contains interesting explanations of the concepts behind the mechanics of a wide range of appliances, machines, and vehicles. Examples of items included are the tricycle, jet airplane, sewing machine, skating rink, saw, ballpoint pen, thermometer, piano, telephone, tape recorder, kaleidoscope, movie projector, television camera, radar, to mention only a few. Detailed color drawings depict each item; some drawings include cutaways to show the working parts or interior. Valuable both to the social studies and science curricula, this book will be pored over by young browsers.

Applied Science

Keen, Martin L. How It Works. New York: Grosset, 1972. 147p. $4.95.

Brief explanations of how things work. Items selected for inclusion are those devices most commonly used in every day life, such as telephones, electric lights, radio, television, ball point pens, locks, elevators, etc. The text is supplemented by a glossary of technical terms and many clear illustrations. The full index is also helpful.

Lodewijk, T. and others. The Way Things Work; An Illustrated Encyclopedia of Technology. Special ed. for young people. New York: Simon and Schuster, 1973. 288p. $9.95.

Adapted from a more technical volume with the same title, this book covers, according to the authors, simple mechanical functions like block and tackle, basic scientific principles such as in supersonic speed, and complex industrial processes as those which convert energy into work and use light to make pictures. Altogether, there are 91 individual entries, each accompanied by a two-color illustration. A subject index helps to locate information in the text.

Stockel, Martin W. Auto Mechanics Fundamentals. South Holland, Ill.: Goodheart-Willcox, 1969. 480p. $9.28.

Bearing the subtitle "The how and why of the design, construction and operation of automotive units," Auto Mechanics Fundamentals is a how-to book written in clear style and illustrated with hundreds of drawings and photographs. Among the many aspects of auto mechanics included are building an engine, ignition systems, cooling systems, automobile brakes, electrical systems, etc. Each automotive unit is approached by starting with the basic theory involved and moving to its practical applications. Each chapter ends with a clear concise summary and questions to test comprehension and retention. Although a rather long "Dictionary of Automotive Terms" appears in the back of the book, the author helpfully defines words as they occur in the text. Throughout the book, he stresses safety precautions and safe working practices. An important chapter explores job possibilities. Junior high school students will find this book both attractive and useful.

Chilton's Auto Repair Manual. Philadelphia: Chilton, 1953- . Annual. $18.00.

First published in 1953, Chilton's Auto Repair Manual is a guide to the repair of American automobiles. For each model of car, the guide describes all systems including detailed instructions for installation and removal of parts. Troubleshooting charts and instructions for assembly and reassembly of various types of transmissions occupies a large part of the text. Filled with illustrations in the form of drawings, diagrams and photographs plus charts and tables of specifications, the book belongs in junior high libraries needing this type of information.

Kleeberg, Irene Cumming. Bicycle Repair. New York: Franklin Watts, 1973. 60p. $3.95.

A title in the Concise Guide Series, Bicycle Repair provides instructions for repairs in various categories, such as tires, common wheel problems, brakes, gear mechanism, chain, seat and handlebars, lights, pedals, and preventive maintenance. Following the text there is a bicycle repair checklist, a glossary, bibliography, and an index. Illustrated throughout with photographs and drawings, this easy to read text will appeal to the slow reader as well as to the bike addict.

Coles, Clarence W. and Harold T. Glenn. Glenn's Complete Bicycle Manual: Selection, Maintenance, Repair. New York: Crown, 1973. 339p. $7.95. $5.95 paper.

Utilizing photographs and drawings and clear step by step directions, the authors show how to assemble, adjust, and maintain American, European, and Japanese bicycles. They also include useful troubleshooting tables and lists of maintenance tasks to be performed monthly, semiannually, and annually. An important section gives tips for choosing a bicycle. Although there is no index, the book has a detailed table of contents and many cross references throughout the text.

PETS

Chrystie, Frances N. Pets. New rev. ed. Boston: Little, Brown, 1974. 269p. $6.95.

A standard title on pets, this book bears the subtitle: "A complete handbook on the care, understanding, and appreciation of all kinds of animal pets." An important introduction discusses the responsibility of owners to pets. It covers dogs, cats, small caged animals, caged birds, aquarium and vivarium pets, wild animals and birds, farm animals, ponies and saddle horses, and first aid and common diseases.

Morgan, Alfred. A Pet Book for Boys and Girls. New York: Scribner, 1951. 254p. $5.95.

This rather complete pet book includes instructions for the care of dogs, cats, rabbits, guinea pigs, golden hamsters, skunks, raccoons, squirrels, flying squirrels, moles and mice, American chameleons, tortoises and turtles, alligators, goldfish, tropical fish, canaries, parrots, and wild bird pets. It also lists some general rules for the care of pets.

Taggart, Jean E. Pet Names. New York: Scarecrow, 1962. 387p. $6.00.

The purpose of this book is to bring together suitable foreign

Applied Science 231

and English names for pets. Included in the various languages are lists of names for birds, cats, dogs, fish, amphibians, salamanders and newts, horses, insects and spiders, and small and other wild animal pets.

SEWING

Zarchy, Jeanette. Sewing. New York: Knopf, 1952. 45p. $3.41.

Written for middle elementary level children, this book in a minimum of words describes the materials and equipment needed for sewing, such as sewing box, needles, thread, thimble, shears and scissors, measuring tape, emery bag, and pins. In addition it shows how to make a variety of work stitches, decorative and embroidery stitches, seams, binding, and how to sew buttons, snaps, and hooks and eyes. Each item appears as a heading in large bold type followed by a paragraph of text and a clear simple illustration. Instructions for sewing a number of things from pincushions to stuffed toys are in the back of the book. The clarity of both text and drawings in this manual makes it an excellent choice for beginners. Although it has no index, all entries are listed in the table of contents on a single page.

Corrigan, Barbara. Of Course You Can Sew! Basics of Sewing for the Young Beginner. Garden City, N.Y.: Doubleday, 1971. 127p. $4.95.

Very simple instructions, casual style, and many illustrations highlight this guide to sewing for young people. Included in the text is information on equipment, fabrics, basic stitches, accessories, ponchos, capes, shifts, robes, skirts, blouses, and patterns. Easy to understand, this book will appeal to both upper elementary and junior high school students.

Rydell, Wendy. The Instant Sewing Handbook. Mundelein, Ill.: Career Institute, 1972. 315p. $2.65.

A pocket-sized handbook, The Instant Sewing Handbook contains a wealth of information for a small cost. Covering nearly every aspect of sewing, it tells how to select styles appropriate to various figures, how to select a pattern size, how to read and alter patterns, fabrics, sewing tools, constructing the garment, pressing the garment, and tailoring. It also includes a section arranged alphabetically which explains in text and illustrations how to perform specific tasks, e.g., easing, facings, fitting, etc. This helpful little book can be used by junior high schools and can also be recommended for purchase by individuals.

Enthoven, Jacqueline. Stitchery for Children: A Manual for Teachers, Parents, and Children. New York: Van Nostrand, 1968. 172p. $7.95.

This manual for teachers should be considered for the elementary and junior high school library particularly if it is called to the attention of teachers. Beginning with two-and-one-half-year-olds and progressing through high school, the author describes with pictured examples stitchery executed by children and teenagers. A section of the book is devoted to the description and variations of stitches with simple drawings illustrating each. Of particular interest might be the chapter discussing stitchery for the physically handicapped, the mentally retarded, the left-handed child, the blind child, the emotionally or socially maladjusted child, and the gifted child. Suggestions are offered for materials--hoops, yarn, needles, fabrics, and so on. An index of stitches is helpful.

Guild, Vera P. Good Housekeeping New Complete Book of Needlecraft. New York: Good Housekeeping, 1971. 548p. $8.95.

This book provides how-to instructions for all major types of needlework. Chapter contents include sewing, embroidery, quilting, smocking, needlepoint, rug making, knitting, crochet, tatting and netting, macrame, hand weaving, sewing for the home, machine embroidery, mending, and gifts to make. More than 1,400 explanatory diagrams and drawings and 24 color photographs illustrate the book. Emphasis throughout the text is on teaching a neophyte basic steps of each type of needlework. The section on gifts to make includes patterns and instructions for creating items ranging from bean bag toys to dog baskets. A full index aids in locating specific items. This book will be much used in junior high library collections.

Klapper, Marvin. Fabric Almanac. 2nd ed. New York: Fairchild, 1971. 191p. $6.95.

This book consists primarily of a glossary of terms. Each entry has a brief two- to five-line definition identifying a type of fabric, a trademark, and so forth. In addition to the definitions in the main body, there are several factual sections discussing techniques, processes, and statistics. Although this reference book would be interesting for most junior high home economics students, it is really essential in junior highs only in support of rather sophisticated sewing classes.

SPACE

Moore, Patrick. Moon Flight Atlas. New rev. and enl. ed. New York: Rand McNally, 1970. 64p. $6.95.

Covering a variety of topics, the book includes two-page spreads for each. Included are, for example, features of the moon, mapping the moon, an atlas of the moon, the far side of the moon, the Apollo plan, the Lunar module, new landing sites, etc. The outstanding color photographs actually utilize more space than the readable text.

Applied Science

Bergaust, Erik, ed. The New Illustrated Space Encyclopedia.
Rev. ed. New York: Putnam, 1970. 190p. $4.29.

Approximately 2,000 astronautical terms are defined in the
revised edition of Bergaust's space encyclopedia. Also included
are facts about the moon landing; logs of all space flights; data on
the sun, moon, stars, planets, and satellites; biographical sketches
of United States astronauts; specifications for launch vehicles; etc.
Illustrated with photographs, it is easily used by upper elementary
and junior high school students.

Jones, Sir Harold Spencer and others. The New Space Encyclopedia; A Guide to Astronomy and Space Exploration. New
rev. ed. New York: Dutton, 1973. 326p. $14.95.

Over 800 entries fill the new revised edition of this space
encyclopedia. Alphabetically arranged, the entries range in length
from a few lines to several pages. Photographs, drawings, and
maps further explain definitions. Topics covered include artificial
satellites, rocketry and missiles, the moon, the planets, the stars,
and space medicine. Although this book is probably too difficult
for most elementary school children, it is a worthwhile addition to
junior high school libraries.

RECREATION AND HOBBIES

Students in elementary and junior high schools should be able to turn to the school library to locate information for recreational activities as well as for class work. Young people of this age become enthusiastically involved in special interests covering a wide gamut of topics. For instance, children aged approximately eight to twelve are notorious for collecting objects, ranging from rocks to baseball cards to coins. Many of these amateur collectors will have six or eight collections going at one time. Some children become avid sports enthusiasts, poring over every book they can find about specific sports, including how to play and improve one's skill, records set by champions, and biographies of outstanding players. Whether it is playing a guitar, making a film, or giving a puppet show, the young student should be able to find necessary materials in his school library.

Reference books per se for this age group are sparse, but trade books drawn from the general book collection can be used to answer students' questions. Whether or not these books should be made non-circulating reference books will depend upon the quantity of the library's resources and the student demand. Included in this chapter are titles covering a wide range of topics. They are arranged under the following subheadings: Hobbies--general works, Hobbies--collecting, Miscellaneous hobbies, Bicycling and motorcycling, Crafts, Games, Model building, Photography, Outdoor recreation, and Sports. Supplementing these books will be many included in the chapters on science and technology, for many youngsters will consider as hobbies seashell collecting, wild flower identification, cooking, needlework, or auto mechanics. In general, children's special interests should be treated as seriously as curriculum-oriented subjects, for through their recreational activities they acquire much knowledge relative to their formal course of study.

HOBBIES--General Works

Liebers, Arthur. <u>Fifty Favorite Hobbies.</u> New York: Hawthorne, 1968. 188p. $4.95.

This easy to read guide describes 50 hobbies for young people. Entries tell how to begin the hobby and give special information such as definitions of terms and a booklist for further reading. The book unfortunately contains no index; however, information can be located without much difficulty through the table of contents.

Vermes, Hal G. Hobbies for Boys. New York: Young Men's Christian Association, 1965. 127p. $2.95.

Suggested hobbies in this book are listed in chapters with broad subject headings. Chapter titles follow: The fun of having a hobby; Let's collect something; "A picture is worth 1000 words"; Let's communicate; Let's explore nature; Let's be a craftsman; Let's look at science; and Let's be a good sport. For each hobby, the author gives a description, a cost estimate, and a bibliography. While the descriptions are good, the costs and booklists are sadly out of date.

Vermes, Jean C. Hobbies for Girls. New York: Young Men's Christian Association, 1965. 128p. $2.95.

Similar to Hobbies for Boys, Hobbies for Girls contains chapters as follows: Everybody has a hobby; Collecting can be fun; Talent can be developed; Nature is all around you; Crafts can be useful; Science can be exciting; Homemaking can be a hobby; Sports can be for you. While each suggestion is carefully described, the cost estimates and bibliographies are dated.

Zarchy, Harry. Here's Your Hobby. New York: Knopf, 1950. 233p. $3.25.

Although this book is relatively old, it is included because it contains hobbies normally omitted from hobby handbooks. Covered in this book are photography, fresh water fishing, salt water fishing, ceramics, stamp collecting, home repair, archery, tropical fish, collecting butterflies and moths, sailing, collecting leaves, and painting. It contains an index as well as a bibliography.

HOBBIES--Collecting

Salny, Roslyn W. Hobby Collections A-Z. New York: Crowell, 1965. 245p. $4.50.

Alphabetically arranged from "autographs" to "toy banks," Hobby Collections A-Z contains whole chapters on each of a number of inexpensive items to collect. For each topic, pertinent information is included, e.g., what to collect, how to start, where to find items, how to store and display them, how to learn more, where to find more information (bibliographies). At the back of the book is an A-Z list of additional things to collect and an adequate index.

Smaridge, Norah and Hilda Hunter. The Teen-ager's Guide to Collecting Practically Anything. New York: Dodd, Mead, 1972. 183p. $4.50.

Emphasizing quality rather than quantity in collections, the authors describe for teenagers various types of things to collect. Among those included are stamps, coins, china, glass, beach treasure, wood, and prints, as well as information on how to catalog, clean, store, and display the material. This book will be quite useful for junior high students.

Johnstone, Kathleen Yerger. Collecting Seashells. New York: Grosset and Dunlap, 1970. 198p. $5.99.

Every aspect of seashell collecting is approached in this manual. From the definition of a seashell to types of shells, the author provides an interesting, well-illustrated text. She discusses how and where to search for shells, collecting equipment, recordkeeping, cleaning and curing, cataloging, storing, displaying, and exhibiting. Appended are lists of suggested reading and museum exhibits.

Young, Helen. Here Is Your Hobby: Doll Collecting. New York: Putnam, 1964. 128p. $4.19.

This book not only describes doll collecting but offers information on how to make dolls of candles, papier-maché, etc. Doll clothing and patterns for making it are included with explicit directions. Repairing dolls and doll houses are discussed as are paper dolls, rag dolls, and wood dolls. A bibliography and an index are included.

Rosenfeld, Sam. The Story of Coins. New York: Harvey, 1968. 126p. $4.95.

The story of how money began and how ancient coins looked provides the introduction for this book. Sections on starting a coin collection and caring for coins follow. Official coins of the United States are described in text and shown in photographs. An interesting chart of key coins tells the value of each coin listed. A coin glossary, a bibliography, a photo index, and a general index conclude this volume.

Reinfeld, Fred. Catalogue of the World's Most Popular Coins. Rev. ed. New York: Doubleday, 1973. $8.95.

Accurate and comprehensive, this book shows coins, modern, medieval, and ancient, which are desirable and available for purchase. Arranged alphabetically by country, it describes each coin with its picture and gives the coin's composition. The book could also provide added stimulus to the study of history and economics.

Reinfeld, Fred. Stamp Collectors' Handbook. Adapted by Burton Hobson. Garden City, N.Y.: Doubleday, 1970. 152p. $4.95.

Following an interesting history of the United States postal system, this book discusses the tools and terms of stamp collecting. The bulk of the text consists of postage stamps arranged chronologically by year, with values given for both used and unused copies.

U.S. Postal Service. Postage Stamps of the United States. Washington, D.C.: U.S. Government Printing Office, 1927- . Biennial. $2.50.

The subtitle states that this inexpensive book is a complete survey of all the United States postage stamps beginning with the first adhesive stamp in 1847. Besides being useful in philately, Postage Stamps of the United States could provide interesting enrichment for social studies classes, particularly American history.

Scott Publications, Inc. Standard Postage Stamp Catalogue: The Encyclopedia of Philately. New York: Scott, 1868- . Annual. 3 vols. $9.00 each vol.

International in scope, this illustrated catalog lists all stamps ever issued by any government. It gives the date of issue, the shape, and the value of each entry. Published annually since 1867, it is updated by Scott's Monthly Stamp Journal.

MISCELLANEOUS HOBBIES

Fenton, Robert S. Chess For You. New York: Grosset and Dunlap, 1973. 84p. $4.95.

Chess For You begins with the chess board itself and then describes each of the chessmen, their power, and how they move. Openings and attacks are discussed as well as advanced rules and suggestions. Carefully illustrated, this book is easy to read and easy to follow.

Levine, Jack and Takeru Iijima. Understanding Musical Instruments; How to Select Your Instrument. Rev. version. New York: Warner, 1971. 124p. $3.95.

Originally published in 1959 by Sterling Press as What Instruments for Me?, this simple well-written book describes each instrument, tells how it is played, and how it plays. Illustrated with drawings and photographs, it covers the piano and organ, the strings, the woodwinds, the brass, the percussion, other instruments, and the voice. It features a selected list of recordings following each grouping of instruments.

Humphrey, Marylou and Ron Humphrey. Cheerleading and Song Leading. Rutland, Vt.: Tuttle, 1970. 143p. $5.75.

This guidebook begins with suggestions for building self-confidence and strengthening leadership qualities. It proceeds to cover the cheerleader's main jobs at school, at the games, and routines. This book, one of few on this popular subject, will be sought after in upper elementary and junior high school by both cheerleaders and aspiring cheerleaders.

Collins, A. Frederick. The Radio Amateur's Handbook. 12th ed. Rev. by Robert Hertzberg. New York: Crowell, 1970. 374p. $5.95.

All the basics for the amateur radio operator are included in this book. Fundamentals of electricity, vacuum-tube principles, power supplies, receiver theory, the FCC amateur licenses, mobile operation, and setting up and operating an amateur station are examples of the topics covered. A 55-page glossary is appended.

Draper, Nancy and Margaret F. Atkinson. Ballet for Beginners. New York: Knopf, 1951. 115p. $3.95.

Ballet is covered in this book from the children's ballet class to the history of ballet. All basic positions are described in the text and photographs with suggestions for home practice. Short biographies of famous ballerinas, brief synopses of popular ballets, a dictionary of ballet terms, and a chronological list of great names in ballet are included.

Alkema, Chester Jay. The Complete Crayon Book in Color. New York: Sterling, 1969. 156p. $8.95.

All aspects of crayon work are covered in this attractive book, beginning with the different kinds of crayons. Included are chapters on design, crayon stencils, mosaic technique, background materials, crayon reliefs, melted wax crayons, crayon resist technique, and crayon etching technique. A final section tells how to mount crayon drawings.

Weiss, Harvey. Pencil, Pen and Brush; Drawing for Beginners. New York: Young Scott, 1961. 64p. $4.50.

Although there are a number of good drawing books, this one is simple and appealing. It includes instructions for drawing animals, the figure, heads, landscapes, scenes, and suggests ways to experiment with pencil, pen, and brush.

Pels, Gertrude. Easy Puppets; Making and Using Hand Puppets. New York: Crowell, 1951. 104p. $3.95.

Hand puppets of all kinds are described in this book complete with instructions for making them. Examples include potato head puppets, rubber ball puppets, paper-bag puppets, sock puppets, wooden spoon puppets, and papier-maché puppets. A number of different stages are shown as well as how to prepare scenery and props.

Adair, Margaret Weeks and Elizabeth Patapoff. Folk Puppet Plays for the Social Studies. New York: Day, 1972. 120p. $6.95.

The main part of this book is devoted to a number of folk puppet plays based on tales and legends from around the world. Each play is followed by study notes tracing the history of the tale, and production notes giving suggestions for scenes, props, and puppets. The final two chapters, "Different Ways to Dramatize Stories," and "Production Pointers: Stage, Lights, Scenery, Making Your Puppets," will be valuable to puppeteers of all ages.

Severn, Bill. Big Book of Magic. New York: McKay, 1973. 238p. $5.95.

Author of a number of books on magic, Bill Severn begins this volume with a brief history of magic. The remainder of the book is filled with tricks: magic with cards, rope magic, money magic, magic with handkerchiefs, close-up magic, stage magic, and things that go with magic. A rather extensive index completes the book.

Wels, Byron G. Here Is Your Hobby: Magic. New York: Putnam, 1967. 95p. $4.19.

Prepared for the beginner, this book of magic includes a number of easy tricks. Card tricks, illusions, mentalist tricks, and scientific magic are all included.

Severn, Bill. Pack of Fun; 101 Unusual Things to Do with Playing Cards and to Know About Them. New York: McKay, 1967. 170p. $3.89.

In this interesting book are a variety of games and stunts involving playing cards. Rules for card games for one, two, and a group of players are given. Also included are telling fortunes with cards, mind reading, solving puzzles, magic tricks, juggling, and card collecting.

BICYCLING AND MOTORCYCLING

Sarnoff, Jane and Reynold Ruffins. A Great Bicycle Book. New York: Scribner, 1973. 31p. $5.95.

Designed to help the non-mechanical bicycle rider, aged eight and up, to maintain, repair, and understand a bicycle. A Great Bicycle Book describes the various parts of the bicycle and tells in simple language how to take care of them. Illustrated in garish, "mod" colors, this book will appeal to children of all ages.

Frankel, Lillian and Godfrey Frankel. Bike-Ways (101 Things to Do with a Bike). Rev. ed. New York: Sterling, 1972. 128p. $3.95.

Consisting of a series of short and easily identified topics on the subject of bicycling, the book includes information on bike clubs; bike games; trips and tours; camping; how to ride; how to select a bike; parts and accessories; bike safety; earning money with a bike; care and repair of a bike; and bike photography. Many photographs illustrate the book.

Lyttle, Richard B. The Complete Beginner's Guide to Bicycling. Garden City, N.Y.: Doubleday, 1974. 127p. $4.95.

This guide to bicycling for junior high age people covers a variety of aspects of cycling. From learning how to ride to caring for and repairing a bicycle, the book provides concise information. Topics such as the benefits of cycling, bike safety, competition, touring, camping, and the history of the bicycle are all included. A bibliography of further reading is appended.

Edmonds, I. G. Motorcycling for Beginners; A Manual for Safe Riding. Philadelphia: Macrae Smith, 1972. 156p. $4.95.

Written throughout with a safety orientation, Motorcycling for Beginners covers choosing and driving a motorcycle, how it works, following the rules of the road, maintenance and repairs, traveling alone or in groups, and participating in competitive sports. A glossary of terms, an index, and a number of black and white photographs increase the value of this book.

CRAFTS

Index to Handicrafts, Model Making, and Workshop Projects: 4th supplement 1962-1967. Comp. by Winifred Alt. Westwood, Mass.: Faxon, 1969. 468p. $14.00.

Designed as an index to popular handicraft and workshop projects for home and school, it indexes books and periodicals. As with all indexes, librarians would check their holdings against the list of materials indexed before purchasing this volume or its predecessors.

Cole, Ann, and others. I Saw a Purple Cow and 100 Other Recipes for Learning. Boston: Little, 1972. 96p. $5.95, $2.95 paper.

This hodge-podge of activities for the preschooler is designed to be a curriculum for the home but will also be helpful to preschool and primary teachers. It includes first the basic recipes for making paste, finger paint, fun dough, and cornstarch clay, and then is divided into sections called Pretending, Creating, Simple crafts, Collecting, Music and rhythm, Rhythm activities, Finger games, Simple experiments, Make a kitchen garden, Learning games, Word games, and Parties.

Boy Scouts of America. The Cub Book. New York: Putnam, 1967. 63p. $3.64.

Utilizing one page for each craft or suggestion of something to do, The Cub Book includes a variety of ideas. From making a puppet show to preparing tin can walkers, to building homemade musical instruments, the book covers a variety of ideas suitable for youngsters in the primary grades.

Foley, Doris E. Art Recipes. Dansville, N.Y.: Owen, 1960. 48p. $1.95 paper.

This valuable little book contains numerous recipes for making materials for art. Included are powder paint, finger paint, printing ink, paste, clay, papier-maché, sawdust modeling clay, dough modeling clay, plus recipes for holidays and nature study. A good index locates specific instructions quickly.

Sattler, Helen Roney. Recipes for Art and Craft Materials. New York: Lothrop, 1973. 128p. $4.50.

Very easy to follow instructions are the feature of this valuable little book. Recipes included tell how to make a variety of pastes, modeling compounds, papier-maché, casting compounds, paint and paint mediums, inks, and other craft materials. This resource is a must for elementary libraries.

Shaw, David. The Girl's Book of Handicrafts. London: Ward Lock, 1970. 160p. $5.95.

Very explicit instructions tell how to do the following crafts: weaving; leatherwork; lampshades, feltwork, and novelties; needlework; raffia, cord and seagrass work; and surface decoration. This book is illustrated with many sketches and some photographs and is indexed.

Beard, Lina and Adelia B. Beard. The American Girls' Handy Book. Rutland, Vt.: Tuttle, 1968. 474p. $6.25.

First published in 1887, this very old book is quite useful despite the flowery text, for it contains simple instructions for things not found in other craft books. Arranged by the seasons: Spring, Summer, Autumn, and Winter, it includes everything from planning nutting parties to making sea-side cottage decorations. Although the old-fashioned illustrations may frighten off today's youngsters, the book will fascinate them once they get into it.

Beard, D. C. The American Boys' Handy Book. Rutland, Vt.: Tuttle, 1966. 391p. $5.50.

Like The American Girls' Handy Book, this book was published long ago and is arranged by seasons. Claiming to tell "what to do and how to do it," it discusses kites, knots, traps, puppets, whirligigs, ice boats, soap bubbles, and numerous items. The very simple instructions for making the various things will offset the old-fashioned illustrations.

Hellegers, Louisa B. and Anne E. Kallem. Family Book of Crafts. New York: Sterling, 1973. 576p. $16.79.

Part I of this excellent book describes the medium of crafts, e.g., beads, crayon, fabric, glass, horseshoe nails, natural materials, paint, papers, plastic foam, string, wood, and wool. Part II describes the various crafts themselves and includes simple to follow instructions for making the items. Typical crafts are candles, collages, creative gifts, decorative masks, etc. Prepared in an excellent, easy to use format, this book has an index and three useful appendixes: Ideas for designs, Suppliers, and a Bibliography.

Di Valentin, Maria and others. Practical Encyclopedia of Crafts. New York: Sterling, 1970. 544p. $20.00.

Similar to the Family Book of Crafts, the Practical Encyclopedia of Crafts contains a completely different set of instructions and lists of crafts. Covered in this volume are art materials; clay; fabric; metal and glass; natural materials; paper; plastic and leather; print; scrap materials; and wood. Carefully illustrated with photographs and drawings, the book is written in a clear style with all information presented logically in easy to understand statements. The large readable type and pleasing page arrangement encourages readers to browse as well as look up specific information. A directory of suppliers, a bibliography, and an index add to the book's usefulness. It is recommended for all age levels.

GAMES

Matterson, Elizabeth. Games for the Very Young; Finger Plays and Nursery Games. New York: American Heritage, 1969. 206p. $3.83.

This fine, large collection lists numerous finger plays, singing games with simple music, and action stories. It is arranged by subjects of interest to primary and preschool children, and contains an index of first lines.

Grayson, Marion. Let's Do Fingerplays. Washington: Luce, 1962. 109p. $5.50.

Arranged by subjects appropriate to the kindergarten set, Let's Do Fingerplays consists of dozens of short finger games, many of which are illustrated with line drawings. The book contains an index of first lines and an index of titles.

Recreation and Hobbies 243

Mulac, Margaret E. and Marian S. Holmes. The School Game Book. New York: Harper, 1950. 131p. $3.95.

Nearly 100 games, activities, songs, and recreation ideas fill this little book which was designed for the classroom teacher. Included are dramatic games, drawing games, guessing and magic games, number and arithmetic games, party and feature programs, seat games and relays, singing games and action songs, songs for little children, treasure hunt games, word and spelling games, and miscellaneous games. Each game is graded and is carefully explained so that young children can understand.

Webb, Marian A. Games for Younger Children. New York: Morrow, 1947. 124p. $4.25.

This book describes eighty very easy games to be played by young children. In addition it includes counting out rhymes, holiday parties, birthday parties, Mother Goose parties, and lists of stories, poetry, and songs. There is no index; however, the games are all listed alphabetically and the holiday parties are arranged according to the school calendar.

Bancroft, Jessie H. Games. Rev. and enl. ed. New York: Macmillan, 1937. 685p. $9.00.

This standard collection of games contains explicit instructions for all types of games for all ages of players. Included are singing games, quiet games, stunts and contests, games for one or two, track and field games, ball games, active games, and more. Each entry tells the number of players, the intended age level, the appropriate play area, and a concise description and rules for playing. The title index locates the games by page and also indicates the grade level.

Harbin, E. O. The Fun Encyclopedia. New York: Abingdon, 1968. 1008p. $6.95.

This favorite book is best described by its subtitle: "An all-purpose plan book for those interested in recreation for clubs, schools, churches, and the home." More than 2,400 activities for all ages are suggested. Included are all types of games, hobbies, outdoor activities, sports, dramatics, puppetry, magic, and parties, to mention only a few. A long bibliography, an alphabetical index, and a classified index follow the main text.

Ickis, Marguerite. The Book of Games and Entertainments the World Over. New York: Dodd, Mead, 1969. 165p. $5.00.

This is an ideal source for locating games and entertainment of other lands in correlation with a social studies project. It covers games, festivals, sports, birthdays, drama, folk dances and ideas for international parties. Although there is no index, all items are listed by section in the contents. The text itself is concise and fairly easy to read.

Hunt, Sarah Ethridge. Games and Sports the World Around. 3rd ed. New York: Ronald, 1964. 271p. $6.00.

This collection of games is arranged geographically, and urges the use of games and sports to develop an understanding of human relationships. Each entry contains the age level, number of players, playing area, necessary supplies, and instructions for playing. Appendices include definition of terms and a bibliography. Indexes include an alphabetical title index, an age level index, degree of activity index, playing area index, and type of activity index.

Harbin, E. O. Games of Many Nations. New York: Abingdon, 1954. 160p. $2.95.

Alphabetically arranged by country, this book lists from one to more than twenty games per country. In addition to instructions for playing, each entry gives the number of players, the formation and equipment, and the action. A game index, a classified index, and a list of forfeits follow the text. This work ideally supplements upper elementary school students' social studies classes.

MODEL BUILDING

Yates, Raymond F. The Boys' Book of Model Railroading. New York: Harper, 1951. 172p. $3.50.

This handbook tells how model railroads are constructed and how the owner of a set of model trains can get the greatest possible enjoyment from them. The easy to follow instructions are illustrated by drawings and photographs. A list of railroad terms is contained in Chapter 13. Unfortunately, the book has no index and a very brief table of contents; therefore, the user must locate the information he needs by browsing.

Arora Plastics Corp. The Complete Handbook of Model Car Racing. Englewood Cliffs, N.J.: Prentice-Hall, 1967. 151p. $7.95.

Following a history of model car racing, this book lists information on scales, gear drives, ratio and friction, suspension, tools, motors, tires and wheels, painting and detailing, electricity and pickups, controllers, ready-to-run cars, drivers' skills, building your own car, race time, and advantages of home racing. Utilizing photographs on nearly every page, the book is attractive even to a non-enthusiast.

Musciano, Walter A. Building and Operating Model Ships. New York: Funk and Wagnalls, 1965. 189p. $4.50.

Provides the reader with a variety of ship model construction techniques so that he can apply his knowledge to projects other

Recreation and Hobbies

than those listed by the author. Arranged in order of complexity beginning with the most simple, the text consists of step-by-step instructions for construction illustrated by drawings and photographs. A glossary of nautical terms is appended.

McEntee, Howard G. The Model Aircraft Handbook. 5th ed. New York: Crowell, 1968. 226p. $6.95.

Based on an earlier edition by William Winter, The Model Aircraft Handbook contains explicit construction details written in a rather difficult style. Contents include types of models, aerodynamics and proportions, preparation of working drawings, construction, landing gears and pontoons, propellers, etc. A rather long glossary and a list of model plane and rocket associations are appended.

Stine, G. Harry. Handbook of Model Rocketry. 3rd ed. completely rev. Chicago: Follett, 1970. 304p. $6.95, $4.95 paper.

The Handbook of Model Rocketry contains detailed, easy to follow instructions written in a clear conversational style. After describing what model rocketry is, the author discusses engines, ignition and launching, model rocket ranges, clubs and contests, and much more. A bibliography, a glossary, and an index follow the main text.

PHOTOGRAPHY

Sussman, Aaron. The Amateur Photographer's Handbook. 8th rev. ed. New York: Crowell, 1973. 562p. $8.95.

A comprehensive standard work on photography, this handbook presents aspects of the topic relevant to the non-professional. Sample chapters include: The magic of light; What the lens does; What camera shall I get; Film and exposure; The picture; People and closeups; Action and flash; All about filters; etc. A fifteen-page glossary of terms and a full index complete this work. Junior high school camera buffs will find this book extremely valuable.

Helfman, Harry. Making Your Own Movies. New York: Morrow, 1970. 95p. $3.95.

Designed for the young person already familiar with film making terminology, this book contains clear instructions in large clear print and is ideal for the elementary and junior high school which utilizes film making in the curriculum. It describes movie equipment and tells how to shoot the movie, design titles, edit the film, make animated movies, produce the sound track, and what subjects to film.

Andersen, Yvonne. Make Your Own Animated Movies; Yellow Ball Workshop Techniques. Boston: Little, Brown, 1970. 101p. $6.95.

This interesting book shows very simply the techniques involved in making animated movies. It discusses cutouts, setting up the camera, animation, projection, editing, sound, flip cards, clay, drawing on film, tearouts, pixillation, film equipment, and art supplies.

OUTDOOR RECREATION

Paul, Aileen. Kids Camping. Garden City, N.Y.: Doubleday, 1973. 128p. $4.95.

For the beginning camper, Kids Camping is a practical guide for making camping fun and safe. It includes information on planning the trip, equipment, camp life, backpacking. It lists menus for seven days and contains a complete grocery shopping list for a party of four people. The "List of Things You Will Need" covers everything from the tent to clothespins.

Boy Scouts of America. Fieldbook; for Boy Scouts, Explorers, Scouters, Educators, Outdoorsmen. 2nd ed. New Brunswick, N.J.: Boy Scouts of America, 1967. 565p. $1.95.

This excellent guide covers hiking, camping, swimming, safety, and first aid, survival, nature, conservation, astronomy, weather, and many other topics. Illustrated with outstanding photographs on nearly every page, this book is not limited to use by Boy Scouts, but is universal in content and appeal. Following the explicit instructions, even an amateur could perform well. Well organized and easy to use, it contains an extensive bibliography and a detailed index.

Lindholm, Mauno A. Guide for Young Campers. New York: Hart, 1961. 192p. $3.95.

This simple guide details every procedure from preliminary preparations for camping, to fire building, outdoor cooking, wire hanger craft, aluminum foil cookery, tools, lamps, knots, hazards, trail marks and nature tips. Easy to use, all directions are listed in numbered sequence, usually with illustrations for each step. A "Day Hike Checklist" and an "Overnight Hike Checklist" precede the index.

Macfarlan, Allan. The Boy's Book of Indian Skills. Harrisburg, Pa.: Stackpole, 1969. 159p. $4.50.

Instructions for "living the Indian way at home and on the trail" include scouting, clothing, storytelling, and staging ceremonies. Whether it is "making gear and regalia for the tribe"

Recreation and Hobbies 247

or "becoming a wary brave," the topics are so interesting that they overcome the book's small print and reading difficulty.

Sparano, Vin T. Complete Outdoors Encyclopedia. New York: Harper, 1972. 622p. $13.95.

This essential source of information will aid the outdoorsman in hunting, fishing, camping, boating, archery, first aid, and related subjects. The profusion of photographs illustrate both equipment and procedures in various activities. The section called "Outdoor Information Guide" lists fish and game departments and state park commissions, national park service regional offices, state travel information, organizations for outdoor recreation, federal recreation symbols, and North American shooting preserves. A bibliography and a lengthy index complete this volume.

SPORTS

Kann, Herbert. The Junior Illustrated Encyclopedia of Sports. 4th ed. New York: Bobbs-Merrill, 1970. 591p. $6.95.

Many photographs illustrate this book which contains long articles on major sports, i.e., auto racing, baseball, golf, ice hockey, basketball, track and field, tennis, boxing, football, bowling, surfing, swimming, and winter skiing. It also includes biographical sketches of important figures, statistics, and records.

Keith, Harold. Sports and Games. 5th ed. rev. New York: Crowell, 1969. 411p. $5.95.

The author has written a chapter each on the following sports: badminton, baseball, basketball, bowling, boxing, football, golf, handball, ice hockey, soccer, softball, swimming and diving, tennis, track and field, volleyball, and wrestling. For each sport he gives its history, some outstanding performers, instructions on how to play, and diagrams of playing areas when appropriate. A rather detailed index completes this work.

Jennison, Keith W., ed. The Concise Encyclopedia of Sports. New York: Watts, 1970. 165p. $6.95.

Appropriate for both upper elementary and junior high students, this encyclopedia is arranged alphabetically from America's Cup and Archery to Winter Sports and Wrestling. It includes the history, development, and rules of more than 50 sports plus instruction, and capsule biographies. Even such minor sports as jai-alai and falconry are described. Many of the articles list a glossary of terms for that sport. Although the articles are unsigned, a list of contributors is appended. Profusely illustrated with photographs, drawings, and diagrams, the book will be very useful for quick reference.

Menke, Frank G. The Encyclopedia of Sports. 5th ed. New
    York: Barnes, 1974. $25.00.

Long a recognized, reliable source book, Menke's fifth edition of the Encyclopedia of Sports is comprehensive and covers a great diversity of subjects. This useful reference book includes records, history, rules, and organizations for over 80 sports. Its brief articles provide information on chess, bob-sledding, and fencing as well as on the more common sports. It also lists such hard-to-find facts as the seating capacity of the various stadiums in the United States.

Pratt, John Lowell and Jim Benagh, eds. The Official Encyclopedia
    of Sports. New York: Watts, 1964. 344, 90p.
    $6.95.

From archery to yachting, this alphabetically arranged encyclopedia contains articles on 34 sports. For each sport the book gives the history, how it is played, the star players, and a list of associations. It has a 90-page section on records in various sports, an appendix on general athletic associations, a bibliography, and a detailed index. The clear photographs and good drawings add to its usefulness.

Dobson, Margaret J. and Becky L. Sisley. Softball for Girls.
    New York: Ronald, 1971. 224p. $6.50.

A guidebook intended to aid in coaching girls to play softball, this book contains instructions in text and in photographs. Each of the various positions are described as well as batting and baserunning. Helpful hints for setting up school and recreation programs are included. A glossary of terms and a rather long bibliography conclude this book.

Liss, Howard. Basketball Talk for Beginners. New York: Messner, 1970. 95p. $4.95.

Both basketball slang and legitimate terminology appear in this small dictionary. Examples and more than 50 drawings and diagrams illustrate the terms. A diagram of the playing court and an explanation of it are included.

Hollander, Zander and Sandy Padwe. Basketball Lingo. New
    York: Grosset & Dunlap, 1971. 121p. $4.95.

This alphabetical dictionary covers from ABA to Zone Defense. The simple, succinct definitions or explanations are rather dignified despite the zany cartoon illustrations on nearly every page. Entries, ranging from one to eight lines, include many references to professional players.

Walker, Henry. Illustrated Baseball Dictionary for Young People. Irvington-on-Hudson, N.Y.: Harvey, 1970. 125p. $4.50.

This alphabetically arranged list of baseball terms is illustrated by Leonard Kessler. Entries range from one sentence to one half page and includes examples. This book is especially for elementary school students.

Archibald, Joe. Baseball Talk for Beginners. New York: Messner, 1969. 90p. $4.64.

Featuring brief highlights of baseball lore and facts, this alphabetically arranged dictionary of terms is illustrated with the author's cartoons. Definitions are written in second person from the player's point of view. Examples are sited to describe further the terms.

Jacobs, G. and J. R. McCrory. Baseball Rules in Pictures. Rev. ed. New York: Grosset and Dunlap, 1965. unp. $2.69, $1.25 paper.

Prepared in cartoon fashion, each page of this book consists of two or three cartoon drawings with one or two lines of text. Each technique is presented in a number of explicit drawings, showing the reader exactly what he is supposed to do.

Liss, Howard. Football Talk for Beginners. New York: Messner, 1970. 94p. $4.95.

This dictionary of football terminology is written in simple, easy to understand language and uses examples to illustrate the terms. More than 40 play diagrams and drawings plus referees signals are included, as is a diagram of the playing field.

Sullivan, George. Pro Football Plays in Pictures. New York: Grosset & Dunlap, 1971. 70p. $3.95, $2.95 paper.

A lengthy introduction explains standard professional football plays. The main body of text includes one play per page with a photograph, description, and illustration. The official's code of signals is appended.

Liss, Howard. Hockey Talk for Beginners. New York: Messner, 1973. 94p. $5.25.

A handbook arranged in dictionary style, this book includes terms and techniques. Numerous drawings, many of them full page, aid in illustrating definitions and descriptions. Both format and text will appeal to the sports-minded youngster.

Scharff, Robert, ed. Ice Hockey Rules in Pictures. New York: Grosset & Dunlap, 1967. 80p. $2.69, $1.95 paper.

Using clear line drawings and brief readable text, Ice Hockey Rules in Pictures provides an introduction to the game. In addition to depicting the rink, the team, the equipment, officials, infractions, techniques, penalties, and fouls, the book includes the official's code of signals, a glossary of terms, and the official rules of the National Hockey League.

Liebers, Arthur. The Complete Book of Winter Sports. Rev. ed. New York: Coward-McCann, 1971. 246p. $6.95.

In this book are sections on skiing, ice skating, sled dog racing, ice hockey, iceboating, snowshoeing, snowmobiling, and others. Appended to the chapters on skiing, dog sled racing, and curling are glossaries of terms. A meter-yards conversion chart is appended, as is a rather long annotated bibliography. Photographs and sketches help to illustrate the detailed instructions for all the sports.

Olney, Ross R. Let's Go Sailing: A Handbook for Young Sailors. Englewood Cliffs, N.J.: Prentice-Hall, 1969. 83p. $4.75.

Covering all aspects of sailing in an elementary fashion, Let's Go Sailing includes sections on parts of a sailboat, boat and sail care, safety, and so forth. It also includes "A Sailor's Dictionary," consisting of 13 pages of terms with simple phrase-type definitions. The index is skimpy, but the book is so well arranged that it is easy to use.

McAllister, Evelyn Ditton. Easy Steps to Safe Swimming; A Swimming Handbook. 5th rev. ed. New York: Barnes, 1969.

Divided into three parts, this book covers elementary strokes, advanced strokes, and diving and water safety. Each stroke is described in a step-by-step method and is carefully illustrated. The use of bold type to indicate important points makes the book easier to read.

Kramp, Harry and George Sullivan. Swimming. Chicago: Follett, 1971. 127p. $3.99.

Swimming is designed for intermediate boys and girls. It includes the basics of swimming safety, swim-breathing, and floating, then progresses to a number of strokes, such as the crawl, the backstroke, the breast stroke, etc. Information on lifesaving, elementary dives, and swimming competition complete this book, which is illustrated by numerous black and white photographs.

Frey, Shaney. The Complete Beginner's Guide to Skin Diving. Garden City, N.Y.: Doubleday, 1965. 114p. $3.95.

Chapters included in this book are Equipment and how to choose it, Learning to skin dive, Exploring history underwater, Underwater photography, Wildlife underwater, Fish for your supper,

Recreation and Hobbies 251

Fun and games underwater, Hobbies for the skin diver, Undersea science, and Safety tips for the skin diver. Illustrated with black and white drawings and photographs, the text is interesting and easy to read.

Harrison, E. J. Junior Judo. Rev. ed. New York: Sterling, 1965. 144p. $2.95.

Beginning with a description of judo, its ranks and its eqiquette, the book includes a number of throws, hold-downs, and breakfalls. Illustrated profusely with drawings and photographs, each position is depicted in pictures as well as in text.

Kozuki, Russell. Junior Karate. New York: Sterling, 1971. 128p. $2.95.

Emphasizing karate as a game and a means for developing good sportsmanship, Junior Karate covers warm-up exercises, balance and stance, power, blocking techniques, the karate fist, strikes, kicks, contests, and katas. Illustrated with photographs, the book contains easy to follow instructions.

Loken, Newton C. Gymnastics. New York: Sterling, 1969. 104p. $3.99.

A small amount of text and many photographs are the unique feature of this instructional book. Specific guidelines are given for stunts and exercises on the parallel bars, the horizontal bar, the rings, the side horse, and the long horse. Appended are the official gymnastic rules and lists of desirable and undesirable performance features.

Burns, Ted. Tumbling Techniques Illustrated. New York: Ronald, 1957. 96p. $5.50.

A variety of tumbling activities are described and illustrated in this book. Beginning with the basic forward roll, the text progresses to very difficult stunts. A glossary of terms precedes the index.

Schuon, Karl. Bowling. New York: Watts, 1966. 66p. $3.95.

This First Book Series title begins with the score sheet and bowling shoes and proceeds to cover all the major techniques of bowling, with emphasis on keeping score. Team and league bowling are mentioned as well as courtesy and safety. A dictionary of bowling terms is appended.

Smith, Parker. Golf Techniques: How to Improve Your Game. New York: Watts, 1973. 63p. $3.95.

The author has written an introduction to the game of golf covering all of the fundamentals. He tells how to buy a set of

clubs; how to improve the grip, stance, alignment, and swing; how
to manipulate difficult shots, how to putt, and how to maintain a
relaxed state of mind. A title in the Concise Guide Series, this
book concludes with a glossary, a bibliography, and an index.

Riessen, Clare. Tennis: A Basic Guide. New York: Lothrop,
1969. 128p. $3.94.

Using many photographs to illustrate points, this guide book
attempts to demonstrate all the basics of tennis. Beginning with
an overall description of how the game is played, the book also
covers equipment, the grips, the service, the forehand, the backhand, the lob, the net game, play on different surfaces, and the
first game. A list of tennis terms follows.

O'Connor, W. Harold. How to Star in Track and Field. New
York: Four Winds, 1961. 64p. $3.27.

Written in easy second person style, this book provides instructions for excelling in sprinting, distance running, hurdling,
long jumping, high jumping, pole vaulting, shot putting, discus
throwing, and javelin throwing. Each sport is demonstrated in a
series of photographs by a champion in the field. In the 1972
second printing of this title, statistics have been updated through
1968.

Mohan, Beverly and Margaret Steinberg. Riding: A Guide to
Horsemanship. Rev. ed. Chicago: Follett, 1972. 128p.
$3.95.

Written for children, this book covers the fundamentals of
horseback riding, care of tack, care of horses, and participation
in horse shows and pony clubs. A guide to horse terms and a
guide to tack are appended. Black and white photographs illustrate
the text.

McNally, Tom. Hunting. Chicago: Follett, 1972. 127p. $3.99.

Written by the outdoor editor of The Chicago Tribune, Hunting is prepared as a basic introduction for the beginning hunter.
Covered in it are safety, learning to shoot, equipment, hunting
small game, hunting waterfowl and deer, selecting a hunting dog,
and conservation and sportsmanship. Over forty black and white
photographs illustrate the work.

Moore, William. Here Is Your Hobby: Fishing. New York: Putnam, 1962. 127p. $4.19.

Using drawings and photographs to illustrate the text, this
book touches lightly upon many aspects of fishing as a hobby.
Sample items covered are cane pole fishing, bait casting, spinning,
landing your fish, cleaning a fish, knot crafts, care of tackle, facts
about fish, salt-water fishing, surf casting, and charter boats.

Roth, Bernhard A. **Here Is Your Hobby: Archery.** New York: Putnam, 1962. 128p. $4.19.

Designed as an introduction for the beginner, this book tells how to select and purchase archery tackle, how to string the bow and shoot it, and how to become involved in competition shooting. Illustrated with photographs, the book contains only the most basic information.

BIBLIOGRAPHIES

Bibliographies serve a basic need in any library. One of the most frequent uses of these tools is in building collections of materials. Whether the library is a brand new one or of several years standing, the librarian can partially determine its balance and completeness by checking it against standard bibliographies. For instance, the library in an elementary school should contain at least all of the Phase 1 titles listed in the Elementary School Library Catalog and probably all of the titles in the Children's Catalog. Since these two lists are only basic ones, however, the librarian should turn to more specific ones to further develop the library's holdings. For example, does the library own most of the primary and intermediate titles suggested in Reading Ladders for Human Relations and Good Reading for Poor Readers?

Besides serving as a checklist for the collection, the bibliographies can function as suggested buying guides. The librarian planning to develop a multimedia literature collection might turn to A Multimedia Approach to Children's Literature to aid in selecting outstanding renditions of stories in a variety of formats. To improve the periodical holdings, she might consult Periodicals for School Libraries or The Dobler World Directory of Youth Periodicals. If she were choosing materials for the culturally disadvantaged, she would surely check I Read, You Read, We Read....

Some bibliographies are designed to be selective, others to be universal. For instance, Children's Books in Print can be helpful in verifying bibliographic data for books selected for purchase. The variety of indexes produced by the National Information Center for Educational Media at the University of Southern California can aid in providing valuable "mediagraphic" information for films, filmstrips, video tapes, records, etc. The purpose of these universal bibliographic tools is to list, in so far as possible, every title available, with the important purchasing data.

Another function of bibliographies relates to the reader guidance aspect of library service. The librarian or teacher, aiding a student in choosing materials, will perhaps want to turn to a selected list. The book High Interest-Easy Reading for Junior and Senior High School Students may suggest a title which will stimulate a reluctant reader to read. A source such as What Is a City may offer titles to assist a student's research on urban living. Some students will turn to bibliographies themselves for aid in making their own selections for recreational as well as curricular reading.

Included in this chapter are bibliographies of a general nature covering a number of subjects and a variety of formats. Audiovisual as well as print materials are represented. The titles are listed in alphabetical order. Throughout the book, bibliographies relating to a specific subject are listed with the materials on that subject; e.g., AAAS Booklist for Children appears in the chapter on science, and American History in Juvenile Books is listed in the history section.

Adventuring with Books; 2,400 Titles for Pre-kindergarten to Grade 8. 2nd ed. By Shelton L. Root, Jr. and others. New York: Citation, 1973. 395p. $1.95 paper.

Prepared by the Committee on the Elementary School Booklist of the National Council of Teachers of English, Adventuring with Books is a subject-arranged bibliography of 2,400 titles for children of preschool level through junior high school. Entries give complete bibliographic information, age suggestions, and annotations ranging in length from two to twelve or so lines. To be considered for inclusion, a title must have high potential for reader involvement or interest and a degree of literary merit that raises it above others of its type.

An Annotated List of Recordings in the Language Arts. Morris Schreiber, comp. and ed. Urbana, Ill.: National Council of Teachers of English, 1971. 107p. $2.00.

More than 500 recordings are evaluated in this guide which is arranged in three main divisions: elementary, secondary, and college. All titles selected are of potential use to the English and language arts teacher. Recordings of varying types are included, such as lectures and speeches, documentaries, authors reading their own works, selections read by others, and anthologies. While the original list was published in 1964, a supplement published in 1971 updates the titles through 1970.

Behavior Patterns in Children's Books: A Bibliography. By Clara J. Kirchner. Washington, D.C.: Catholic University of America Press, 1966. 132p. $3.75. $1.95 paper.

Designed as a list for bibliotherapy, Behavior Patterns in Children's Books is arranged by 24 broad subject categories, e.g., general behavior patterns, "little" problems of small children, value of honesty, spirit of generosity, orphans and adopted children, etc. The 507 entries give author, title, publisher, date, price, a brief annotation, grade level, and subject headings. Appended materials include an annotated list of readings in bibliotherapy for adults, a behavior index (alphabetically arranged by behaviors), an author index, a title index, and a directory of publishers.

Bibliography of Books for Children. Washington, D. C. : Association for Childhood Education International, 1974. 112p. $2.75 paper.

Revised every three years, this bibliography purports to list the best children's books according to commonly accepted literary standards. Included are titles for preschool through junior high school. Arranged by subjects, it provides a fine list of new titles, old favorites, and especially trade books, to complement classroom instruction. Author, title, and publisher indexes follow the annotations.

Book and Non-Book Media: Annotated Guide to Selection Aids for Educational Materials. By Flossie L. Perkins. Urbana, Ill. : National Council of Teachers of English, 1972. 298p. $4.25 paper.

A revision of the 1967 publication, Book Selection Media by Ralph Perkins, this contains one-page analyses of 271 different selection tools. Arranged alphabetically by title, the entries give author-publisher, publication data, purpose, scope, subject headings, similar tools, special features, usefulness, and cost. Indexes include aids to making selections for children, aids to making selections for teenagers, selection aids for college students and adults, selection aids for teacher-parent background, selection aids for librarians, title index, and author-publisher index. While this list identifies a number of bibliographies, it makes no comparisons and devotes equal space to free leaflets and expensive standard works. School librarians may find it helpful, but will have to rely on other sources, especially for non-print materials.

Books for Friendship, A List of Books Recommended for Children. 4th ed. Mary Esther McWhirter, ed. Philadelphia: American Friends Service and Anti-Defamation League of B'nai B'rith, 1968. Dist. by Children's Program Publications, Philadelphia, Pa. 46p. $1.25.

Arranged by categories and subdivided by age levels, this bibliography contains more than 300 titles selected because they are "consistent with the purposes of the two sponsoring organizations dedicated to the cause of brotherhood and peace as embodied in the Jewish and Christian traditions." Entries provide complete bibliographic data plus brief annotations which unobtrusively show the friendship theme.

Books in Print. New York: Bowker, 1948- . 4 vols. Annual. $64.50. Supplement. $27.95.
Subject Guide to Books in Print. New York: Bowker, 1957- . 2 vols. Annual. $47.00.

Books in Print is a valuable aid in verifying bibliographic information. Consisting of an author index and a title index, both alphabetically arranged, it records all the books currently in print and for sale by most of the major publishing houses in the United States. It is issued in the fall of each year with a supplement appearing in late spring. Subject Guide to Books in Print omits poetry, fiction, and drama, but indexes titles under nearly 70,000 subject headings with numerous cross references.

Books to Help Children Adjust to a Hospital Situation. Vera S. Flandorf, comp. Chicago: American Library Association, 1967. 56p. $.50.

This small but useful bibliography, prepared by the Association of Hospital and Institution Libraries, attempts to point out books meeting the emotional, intellectual, and recreational needs of hospitalized children. It is arranged by topics, such as adjustment and understanding, fear and reassurance, loneliness and homesickness, etc. Each topic is subdivided by age level ranging from three to 16 years.

Children's Books in Print. New York: Bowker, 1969- . Annual. $17.95.
Subject Guide to Children's Books in Print. New York: Bowker, 1970- . Annual. $17.95.

These two companion volumes represent the first organized attempt at comprehensive bibliographic control of juvenile books. Children's Books in Print contains three indexes: author, title, and illustrator. The hard and soft cover titles included are gleaned from more than 500 United States publishers. The lists are comprehensive rather than selective and are intended to serve as verification tools. The Subject Guide to Children's Books in Print serves as an index to the other volume. It arranges titles under some 7,000 subject headings. These two books can be used advantageously as a supplement to the card catalog and as such should be considered part of the reference collection as well as an acquisition tool.

Children's Catalog. 12th ed. Estelle A. Fidell, ed. New York: Wilson, 1971. 1156p. $25.00 with four annual supplements.

First published in 1909 and revised regularly, this highly selective tool attempts to list the best fiction and nonfiction for children and to serve as a buying guide, a cataloging aid, and a checklist for librarians purchasing books for children. More than 5,100 titles appear in the twelfth edition. Arranged by Dewey classification, the entries provide complete bibliographic data. Perhaps the most valuable feature of the Children's Catalog is the Author, Title, Subject and Analytical Index. The 13,000-plus analytical entries index story, folk tale, play, and biography collections. Many of the collections analyzed in this tool are not indexed in any other reference work; therefore, this bibliography should be housed with other indexes for use as a ready reference source.

The Dobler World Directory of Youth Periodicals. 3rd enl. ed.
Lavinia Dobler, ed. New York: Citation, 1970. 108p.
$4.25 paper.

Nearly 1,000 periodicals are included in the third edition of the Dobler World Directory of Youth Periodicals. The first section of the book, "Youth Periodicals in the United States," is arranged by subject and curriculum interest. Entries include title, circulation, advertising, number of issues, number of pages, price, age range, editor, publisher, type material purchased and prices, main emphasis. Part II, "Periodicals in English Published Outside the United States," gives essentially the same information. Two other sections are called "Agents to Foreign Periodical Subscriptions" and "Periodicals Published in Non-English Languages." A section in the back lists cessations and title changes. A title index is also present. The list itself is helpful but is too old to be totally accurate as to titles still in publication and their prices.

8mm Film Directory. Grace Ann Kone, comp. and ed. New York: Educational Films Library Association, 1969. 532p. $10.50. Dist. by Comprehensive Service Corp., 250 W. 64th St., New York, N.Y. 10023.

A comprehensive, non-selective list of more than 5,000 8mm films, this directory includes all 8mm film formats: standard, super, silent, sound, cartridge, or reel-to-reel. Subject arranged with titles listed alphabetically under each topic, the bibliography includes pertinent information for entries, e.g., title, series title, production date, Dewey classification number, running time, grade level, format, producer or distributor, length in minutes or feet, and a brief annotation. Major subjects covered are arts, education, fiction, language, recreation, religion, sciences, society and environment, and technology.

The Elementary School Library Collection: A Guide to Books and Other Media, Phases 1-2-3. 8th ed. Mary V. Gaver, gen. ed. Newark: Bro-Dart Foundation, 1973. 780p. $20.00.

Intending "to list the media which should be provided in any elementary school serving preschool through sixth grade" and "meeting as nearly as possible the standards recommended by Standards for School Media Programs," this bibliography lists 7,635 trade books, 1,743 audio-visual titles, plus periodicals, reference books, and professional tools. Keyed for first, second, and third purchase, it is arranged by Dewey classification. Entries provide bibliographic information, a brief annotation, approximate reading level, and suggested subject headings to be used by the cataloger. Three separate indexes appear in Section II: Author Index, Title Index, and Subject Index. The Subject Index can be especially helpful in locating both fiction and non-fiction titles on a particular subject; in this regard the Elementary School Library Collection should be considered as a valuable part of the reference collection as well as a selection tool and checklist. Published annually, it is an up-to-date and reliable guide.

Bibliographies 259

El-Hi Textbooks in Print. New York: Bowker, 1965- . Annual. $17.50.

First published in 1956 as Textbooks in Print, this annual bibliography lists nearly 17,000 textbooks currently in print for elementary, junior high, and senior high school levels. Titles are arranged under 20 curriculum headings with nearly 200 subheadings. Author, title, and series indexes provide other approaches to locating titles. In addition to the textbooks published by the 270-plus textbook firms, this bibliography lists programmed learning materials in book form, related audio-visual aids, and professional tools. It is a valuable non-selective source for verifying in-print information.

Feature Films on 8 and 16: A Directory of Sound Feature Films Available for Rental, Sale and Lease in the United States. 4th ed. James L. Limbacher, ed. New York: Bowker, 1974. 400p. $16.50.

Previously published by the Educational Film Library Association, this directory lists about 16,000 commercial productions, documentaries, experimental films and animations available for rental, sale, or lease in the United States. Titles span from early silent classics to 1973 releases. Entries give running time, studio, director, actors and distributors. Also included are a geographical index to film distributors, an index to directors and an index to film serials. An individual school considering this volume for purchase should analyze carefully the amount of use it will receive. Smaller libraries will probably want to borrow a copy from a district media center rather than buy their own.

Films for Children. New York: Educational Film Library Association, 1961. 59p. Supplement. 1965. 14p. $2.00 (available only in combined edition).

Films for Children is a selected list of 272 16mm films chosen for their outstanding entertainment value rather than for classroom or informational use. Titles are arranged alphabetically under the following subject categories: animation, circus, farm and zoo, fables, legends, fairy tales, holidays, nature and wildlife, pets, puppets, real life adventure, story films, and silent film comedies. Entries give title, producer/distributors, running time, color or black and white, date, and a short annotation.

Films for Children: A Selected List. Prepared by the New York Library Association, Children's and Young Adult Services Section. Rev. ed. Available from New York Library Association, P. O. Box 521, Woodside, N.Y. 11377. 1969. $1.00.

Included in this list are about 100 well-chosen 16mm films considered to be of outstanding quality. Alphabetically arranged by title, the entries give the title, producer/distributor, date, running time, color or black and white, sales price, and rather complete annotation. Preceding the main text is an introduction telling how to plan and execute a successful film program. A bibliography, a subject index, and a directory of distributors are also included.

Films for Young Adults: A Selected List. Prepared by New York Library Association, Children's and Young Adult Services Section. Rev. ed. New York: Educational Film Library Association, 1970. 54p. $2.00.

A collection of 125 16mm films of exceptional quality and of interest to junior and senior high school students is incorporated in this book. Alphabetically arranged by title, entries provide title, producer/distributor, date, running time, color or black and white, sales price, and lengthy annotation. Special features of this list are the subject index, a bibliography of articles about films and film programs, recommended periodicals, an alphabetical list of film makers, and a list of distributors with addresses. While the films in this bibliography are not classroom oriented, many of them can advantageously be correlated with art, language arts, science, and social studies.

Films Kids Like: A Catalog of Short Films for Children. Susan Rice, ed. Chicago: Published for Center for Understanding Media by American Library Association, 1973. 150p. $4.95 paper.

This collection of 229 short films for children up to age twelve was selected by the staff of the Children's Film Theater in New York. Arranged alphabetically by film title, the list contains rather long annotations often based on the children's reactions. Each entry gives, besides title and annotation, a technical description, distributor, and the country where it originated. Films are not curriculum oriented but most could be used advantageously in the classroom.

General Encyclopedias in Print 1973-74: A Comparative Analysis. 9th ed. S. Padraig Walsh, comp. New York: Bowker, 1973. 239p. $10.95.

An informative, evaluative guide, this book compares and analyzes the major general encyclopedias in print in the English language. It establishes guidelines for purchasing sets and presents excerpts from critical reviews. Including a number of comparative charts, it ranks the major encyclopedias in order of quality. This source is not only helpful for the librarian buying sets, but is also valuable to give to parents wishing to acquire encyclopedias for home use.

General World Atlases in Print 1972/1973. 4th ed. S. Padraig Walsh, ed. New York: Bowker, 1973. 211p. $12.50.

As a companion to General Encyclopedias in Print, this

guide compares and evaluates the major world atlases on the market today. It offers a number of easy to read comparative charts, and ranks the titles in order of quality. In addition, it maintains a list of briefly described inexpensive atlases and a list of discontinued ones.

Good Reading for Poor Readers. 8th ed. By George Spache. Champaign, Ill.: Garrard, 1972. 300p. $4.95 paper.

Following four chapters which tell how to choose books to match a child's reading level are eight chapters listing about 1,800 titles suitable for remedial reading. Materials included are textbooks, trade books, magazines, series, programmed materials, games, adapted and simplified materials, and visual aids. Besides providing bibliographic data, entries give a brief annotation, the reading level, and the interest level. The Spache Readability Formula appears in an appendix.

Guide to Reference Books for School Media Centers. By Christine L. Wynar. Littleton, Colo.: Libraries Unlimited, 1973. 473p. $17.50.

This mammoth bibliography attempts to evaluate reference books for elementary, junior high, and high school media centers as well as for vocational programs and junior colleges. In it 2,575 titles are arranged under 54 subjects. Under each subject are subdivisions representing types of reference works, e.g., directories, indexes, handbooks, etc., and specific areas of the general subject. Entries give bibliographic data, price, a critical annotation, and sources of reviews. The full index is necessary to locate titles in this rather complicated arrangement of the text. Up to date and comprehensive, the list should serve quite well as a guide for junior high librarians and extremely well for senior high school and junior college librarians. The list's weakest point, however, is in aiding elementary school librarians, especially in primary schools. While considerable material included in the list will be of value to elementary school libraries, librarians will find difficulty in sifting it out of the massive listing of mature, adult materials. Reference books for the very young are sparse. It is unfortunate that some special effort was not made to indicate reference sources for elementary schools, for this omission mars an otherwise fine bibliography.

Guides to Educational Media. 3rd ed. Margaret I. Rufsvold and Carolyn Guss, eds. Chicago: American Library Association, 1971. 116p. $3.00 paper.

Revised from Guides to Newer Educational Media (1967), this source provides a comprehensive list of 153 bibliographies on films, filmstrips, kinescopes, phonodiscs, phonotapes, programmed instruction materials, slides, transparencies, and videotapes. Entries give bibliographic data, price, scope, arrangement, description of entries, and special features. Additional information in the book includes professional organizations in the educational media field, periodicals in the educational media field--a selected list, and educational media catalogs and lists published since 1957 but unavailable in 1971. An index provides access to the text by title, author, and subject. The non-selective list is helpful in identifying specific bibliographies, but since no comparisons are made, school librarians will still have to rely upon their own judgment as to the relative value of each entry.

High Interest-Easy Reading for Junior and Senior High School Students. 2nd ed. Marian E. White, ed. chairman and the Committee on the High Interest-Easy Reading Booklist. New York: Citation, 1972. 144p. $.95.

Prepared by a committee of the National Council of Teachers of English, this valuable bibliography is designed to entice reluctant readers to read. Materials selected cover a wide range of topics excluding textbooks, classics, and other classroom type titles. Annotations are written for the teenager rather than the teacher or librarian.

I Read, You Read, We Read, I See, You See, We See, I Hear, You Hear, We Hear, I Learn, You Learn, We Learn. Chicago: Children's Services Division, American Library Association, 1971. 104p. $2.00 paper.

Prepared essentially for use with the culturally disadvantaged, this list is an outgrowth of the 1966 publication We Read. Arranged by age levels from preschool through 14 years, the list includes books, poems, stories, films, and recordings for each group. Entries for books give author, title, publisher, date, price, annotation, and symbols indicating other formats. Film and recording entries give title, illustrator if there is one, publisher, date, time, color or black and white, distributor, annotation, and symbols for other formats. A useful final section suggests program resources to use with preschool children and for adult storytellers to use with children ages 5 to 11. Volunteers will find this book especially helpful.

Junior High School Library Catalog. 2nd ed. Estelle A. Fidell and Gary L. Bogart, eds. New York: Wilson, 1970. 808p. $30.00 with four annual supplements.

Organized identically to the Children's Catalog, the Junior High School Library Catalog lists more than 3,400 titles. The newest of the Wilson Standard Catalog series, this one attempts to bridge the gap between elementary and senior high level reading materials. In this volume the analytical entries in the Author, Title, Subject, and Analytical Index are valuable for locating specific titles in collected works.

Large Type Books in Print. Robert A. Landau and Judith Nyren, eds. New York: Bowker, 1970. 193p. $12.50.

Printed in large type itself, this book is a listing of about 1,500 titles representing fiction, nonfiction, and textbooks that are printed in large type for visually and physically handicapped readers. Entries give title, author, audience level, binding other than cloth, publisher of large type edition, whether accompanying workbook is available, price, and type size if over 18 point. An author-title index and a directory of publishers are included.

Learning Directory. New York: Westinghouse Learning Corp., 1970-71. 7 vols. plus 1 vol. Supplement 1972. $99.50.

A finding tool for instructional materials, the Learning Directory includes 205,000 different items in various formats including books, films, games, videotapes, programmed material, microforms, and computer-assisted instruction programs. Covering all subjects in the curriculum, the list ranges from preschool through college and adult materials. Although there are omissions and inconsistencies, the directory is the first major attempt to list both book and nonbook materials in one index. Volume one of the set contains a publishers directory and a portion of the main body; volumes two to seven contain the rest of the main text. Entries include topic; audience level; type of medium; title; color or black and white; sound; size; running time; number of frames, pages, sides, or reels; date; price; free, loan or purchase options; and source. Before purchasing this tool, librarians should determine if the information they need is available in other less expensive sources.

Library of Congress Catalog: Films and Other Materials for Projection; A Cumulative List of Works Represented by Library of Congress Printed Cards. Washington, D.C.: Card Division, Library of Congress, 1953- . 3 current quarterly issues with annual cumulation. $40.00/yr.

Covering all motion pictures and materials for projection that are of educational value released in the United States or Canada and cataloged by the Library of Congress, this is a comprehensive listing. Entries are arranged by title and give both content and technical descriptions, subject headings, and LC card number. More than 67,000 films and filmstrips were cataloged by the Library of Congress between 1952 and 1968 with an average of nearly 11,000 more being produced annually. This volume is included in a subscription to the National Union Catalog. It is a necessary tool for the district media center.

Library of Congress Catalog: Music and Phonorecords: A Cumulative List of Works Represented by Library of Congress Printed Cards. Washington, D.C.: Card Division, Library of Congress, 1953- . Current issue and annual cumulation. $30.00/year.

Arranged alphabetically by composer or author, this list includes music scores intended for performance, sound phonorecords (both musical and non-musical), and books about music and librettos (since 1963). Entries include composer or author, title, type of medium, publisher or source, catalog number, date, physical description, suggested subject headings, and LC card number. Part of the National Union Catalog, this bibliography should be available in district media centers.

Matters of Fact: Aspects of Non-Fiction for Children. By Margery Fisher. New York: Crowell, 1972. 488p. $11.95.

This British publication consists mainly of analyses of information books and the criteria necessary to make them works of distinction. Utilizing specific topics to illustrate general discussions, the author approaches non-fiction books in the following categories: Foundations (bread, the postal system, Holland, honeybees, cowboys, time); The Multiple Subject (London, atoms); Biography (Johann Sebastian Bach, Helen Keller, Abraham Lincoln); Careers (nursing, journalism). Each topic is followed by long bibliographies of related titles. Writers and parents as well as teachers and librarians will benefit from studying the criteria listed in this book for outstanding nonfiction books for children.

A Multimedia Approach to Children's Literature; A Selective List of Films, Filmstrips, and Recordings Based on Children's Books. Ellin Green and Madalynne Schoenfeld, eds. Chicago: American Library Association, 1972. 262p. $3.75 paper.

This source claims to be a "buying guide to a quality collection of book-related nonprint materials to use with children from preschool to grade eight." Approximately 425 books, 175 16mm films, 175 silent and sound filmstrips, and 300 recordings (33rpm disc and tape cassette) are listed. Entries are arranged alphabetically by book title with related audiovisual materials following each title. Bibliographic information and an annotation are provided for each. A useful section on resources contains lists of related readings, selection aids, program aids, realia, figurines, stuffed animals, portfolios of posters. Particularly helpful are the lists following the main text. They include directory of distributors, index of authors, index to film titles, index to filmstrip titles, index to media about or presented by authors and illustrators, index to record titles, and index to subjects. This bibliography is essential for building a children's literature collection in a variety of formats.

National Center for Audio Tapes: 1974-76 Catalog. Boulder, Colo.: National Center for Audio Tapes, 1974. 329p. $4.50.

This bibliography of 14,000 titles of curriculum related audio tapes represents the holdings of the National Center for Audio Tapes at the University of Colorado. Titles will be dubbed onto new reel or cassette tape for single copy costs ranging from $2.40

to $5.00 depending upon the length of the tape. Spanning grade levels from elementary school through college, they cover all curriculum areas. The catalog contains three separate indexes, the first being a subject index with the following major divisions: Arts, Education, Language and literature, Mathematics, Physical education and recreation, Science, Social Sciences, and Vocational-Technical. A numeric index and an alphabetical index follow.

NICEM Index to 16mm Educational Films. 5th ed. Los Angeles: National Information Center for Educational Media, 1974. 3 vols. $99.50 bookcopy. $79.50 microfiche. (90,000 entries)

NICEM Index to 35mm Filmstrips. 5th ed. Los Angeles: National Information Center for Educational Media, 1974. 2 vols. $68.50 bookcopy. $59.50 microfiche. (52,000 entries)

NICEM Index to Educational Video Tapes. 3rd ed. Los Angeles: National Information Center for Educational Media, 1974. $26.50 bookcopy. $18.50 microfiche. (12,000 entries)

NICEM Educational Audio Tapes. 3rd ed. Los Angeles: National Information Center for Educational Media, 1974. $42.40 bookcopy. $28.50 microfiche. (24,000 entries)

NICEM Index to Educational Overhead Transparencies. 4th ed. Los Angeles: National Information Center for Educational Media, 1974. 2 vols. $68.50 bookcopy. $49.50 microfiche. (50,000 entries)

NICEM Index to Educational Records. 3rd ed. Los Angeles: National Information Center for Educational Media, 1974. $42.50 bookcopy. $28.50 microfiche. (22,000 entries)

NICEM Index to 8mm Motion Cartridges. 4th ed. Los Angeles: National Information Center for Educational Media, 1974. $42.50 bookcopy. $28.50 microfiche. (22,000 entries)

NICEM Index to Educational Slides. 2nd ed. Los Angeles: National Information Center for Educational Media, 1974. $38.50 bookcopy. $26.50 microfiche. (18,000 entries)

NICEM Index to Producers and Distributors. 3rd ed. Los Angeles: National Information Center for Educational Media, 1974. $19.50 bookcopy. $12.50 microfiche. (10,000 entries)

Emanating from the National Information Center for Educational Media of the University of Southern California, these comprehensive indexes represent an attempt to provide a uniform guide to commercially prepared educational media in nonprint formats. Arranged similarly, the indexes all have a subject index which arranges titles under curriculum related subject headings. They also have an alphabetical listing which contains bibliographic data, such as, title, series, release date, content description, technical description, and producer/distributor. Unfortunately, no prices are given. The third section consists of a directory of producers and distributors. These computer-produced bibliographic aids draw from nearly 400,000 entries of non-book media. NICEM has, in addition to these general bibliographies, produced multi-media subject lists in the areas of psychology, vocational and technical education, health and safety education, Black history and studies, and ecology. Also available in both book format and on microfiche is the NICEM Update of Nonbook Media, a bi-monthly volume issued four times each year to keep the indexes current. The entire series is revised frequently. These helpful bibliographic tools are a recommended purchase for system media centers; unless an individual school will make great use of them, a librarian could hardly justify the excessive expense. If, however, he could borrow them from a centralized media center, he probably could use them advantageously in building his own school's collection.

Periodicals for School Libraries: A Guide to Magazines, Newspapers, and Periodical Indexes. Rev. ed. Marian H. Scott, ed. Chicago: American Library Association, 1973. 292p. $4.50 paper.

Revised from the 1969 edition, Periodicals for School Libraries reviews 520 newspapers and magazines for kindergarten through grade 12. In the new edition are 136 new titles while 49 were deleted from the original list. Alphabetically arranged, the entries give the address, grade level, frequency, price, descriptive annotation, and where abstracted. Some foreign and ethnic periodicals are included. Guidelines for inclusion in the listing are "the realities of curricular demands and the wide range of reading levels and personal interests of students." This book will be a helpful guide for developing the periodical collection.

Picture Books for Children. Patricia Jean Cianciolo, ed. and the Picture Book Committee, National Council of Teachers of English. Chicago: American Library Association, 1973. 159p. $5.95 paper.

This book is intended "to serve as a resource and guide for teachers of children, from nursery school through junior high school, day-care center personnel, librarians in school and public libraries, parents, and any other adult concerned with the selection of well-written, imaginatively illustrated picture books that are of interest to all ages and backgrounds." Arranged alphabetically by the author in four categories, the entries contain bibliographic data, age level, and well written annotations. Illustrated with black and white reproductions from picture books, this booklist is important for all libraries.

Reading Ladders for Human Relations. 5th ed. Virginia M. Reid, ed. Washington, D.C.: American Council on Education, 1972. 346p. $3.95 paper.

The new edition of this standard title is a complete revision and should supplement old editions rather than replace them. Only four reading themes appear in this fifth edition: creating a self-image, living with others, appreciating different cultures, and coping with change. Within each theme are a number of subcategories with each listing books for primary, intermediate, junior, senior, and mature reading levels. This is an excellent tool for reader guidance and should be available in all school libraries.

Recordings for Children: A Selected List of Records and Cassettes. 3rd ed. Prepared by New York Library Association, Children and Young Adult Services Section. New York: New York Library Association, 1972. 40p. $2.50 paper (prepaid)

Approximately 450 highly selective titles are included in this subject arranged bibliography. Both disc recordings and cassettes are chosen for children ranging in age from preschool to age 13. Prepared with emphasis on recordings for home and recreational use, the list covers a wide range of subjects and includes both musical and nonmusical recordings. Entries give album title, composer/author, performing group, narrator, producer/recording company, record number, and a brief annotation.

Resources for Learning; A Core Media Collection for Elementary Schools. Roderick McDaniel, ed. New York: Bowker, 1971. 365p. $16.50.

This selective guide lists some 4,000 recommended titles in various formats which will complement the curriculum of the elementary school. Chosen from approved lists, reviews in periodicals, and collections of several public school systems, the titles include 576 items starred to indicate materials necessary for a basic core collection. All types of media are included, e.g., 8 and 16mm films, filmstrips, study prints, phonodiscs, models, transparencies, etc. Main entries are alphabetically arranged by title and provide author, release date, media, producer, grade level, price, Dewey classification, recommending sources, and annotation. Contents of this bibliography include the following sections: Introduction (describing the recommendation sources), Media indexed by subject, Media indexed by title/author, Producer/distributor directory, and Index of subject headings. This valuable guide, despite the need for annual revisions, will greatly simplify the task of an elementary school librarian who is trying to develop a strong media collection.

Spoken Records. 3rd ed. By Helen Roach. Metuchen, N.J.: Scarecrow Press, 1970. 288p. $7.50.

A collection of more than 500 spoken recordings, this list includes documentaries, lectures, and interviews; readings by authors; readings by other than authors in English, American, Scottish, and Irish; children's literature; religious and biblical works; and plays of Shakespeare and others. Entries give title, producer/distributor, size and number of recordings, phonodisc number and a critical annotation. While the material listed for children is sparse (the most obvious exclusions being the excellent story recordings by Weston Woods Studios), the list is a fine one for junior and senior high schools.

Senior High School Library Catalog. 10th ed. Estelle A. Fidell
and Toby M. Berger, eds. New York: Wilson, 1972.
1214p. $30.00 with five annual supplements. $35.00 with
Catholic Supplement.

Formerly titled Standard Catalog for High School Libraries, this member of the Wilson catalog series contains 4,760 fiction and nonfiction titles selected to complement the high school curriculum. It is arranged similarly to the Children's Catalog and the Junior High School Library Catalog. The tenth edition offers a special edition in which the Catholic Supplement of 658 titles selected by the Catholic Library Association is bound with the regular text. The Senior High School Library Catalog should be considered for junior high schools as a checklist for more mature material.

What Is a City? A Multi-Media Guide on Urban Living. Rose
Moorachian, ed. Boston: Boston Public Library, 1969.
152p. $2.00 paper.

Containing materials for young people from preschool through senior high school, this list includes only items which explain or illuminate some facet of city life, primarily contemporary themes and issues. Arranged by 14 topics, the bibliography spans such subjects as what is a city, transportation, government and services, and music and art. Under each heading are lists of books, films, filmstrips, slides, pictures and transparencies, recordings, tapes, and activities. For each entry there is bibliographic data, technical description, grade level, and an annotation. This unique specialized reference work is valuable in that it brings together considerable amounts of material in a variety of formats on specific subjects.

Young People's Literature in Series: Fiction; An Annotated Bibliographic Guide. By Judith K. Rosenberg and Kenyon C.
Rosenberg. Littleton, Colo.: Libraries Unlimited, 1972.
176p. $7.50.

This very arbitrary list of books for elementary and junior high school children will be of some use to libraries. Arranged alphabetically by author, it lists the books in an author's series and gives brief covering notes concerning the whole series. A series title index and a title index are included. The 1,428 entries represent a wide range of series although there is no apparent reason for inclusions or omissions. Since it is the only source of its kind, however, it will probably be wanted in larger libraries.

Young People's Literature in Series: Publishers' and Non-Fiction
Series; An Annotated Bibliographical Guide. By Judith K.
Rosenberg and Kenyon C. Rosenberg. Littleton, Colo.:
Libraries Unlimited, 1973. 280p. $10.00.

Similar to the authors' list of fiction series books, this bibliography is arranged alphabetically by the names of the series with titles arranged chronologically for each series. Over 6,000 entries are in the list. Author and title indexes help locate specific books.

REVIEW SOURCES

Appraisal. Longfellow Hall, 13 Appian Way, Cambridge, Mass. : Children's Science Book Review Committee, Harvard Graduate School of Education, 1967-   . 3 times/yr. $4.00.

Approximately 75 titles are rated and reviewed in each issue of Appraisal. Uniquely, each title is reviewed twice--once by a librarian and once by a subject specialist. The signed reviews contain approximate age levels and a rating code ranging from excellent to unsatisfactory.

The Booklist. Chicago: American Library Association, 1905-   . Semimonthly (only one issue in August). $15.00.

Books, reference books, films, filmstrips, recordings, pamphlets, and paperbacks are reviewed in this periodical. Containing no articles, this source contains brief reviews including grade levels. Only recommended materials are included. Although basically conservative in its selection of titles, The Booklist is a reliable medium for evaluations of new materials.

Bulletin of the Center for Children's Books. Zena Sutherland, ed. Chicago: Published for the University of Chicago Graduate Library School by the University of Chicago Press, 1945-   . Monthly (except August). $6.00.

Both recommended and not recommended titles are included in this review periodical. Highly regarded for its critical evaluations of books, this source contains reviews for about 70 books in each issue. Entries contain grade level indications and ratings including the following: recommended, additional book of acceptable quality for collections needing more material in this area, marginal book that is slight in content or weak in style or format, not recommended, subject matter or treatment will tend to limit the book to specialized collections, and a book that will have appeal for the unusual reader only.

Childhood Education: A Journal for Teachers, Administrators, Church-School Workers, Librarians, Pediatricians. Washington, D.C.: Association for Childhood Education, 1924-   . Monthly (except June, July, and August). $6.00.

Review Sources   271

   This journal, while covering many aspects of childhood education in scholarly articles, contains sections of book reviews. The rather long reviews are arranged by broad subjects in the curriculum.

Educational Screen and Audiovisual Guide.   Henry C. Ruark, Jr.
   Chicago: Educational Screen, 1922-   .   Monthly. $6.00.

   Reviews of films, filmstrips, recordings, and equipment appear in each issue of this source, along with articles describing audio-visual instruction. The annual "Blue Book," the July-August issue, lists over 1,000 titles produced during the past year.

Elementary English; A Magazine of the Language Arts.   Champaign, Ill.: National Council of Teachers of English, 1925-   .
   Monthly (except June, July, and August). $10.00.

   This outstanding journal contains both articles concerned with reading and the language arts and an excellent review column. Reviews are rather long and thoughtfully written. Although it does not review as many titles as some periodicals, its evaluations are reliable.

The Horn Book Magazine.   Boston: The Horn Book, 1924-   .
   Bimonthly. $7.50.

   A journal of highest standards devoted entirely to children's literature, The Horn Book contains qualitative articles concerning books and authors. Each issue includes reviews of 70 to 120 books, arranged by subject. Although nonfiction is covered, emphasis is placed on fiction, picture books, and folklore.

Instructor.   Dansville, N.Y.: F. A. Owen, 1891-   .   Monthly (except July and August). $8.00.

   While the main function of Instructor is to provide practical articles of value to the classroom teacher, it does contain review columns. Each issue reviews a small number of professional tools, children's books for preschool through junior high, and educational media including a variety of formats from 16mm films to maps.

Interracial Books for Children.   New York: Council on Interracial Books for Children, 1970-   .   Quarterly. $2.00.

   Concerned with children's literature for minority groups, Interracial Books for Children contains articles as well as reviews of books. Reviews are forcefully written and do not reflect the opinions of other review sources (e.g., reviews of The Cay and Sounder). This periodical is valuable for selecting books through junior high school.

Kirkus Reviews.   60 W. 13th St., New York: The Kirkus Service, 1934-   .   Semimonthly.   Apply for rate schedule.   Looseleaf.   (Juvenile Reviews may be subscribed separately.)

Highly critical reviews of about 70 children's books and 140 adult books are contained in each issue of this book review service. A major advantage of this source is that it reviews titles early, often before publication of the book. Each issue is indexed with indexes cumulating at three and six month intervals.

Landers Film Reviews.   P. O. Box 69760, Los Angeles: Landers Associates, 1956- .   Monthly (except July and August). $35.00.   Looseleaf.

About 700 to 800 16mm film titles are reviewed each year in this periodical. Instructional films, training films, TV documentary and short subject films, and children's fiction films are reviewed. This source should probably be purchased by the district media center and shared by several individual schools.

Library Journal.   John N. Berry, III, ed.   New York: Bowker, 1876- .   Semimonthly (monthly in July and August). $16.20.

An important periodical carrying articles on all aspects of librarianship, Library Journal annually reviews about 5,700 adult and 2,200 children's books. Reviews are written by practicing librarians and specialists and therefore vary somewhat in standards of quality. School Library Journal was incorporated in the midmonthly issues from September through May until the end of 1974, but now appears only as a separate.

Previews: News and Reviews of Non-Print Media.   New York: Bowker, 1972- .   Monthly (September through May). $9.00.

Previews consists primarily of reviews of various types of audio-visual materials which, before September 1971, appeared in separate columns in Library Journal. Covered in reviews are 16mm films, 8mm silent films, 35mm filmstrips, transparencies, slides, prints, maps, charts, games, and multimedia kits. About 130 titles appear in each issue. The "Audiovisual Guide: A Multimedia Subject List" announces new titles in advance of their release dates.

Reference Services Review.   Ann Arbor, Mich.: Pierian Press, 1973- .   Quarterly. $10.00.

Devoted entirely to reviews of reference books, Reference Services Review contains regular features including the following: Recent reference books, Reference book review index, and Reference books in print. Although many titles covered are scholarly and technical, this source should be considered by libraries building large reference collections and by district media centers to share with a number of schools.

Review Sources 273

RQ. Chicago: American Library Association, 1960-   . Quarterly. Not available by subscription; sent only to members of Reference and Adult Services Division.

The official journal of the Reference and Adult Services Division of the American Library Association, RQ contains both articles and reviews of reference books. While most articles are technical, some are specifically dealing with service to children, e.g., "Reference Materials Found in Sample of Illinois School Library/Media Centers." The same is true for the reference books reviewed; most are adult and scholarly, but some are definitely suitable for children.

School Library Journal. Lillian N. Gerhardt, ed. New York: Bowker, 1954-   . Monthly (September through May). $10.80.

Containing articles on topics concerning school libraries and children's work in public libraries, this journal also appeared in the mid-monthly issue of Library Journal up to the end of 1974. It includes a large book review section, covering about 250 titles each issue. Reviews are arranged by reading levels: preschool-primary, grades 3-6, Junior high and up, and adult books for young adults.

Science and Children. Washington, D.C.: National Science Teachers Association, 1963-   . 8 issues per year. $5.00.

A periodical designed specifically for teachers of elementary school science, Science and Children contains articles dealing with practical suggestions for the teacher. It also lists reviews of books and audio-visual materials suitable for use with children.

Science Books: A Quarterly Review. Washington, D.C.: American Association for the Advancement of Science, 1965-   . Quarterly. $6.50.

Approximately 250 titles are reviewed in each issue. All age levels are included from primary through adult. This periodical serves to update such bibliographies as the AAAS Science Book List for Children and the AAAS Science Book List.

Wilson Library Bulletin. New York: Wilson, 1914-   . Monthly (except July and August). $9.00.

A periodical containing articles of general interest to librarians, Wilson Library Bulletin includes a monthly column, "Current Reference Books." In it are reviews of about 25 reference books, many of interest to school librarians.

DIRECTORY OF PUBLISHERS

Abingdon Press
201 Eighth Ave. S.
Nashville, TN 37203

Abrams, Harry N., Inc.
110 E. 59th St.
New York, NY 10022

Aldine Pub. Co.
529 S. Wabash Ave.
Chicago, IL 60605

American Association for the Advancement of Science
1776 Massachusetts Ave., NW
Washington, D. C. 20036

American Book Co.
450 W. 33rd St.
New York, NY 10001

American Council on Education
One Dupont Circle, NW
Washington, D. C. 20036

American Educational Publications
Xerox Family Education Services
Education Circle
Columbus, OH 43216

American Elsevier Pub. Co.
52 Vanderbilt Ave.
New York, NY 10017

American Heritage Pub. Co.
1221 Ave. of the Americas
New York, NY 10020

American Library Association
50 E. Huron St.
Chicago, IL 60611

Americana Corp.
575 Lexington Ave.
New York, NY 10022

Appleton-Century-Crofts
440 Park Ave. S.
New York, NY 10016

Association for Childhood Educational International
3615 Wisconsin Ave., NW
Washington, D. C. 20016

Atheneum Pubs.
122 E. 42nd St.
New York, NY 10017

Ayer Press
W. Washington Sq.
Philadelphia, PA 19106

Barnes & Noble
10 E. 53rd St.
New York, NY 10022

Bellwether Pub. Co.
167 E. 67th St.
New York, NY 10021

Benefic Press
10300 W. Roosevelt Rd.
Westchester, IL 60153

Bloch Pub. Co.
915 Broadway
New York, NY 10010

Bobbs-Merrill Co.
4300 W. 62nd St.
Indianapolis, IN 46268

Bowker, R. R., Co.
1180 Ave. of the Americas
New York, NY 10036

Branford, Charles T., Co.
28 Union St.
Newton Centre, MA 02159

Bro-Dart Foundation
Box 306
Montoursville, PA 17754

Brown, William C. & Co.
2460 Kerper Blvd.
Dubuque, IA 52001

Career Institute
555 E. Lange St.
Mundelein, IL 60060

Carroll Book Service, Inc.
P. O. Box 1776
N. Tarrytown, NY 10591

Catholic Univ. of America
Press
620 Michigan Ave., NE
Washington, D.C. 20017

Cavanagh, Gladys
2223 Chamberlain Ave.
Madison, WI 53705

Centennial Press
1320 Q St., Box 428
Lincoln, NE 68501

Chemical Rubber Co.
CRC Press
18901 Cranwood Pkwy
Cleveland, OH 55128

Chicorel Library Pub. Co.
330 W. 58th St.
New York, NY 10019

Children's Press
1224 W. Van Buren St.
Chicago, IL 60607

Chilton Book Co.
Chilton Way
Radnor, PA 19089

Citadel Press, Inc.
120 Enterprise Ave.
Secaucas, NJ 07094

Citation Press
50 W. 44th St.
New York, NY 10036

Collins, William, Sons & Co.
215 Park Ave. S.
New York, NY 10003

Columbia Univ. Press
562 W. 113rd St.
New York, NY 10025

Compton, F. E., Co.
425 N. Michigan Ave.
Chicago, IL 60611

Comstock Pub. Associates
Div. of Cornell Univ. Press
124 Roberts Pl.
Ithaca, NY 14850

Council of State Governments
Iron Works Pike
Lexington, KY 40505

Coward, McCann and Geoghegan, Inc.
200 Madison Ave.
New York, NY 10016

Creative Education Press
500 Kappock St.
Bronx, NY 10463

Criterion Books
257 Park Ave. S.
New York, NY 10010

Crowell Collier Educ. Corp
866 Third St.
New York, NY 10022

Crowell, Thomas Y., Co.
666 Fifth Ave.
New York, NY 10019

Directory of Publishers

Crown Pubs., Inc.
419 Park Ave. S.
New York, NY 10016

Curtis Books, Inc.
The Chestnut Bldg.
Philadelphia, PA 19107

Day, John, Co.
257 Park Ave. S.
New York, NY 10010

Dodd, Mead & Co.
79 Madison Ave.
New York, NY 10016

Doubleday & Co., Inc.
277 Park Ave.
New York, NY 10017

Dover Publications
180 Varick St.
New York, NY 10014

Dutton, E. P., & Co., Inc.
201 Park Ave. S.
New York, NY 10003

Educational Film Library
  Association, Inc.
17 W. 60th St.
New York, NY 10023

Elk Grove Press
620 West Rd.
La Habra, CA 90631

Encyclopaedia Britannica
Educational Corp.
425 N. Michigan Ave.
Chicago, IL 60611

Facts on File, Inc.
119 W. 57th St.
New York, NY 10019

Fairchild Publications, Inc.
7 E. 12th St.
New York, NY 10003

Faxon, F. W., Co., Inc.
15 Southwest Park
Westwood, MA 02090

Ferguson, J. G., Pub. Co.
6 N. Michigan Ave.
Chicago, IL 60602

Field Enterprises Educational
  Corp.
510 Merchandise Mart Pl.
Chicago, IL 60654

Fleet Press Corp.
156 Fifth Ave.
New York, NY 10010

Follett Pub. Co.
1010 W. Washington Blvd.
Chicago, IL 60607

Free Press
866 Third Ave.
New York, NY 10022

Frontier Press Co.
250 E. Town St.
Columbus, OH 43215

Funk & Wagnalls Pub. Co.
666 Fifth Ave.
New York, NY 10019

Gale Research Co.
Book Tower
Detroit, MI 48226

Gambit, Inc.
53 Beacon St.
Boston, MA 02108

Garrard Pub. Co.
1607 N. Market St.
Champaign, IL 61820

Golden Press
Western Pub. Co., Inc.
1220 Mound Ave.
Racine, WI 53404

Goodhousekeeping Books
250 W. 55th St.
New York, NY 10019

Goodheart-Willcox Co.
123 W. Taft Dr. South
Holland, IL 60473

Greystone Corp.
225 Park Ave. S.
New York, NY 10003

Grolier, Inc.
575 Lexington Ave.
New York, NY 10022

Grosset & Dunlap, Inc.
51 Madison Ave.
New York, NY 10010

Hammond Inc.
Maplewood, NJ 07040

Harcourt, Brace, Jovanovich, Inc.
757 Third Ave.
New York, NY 10017

Harper & Row, Pubs.
10 E. 53rd St.
New York, NY 10022

Harvard Univ. Press
79 Garden St.
Cambridge, MA 02138

Hawthorne Books, Inc.
260 Madison Ave.
New York, NY 10016

Herder & Herder, Inc.
815 Second Ave.
New York, NY 10017

Hill & Wang, Inc.
19 Union Sq.
New York, NY 10003

Hippocrene Books, Inc.
171 Madison Ave.
New York, NY 10016

Holt, Rinehart & Winston, Inc.
383 Madison Ave.
New York, NY 10017

Houghton Mifflin Co.
1 Beacon St.
Boston, MA 02108

Jewish Publication Society of America
222 N. 15th St.
Philadelphia, PA 19102

Johnson Pub. Co.
1820 E. Michigan Ave.
Chicago, IL 60616

Knopf, Alfred A.
201 E. 50th St.
New York, NY 10022

Larousse & Co., Inc.
572 Fifth Ave.
New York, NY 10036

Lerner Publications Co.
241 First Ave. N.
Minneapolis, MN 55401

Lexington, Andrews, Inc.
866 Third Ave.
New York, NY 10022

Libraries Unlimited
Colorado Bibliographic Institute
Box 263
Littleton, CO 80120

Library of Congress
Washington, D.C. 20540

Lippincott, J. B., Co.
E. Washington Square
Philadelphia, PA 19105

Little, Brown & Co.
34 Beacon St.
Boston, MA 02106

Littlefield, Adams & Co.
81 Adams Dr.
Totowa, NJ 07512

Lothrop, Lee & Shephard Co.
105 Madison Ave.
New York, NY 10016

McGraw-Hill Book Co.
1221 Ave. of the Americas
New York, NY 10020

Directory of Publishers

McKay, David, Co., Inc.
750 Third Ave.
New York, NY 10017

McKinley Pub. Co.
112 S. New Broadway
Brooklawn, NJ 08030

Macmillan Educational Corp.
866 Third Ave.
New York, NY 10022

Macrae Smith Co.
225 S. 15th St.
Philadelphia, PA 19102

Marquis-Who's Who, Inc.
200 E. Ohio St.
Chicago, IL 60611

Meredith Corp. --Better Homes
& Gardens Books
1716 Locust St.
Des Moines, IA 50303

Merriam, G. & C., Co.
47 Federal St.
Springfield, MA 01101

Messner, Julian
1 W. 39th St.
New York, NY 10018

Morrow, William, & Co., Inc.
105 Madison Ave.
New York, NY 10016

Mosby, C. V., The, Co.
11830 Westline Industrial Dr.
St. Louis, MO 63141

National Center for Audio Tapes
University of Colorado
Boulder, CO 80301

National Council for the Social Studies
1201 16th St., NW
Washington, D. C. 20036

National Council of Teachers
of English
1111 Kenyon Rd.
Urbana, IL 61801

National Council of Teachers
of Mathematics
1906 Association Dr.
Reston, VA 22091

National Education Ass'n Pub.
1201 16th St., NW
Washington, D. C. 20036

National Geographic Society
17 & "M" Sts., NW
Washington, D. C. 20036

National Information Center
for Educational Media
University of Southern Calif.
University Park
Los Angeles, CA 90007

National Press Books
850 Hansen Way
Palo Alto, CA 94304

Nelson, Thomas, Inc.
407 Seventh Ave., S.
Nashville, TN 37203

New York Public Library
Fifth Ave. & 42nd St.
New York, NY 10018

New York Times Book Co.
10 E. 53rd St.
New York, NY 10022

Newspaper Enterprise Ass'n
230 Park Ave.
New York, NY 10017

Norton, W. W., & Co., Inc.
55 5th Ave.
New York, NY 10003

Oceana Publications, Inc.
Dobbs Ferry, NY 10522

Ocelot Press
Box 504
Claremont, CA 91711

Odyssey Press
4300 W. 62nd St.
Indianapolis, IN 46268

Oxford University Press, Inc.
200 Madison Ave.
New York, NY 10016

Palo Verde Pub. Co.
Box 5783
Tucson, AZ 85703

Pantheon Books, Inc.
201 E. 50th St.
New York, NY 10022

Philosophical Library, Inc.
15 E. 40th St.
New York, NY 10016

Pierian Press
Box 1808
Ann Arbor, MI 48106

Platt & Munk, Inc.
1055 Bronx River Ave.
Bronx, NY 10472

Praeger Pubs., Inc.
111 Fourth Ave.
New York, NY 10003

Prentice-Hall, Inc.
Englewood Cliffs, NJ 07632

Public Affairs Press
419 New Jersey Ave., SE
Washington, D.C. 20003

Purnell Library Service
850 Seventh Ave.
New York, NY 10019

Putnam's, G. P., Sons
200 Madison Ave.
New York, NY 10016

Quadrangle/The New York
    Times Book Co.
10 E. 53rd St.
New York, NY 10022

Quality Books
Box 6421, 2013 S. 20th St.
Philadelphia, PA 19145

Rand McNally & Co.
8255 Central Park Ave.
Skokie, IL 60076
Mailing address:
Box 7600
Chicago, IL 60680

Random House, Inc.
201 E. 50th St.
New York, NY 10022

Reader's Digest Association
Pleasantville, NY 10570

St. Martin's Press, Inc.
175 Fifth Ave.
New York, NY 10010

Scarecrow Press, Inc.
52 Liberty St., Box 656
Metuchen, NJ 08840

Schirmer, G., Inc.
866 Third Ave.
New York, NY 10022

Scott, Foresman & Co.
1900 E. Lake Ave.
Glenview, IL 60025

Scribner's, Charles, Sons
597 Fifth Ave.
New York, NY 10017

Shengold Pubs., Inc.
45 W. 45th St.
New York, NY 10036

Simon & Schuster, Inc.
630 Fifth Ave.
New York, NY 10020

Southwestern Co.
I-65 at Moore's Lane
Box 820
Nashville, TN 37202

Directory of Publishers

Stein and Day Pubs.
7 E. 48th St.
New York, NY 10017

Sterling Pub. Co.
419 Park Ave., S.
New York, NY 10016

Teachers College Press
Teachers College
Columbia University
1234 Amsterdam Ave.
New York, NY 10027

Tudor Pub. Co.
221 Park Ave. S.
New York, NY 10003

Two Continents Pub. Group
30 E. 42nd St.
New York, NY 10017

U. S. Government Printing Office
Div. of Public Documents
Washington, D. C. 20402

University of Pittsburgh Press
127 N. Bellefield Ave.
Pittsburgh, PA 15213

Van Nostrand Reinhold Co.
450 W. 33rd St.
New York, NY 10001

Viking Press, Inc.
625 Madison Ave.
New York, NY 10022

Walck, Henry Z., Inc.
3 E. 54th St.
New York, NY 10022

Warne, Frederick, & Co., Inc.
101 Fifth Ave.
New York, NY 10003

Washburn, Ives, Inc.
750 Third Ave.
New York, NY 10017

Watts, Franklin, Inc.
845 Third Ave.
New York, NY 10022

Western Pub. Co., Inc.
1220 Mound Ave.
Racine, WI 53404

Westminster Press
Witherspoon Bldg.
Philadelphia, PA 19107

William Penn Pub. Corp.
221 Park Ave., S.
New York, NY 10003

Wilson, H. W., Co.
950 University Ave.
Bronx, NY 10452

World Pub. Co.
110 E. 59th St.
New York, NY 10022

Worldmark Press, Inc.
242 E. 50th St.
New York, NY 10022

The Writer, Inc.
8 Arlington St.
Boston, MA 02116

Zondervan Pub. House
1415 Lake Dr., SE
Grand Rapids, MI 49506

AUTHOR AND TITLE INDEX

AAAS Science Book List 197, 273
AAAS Science Book List for Children 197, 255, 273
ABC Book of Early Americana 162
ABC's of Astronomy 9, 14, 216
ABC's of Chemistry 9, 14, 216
Abbott, R. Tucker 208
Abbreviations Dictionary 10, 49
Abingdon Bible Commentary 134
Abridged Readers' Guide to Periodical Literature 7, 11, 55
Ackner, Joseph 215
Adair, Margaret Weeks 239
Adams, George F. 218
Adams, James Truslow 75, 159, 160
Addington, Richard 108
Adler, Mortimer J. 163, 193
Adventures in Discovery 197
Adventuring with Books 255
Africa South of the Sahara 1974 144
Ahnstrom, D. N. 179
Air Facts and Feats 179-180
Aircraft 179
Album of American History 13, 157, 159
Album of Jews in America 188
Album of Puerto Ricans in the United States 188
Album of the American Indian 188
Album of the Irish Americans 188
Album of the Italian-American 188
Alexander, Gerald L. 147
Alexander, Taylor R. 211
Alkema, Chester Jay 238
All About American Holidays 172
Almanac of American Politics 13, 177
Alt, Winifred 240
Altman, Addie Richman 131
Alvarez, Joseph A. 175

Amateur Photographer's Handbook 245
America Is Also Irish 186-187
America Is Also Italian 186-187
America Is Also Jewish 186-187
America Is Also Scandinavian 186-187
America Is Also Series 186-187
America Is My Country 9, 168
American Association for the Advancement of Science 197, 255, 273
American Authors, 1600-1900 11, 86
American Book of Days 9, 13, 173-174
American Boys' Handy Book 241-242
American Citizens Handbook 13, 168-169
American College Dictionary 40
American Composers Today 89
American Counties 147
American Forts 161
American Girls' Handy Book 241
American Heritage Book of Natural Wonders 146
American Heritage Dictionary of the English Language 7, 10, 40, 114
American Heritage Guide to Archaeology 152
American Heritage New Pictorial Encyclopedic Guide to the United States 8, 13, 144-145
American Heritage Pictorial Atlas of United States History 7, 11, 75
American Heritage School Dictionary 10, 36
American Heritage Songbook 8, 123
American Historical Fiction and Biography for Children and Young People 156-157

283

American History in Juvenile Books 157, 255
American Indian in America 188, 190
American Indians, Yesterday and Today 189
American Men and Women of Science: Physical and Biological Sciences 88-89
American Men and Women of Science: Social and Behavioral Sciences 88
American Negro Reference Book 14, 190-191
American Nicknames 49-50
American Political Dictionary 177
American Red Cross 225
American Revolution 160
American Symbols 164
American Thesaurus of Slang 116-117
Americana Annual 22, 52
America's Historylands 146
America's Natural Wonders 146
Ames, Delano 108
Ammer, Christine 120
Andersen, Yvonne 246
Animal Atlas of the World 9, 14, 204
Animals Next Door 203
Annals of America 158, 163-164, 193
Anniversaries and Holidays 173
Annotated List of Recordings in the Language Arts 255
Answer Book 48
Answers and More Answers 48
Anthony, Catherine Parker 226
Antonyms 112-113
Apel, Willi 120
Appleton's New Cuyas English-Spanish, Spanish-English Dictionary 11, 96
Appraisal 270
Aquino-Bermudex, Frederico 95
Arbuthnot, May Hill 108-109
Archibald, Joe 249
Arnold, Pauline 164
Arora Plastics Corp. 244
Art Recipes 241
Art Through the Ages 125-126
Asimov, Isaac 61, 89, 105, 197
Asimov's Biographical Encyclopedia of Science and Technology 7, 11, 89
Atkinson, Margaret F. 238
Atlas Moderno Universal 7, 11, 72

Atlas of American History 75, 157, 159
Atlas of Animal Migration 205, 211
Atlas of Discovery 8, 13, 155
Atlas of Plant Life 211-212
Atlas of the Bible Lands 12, 67, 132
Atlas of the Presidents 87
Atlas of Wildlife 205, 211
Atlas of World History: From the Beginning to Alexander the Great 152
Atlas of World History: The Classical World 74
Atlas of World History: The Dark Ages 154
Audubon Nature Encyclopedia 14, 201
Authors and Illustrators of Children's Books 85
Authors of Books for Young People 83-84
Authors of Today and Yesterday 85
Auto Mechanics Fundamentals 229
Avery, Catherine B. 152
Ayer Directory of Publications 11, 56

Bagai, Leona B. 187
Bailard, Virginia 175
Baker, Augusta 190
Baker, Robert H. 215
Baker's Biographical Dictionary of Musicians 90
Ballet for Beginners 238
Bancroft, Jessie H. 243
Banks, Arthur 153
Barber, Anson B. 23
Barnhart, Clarence L. 35, 38-40, 45, 50, 97
Barnhart Dictionary of New English Since 1963 7, 10, 39-40
Barone, Michael 177
Barraclough, E. M. C. 165
Bartholomew, John 72, 138
Bartlett, John 110
Baseball Rules in Pictures 249
Baseball Talk for Beginners 249
Basketball Lingo 248
Basketball Talk for Beginners 248
Beard, Adelia B. 241
Beard, D. C. 241
Beard, Lina 241
Beginner's Guide to Wild Flowers 213-214

Author and Title Index 285

Beginning Knowledge Book of
  Backyard Flowers 6, 212
Beginning Knowledge Book of
  Snakes 6, 207
Beginning Knowledge Book of
  Stars and Constellations 6,
  215
Beginning Knowledge Book of
  Turtles 6, 207
Beginning Knowledge Book Series
  207, 212, 215
Behavior Patterns in Children's
  Books 255
Bell, Melville 146
Belpre, Pura 194
Benagh, Jim 248
Ben-Asher, Naomi 193
Bendick, Jeanne 214
Benét, William Rose 98
Benson, Brian 180
Bergaust, Erik 233
Berger, Toby M. 268
Berrey, Lester V. 116
Berry, John N., III 272
Bertin, Leon 217
Better Homes and Gardens
  Junior Cook Book for the
  Hostess and Host of Tomor-
  row 222
Better Homes and Gardens New
  Cook Book 223
Betteridge, Harold T. 93
Bettman, Otto 119
Betty Crocker's New Boys and
  Girls Cookbook 222
Bevans, Michael H. 207
The Bible 129, 133
Bible Book by Book 135
Bible Encyclopedia for Children
  8, 133
Bibliography of Books for Children
  256
Bibliography of Negro History and
  Culture for Young Readers
  192
Bicycle Repair 230
Big Book of Magic 239
Bike-Ways 239-240
Biography Index 78
Birds 6, 9, 14, 206-207
Birnbaum, Max 182, 183
Black Experience in Children's
  Audio Visual Materials 6,
  9, 190
Black Experience in Children's
  Books 6, 9, 190
Blackburn, G. Meredith, III 109
Boatner, Mark Mayo, III 160

Bogart, Gary L. 262
Bohle, Bruce 111
Bolander, Donald O. 111
Book and Non-book Media 256
Book of Art 8, 126
Book of Europe 142-143
Book of Games and Entertainments
  the World Over 243
Book of Popular Science 9, 14,
  199
Book of Reptiles and Amphibians
  207
Book of Saints 136
Book of States 13, 177
Book Review Digest 11, 56
Book Review Index 56
Book Selection Media 256
Booklist 270
Books About Negro Life for Chil-
  dren 190
Books Are by People 84
Books in Print 14, 256-257
Books for Friendship 256
Books to Help Children Adjust to
  a Hospital Situation 257
Botany 9, 14, 211
Bouquet, A. C. 132
Bowling 251
Boy Scouts of America 241, 246
Boys' Book of Indian Skills 246-
  247
Boys' Book of Model Railroading
  244
Brahs, Stuart 188
Bray, Leonard 56
Bray, Warwick 152
Brett, Lewis E. 96
Breul, Karl 93
Brewer's Dictionary of Phrase and
  Fable 12, 98
Brewton, John E. 109
Brewton, Sara W. 109
Bridges of Understanding 185
Britannica Atlas 11, 71-72
Britannica Book of the Year 17,
  47, 52-53
Britannica Encyclopedia of Ameri-
  can Art 8, 12, 126-127
Britannica Junior Encyclopaedia for
  Boys and Girls 5-6, 15-16,
  52
Britannica 3 25
Britannica Yearbook of Science and
  the Future 198
British Authors Before 1800 11,
  86
British Authors of the Nineteenth
  Century 11, 86

Brockman, C. Frank 212
Broido, A. 118-120
Bronowski, J. 220
Brown, Harriett M. 168
Brown, J. A. C. 226
Brownrigg, Ronald 136
Buchanan, Fannie R. 118
Buchwald, Ann 171
Bucknall, Rixon 179
Building and Operating Model Ships 244-245
Building Bridges of Understanding Between Cultures 6, 9, 13, 185
Bulla, Clyde Robert 121
Bulletin of the Center for Children's Books 270
Burnett, R. Will 203, 211
Burns, Ted 251
Burton, Maurice 202
Burton, Robert 202
Bush-Brown, Louise 224
Butterflies and Moths 209
Butterfly Book 210
Butwin, Frances 187

Cabinet 176
Carlson, Ruth Kearney 184
Carpenter, Rhys 148, 151
Carr, C. T. 41
Carruth, Gordon 158
Cass, James 182, 183
Cassell's Beyond the Dictionary in French 93
Cassell's Beyond the Dictionary in Spanish 96
Cassell's Encyclopedia of World Literature 98
Cassell's Italian Dictionary 11, 94
Cassell's New French Dictionary 11, 92-93
Cassell's New German Dictionary 11, 93
Cassell's New Latin Dictionary 11, 94
Cassell's Spanish Dictionary 96
Cassidy, Fredric G. 41
Cat in the Hat Beginner Book Dictionary 32
Cat in the Hat Beginner Book Dictionary in French 5, 91
Cat in the Hat Beginner Book Dictionary in Spanish 95
Catalogue of the World's Most Popular Coins 236
Cates, Edwin H. 187

Cauman, Samuel 124
Cavanagh, Gladys 59
Cavanah, Frances 161
Cayne, Bernard S. 21
Chamberlin, Waldo 174
Chamber's Biographical Dictionary 80
Charles-Picard, Gilbert 152
Charlie Brown Dictionary 5-6, 33
Chase, Alice Elizabeth 118, 123-124
Cheerleading and Song Leading 237-238
Chess for You 237
Chicorel, Marietta 101
Chicorel Theater Index to Children's Plays 101-102
Childcraft 5, 17
Childhood Education 270-271
Children's Books in Print 6, 10, 254, 257
Children's Catalog 6, 10, 254, 257, 262, 268
Chilton's Auto Repair Manual 229
Chinery, Michael 200, 204, 211
Chinese in America 187-188
Chronology and Fact Book of the United Nations, 1941-1969 13, 174
Chronology of the Expanding World 1492 to 1762 13, 154
Chronology of the Medieval World 800 to 1491 154
Chronology of the Modern World; 1763 to the Present Time 13, 156
Chrystie, Frances N. 230
Chu, Daniel 190
Chu, Samuel 190
Cianciolo, Patricia Jean 266
Civil War Dictionary 160-161
Clement, Roland C. 202
Cochran, Doris M. 207
Cochran, Thomas 159
Cohen, John Michael 110
Cohen, Mark J. 110
Cohen, Saul B. 69
Cohen, Selma Jeanne 122
Colby, C. B. 146, 162
Colby, Vineta 85-86
Cole, Ann 240
Coles, Clarence W. 230
Collecting Seashells 236
Collector's Encyclopedia of Rocks and Minerals 217
Colley, C. Earl 141
Collier's Encyclopedia 6, 10, 18, 53

Author and Title Index 287

Collier's Year Book 10, 19, 24, 53
Collins, A. Frederick 238
Colonial America 159
Columbia-Lippincott Gazetteer of the World 12, 138
Comay, Joan 136, 194
Commager, Henry Steele 163
Commire, Anne 83
Common Bible with the Apocrypha/Deuterocanonical Books 8, 12, 133
Comparative Guide to American Colleges 183
Comparative Guide to Junior and Two-Year Community Colleges 182-183
Complete Beginner's Guide to Bicycling 240
Complete Beginner's Guide to Skin Diving 250-251
Complete Book of Home Repairs and Maintenance 228
Complete Book of Jets and Rockets 179
Complete Book of Winter Sports 250
Complete Concordance to the Bible 135
Complete Crayon Book in Color 238
Complete Ecology Fact Book 14, 224
Complete Encyclopedia of Motorcars 179
Complete Handbook of Model Car Racing 244
Complete Junior Encyclopedia of Transportation 9, 13, 178
Complete Outdoors Encyclopedia 247
Complete Rhyming Dictionary 12, 116
Composers of Today 89
Composers Since 1900 7, 11, 89-90
Compton, Helen Douglas 173
Compton Yearbook 7, 10, 20, 51-52
Compton's Dictionary of the Natural Sciences 201
Compton's Encyclopedia and Fact Index 6, 10, 19, 51
Compton's Precyclopedia 5, 20
Comstock, Anna Botsford 200
Concise Color Encyclopedia of Nature 9, 200
Concise Dictionary of American Biography 7, 11, 81-82
Concise Dictionary of American History 159
Concise Dictionary of Music 12, 119-120
Concise Dictionary of National Biography 82-83
Concise Encyclopedia of Explorations 155
Concise Encyclopedia of Greek and Roman Mythology 107
Concise Encyclopedia of Sports 10, 14, 247
Concise Encyclopedia of the Middle East 143
Concise Guide Series 170, 221, 230
Concise Handbook of Occupations 9, 181
Concise Oxford Companion to English Literature 12, 98-99
Concise Oxford Dictionary of Current English 40-41
Concise Oxford Dictionary of Opera 121
Congress 176
Connor, Billie M. 102
Connor, John M. 102
Contemporary Authors 86-87
Contributions of Ethnic Groups 184-185
Conwell, Mary K. 194
Cook, Dorothy Elizabeth 104
Cookbook for Girls and Boys 222
Cooke, Donald E. 87, 163
Cornett, Frederick D. 225
Corrigan, Barbara 231
Costume Book 6, 9, 169
Costumes and Styles 169
Costumes for School Plays 169
Costumes for You to Make 169
Cottam, Clarence 209
Coughlan, Margaret N. 156
Coulson, J. 41
Courtis, Stuart A. 33, 35
Courtis-Watters Illustrated Golden Dictionary for Young Readers 33, 35
Cowboy Encyclopedia 161
Coy, Harold 87-88
Crandall, Elizabeth L. 161
Craven, Thomas 125
Creating Independence, 1763-1789 156
Crispin, Frederic Swing 220
Crocker, Betty 222
Cross, Milton 121
Crouthers, David D. 166

Crowell's Handbook of Classical
    Literature 99
Crowell's Handbook of Classical
    Mythology 107
Cruden, Alexander 134
Cruden's Complete Concordance
    to the Old and New Testa-
    ments 134-135
Cub Book 241
Curora, Maria Lucia 96
Current Biography Yearbook 7,
    11, 79
Customs and Holidays Around the
    World 9, 13, 173
Cuyas, Arturo 96
Cyclopedia of Literary Characters
    100
Cyclopedia of World Authors 85
Cynar, Robert 227
Czechs and Slovaks in America
    184, 188

Daniels, Leo Francis 34
Darby, Gene 228
Daroqui, Julia 95
Daves, Michael 135
Davis, John Preston 190
Davis, Marilyn Kornreich 118-120
Days to Remember 173
DeAngeli, Marguerite 97, 108,
    133
Deason, Hilary J. 197
Deedy, John 224
Deeson, A. F. L. 217
Deford, Miriam A. 81
De la Croix, Horst 125
Delury, George E. 54
DeMontreville, Doris 84
Demske, Dick 228
DeSola, Dorothy 223
DeSola, Ralph 49, 223
Deutsch, Babette 110
Dictionary of American Biography
    75, 81, 157, 159-160
Dictionary of American History
    75, 157, 159-160
Dictionary of American Homo-
    phones and Homographs 115
Dictionary of American Politics
    176-177
Dictionary of American Slang
    12, 117
Dictionary of Basic Words 34-35
Dictionary of Biological Terms
    202
Dictionary of Chivalry 8, 13, 153
Dictionary of Classical Mythology
    107
Dictionary of Cooking 223
Dictionary of Costume 9, 13, 170
Dictionary of Fictional Characters
    12, 99
Dictionary of Geography 138
Dictionary of Literary Terms 12,
    100-101
Dictionary of Modern Ballet 12,
    122
Dictionary of Music and Musicians
    118, 120
Dictionary of Mythology, Mainly
    Classical 8, 12, 107
Dictionary of National Biography
    82
Dictionary of Non-Christian Reli-
    gions 12, 131
Dictionary of Philosophy 129-130
Dictionary of Political Science 13,
    176
Dictionary of Spoken Russian 11,
    95
Dictionary of Technical Terms
    220-221
Dictionary of the American Indian
    189
Dictionary of the Environmental
    Sciences 223-224
Dictionary of the Social Sciences
    167
Dictionary of Word Origins 116
Dictionary of World Literary Terms
    101
Dictionary of World Literature 101
Dictionnaire Universel de l'Art et
    des Artistes 127
Dinosaur Dictionary 210-211
Discovering Natural Science 9, 201
DiValentin, Maria 242
Doane, Pelagie 105
Dobler, Lavinia 173, 258
Dobler World Directory of Youth
    Periodicals 258
Dobrin, Arnold 194
Dobson, Margaret J. 248
Documents of American History
    13, 163
Doubleday, Nelson 141
Doubleday First Guide Series 209,
    212-213, 217
Doubleday First Guide to Insects
    6, 209
Doubleday First Guide to Rocks
    6, 217
Doubleday First Guide to Trees 6,
    212
Doubleday First Guide to Wild

Flowers 6, 213
Doubleday Pictorial Library of Technology 220
Dougherty, Margaret M. 112
Douglas, George William 173
Dowdell, Dorothy 187
Dowdell, Joseph 187
Downey, D. G. 134
Dragons, Unicorns, and Other Magical Beasts 8, 105
Draper, Nancy 238
Driscoll, Timothy 188
Drugs from A to Z 14, 226-227
Drury's Guide to Best Plays 102
Dubois, Marguerite-Marie 93
Ducas, George 193
Dunan, Marcel 153
Duncan, Marcel 155
Dunner, Joseph 176
Dupuy, Ernest 88
Durrenberger, Robert W. 223
Dutch in America 188

Eagle, D. S. 41
Eagle, Dorothy 98
Eakin, Mary K. 58, 59
Earl of Harewood 122
Earle, Olive L. 165
Earth and Man 65, 68-69
Earth and Space 9, 215
East Indians and Pakistanis in America 187-188
Eastern Religions 12, 130
Eastman, Mary Huse 105-106
Eastman, Philip D. 32, 91, 95
Easy Puppets 238
Easy Steps to Safe Swimming 250
Eaton, Helen S. 96
Ebony 191
Ebony Pictorial History of Black America 14, 191
Ebony Success Library 14, 191
Economics Reference Book 13, 170-171
Edlin, Herbert Leeson 211
Edmonds, I. G. 240
Educational Screen and Audiovisual Guide 271
Edwards, Paul 129
8mm Film Directory 258
Eiselen, F. C. 134
Eiseman, Alberta 195
Elementary English 271
Elementary School Library Collection 6, 10, 254, 258
El-Hi Textbooks in Print 259

Ellis, Hamilton 179
Ellison, John W. 135
Elting, Mary 48
Emerging Humanity 184
Emily Post Book of Etiquette for Young People 9, 171
Encyclopedia Americana 10, 21, 52
Encyclopedia International 6, 10, 16, 22, 51, 131
Encyclopedia of American Biography 11, 82
Encyclopedia of American Facts and Dates 13, 158-159
Encyclopedia of American History 9, 13, 156, 158
Encyclopedia of Art 8, 12, 125
Encyclopedia of Careers and Vocational Guidance 13, 167, 181-182
Encyclopedia of Discovery and Exploration 155
Encyclopedia of Philosophy 129
Encyclopedia of Sports 14, 248
Encyclopedia of the American Revolution 160
Encyclopedia of the Biological Sciences 202
Encyclopedia of World Art 118, 126, 128
Encyclopedia of World Geography 8, 12, 139
Encyclopedia of World History 8, 13, 148, 150
Encyclopedia of World Travel 141
Encyclopedia Science Supplement 199
Encyclopedia Year Book 23, 51
English in America 187-188
Enthoven, Jacqueline 231
Epstein, Edna 174
Ertel, James 32
Espenshade, Edward B., Jr. 64
Essay and General Literature Index 56-57
Etiquette 6, 9, 171
Eubank, Nancy 187
Europa Yearbook 8, 13, 142
European Authors, 1000-1900 11, 86
European Composers Today 89
European Historical Fiction and Biography for Children and Young People 148
Evans, Bergen 107
Evans, Ivor H. 98
Everyday Life in Ancient Times 148, 151

Everyday Life in New Testament Times 132-133
Everyday Life in Old Testament Times 132-133
Ewen, David 89-90, 121-122

Faber Junior Dictionary 36
Fabric Almanac 232
Fact Book of the Countries of the World 13, 141-142
Facts about the Presidents 7, 11, 87-88
Facts on File 10, 53
Facts on File Yearbook 53
Fairy Elves 5, 8, 105
Falls, C. B. 151
Familiar Quotations 8, 12, 110
Family Book of Crafts 242
Famous Artists of the Past 124
Famous First Facts 7, 10, 48-49
Famous Paintings 6, 8, 118, 123-124
Far East and Australasia 1973 143
Feature Films on 8 and 16 259
Feder, Lillian 99
Feerick, Emalie P. 88
Feerick, John D. 88
Fenton, Carroll Lane 210
Fenton, Mildred Adams 210
Fenton, Robert S. 237
Ferguson, J. G. 181
Festivals U. S. A. and Canada 172
Fichter, George S. 210
Fidell, Estelle A. 102, 104, 257, 262, 268
Field Guide to Butterflies of North America 210
Fieldbook 246
Fifty Favorite Hobbies 234-235
Films for Children (EFLA) 259
Films for Children (NYPL) 259-260
Films for Young Adults 260
Films Kids Like 260
Fines, John 153
First Book Atlas 63
First Book of Facts and How to Find Them 7, 47
First Book of Festivals Around the World 172
First Book of How to Run a Meeting 9, 174
First 3000 Years 151
Fisher, Harvey I. 203

Fisher, Margery 264
Fishes 9, 14, 208
Fitch, Florence Mary 130
Five Centuries of American Costume 170
Flag Book of the United States 9, 13, 166
Flags of American History 166
Flags of the World 9, 13, 165-166
Flandorf, Vera S. 257
Flexner, Stuart Berg 38, 41, 117
Flory, Esther V. 104
Flowers 213
Fogel, Barbara R. 49
Foley, Doris 241
Folk Puppet Plays for the Social Studies 239
Folk Songs of the World 12, 123
Folklore: An Annotated Bibliography and Index to Single Editions 8, 12, 106
Folklore of the North American Indians 106
Fonteneau, Marthe 92, 96
Football Talk for Beginners 249
Fossil Book 14, 210
Fossils 9, 210
Fowler, F. G. 40
Fowler, H. W. 40
Frankel, Godfrey 239
Frankel, Lillian 239
Franklin Watts Concise Guide to Baby-Sitting 221
Freedom Encyclopedia 9, 13, 161
Freeman, William 99
Freidrichsen, E. 40
French in America 188
Frey, Shaney 250
Fried, Jerome 108
Frome, Michael 145
Fullard, Harold 74
Fuller, Muriel 84
Fun Encyclopedia 243
Fun with Tools 227
Funk, Charles Earle 44
Funk, Isaac K. 43
Funk and Wagnalls Guide to Modern World Literature 100
Funk and Wagnalls Modern Guide to Synonyms and Related Words 115
Funk and Wagnalls New "Standard" Bible Dictionary 134
Funk and Wagnalls New Standard Dictionary of the English Language 43
Funk and Wagnalls Standard College

Dictionary 10, 41
Funk and Wagnalls Standard Dictionary of Folklore, Mythology, and Legend 12, 107-108
Funk and Wagnalls Standard Dictionary of the English Language: International Edition 10, 41, 44

Gabrielson, Ira N. 206
Gadan, Francis 122
Gaer, Joseph 130
Gail, Marzieh 154
Gallant, Roy A. 216
Gamebirds 206
Games 10, 14, 243
Games and Sports the World Around 244
Games for the Very Young 242
Games for Younger Children 243
Games of Many Nations 244
Gardner, Helen 125
Garraty, John A. 82
Gassner, John 103
Gauvin, Claude 92
Gaver, Mary V. 258
Gay, Kathlyn 187
Geisel, T. S. 32, 91, 95
General Encyclopedias in Print 1973-1974 260
General World Atlases in Print 1972/1973 260-261
Geology 218
Georgano, G. N. 179
Gephert, Joseph C. 57
Gerhardt, Lillian N. 273
Germans Helped Build America 187
Germans in America 188
Gerrand, A. Bryson 96
Gerrish, Howard H. 221
Gerrish's Technical Dictionary 14, 221
Gersh, Harry 203
Getting to Know American Indians Today 189-190
Giant Nursery Book of Things That Go 6, 178
Gillespie, John 104
Gilliard, E. Thomas 206
Ginn Beginning Dictionary 34
Girard, Denis 92
Girl's Book of Handicrafts 241
Glenn, Harold T. 230
Glenn's Complete Bicycle Manual 230
Glut, Donald F. 210

Goetz, Delia 146
Goin, Coleman 207
Golden Bible Atlas 8, 132
Golden Book of Quotations 8, 110
Golden Dictionary 33
Golden Encyclopedia of Music 8, 12, 119
Golden History of the United States 157
Golden Nature Guide Series 201, 203-204, 206-210, 212-213, 216-217
Golden Science Guide Series 211-212, 218
Golden Song Book 6, 122-123
Golden Treasury of Myths and Legends 105
Goldhurst, Richard 186
Golenpaul, Dan 53
Golf Techniques 251-252
Good Housekeeping New Complete Book of Needlecraft 232
Good Reading for Poor Readers 254, 261
Good Reading for the Disadvantaged Reader 186
Goode, John P. 64
Goode's World Atlas 5, 7, 11, 64
Goodman, Morris C. 191
Gorsline, Douglas 170
Gould, Julius 167
Goulden, Shirley 122
Gove, Philip Babcock 36, 45
Gracza, Margaret 187
Gracza, Rezsoe 187
Granger's Index to Poetry 12, 109-110
Grant, Bruce 161, 189
Gray, Peter 202
Grayson, Marion 242
Great Bicycle Book 239
Great Composers 1300-1900 7, 11, 89
Great Indian Tribes 9, 14, 189
Great Religions of the World 131
Greeks in America 187-188
Green, Ellin 264
Greenberg, Milton 177
Greer, Roger C. 57
Greet, W. Cabell 31, 113
Greisman, Joan 111, 114
Gresswell, R. Kay 139
Grosset World Atlas 64
Grossman, Ronald 187
Grosvenor, Melville Bell 66
Grove, Sir George 118, 120
Gruenberg, Sidonie Matsner 221
Guadagnolo, Joseph F. 168

Guide for Young Campers 246
Guide to Garden Flowers 225
Guide to Historical Fiction 149
Guide to Historical Reading: Nonfiction 149
Guide to Media and Materials on Ethnic American Minorities 185
Guide to Reference Books for School Media Centers 261
Guides to Educational Media 261-262
Guides to Newer Educational Media 261
Guild, Vera P. 232
Guinness Book of World Records 7, 10, 49
Guralnik, David B. 37, 43
Guss, Carolyn 261
Gymnastics 251

Halsey, William D. 18, 24, 50
Hammond, N. G. L. 99
Hammond Ambassador World Atlas 65-66, 73
Hammond Atlas of United States History 7, 11, 67, 75-76
Hammond Citation World Atlas 5, 64-66
Hammond Comparative World Atlas 7, 11, 73
Hammond Headline World Atlas 11, 64
Hammond Illustrated Atlas for Young America 7, 11, 62
Hammond International World Atlas 64, 73-74
Hammond Medallion World Atlas 7, 11, 64-67, 73
Hammond Nature Atlas of America 202
Hammond's Atlas of World History 7, 11, 67, 75
Hammond's Historical Atlas 67, 75
Hammond's United States History Atlas 67, 76
Hand, Jackson 228
Handbook of Chemistry and Physics 14, 217
Handbook of Model Rocketry 245
Handbook of Nature-Study 200-201
Handbook of New Nations 142
Handbook of Pseudonyms and Personal Nicknames 10, 50
Handbook of the World's Religions 8, 12, 131
Handbook to Literature 97, 101
Hansen, Henny Harald 169
Hanson, Joan 112-113
Harbin, E. O. 243-244
Harcourt Brace School Dictionary 37
Hardgrove, Clarence Ethel 214
Harper Encyclopedia of Science 199-200
Harper Encyclopedia of the Modern World 13, 156
Harper's Bible Dictionary 12, 133-134
Harper's Dictionary of Music 120
Harrison, E. J. 251
Hart, James D. 99
Hartnoll, Phyllis 103
Harvard Dictionary of Music 120
Harvey, Sir Paul 98-99
Hathaway, Polly 212
Haupt, Enid A. 171
Hausman, Ethel Hindkley 213
Hayakawa, S. I. 41, 115
Haycraft, Howard 84-86
Haywood, Charles 123
Hazeltine, Mary Emogene 173
Heaton, E. W. 132
Helfman, Harry 245
Hellegers, Louisa B. 242
Helped Build America Series 187
Hems, Jack 208
Henderson, Isabella 202
Henderson, William D. 202
Henshaw, Edmund L., Jr. 87
Herald, Earl S. 208
Here Is Your Hobby: Archery 253
Here Is Your Hobby: Doll Collecting 236
Here Is Your Hobby: Fishing 252
Here Is Your Hobby: Magic 239
Here's Your Hobby 235
Hervey, George 208
Herzberg, Max J. 100
Hibbard, Addison 97, 101
High Interest--Easy Reading for Junior and Senior High School Students 254, 262
Hill, Donna 84
Hillbrand, Percie V. 187
Hindley, Geoffrey 120
Historical American Landmarks 162
Historical Fiction 149
Historical Nonfiction 149
History Atlas of America 7, 76
History in Children's Books 149-150

Author and Title Index

History of Art for Young People 8, 12, 124
Hobbies for Boys 235
Hobbies for Girls 235
Hobby Collections A-Z 9, 235
Hockey Talk for Beginners 249
Hoffman, Miriam 85
Hoffmeister, Donald F. 203-204
Hoke, Helen 171
Holland, W. J. 210
Hollander, Zander 248
Holman, C. Hugh 101
Holmes, Marian D. 243
Holt Basic Dictionary of American English 36-37
Holy Land in the Time of Jesus 132
Holy Scriptures According to the Masoretic Text 8, 12, 133
Home Book of American Quotations 111
Home Book of Bible Quotations 12, 135-136
Home Book of Quotations, Classical and Modern 12, 110-111
Homographic Homophones 112-113
Homographs 112-113
Homonyms 113
Hopke, William E. 181
Hopkins, Joseph G. E. 81
Hopkins, Lee Bennett 84, 192
Horn Book Magazine 271
Hotchkiss, Jeanette 148, 156
How Documents Preserve Freedom 9, 162
How It Works 229
How Man Made Music 8, 118-119
How Much and How Many 214
How the Great Religions Began 130-131
How to Read a City Map 5, 7, 61
How to Read a Highway Map 5, 7, 61
How to Star in Track and Field 252
How We Named Our States 164-165
How We Use Maps and Globes 5, 7, 60-61
Howard, Neal E. 216
Howat, Gerald 80
Human Physiology 225-226
Humphrey, Edward 22

Humphrey, Marylou 237
Humphrey, Ron 237
Hungarians in America 187-188
Hunt, Sarah Ethridge 244
Hunter, Hilda 235
Hunting 252
Hutchinson, M. L. 41
Huxley, Anthony 138-139
Hylander, Clarence J. 213

I Read, You Read, We Read 6, 10, 14, 254, 262
I Saw a Purple Cow 240
Ice Hockey Rules in Pictures 249-250
Ickis, Marguerite 243
Iijima, Takeru 237
Illustrated Baseball Dictionary for Young People 249
Illustrated Encyclopedia of Freshwater Fishes 208
Illustrated Encyclopedia of the Animal Kingdon 14, 205
Illustration Index 57
Illustrators of Books for Young People 85
Important Dates in Afro-American History 192
In America Series 9, 187-188
In Other Words 5, 8, 97, 113
Index to Children's Plays in Collections 8, 101
Index to Children's Poetry 5, 8, 12, 109
Index to Children's Poetry, First Supplement 5, 8, 12, 109
Index to Children's Poetry, Second Supplement 5, 8, 12, 109
Index to Fairy Tales, Myths, and Legends 8, 12, 105-106
Index to Fairy Tales, Myths, and Legends, Supplement 8, 12, 106
Index to Fairy Tales, Myths, and Legends, Second Supplement 8, 12, 106
Index to Fairy Tales, 1949-1972 8, 12, 106
Index to Handicrafts, Model Making, and Workshop Projects 240
Index to Poetry 12, 109-110
Index to Poetry and Recitations 110
Index to Poetry for Children and Young People 5, 8, 12, 108-109

Index to Scientists of the World from Ancient to Modern Times 79
Index to Short Biographies 7, 11, 78
Index to Women of the World 78-79
Index to Young Readers' Collective Biographies 7, 11, 78
Information Please Almanac, Atlas and Yearbook 7, 10, 47, 53
Ingle, Lester 209
Insect Pests 210
Insects 9, 14, 209
Instant English Handbook 8, 12, 111
Instant Home Repair Handbook 228
Instant Medical Advisor 226
Instant Sewing Handbook 231
Instant Spelling Dictionary 112
Instructor 271
Intermediate World Atlas 7, 63-64
International Atlas 71-72
International Cyclopedia of Music and Musicians 121
International Encyclopedia of the Social Sciences 168
International Relations Dictionary 174
International Visual Dictionary 34
International Wildlife Encyclopedia 202-203
Interracial Books for Children 271
Introducing Books 104
Introduction to Birds 206
Introduction to Trees 212
Introduction to Wild Flowers 213
Ireland, Norma Olin 78-79, 106
Irish Helped Build America 187
Irish in America 187-188
Irwin, Graham W. 156
Irwin, Leonard B. 149
Ish-Kishor, Sulamith 131
Italians in America 187-188
Ivins, Ann 207, 215

Jackson, Anne 184
Jackson, Joseph Hollister 216
Jackson, Miles M., Jr., 192
Jacobs, G. 249
Jacobson, Daniel 189
Jacobus, Melancthon W. 134

James, Glenn 214
James, Robert C. 214
Janson, Dora Jane 124
Janson, H. W. 124
Japanese Helped Build America 187
Japanese in America 188
Jarman, Catherine 205, 211
Jenkins, Williams A. 113
Jennison, Keith W. 247
Jewish Child's Bible Stories 131
Jews Helped Build America 187
Jews in America 187-188
Joe Kaufman's What Makes It Go? 6, 9, 228
Johnson, Allen 81
Johnson, Gerald W. 175-176
Johnson, Harry A. 185, 192
Johnson, James E. 187
Johnson, Thomas H. 158
Johnstone, Kathleen Yerger 236
Jones, Claire 187
Jones, Sir Harold Spencer 233
Jones, Jayne 187-188, 190
Joquel, Arthur Louis, II 26
Jordan, E. L. 145, 204
Josephy, Alvin M., Jr. 146
Joslin, Sesyle 93
Joy of Cooking 222
Junior Book of Authors 7, 11, 84
Junior High School Library Catalog 14, 262, 268
Junior History of the American Negro 9, 191-192
Junior Illustrated Encyclopedia of Sports 10, 247
Junior Jewish Encyclopedia 9, 14, 193-194
Junior Judo 251
Junior Karate 251
Junior Thesaurus 8, 113-114
Juniorplots 104

Kainz, Luise C. 124
Kaiser, Ernest 193
Kallem, Anne E. 242
Kane, Joseph Nathan 48, 87, 147
Kann, Herbert 248
Kaufman, Joe 228
Keating, Charlotte Matthews 185
Keen, Martin L. 229
Keith, Harold 247
Kelly, Gerard W. 215
Kenneth, John H. 202
Kenward, James 36
Kids Camping 246
Kids Gardening 224

Author and Title Index

Kieran, John 206, 212-213
Kinsman, Clare D. 86
Kircher, Clara J. 255
Kirkus Review 271-272
Klapper, Marvin 232
Kleeberg, Irene Cumming 230
Klinge, Paul 201
Klots, Alexander B. 209-210
Klots, Elsie 209
Knight, Frank 180
Kobbe, Gustav 122
Kobbe's Complete Opera Book 122
Kohn, Bernice 223
Kolb, W. L. 167
Kone, Grace Ann 258
Konversations-Lexikon 21
Kotker, Norman 132
Kozuki, Russell 251
Kramp, Harry 250
Kreider, Barbara 101
Krythe, Mayme R. 164, 172
Kunitz, Stanley J. 84-86
Kunz, Virginia Brainard 188
Kuropas, Myron B. 188
Kurtis, Arlene Harris 187

Labor Reference Book 171
LaFarge, Oliver 189
LaGumina, John 188
Laird, Charlton 114
Lamb, Ruth S. 195
Landau, Robert A. 262
Landers Film Reviews 272
Landforms 218
Landmarks of Liberty 162
Lands and Peoples 8, 13, 140
Lands of the Bible 132
Lane, Elbert C. 134
Lang, Paul Henry 119
Langer, William L. 148, 150
Large Type Books in Print 262-263
Large Type Hammond-Jennison World Atlas 73
Larousse Encyclopedia of Ancient and Medieval History 153
Larousse Encyclopedia of Archaeology 152
Larousse Encyclopedia of Modern History 155-156
Larousse Encyclopedia of Music 120
Larousse Encyclopedia of the Earth 14, 217-218
Larousse Illustrated French-English/English-French Dictionary for Young Readers 8, 92
Larousse Modern French-English, English-French Dictionary 93
Larsen, Ronald J. 188
Latin America and the Caribbean 144
Lawson, Donald E. 19
Leach, Maria 108
Leaf, Hayim 193
Learning Directory 263
Leathers, Noel L. 188
Leaves 212
Leeming, Joseph 169
Lehner, Ernst 164
Lembo, Diana 104
Leokum, Arkady 48
LeSueur, Richard 57
Let's Do Fingerplays 242
Let's Go Sailing 250
Levieux, Eleanor 93
Levieux, Michel 93
Levin, Marcia 214
Levine, Jack 237
Lewis, E. 134
Lewis, Norman 115
Library Journal 272
Library of Congress Catalog: Films and Other Materials for Projection 263
Library of Congress Catalog: Music and Phonorecords 263-264
Libros en Espanol 6, 9, 194
Liebers, Arthur 234, 250
Life in the Middle Ages 153
Life in the Renaissance 154
Limbacher, James L. 259
Lincoln Library of Essential Information 10, 23, 100, 168
Lincoln Library of Language Arts 8, 12, 23, 100
Lincoln Library of the Fine Arts 23
Lincoln Library of the Social Sciences 13, 168
Lindholm, Mauno A. 246
Lingeman, Richard R. 226
Lipkind, William 173
Liss, Howard 248-249
Living Amphibians of the World 207
Living Authors 85
Living Birds of the World 206
Living Fishes of the World 208
Living Insects of the World 209
Living Mammals of the World 204
Lloyd, Norman 119

Lodewijk, T. 229
Logasa, Hannah 149, 196
Loken, Newton C. 251
Lots More Tell Me Why 48
Lovejoy, Clarence E. 182
Lovejoy's Career and Vocational School Guide 13, 182
Lovejoy's College Guide 13, 182
Lowndes, Marion 207, 221
Luchenbill, Charles L. 118
Lyttle, Richard B. 240

McAllister, Evelyn Ditton 250
McCarthy, Joseph F. X. 157
McCrory, J. R. 249
McDaniel, Roderick 267
McDonnell, Virginia B. 187
McEntee, Howard G. 245
McEvedy, Colin 74, 152, 154
McEvedy, Sarah 74, 152, 154
Macfarlan, Allan 246
McGraw-Hill Bibliography of Science and Technology 200
McGraw-Hill Dictionary of Art 12, 127
McGraw-Hill Encyclopedia of Science and Technology 89, 200
McGraw-Hill Encyclopedia of World Biography 11, 81
McGraw-Hill Encyclopedia of World Drama 12, 103
McGraw-Hill Modern Men of Science 11, 89, 200
McKechnie, Jean L. 45
McKnown, Harry C. 175
McMillan, James B. 41
Macmillan Wild Flower Book 213
McNally, Tom 252
McWhirter, Mary Esther 256
McWhirter, Norris 49
McWhirter, Ross 49
Magill, Frank N. 85, 100
Maillard, Robert 122
Make Your Own Animated Movies 246
Makers of America 14, 184-186
Making Your Own Movies 245
Malmberg, Carl 186
Malone, Dumas 81
Mammals 6, 9, 14, 204
Man and History 150
Manana Is Now 9, 14, 184, 195
Mangoine, Jerre 186
Manual for Baby Sitters 221
Marckwardt, Albert H. 41
Margolis, Max L. 133

Marguerite DeAngeli's Book of Nursery and Mother Goose Rhymes 5, 97, 108
Marquardt, Dorothy 83, 85
Martin, Alexander C. 212, 213
Masterpieces of World Literature in Digest Form 85
Mathematics Dictionary 14, 214
Mathematics Illustrated Dictionary 9, 14, 214
Mathematics Library 214
Matters of Fact 264
Matterson, Elizabeth 242
Media Review Digest 55, 57
Melrose, Margaret 92
Menke, Frank G. 248
Meravi, Mehdi 143
Merit Atlas 7, 11, 68
Merit Students Encyclopedia 6, 10, 16, 24, 53, 68
Merit Students Year Book 24
Merlick, Arden Davis 88
Merritt, Eleanor 59
Metric System Simplified 9, 14, 215
Metzner, Seymour 149, 157
Mexican Americans: Sons of the Southwest 195
Mexicans in America 188
Meyer, Robert 172
Mi Diccionario Illustrado 5, 8, 95
Mi Primer Diccionario 8, 91, 95
Mi Primer Larousse en Colores 96
Middle East and North Africa 1974-75 143-144
Miers, Earl Schenk 157
Miles, Betty 223
Miller, Herbert F. 214
Miller, J. Lane 133
Miller, Madeleine S. 133
Milton Cross New Encyclopedia of the Great Composers and Their Music 121
Mirkin, Stanford M. 150
Misspeller's Dictionary 12, 112
Mitchell, Robert T. 209
Model Aircraft Handbook 245
Mohan, Beverly 252
Mon Larousse en Images 92
Mon Premier Dictionnaire 92
Mon Premier Larousse en Couleurs 92
Mondey, David 179
Monkhouse, F. J. 138
Monro, Isabel S. 104
Monroe, Marion 31, 95
Moon Flight Atlas 232

Author and Title Index

Moorachian, Rose 268
Moore, Patrick 232
Moore, William 227, 252
Moquin, Wayne 185
More Antonyms 112-113
More Books by More People 84
More Homonyms 113
More Junior Authors 7, 11, 84
More Stories of Favorite Operas 5, 8, 121
More Synonyms 113
More Tell Me Why 48
More Words of Science 197-198
Morehead, Albert H. 115
Morgan, Alfred 230
Morgan, Joy Elmer 168
Moritz, Charles 79
Morris, Richard B. 156, 158, 162
Morris, William 34, 40, 114
Morrison, Joel L. 64
Morrison, Thomas F. 225
Motorcycling for Beginners 240
Muir's Atlas of Ancient and Classical History 74
Muir's Historical Atlas 11, 74
Muir's Historical Atlas--Medieval and Modern 74
Mulac, Margaret E. 243
Multi Media Review Index 57
Multicultural Bibliography for Preschool Through Second Grade 6, 186
Multimedia Approach To Children's Literature 6, 10, 254, 264
Multimedia Materials for Afro-American Studies 14, 185, 192-193
Munro, Eleanor C. 125
Munson, Kenneth 179
Murphy, Eugene 188
Musciano, Walter A. 244
Music Dictionary 5, 8, 118-120
Music in Western Civilization 119
My-Fun-With-Words Dictionary 5, 32
My Pictionary 5, 31, 95
My First Picture Dictionary 5, 31
My First World Atlas 5, 62
My Second Picture Dictionary 5, 31
My Weekly Reader 28
My World 5, 47-48
Myers, Bernard S. 127

National Center for Audio Tapes: 1974-76 Catalog 264-265
National Education Association of the United States 140
National Encyclopedia 53
National Geographic Atlas of the World 11, 66
National Geographic Society 66, 131
National Holidays Around the World 13, 173
National Information Center for Educational Media 180, 193, 224, 227, 265
National Park Guide 145
National Union Catalog 263-264
National Yearbook 53
Nault, William H. 27
Nayman, Jacqueline 205, 211
Negro Almanac 9, 14, 193
Negro in America 188
Negro in American History 193
Nelson's Complete Concordance of the Revised Standard Version Bible 135
New American Roget's College Thesaurus in Dictionary Form 115-116
New Book of Knowledge 5, 6, 10, 15-16, 24, 178
New Book of Knowledge Annual 5, 7, 10, 25, 47, 51
New Century Classical Handbook 13, 152
New Century Cyclopedia of Names 10, 50-51, 98
New Century Handbook of English Literature 97-98
New Encyclopaedia Britannica 10, 15, 17, 25, 52
New Encyclopedia of Child Care and Guidance 14, 221-222
New Encyclopedia of the Opera 12, 122
New Field Book of Reptiles and Amphibians 207-208
New Golden Dictionary 5, 32-33
New Illustrated Space Encyclopedia 9, 233
New International Illustrated Encyclopedia of Art 127
New Larousse Encyclopedia of Mythology 108
New Life--La Vida Nueva 194
New Roget's Thesaurus of the English Language in Dictionary Form 8, 12, 115

New Seventeen Book of Etiquette and Young Living 13, 171-172
New Space Encyclopedia 14, 233
New Standard Bible Dictionary 134
New York Library Association, Children's and Young Adult Services Section 259-260, 267
New York Times Atlas of the World 11, 70-71
New York Times Encyclopedia Almanac 54
New York Times Index 57-58
Newman, James R. 199
NICEM Educational Audio Tapes 265-266
NICEM Index to Black History and Studies--Multimedia 193
NICEM Index to Ecology--Multimedia 224
NICEM Index to Educational Overhead Transparencies 265-266
NICEM Index to Educational Records 265-266
NICEM Index to Educational Slides 265-266
NICEM Index to Educational Video Tapes 265-266
NICEM Index to 8mm Motion Cartridges 265-266
NICEM Index to Health and Safety Education--Multimedia 227
NICEM Index to Producers and Distributors 265-266
NICEM Index to 16mm Educational Films 265-266
NICEM Index to 35mm Filmstrips 265-266
NICEM Index to Vocational and Technical Education --Multimedia 167, 180
NICEM Update of Nonbook Media 266
Nichols, Margaret S. 186
Nicholsen, Margaret E. 79
Nicknames and Sobriquets of U.S. Cities and States 147
Nobile, Philip 224
Non-flowering Plants 213
Norback, Craig 112
Norback, Peter 112
Northcott, Cecil 133
Northern, B. Penny 57
Norwegians in America 187-188
Now You Know About Animals 6, 203
Now You Know About People at Work 6, 9, 167, 181
Now You Know About Plants 6, 211
Nyren, Judith 262

Ocean World of Jacques Cousteau 218-219
Oceanography 218
O'Connor, W. Harold 252
Occupational Outlook Handbook 13, 182
O'Donnell, Mabel 31
Of Course You Can Sew! 231
Official Associated Press Almanac 54
Official Congressional Directory 13, 177
Official Encyclopedia of Sports 248
Old Testament 133
Olney, Ross R. 250
Olten, Roy 174
101 Things a Boy Can Do Around the House 227
One Thousand Poems for Children 8, 108-109
O'Neill, Margaret N. 186
Organic Living Book 223
Oswalt, Sabine G. 107
Other Lands, Other Peoples 8, 13, 140
Ottemiller's Index to Plays in Collections 102-103
Our Nation's Great Heritage 163
Our Wonderful World 26
Oxford Classical Dictionary 12, 99
Oxford Companion to American History 13, 158
Oxford Companion to American Literature 12, 99
Oxford Companion to Classical Literature 12, 99
Oxford Companion to English Literature 98
Oxford Companion to the Theatre 103
Oxford Dictionary of Quotations 111
Oxford English Dictionary 40
Oxford Illustrated Dictionary 41
Oxford Junior Companion to Music 119
Oxford World Atlas 69-70

Pack of Fun 239

Author and Title Index

Padwe, Sandy 248
Palmer, R. R. 74
Palmer, Robin 105
Pantheon Story of Art for Young People 125
Paradis, Adrian A. 170-171
Parker, Bertha Morris 32, 212
Parker, Fan 94
Parrinder, Geoffrey 131
Passage to the Golden Gate 190
Patapoff, Elizabeth 239
Pathways Through the Jewish Holidays 131-132
Paul, Aileen 224, 246
Payton, Geoffrey 50
Peake, Dorothy Margaret 102
Pearcy, G. Etzel 142
Peers, Edgar Allison 96
Pels, Gertrude 238
Pencil, Pen and Brush 238
Penguin Dictionary of Quotations 110
People in Books 79
Peoples of the Earth 140-141
Perfect Speller 8, 12, 111-112
Periodicals for School Libraries 10, 14, 254, 266
Perkins, Flossie L. 256
Perkins, Ralph 256
Perry, Day A. 34
Pet Book for Boys and Girls 230
Pet Names 230-231
Peterson Field Guide Series 210
Pets 230
Pictorial Encyclopedia of Railways 179
Pictorial Guide to the Planets 216
Pictorial History of Music 119
Pictorial History of the American Indian 189
Pictorial Travel Atlas of Scenic America 13, 145
Picture Album Series 188
Picture Books for Children 266
Picture Dictionary for Children 33
Pillet, Roger 92
Pinchot, Jane 188
Plano, Jack C. 174, 177
Platt, Harrison Gray 37
Play Index, 1949-52 12, 102
Play Index, 1953-60 12, 102
Play Index, 1961-67 12, 102
Play Index, 1968-72 12, 102
Ploski, Harry A. 193
Pocket Encyclopedia of Physical Science 14, 215

Poetry Handbook 12, 110
Poirie, Helene 92
Poles in America 188
Politics in America 175
Pond Life 201
Popular American Composers 90
Popular American Composers, First Supplement 90
Portraits and Personalities 124
Post, Elizabeth L. 171
Postage Stamps of the United States 237
Powers, David Guy 174
Practical Encyclopedia of Crafts 242
Praeger Encyclopedia of Art 127-128
Praeger Picture Encyclopedia of Art 126
Pratt, John Lowell 248
Preece, Warren E. 25
Presidency 175
Presidents 5, 87-88
Previews 272
Pro Football Plays in Pictures 249
Puerto Ricans in America 188
Purdy, Susan 169
Purnell's History of the 20th Century 151

Quinn, Edward 103

Radice, Betty 151
Radio Amateur's Handbook 238
Rainbow Book of Art 125
Rainbow Dictionary for Young Readers 5, 7, 33, 92
Rand McNally Answer Atlas 61-62
Rand McNally Atlas of World History 74
Rand McNally Atlas of World Wildlife 205-206
Rand McNally Classroom Atlas Indexed 5, 7, 63
Rand McNally New Cosmopolitan World Atlas 7, 11, 67
Rand McNally World Atlas, Family Edition 65
Randel, William Pierce 160
Random House Dictionary of the English Language: College Edition 38, 41-42
Random House Dictionary of the English Language: School Edition 38

Random House Dictionary of the English Language: Unabridged Edition 38, 42, 44
Read, Sir Herbert 126
Reader's Digest Almanac 7, 10, 54
Reader's Encyclopedia 8, 12, 98
Reader's Encyclopedia of American Literature 100
Reader's Encyclopedia of World Drama 103
Readers' Guide to Periodical Literature 55, 58
Reading Ladders for Human Relations 6, 10, 14, 254, 266-267
Recipes for Art and Craft Materials 6, 10, 241
Reck, Alma Kehoe 172
Record of America 9, 13, 157
Recordings for Children 267
Red Letter Days 9, 172
Reference Services Review 272
Reid, George K. 201
Reid, Virginia 266
Reinfeld, Fred 236
Reit, Ann 110
Reptiles and Amphibians 9, 14, 207
Resources for Learning 6, 10, 267
Reuben, Gabriel H. 162
Rhodes, Dorothy 61
Rhodes, Frank H. T. 210, 218
Ribora, Peiro 94
Rice, Susan 260
Richard Scarry's Best Word Book Ever 32
Richard Scarry's Hop Aboard: Here We Go! 6, 178
Richard Scarry's Storybook Dictionary 32
Richard Scarry's What Do People Do All Day? 6, 167, 181
Riding 252
Riessen, Clare 252
Rigg, Cynthia 57
Riley, Olive L. 124
Riverain, Jean 155
Roach, Helen 267
Robert, Henry M. 175
Robert, Sarah Corbin 175
Roberts, Gail 155
Robert's Rules of Order 13, 175
Rock Encyclopedia 12, 123
Rocks and Minerals 9, 217
Roget's International Thesaurus 116

Rollock, Barbara 190
Rombauer, Irma S. 222
Root, Shelton L., Jr. 108, 255
Rosenberg, Judith K. 268
Rosenberg, Kenyon C. 268
Rosenfeld, Sam 236
Rosenthal, Harold 121
Ross, Frank, Jr. 164
Rossman, Isadore 226
Roth, Bernhard A. 253
Rothenstein, Sir John 127
Roucek, Joseph S. 188
Roxon, Lillian 123
Royal Book of Ballet 6, 8, 122
RQ 273
Ruark, Henry C., Jr. 271
Ruffins, Reynold 239
Rufsvold, Margaret I. 261
Runes, Dagobert D. 129
Ruskin, Ariane 125
Russian Alphabet Book 94
Russians in America 187-188
Rydell, Wendy 231

Sabin, Robert 121
Sachs, Moshe Y. 141
Salem, James M. 102
Sainy, Roslyn W. 235
Samuels, Eva 85
Sanderson, Ivan T. 204
Sarnoff, Jane 239
Sattler, Helen Roney 241
Saunders, Rubie 170, 221
Save the Earth! 223
Scarry, Richard 32, 167, 178, 181
Scharff, Robert 249
Schiller, Andrew 31, 113
Schoenfeld, Madalynne 264
Scholastic Dictionary of American English 36-37
Scholes, Percy A. 119
School Game Book 243
School Library Journal 272-273
Schreiber, Morris 255
Schultz, Charles 33
Schuon, Karl 251
Science and Children 273
Science Books 197, 273
Science Dictionary of the Animal World 204
Science Dictionary of the Plant World 211
Science for Youth 196
Science Year 198
Scots and Scotch-Irish in America 187-188

Author and Title Index 301

Scott, Marian H. 266
Scott Publications, Inc. 237
Scott's Monthly Stamp Journal 237
Scullard, H. H. 99
Sea Shells of the World 208-209
Seashores 209
Sechrist, Elizabeth Hough 108, 172
Seeger, Elizabeth 130
Sell, Violet 109
Selsam, Millicent 213
Seltzer, L. E. 138
Semmelmeyer, Madeline 111
Senior High School Library Catalog 14, 268
Severn, Bill 239
Sewing 231
Seymour-Smith, Martin 100
Shaffer, Paul R. 210, 217
Shankle, George Earlie 49, 165
Shapp, Martha Glauber 24, 140
Sharp, Harold S. 50
Shaw, David 241
Shaw, Harry 100
Shepherd, William 74
Shepherd's Historical Atlas 11, 74-75
Shipley, Joseph T. 101, 116
Ships 180
Shoemaker, Hurst H. 208
Shores, Louis 18, 24
Short Story Index 12, 104-105
Short Story Index, Supplement 1950-1954 12, 104-105
Short Story Index, Supplement 1955-1958 12, 104-105
Short Story Index, Supplement 1959-1963 12, 104-105
Short Story Index, Supplement 1964-1968 12, 104-105
Shuttlesworth, Dorothy 217
Shuttlesworth, Floyd S. 213
Sills, David L. 168
Silverman, Judith 78
Simpson, D. P. 94
Sisley, Becky L. 248
Sloane, Eric 162
Slonimsky, Nicolas 90
Smaridge, Norah 235
Smart Shopping and Consumerism 170
Smith, Edward C. 176
Smith, Hobart M. 207
Smith, Jeanne 226
Smith, Parker 251
Smith, Whitney 166
Smith, William James 109
Snook, Barbara 169

So You Were Elected! 175
Softball for Girls 248
Sollenberger, Judith K. 173
Something About the Author 5, 7, 11, 83
Song and Garden Birds of North America 206
Spache, George 186, 261
Spaghetti for Breakfast 93-94
Spangler, Earl 188
Sparano, Vin T. 247
Speech Index 58
Splaver, Sarah 182
Spoken Records 14, 267
Sports and Games 247
Sprint, Alexander 206
Stamp Collectors' Handbook 236-237
Stand Up, Shake Hands, Say "How Do You Do." 171
Standard Catalog for High School Libraries 268
Standard Dictionary 43
Standard Encyclopedia of the World's Mountains 138-139
Standard Encyclopedia of the World's Oceans and Islands 139
Standard Encyclopedia of the World's Rivers and Lakes 139
Standard First Aid and Personal Safety 9, 14, 225
Standard Postage Stamp Catalogue 237
Standards for School Media Programs 258
Stanek, Muriel 60
Stanius, Ellen J. 78
Stars 215-216
State Birds and Flowers 165
State Capital Cities 146
State Names, Flags, Seals, Songs, Birds, Flowers, and Other Symbols 165
State Trees 165
Statesman's Year Book 54
Stein, Jess 44
Stein and Day International Medical Encyclopedia 14, 226
Steinberg, Margaret 252
Steinberg, S. H. 98
Stevenson, Burton 110, 135
Still More Tell Me Why 48
Stine, G. Harry 245
Stitchery for Children 231-232
Stockel, Martin W. 229
Stoneman, Elvyn A. 142

Storey, R. L. 154
Stories of Favorite Operas 5, 8, 121
Stories of the States 9, 13, 164
Story of Coins 236
Story of Painting for Young People 124
Stoutenburgh, John L., Jr. 189
Structure and Function of the Body 226
Student Dictionary of Biology 202
Subject and Title Index to Short Stories for Children 8, 103-104
Subject Guide to Books in Print 14, 256-257
Subject Guide to Children's Books in Print 6, 10, 257
Subject Index to Books for Intermediate Grades 7, 55, 58-59
Subject Index to Books for Primary Grades 5, 58-59
Subject Index to Children's Magazines 5, 7, 59
Subject Index to Poetry for Children and Young People 109
Suhl, Yuri 188
Sullivan, George 249-250
Supreme Court 176
Sussman, Aaron 245
Sutherland, Zena 149, 270
Sutton, Roberta Briggs 58
Swain, Su Zan Noguchi 209
Swedes in America 187-188
Swimming 250
Symons, Arthur 227
Synonyms 113

Taggart, Jean E. 230
Tansey, Richard G. 125
Taylor, A. J. O. 151
Taylor, John W. R. 179
Taylor, Michael J. H. 179
Taylor, Norman 225
Teen-ager's Guide to Collecting Practically Anything 14, 235-236
Telescope Handbook and Star Atlas 216
Tell Me Why 48
Tell Me Why Library 48
Tennenhouse, Mary Ann 86
Tennis 252
tenZythoff, Gerrit 188
Terres, John D. 201

Terrien, Samuel 132
Tether, J. Edward 225
Textbooks in Print 259
Their Search for God 130
Theis, Paul A. 87
Theureau, S. 92, 96
Third Book of Junior Authors 7, 11, 84
Thompson, Hildegard 189
Thompson, Newton 135
Thompson, Oscar 121
Thorndike, E. L. 35, 38-39
Thorndike-Barnhart Advanced Dictionary 10, 39
Thorndike-Barnhart Beginning Dictionary 7, 31, 35
Thorndike-Barnhart High School Dictionary 39
Thorndike-Barnhart Intermediate Dictionary 7, 10, 38
Thorne, J. O. 80
Thrall, William Flint 97, 101
Time for Poetry 5, 8, 108-109
Times Atlas of the World 138
Times Atlas of the World: Comprehensive Edition 70, 72
Times Concise Atlas of the World 70
Times Index-Gazetteer of the World 138
Townes, Willmina 31
Trains 179
Trees 212
Trees of North America 212
Treharne, R. F. 74
Tripp, Edward 107
Trump, David H. 152
Tumbling Techniques Illustrated 251
Twentieth Century Authors 11, 85
Twentieth Century Authors: First Supplement 11, 85

Uden, Grant 153
Ukrainians in America 188
Ullom, Judith 106
Understanding Art 124-125
Understanding Musical Instruments 237
United Nations 174
United States Bureau of Labor Statistics 182
United States Congress 177
United States Government Organization Manual 13, 177-178
United States National Archives and Records Service 177

Author and Title Index

United States Postal Service 237
Unstead, R. J. 47
Urdang, Laurence 41, 54
Urquiljo, Elena 96
Usherwood, Stephen 135

Van Den Bark, Melvin 116
Van Doren, Charles 163, 193
Van Nostrand's Scientific Encyclopedia 199
Veliz, Claudio 144
Vermes, Hal G. 235
Vermes, Jean 235
Vertical File Index 11, 59
Vice-Presidents of the United States 88
Voices from America's Past 9, 13, 162-163
Voss, Gilbert L. 218

Walker, Henry 249
Wall, C. Edward 57
Walpole, Ellen Wales 33
Walsh, S. Padraig 260
Ward, Martha E. 83, 85
Warrack, John 121
Watson, Corinne 119
Watson, Jack M. 119
Watt, May Theilgaard 212
Watters, Garnette 33, 35
Way Things Work 9, 14, 229
We Read 262
Wease, Robert C. 217
Webb, Marian A. 243
Webb, Robert N. 186
Webster, Noah 45
Webster's Biographical Dictionary 7, 11, 80
Webster's Dictionary of Proper Names 7, 10, 50
Webster's Dictionary of Synonyms 115
Webster's Elementary Dictionary 7, 35
Webster's Guide to American History 13, 158
Webster's Instant Word Guide 112
Webster's Intermediate Dictionary 10, 38-39
Webster's New Collegiate Dictionary 7, 10, 42
Webster's New Dictionary of Synonyms 12, 114-115
Webster's New Elementary School Dictionary 36, 38
Webster's New Geographical

303

Dictionary 8, 12, 137
Webster's New Ideal Dictionary 42
Webster's New Students Dictionary 38-39
Webster's New Twentieth Century Dictionary of the English Language 45
Webster's New World Dictionary 7, 10, 37, 43
Webster's New World Dictionary for Young Readers 37
Webster's New World Thesaurus 97, 114
Webster's Seventh New Collegiate Dictionary 39, 42
Webster's Student Dictionary 39
Webster's Third New International Dictionary of the English Language 7, 10, 36, 39, 45
Weedon's Encyclopedia 17
Weekly Reader Beginning Dictionary 5, 34
Weiss, Harvey 238
Wels, Byron G. 239
Wentworth, Harold 117
Wessells, Katharine Tyler 122
West, Dorothy Herbert 102
Wetmore, Alexander 206
What Happened When 150
What Instrument for Me? 237
What Is a City 254, 268
What Is a Simple Machine 6, 228
What People Wore 13, 170
What So Proudly We Hail 9, 13, 164
What's the Biggest 49
When Did It Happen? 150
White, Anne Terry 105
White, Marian E. 262
White, Percival 164
Whitford, Harold Crandall 115
Whitney, David C. 47
Who Did That 80
Who Was When? 81
Who Was Who 83
Who Was Who in America 82
Who's Who 83
Who's Who in America 82
Who's Who in American Politics 11, 87
Who's Who in Jewish History After the Period of the Old Testament 77, 194
Who's Who in the Ancient World 13, 151-152
Who's Who in the Middle Ages 13, 77, 153

Who's Who in the New Testament 12, 136
Who's Who in the Old Testament 12, 136
Who's Who in the World 11, 80
Wilcox, R. Turner 170
Wild Animals of North America 204
Williams, Jay 153
Williams, Neville 154, 156
Wilson Library Bulletin 274
Winston Dictionary for Schools 37-38
Wittels, Harriet 111, 114
Wives of the Presidents 88
Wolfson, George H. 28
Wood, Clement 116
Woodress, James 162
Words from the Myths 105
Words I Like to Read and Write 31-32
Words of Science 197-198
Words on the Map 61
Words to Read, Write, and Spell 31-32
World Almanac and Book of Facts 7, 11, 47, 53-54
World Atlas of Military History, Vol. 1, to 1485 153
World Book Atlas 7, 11, 69
World Book Dictionary 5, 7, 10, 45-46, 52
World Book Encyclopedia 6, 10, 27, 46, 52, 69, 198
World Book Year Book 7, 10, 28, 46, 52
World Culture 149
World History in Juvenile Books 149
World of Nature Series 204, 206-209
Worldmark Encyclopedia of Nations 8, 13, 141
World's Great Religions 8, 130
Wright, Wendell W. 33, 92
Wyckoff, Jerome 218
Wynar, Christine L. 261
Wytrwal, Joseph 188

Yates, Raymond F. 244
Yellow Robe, Rosebud 188
Young, Helen 236
Young, Marjabelle 171
Young, Robert 134
Young America's Garden Book 224-225
Young Children's Encyclopedia 20
Young People's Literature in Series: Fiction 268
Young People's Literature in Series: Publishers' and Non-Fiction Series 268-269
Young People's Science Encyclopedia 198-199
Young People's Thesaurus Dictionary 8, 12, 114
Young Readers Book of Christian Symbolism 135
Young Students Encyclopedia 16, 28
Young's Analytical Concordance to the Bible 134
Your Career if You're Not Going to College 182

Zaffo, George 178
Zarchy, Jeanette 231
Zarchy, Harry 235
Zehavi, A. M. 131, 178
Zenos, Andrew C. 134
Ziegler, Elsie B. 106
Zim, Herbert S. 203-204, 206-213, 215, 217
Zimmerman, John E. 107
Zoo Animals 203
Zoology 203
Zurcher, Arnold J. 176

SUBJECT INDEX

Abbreviations 49, 112
Adult dictionaries 39-43
Africa 108, 139-144, 165-166,
    185, 190, 192-193, 205-206
Afro-Americans 184-186, 188,
    190-193
Agriculture 200-201, 210, 212,
    220, 223, 225
Aircraft 178-180, 244-245
Airplanes 178
Almanacs 47, 53-54
American history
  Art 126-127
  Atlases 75-76
  Bibliographies 156-157
  General 157-165, 168-170,
    172-178, 184-185
American Indians 106, 170,
    184-186, 188-190, 246-247
American literature 99-100
American Revolution 145, 156,
    160
Amphibians 202-203, 205, 207-208
Anatomy 225-226
Ancient history 67, 74-75, 132-133, 136, 151-153, 169-170, 194
Animals 200-211, 218-219
Anniversaries 173
Antarctica 139, 205-206
Anthropology 140-141
Antonyms 112-115
Applied sciences 168, 220-233
Aquariums 203, 208
Archaeology 152
Archery 247, 253
Arctic 140-141, 205-206
Arithmetic 214-215
Art 123-128
  Artists 124, 152
  Drawing 238
  History 98, 124-128
  Paintings 123-124
  Recipes 240-241
  Works of 50-51

Artists 124, 152
Asia 108, 130, 139-143, 152-153,
    165-166, 185, 205-206
Asian-Americans 184-186, 187-188, 190
Astronauts 233
Astronomy 199, 215-216, 233
Athletics 244, 247-253
  Archery 253
  Baseball 249
  Basketball 248
  Bowling 251
  Fishing 252
  Football 249
  General 247-248
  Golf 251-252
  Gymnastics 251
  Hockey 249-250
  Horsemanship 252
  Hunting 252
  Judo 251
  Karate 251
  Sailing 250
  Skiing 250
  Skin diving 250-251
  Softball 248
  Swimming 250-251
  Tennis 252
  Track and field 252
  Tumbling 251
  Water 250-251
  Winter 250
Atlases 60-76
  Evaluation of 60, 260-261
  Foreign language 71-72
  Historical
    American 67, 75-76
    Biblical 67, 132
    World 67, 74-75, 152, 154-155
  Juvenile 62-64
  Large type 73
  Map skills 60-62
  Science 202, 204-206, 211-212, 216
Audio visual materials

Audio visual materials (cont.)
   Bibliographies 184-185, 190, 192-193, 255-256, 258-268
   Indexes 57, 180, 193, 224, 227
   Reviews 57, 270-273
Australasia 140-143, 205-206
Authors 83-87, 97-98, 100, 103
Auto repair 229
Automobiles 178-179, 229
Aviation 179-180

Baby-sitting 221
Ballet 122, 238
Baseball 248-249
The Bible 133-136
Bibliographies 254-269
   Atlases 260-261
   Audio visual 254-269
   Biography 148, 156-157
   Encyclopedias 260
   English 255
   Ethnic groups in America 184-186, 190-195
   Fiction 148-150, 156-157, 255
   Folklore 106
   General 255-259, 261-262, 264-269
   History 148-150, 156-157
   Hospitals 257
   Mathematics 197, 214
   Media 184-185, 190, 192-193, 255-256, 258-268
   Periodicals 258
   Reference books 260-261
   Science 196-197
   Spanish language 194
   Textbooks 259
Bibliotherapy 255, 266
Bicycle repair 230, 239
Bicycles 230, 239-240
Biography 77-90
   American Indians 189
   Astronauts 233
   Authors 97-98, 100, 103
   Ballerinas 238
   Bibliographies 148, 156-157
   Black Americans 191-192
   Dictionaries
      American 81-82
      Artists 124
      Authors 83-87
      British 82-83
      Composers 89-90, 120-121, 123

   Current 79
   Evaluation of 77
   General 79-81, 83, 100
   Illustrators 83-85
   Jews 194
   Politicians 87-88
   Presidents 87-88
   Religious personalities 136
   Retrospective 81-83, 99, 151-153
   Scientists 88-89
   Encyclopedias 81-82
   Explorers 155
   General 168
   Indexes 77-79
   Politicans 177
   Scientists 79, 196-197, 199-200
   Women 78-79
Biology 200-214
Birds 165, 202-203, 205-207
Black Americans
   Bibliographies 184-186, 190, 192-193
   Biographies 191
   History 188, 190-193
   Indexes 193
Boating 247
Boats 178, 180
Book reviews 56, 270-274
Book selection
   Aids 270-274
   Atlases 60, 260-261
   Biographical dictionaries 77
   Dictionaries 30
   Encyclopedias 15-16, 260
   General 4, 256, 261
   Reference books, general 4, 256, 261
Book talks 104
Botany 199-202, 211-214, 224-225
Bowling 251
Buddhism 130-131
Buses 178
Butterflies 209-210

The Cabinet 176-178
Camping 246-247
Canada 100, 172
Capital cities 146
Car repair 229
Cards 239
Careers 79, 180-183, 191
The Caribbean 144, 185, 190
Carpentry 227
Cars 178-179, 229, 244
Central America 140-142, 144
Cheerleading 237-238

Subject Index

Chemistry 199, 215-217, 220
Chess 237
Chicanos 194-195
Child care 221-222
Children's literature 101, 103-105, 108-109, 148-150, 184-186, 190, 192, 194, 196-197, 214, 255-258, 261-264, 266-269
Chinese Americans 187-188, 190
Chivalry 153
Christianity 130-131, 135
Cities of the United States 56, 146-147
Citizenship 168-169
City maps 61
Civics 168-169
Civil rights 161, 191-193, 195
Civil War 160-161
Classical history 74-75, 151-153
Classical literature 99
Classical mythology 99, 105-108, 152
Coins 236
College dictionaries 39-43
Colleges and universities 182-183
Colonial period in America 159, 169-170
Color 197
Communications 220
Community helpers 181
Composers 89-90, 120-121, 123
Confucianism 130-131
The Congress 176-178
Conservation 200-201
Constellations 215-216
The Constitution 163
Consumerism 170-171
Cooking 222-223
Costume 169-170
Counties of the United States 147
Cousteau, Jacques 218-219
Cowboys 161
Crafts 240-242
Cubans 195
Customs 172-174, 193-194
Cycling 230, 239-240
Czech Americans 188

Dates 150, 158-159
Declaration of Independence 163
Dictionaries
 Abbreviations 49, 112
 Biography 79-90, 136, 151-153
 Cooking 223

English language 30-46
 Adult 39-43
 College 39-43
 Evaluation of 30
 Picture 31-34
 School 34-39
 Unabridged 43-46
 Folklore 107-108
 French language 91-93
 Geography 137-138
 German language 93
 History 158-159, 161
 Italian language 93-94
 Latin language 94
 Literature 97-101
 Mathematics 214
 Music 119-121
 Mythology 107-108
 Names 49-51
 Philosophy 129-130
 Poetry 110
 Political science 176-177
 Pseudonyms 50
 Quotations 110-111
 Religion 131, 133-134
 Rhymes 116
 Russian language 94-95
 Science 197-198, 201, 202, 204, 210-211, 216, 223-224, 226-227
 Slang 116-117
 Social sciences 167
 Spanish language 95-96
 Spelling 111-112
 Sports 248-249
 Synonyms 114-115
 Technology 220-221, 223-224
 Word origins 116
Dictionary, defined 30
Dinosaurs 210-211
Diseases 226
Documents 162-164, 168-169, 185-186, 193
Doll collecting 236
Domestic animals 200-201, 230-231
Domestic plants 200-201, 212-214
Drama 99-103, 169, 239
Drawing 238
Drugs 226-227
Dutch Americans 188

Earth sciences 200-201, 217-218
East Indians in America 187-188
Ecology 65-66, 68-70, 200, 202, 215, 223-224
Economics 168, 170-171, 190-191
Egypt 107-108, 151-152

Electronics 199, 238
Elementary dictionaries 31-39
Encyclopedia, defined 15
Encyclopedias
  Adult 18, 21, 23, 25
  Biography 81-82
  Evaluation of 15-16, 260
  General 15-29
  Geography 139
  History 150, 153, 155-157
  Juvenile 16-17, 19-20, 22, 24, 26-28, 47-48
  Literature 98, 100, 103
  Science 198-203, 205, 217-218, 226
  Sports 247-248
  Topical 17, 26
  Vocations 181-182
  Yearbooks 51-53
Endangered species 203, 205-206, 224
Engineering 199-200, 218, 220
English 97-117, 255
English Americans 187-188
English language 30-46, 61, 105, 116, 197-198
English language dictionaries 30-46
English literature 97-98, 107
Entertainment 243
Environment 65-66, 68-70, 223-224
Eskimos 185
Essays 56-57, 99
Ethnic groups in America 184-195
Etiquette 171-172, 222-223
Europe 108, 139-143, 148, 152-153, 165-166, 170, 205-206
Evaluation
  Aids 270-274
  Atlases 60, 260-261
  Biographical dictionaries 77
  Dictionaries 30
  Encyclopedias 15-16, 260
  General 256, 261
  Reference books, general 4
Exploration 155

Fabrics 232
Fact books 47-51
Fairy tales 105-106
Farm animals 200-201
Festivals 172-174, 243
Fiction
  Children's 103-105, 190, 192, 196-197
  Dictionaries 99-100
  General 100-101
  Historical 148-150, 156-157
  Indexes 103-105
  Novels 100, 148-150
  Stories 100, 103-105
Films 245-246, 258-260, 261-268
Finger plays 242
Fire engines 178
First aid 225-226, 246-247
Fishes 201-202, 205, 208
Fishing 247, 252
Flags 164-166
Flowers 165, 200-202, 212-214, 224-225
Folk songs 107-108, 123
Folklore 105-108
Food 200, 220, 222-224
Football 249
Foreign languages
  Atlases 71-72
  Dictionaries 91-96
Forestry 200
Forts 161
Fossils 210
Freedom 161, 168-169
French Americans 188
French language 71, 91-93
Frogs 207-208
Fruit 224-225

Gamebirds 206
Games 237, 242-244, 247-248
Gardening 223-225
Gazetteers 56, 138
Genetics 202
Geography 137-147
  Africa 139-144
  Asia 139-143
  Atlases 60-74
  Australasia 140-143
  Classical 99
  Dictionaries 137-138
  Encyclopedias 139
  Europe 139-143
  Gazetteers 56, 138
  General 54, 98, 138-142, 168, 172-174, 243-244
  Map skills 60-62
  Middle East 141, 143-144
  North America 56, 139-142, 145-147
  Place names 50-51
  South America 139-142, 144
Geology 199, 215, 217-218, 220-221

Subject Index

German Americans 187-188
German language 71, 93
Globes 60-61
Golf 251-252
Government 54, 168, 175-178
Grammar 100, 111
Greek Americans 187-188
Greek mythology 99, 105-108
Gymnastics 251

Handicrafts 241-242
Health 225-226, 257
Highway maps 61
Hiking 246
Hinduism 130-131
Historical fiction 148-150, 156-157
History 137-166
  Ancient 132-133, 136, 151-153, 169-170
  Art 98, 124-128
  Atlases 67, 74-76, 152, 154-155
  Bibliographies 148-150, 156-157
  Black Americans 190-193
  Classical 151-153
  General 98, 150, 155, 168
  Medieval 153-154, 169-170
  Modern 151, 154-156, 169-170
  Music 98, 118-120
  United States 126-127, 156-165, 168-169, 172-178, 184-195
  World 150-155, 165-166, 169-170
Hobbies 234-253
  Art 238
  Ballet 238
  Camping 246-247
  Coins 236
  Collections 210, 235-236
  Crafts 240-242
  Cycling 230, 239-240
  Doll collecting 236
  Games 237, 239, 242-244, 247-248
  General works 234-236
  Indexes 240
  Magic 239
  Models 244-245
  Music 237-238
  Outdoor recreation 246-247
  Photography 245-246
  Puppetry 238-239
  Radio 238
  Shell collecting 208-209, 236
  Sports 247-253
  Stamps 236-237
Hockey 249-250
Holidays 168, 172-174
Home repairs 227-228
Homographs 112-113, 115
Homonyms 113
Homophones 112-113, 115
Horsemanship 252
Hospitals 257
Human body 225-226
Human rights 161-164, 168
Hungarian Americans 187-188
Hunting 247, 252

Ice hockey 249-250
Ice skating 250
Illustrations 57, 159
Illustrators 83-85
Immigrants 185-186
Indexes 55-59
  Biography
    General 77-79, 257
    Scientists 79
    Women 78-79
  Black history 193
  Book reviews 56
  Books 58-59
  Drama 101-103
  Essays 56-57
  Fairy tales 105-106
  Folklore 105-106, 257
  Handicrafts 240
  Hobbies 240
  Illustrations 57
  Media 57, 180, 193, 224, 227
  Mythology 105-106
  Newspapers 57-58
  Pamphlets 59
  Periodicals 55, 57-59
  Plays 101-103, 257
  Poetry 109-110
  Short stories 103-105, 257
  Speeches 58
  Vocations 180
Indians, American 106, 170, 184-186, 188-190, 246-247
Industry 220-221
Insects 201-202, 205, 209-210
Intermediate grades, sample basic reference collection 6-10
International relations 174
Invertebrates 205
Irish Americans 186-188
Islam 130-131
Islands 139

Italian Americans 186-188
Italian language 93-94

Japanese Americans 187-188
Jewish Americans 185-188,
  193-194
Jewish history 194
Judaism 130-132, 133, 193-194
Judo 251
Junior high schools, sample basic
  reference collection 10-14
Karate 251

Labor 171
Lakes 139, 201
Landforms 218
Landmarks 162, 168, 172
Language arts 97-117, 255
Languages
  English 30-46, 61, 105, 116,
    197-198
  French 71, 91-93
  German 71, 93
  Italian 93-94
  Latin 94
  Russian 94-95
  Spanish 71-72, 95-96, 181,
    211
Large type books 262-263
Latin America 108, 139-142,
  144, 152, 165-166, 170,
  190, 205-206
Latin language 94
Leaves 212
Legislators 177
Liberty 161-164, 168-169
Literary characters 98-100
Literary criticism 57, 100
Literary terms 98, 100-101, 103,
  110, 116
Literature
  American 99-100, 267
  Bibliographies 148-150, 156-
    157, 184-186, 190, 192,
    194, 214, 255-258, 261-
    264, 266-269
  Classical 99, 107, 152
  Drama 99-103
  English 97-98, 107, 267
  Fiction 99-101, 103-105,
    148-150, 156-157
  Folklore 105-108
  General 98, 100
  Historical fiction 148-150, 156-
    157
  Mythology 98-99, 105-108

Poetry 99-100, 108-110
Quotations 110-111
Works of 50-51

Machines 228-229
Magazines
  Bibliographies 258, 261, 266
  Directories 56, 258
  Indexes 55, 57-59
Magic 239
Mammals 202-203, 205
Manners 171-172, 222-223
Map skills 60-62
Maps 60-76
Mathematics
  Bibliographies 197, 214
  Dictionaries 214
  General 197, 199-200
  Measurement 197, 214-215, 220
  Metric system 214-215
Measurement 197, 214-215, 220
Mechanics 228-229
Media
  Bibliographies 184-185, 190,
    192-193, 255-256, 258-268
  Indexes 57, 180, 193, 224, 227
  Reviews 57, 270-273
Medicine 199, 226, 257
Medieval history 153-154, 169-170
Mesopotamia 151
Meteorology 199, 215
Metric system 214-215
Mexican Americans 184-186, 188,
  194-195
Middle Ages 153-154, 169-170
Middle East 130-131, 141, 143-
  144, 153
Migration 205-207
Minerals 202, 217-218
Minorities 184-195
Model building 244-245
  Aircraft 245
  Cars 244
  Railroads 244
  Rockets 245
  Ships 244-245
Mollusks 205
Monuments 162, 164, 168-169
Moon 67, 69, 232-233
Mother Goose rhymes 108, 122-
  123
Moths 209-210
Motorcars 179
Motorcycles 240
Mountaineering 138-139
Mountains 138-139, 218
Movies 245-246

Subject Index 311

Music 118-123
 Ballet 122
 Bibliographies 263-264
 Composers 89-90, 120-121
 Dictionaries 119-121
 History 98, 118-120
 Instruments 237
 Operas 121-122
 Rock 123
 Songs 122-123
 Works of 50-51
Musical instruments 237
Musicians 89-90, 120-121
Mythology 98-99, 105-108, 152

Names 49-51, 164-165, 230-231
National parks 145-146, 172
Natural science 198-214
Nature 197, 200-214
Needlework 231-232
Negroes 184-186, 188, 190-193
Newspapers
 Digests 53
 Directories 56
 Indexes 57-58
Nicknames 49-50, 147, 164-165
Non-flowering plants 213
Norse mythology 105-107
North America 108, 139-142, 145-147, 152, 170, 190, 205-206
Nursery rhymes 108, 122-123

Occupations 79, 180-183, 191
Oceania 139-141, 205-206
Oceanography 215, 218-219
Oceans 139, 217-219
Operas 121-122
Organic cooking 223
Organic gardening 223
Oriental Americans 184-188, 190
Outdoor recreation 145, 246-247

Paintings 123-124
Pakistanis in America 187-188
Pamphlets 59
Parks 145-146
Parliamentary procedure 174-175
Patterns 169
Periodicals
 Bibliographies 258, 261, 266
 Directories 56, 258
 Indexes 55, 57-59
Pests 210
Pets 207, 230-231

Philosophy 99, 129-130
Photography 199, 245-246
Physical science 197-201, 215-219
Physics 199, 215, 217
Physiology 202, 225-226
Picture dictionaries 31-34
Planets 215-216
Plants 200-202, 208-208, 211-214, 224-225
Plays 99, 103, 169, 239
Poetry 99-100, 108-110, 116, 152, 196
Polish Americans 188
Political science 175-178
Politicians 87-88, 177
Politics 168, 175-178, 190-191
Pollution 68, 205-206, 223-224
Ponds 201
Population 224
Postage stamps 236-237
Prehistoric life 210-211
The Presidency 175, 177-178
Presidents of the United States 87-88
Primary grades, sample basic reference collection 5-6
Pseudonyms 50
Puerto Ricans 186, 188, 195
Punctuation 111-112
Puppetry 238-239

Quotations 110-111, 135-136
Radio 238
Railroads 178-179, 244
Recipes 222-223, 240-241
Recordings 255, 258, 261-268
Records, world 49
Recreation 243
Reference books, defined 3
Reference books, evaluation of 4, 258, 260-261
Reference collection
 Evaluation of 3-4
 Sample basic, for primary grades 5-6
 Sample basic, for intermediate grades 6-10
 Sample basic, for junior high schools 10-14
Reference interview 2-3
Reference service 2-3
Religion 130-136
 Atlases 67, 132
 The Bible 133-136
 Biography 136
 Buddhism 130-131
 Christianity 130-131, 135

Religion (cont.)
　Classical　99
　Comparative　130-131
　Confucianism　130-131
　Dictionaries　131, 133-134
　Hinduism　130-131
　Holy Land　132-133
　Islam　130-131
　Judaism　130-132, 193-194
　Shinto　130
　Taoism　130
Renaissance　154
Repair
　Auto　229
　Bicycle　230
　Home　227-228
　Motorcycle　240
Reptiles　202-203, 205, 207-208
Reviews　270-274
Revolutionary War　145, 156, 160
Rhyming dictionaries　116
Riding　252
Rivers　139
Rock music　123
Rocketry　233, 245
Rocks　202, 217-218
Roman mythology　99, 105-108
Russian Americans　187-188
Russian language　94-95

Safety　225, 227, 239-240, 246
Sailing　250
Sample basic reference collections
　Intermediate grades　6-10
　Junior high schools　10-14
　Primary grades　5-6
Scandinavian Americans　186-188
Scholarships　182-183, 191
School dictionaries　34-39
Schools　182-183
Science　196-233
　Applied　168, 220-233
　Astronomy　215-216
　Atlases　202, 204-206, 211-212, 216
　Bibliographies　196-197
　Biology　200-214
　Botany　211-214
　Chemistry　216-217
　Dictionaries　197-198, 201-202, 204, 210-211, 216, 226-227
　Encyclopedias　198-203, 205, 217-218, 226
　General　197-200
　Geology　217-218
　Mathematics　214-215
　Medicine　226
　Natural　200-214
　Oceanography　218-219
　Physical　215-219
　Physics　217
　Technology　220-221
　Yearbooks　198-199
　Zoology　203-211
Scientists　79, 88-89
Scots Americans　187-188
Sea　208-209, 218-219
Sea shells　208-209, 236
Selection
　Aids　270-274
　Atlases　60, 260-261
　Biographical dictionaries　77
　Dictionaries　30
　Encyclopedias　15-16, 260
　General　256, 261
　Reference books, general　4
Sewing　169, 231-232
Shapes　197
Shell collecting　236
Shells　208-209, 236
Shinto　130
Ships　178, 180, 244-245
Short stories　103-105
Simple machines　228
Sizes　197
Skiing　250
Skin diving　250-251
Slang　98, 116-117
Slovak Americans　188
Snakes　207-208
Social sciences　167-183
　Citizenship　168-169
　Costume　169-170
　Dictionaries　167
　Economics　170-171
　Encyclopedias　168
　Etiquette　171-172
　Festivals　172-174
　General　167-168, 239, 243-244
　Government　175-178
　Holidays　172-174
　International relations　174
　Parliamentary procedure　174-175
　Political science　175-178
　Transportation　178-180
　Vocations　180-183
Softball　248
Solar system　215-216
Song leading　237-238
Songs　122-123, 242-243
Sound　197
South America　108, 139-142, 144, 152, 165-166, 170, 190, 205-206

Subject Index

Space 199, 216, 232-233
Space travel 155, 178-180, 216
Spacecraft 178-180
Spanish Americans 184-186, 188, 194-195
Spanish language
  Atlases 71-72
  Bibliographies 194
  Dictionaries 95-96
  Science 211
  Vocations 181
Speeches 58, 100-101
Spelling 100, 111-112
Sports 244, 247-253
  Archery 253
  Baseball 249
  Basketball 248
  Bowling 251
  Fishing 252
  Football 249
  General 247-248
  Golf 251-252
  Gymnastics 251
  Hockey 249-250
  Horsemanship 252
  Hunting 252
  Judo 251
  Karate 251
  Sailing 250
  Skiing 250
  Skin diving 250-251
  Softball 248
  Swimming 250-251
  Tennis 252
  Track and field 252
  Tumbling 251
  Water 250-251
  Winter 250
Stamps 236-237
Stars 215-216
States of the United States 146-147, 164-166, 177
Stitchery 231-232
Stories 103-105, 148-150, 156-157, 255-257
Storytelling 246-247
Superstition 98
Supreme Court 176
Swimming 250-251
Symbols 135, 164-165, 168, 197
Synonyms 113-116

Taoism 130
Tape recordings 261-262, 264-267
Technology 220-233
  Child care 221-222

Cooking 222-223
Dictionaries 220-221
Ecology 65-66, 68-70, 200, 202, 215, 223-224
Gardening 224-225
General 168, 199-200, 217-218, 220, 228-229
Health 225-227
Home repairs 227-228
Mechanics 228-230
Medicine 226
Sewing 231-232
Space 232-233
Telescopes 216
Tennis 252
Terrariums 224
Textbooks 259, 263
Theater 102-103
Thesauri 113-116
Time 197
Toads 207-208
Tools 227-228
Track and field 252
Trains 178-179
Transportation 178-180, 220, 228
Travel 141-143, 145-146, 168
Trees 165, 202, 212
Trucks 178
Tumbling 251
Turtles 207-208

Ukrainian Americans 188
Unabridged dictionaries 43-46
United Nations 141-142, 174
United States
  Biography 177
  Geography 145-147
  Government 175-178
  History 75-76, 146, 156-165, 168-170, 172-174, 184-195
  Politics 175-178
Useful Arts 168, 220-233

Vegetables 224-225
Vertical file material 59
Vice-Presidents of the United States 88
Vocations 79, 180-183, 191, 221

War Between the States 160-161
Water sports 250-251
Westward expansion 161
Wildflowers 200-202, 213-214
Winter sports 250
Women 78-79, 88

Word origins 116
World history
    Ancient 151-153
    Atlases 67, 74-75, 152, 154-155
    Bibliographies 148-150
    Costume 169-170
    Encyclopedias 150, 156
    Flags 165-166
    General 150, 153, 155
    Holidays 173-174
    Medieval 153-154
    Modern 151, 154-156
World records 49
Yearbooks 47, 51-54, 142, 198-199

Zoological gardens 203
Zoology 199-211